Measurement Theory in Action

This book helps readers apply testing and measurement theories. Featuring 22 self-contained modules, instructors can pick and choose the ones that are most appropriate for their course. Each module features an overview of a measurement issue and a step-by-step application of that theory. *Best Practices* provide recommendations for ensuring the appropriate application of the theory. *Practical Questions* help students assess their understanding of the topic, while the *Examples* allow them to apply the material using real data. *Case Studies* in each module depict typical dilemmas faced when applying measurement theory followed by *Questions to Ponder* to encourage critical examination of the issues noted in the cases. Each module contains exercises, some of which require no computer access, while others involve the use of statistical packages to solve the problem. The book's website houses the data sets, additional exercises, PowerPoints, and more. The book also features suggested readings, a glossary, and a continuing exercise in Appendix A that incorporates many of the steps in the development of a measure of typical performance.

Updated throughout to reflect recent changes in the field, the new edition also features:

- A new co-author, Michael Zickar, who updated the advanced topics and added the new module on generalizability theory (Module 22)
- Expanded coverage of reliability (Modules 5 and 6) and exploratory and confirmatory factor analysis (Modules 18 and 19) to help readers interpret results presented in journal articles
- Expanded web resources at www.routledge.com/9780415644792. Instructors will now find: suggested answers to the book's questions and exercises; detailed solutions to the exercises; and PowerPoint slides. Students and instructors can access the SPSS data sets; additional exercises; the glossary; and web links that are helpful in understanding psychometric concepts.

Ideal as a text for any psychometrics, testing and measurement, or multivariate statistics course taught in psychology, education, marketing and management, and professional researchers in need of a quick refresher on applying measurement theory will also find this an invaluable reference.

Kenneth S. Shultz is Professor of Psychology at California State University, San Bernardino.

David J. Whitney is Professor and Department Chair of Psychology at California State University, Long Beach.

Michael J. Zickar is Professor and Department Chair of Psychology at Bowling Green State University in Ohio.

Measurement Theory in Action

Case Studies and Exercises

Second Edition

Kenneth S. Shultz

David J. Whitney

Michael J. Zickar

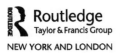
Routledge
Taylor & Francis Group

NEW YORK AND LONDON

Second edition published 2014
by Routledge
711 Third Avenue, New York, NY 10017

and by Routledge
27 Church Road, Hove, East Sussex BN3 2FA

First edition published by Sage Publications, Inc. 2005

Library of Congress Cataloging-in-Publication Data

Shultz, Kenneth S.
Measurement theory in action : case studies and exercises / Kenneth S. Shultz,
David J. Whitney, and Michael J. Zickar. — Second Edition.
    pages cm
1. Psychometrics—Case studies.   2. Psychometrics—Problems, exercises, etc.
I. Whitney, David J.   II. Zickar, Michael J.   III. Title.
BF39.S55   2014
150.28'7—dc23   2013021780

ISBN: 978-0-415-63362-8 (hbk)
ISBN: 978-0-415-64479-2 (pbk)
ISBN: 978-1-315-86983-4 (ebk)

Typeset in Times
by Apex CoVantage, LLC

Contents

x   Contents

About the Authors

Kenneth S. Shultz, PhD, earned his BA in Honors Psychology from the State University of New York College at Potsdam. He also earned his MA and PhD degrees in Industrial/Organizational (I/O) Psychology from Wayne State University in Detroit, Michigan. He is currently a professor in the Psychology Department at California State University, San Bernardino (CSUSB). He regularly teaches classes in undergraduate basic and advanced psychological statistics, tests and measurements, and I/O psychology. He also teaches graduate classes in correlation and regression statistics, applied psychological measurement, and personnel selection and test validation. Prior to joining CSUSB, he worked for four years for the City of Los Angeles as a personnel research analyst, where he conducted applied psychological measurement projects in job analysis, test validation, and other applied personnel psychology areas. He has also completed applied internships with United Airlines and UNISYS Corporation. He continues to engage in consulting assignments related to applied measurement issues for a variety of public and private agencies. He has presented papers and published articles on a variety of applied measurement and test construction issues, in addition to his substantive work in the areas of personnel selection, aging workforce issues, and retirement. When not teaching or writing, he enjoys running, watching sports, and generally hanging out with his wife and children. His website can be found at www.psychology.csusb.edu/facultyStaff/kenneth_shultz.htm.

David J. Whitney, PhD, earned his BS degree from Union College New York and his MA and PhD degrees in Industrial/Organizational Psychology from Michigan State University. He is currently a professor at California State University, Long Beach. He regularly teaches graduate courses in personnel selection, test construction, and employee training, as well as undergraduate courses in autism spectrum disorders and I/O psychology. He has served as a program evaluator for numerous grant-supported and institutional research projects. In addition to research interests in employment testing and employment coaching, he has collaborated with local regional centers to examine factors that might facilitate employment opportunities for individuals with developmental disabilities. While he very much enjoys his adopted home of southern California, his childhood roots are reflected in his undying (and some might say undeserved) devotion to New York Jets football.

His website can be found at www.csulb.edu/colleges/cla/departments/psychology/faculty/whitney/.

Michael J. Zickar, PhD, earned his BA, MA, and PhD degrees, all in psychology, from the University of Illinois at Urbana-Champaign. He currently is a professor and Department Chair of Psychology at Bowling Green State University in Ohio. He regularly teaches undergraduate and graduate courses in psychological testing, statistics, and personnel selection. His research focuses on personality testing and item response theory, as well as historical investigations in applied psychology. In addition to consulting with private and public sector organizations on testing issues such as computer adaptive testing and measurement bias, Dr. Zickar has served as an expert witness on issues related to discrimination using employment tests for hiring and promotion. He is currently on the Executive Board of the Society of Industrial/Organizational Psychology where he is also a Fellow. In his spare time, Dr. Zickar is obsessed with politics (he is the Party Chair for his county) and cats. His web page can be found at www.bgsu.edu/departments/psych/page33128.html.

Preface

Psychometric Theory. Test Theory. Measurement Theory. A quick perusal of the major titles of advanced psychometrics textbooks reveals that most include the word *theory*, and this is for good reason. Upon opening these textbooks, we see clear evidence that the major emphasis of most advanced measurement texts is on explaining test theory. We acknowledge that this should be the case. Students certainly need a solid foundation in measurement theory in order to even begin to hope to apply what they have learned to actual test construction. In teaching our own advanced measurement classes, however, we have often sought to complement our consideration of test theory with applied examples and exercises. Doing such has not always been easy. Until we published the first edition of this book in 2005, few texts had provided students with much practice actually implementing the measurement theory they are so diligently learning about. The title of this book, *Measurement Theory in Action: Case Studies and Exercises*, discloses our major purpose as providing opportunities for students to apply and reinforce their newly found knowledge of psychometric theory. As such, our hope is that this revised version of our 2005 text will be a great complement to the theoretical material that students are exposed to elsewhere in their psychometrics class. The following sections explain how this text is organized to help achieve this goal.

Modules

The 22 modules that make up this text each focus on a specific issue associated with test construction. It was our goal to ensure that these modules corresponded to entire chapters in most typical measurement theory texts. Our goal in developing this book was not to supplant comprehensive textbooks on psychometric theory, but to provide an invaluable supplement that distills the exhaustive information contained in such texts and provide hands-on practice with implementation of measurement theory through the presentation of case studies and exercises. Therefore, each module "stands alone," in that information from previous modules is not assumed in subsequent modules (though linkages are made when appropriate). This is intended to allow instructors to assign only those modules that seem relevant or to assign modules in an order that better fits their own course goals.

The initial four modules introduce the concept of measurement theory (Module 1), review essential foundational statistics (Module 2), explain the concept of psychological scaling (Module 3), and provide an overview of the necessity of developing clear test specifications in the development of a psychological measure (Module 4). Modules 5 through 11 discuss issues related to test reliability and validation. Module 5 discusses classical test theory (CTT) of reliability, and Module 6 discusses estimating reliability in practice. Modules 7, 8, and 9 present issues related to traditional conceptions of content validation, criterion-related validation, and construct validation, respectively. However, we emphasize the contemporary approach, which asserts that all evidence examined in relation to the inferences and conclusions of test scores contributes to the same process, namely, validation. Module 10 examines validity generalization/meta-analysis, while Module 11 examines the psychometric conception of test bias. Practical issues in the construction of tests are examined in Modules 12 through 16. These issues include the development of measures of maximal performance (Module 12), CTT item analysis (Module 13), the scoring of tests (Module 14), development of measures of typical performance (Module 15), and concerns related to response styles and guessing (Module 16). Modules 17 through 22 present more advanced topics in measurement theory, including multiple regression (Module 17), exploratory factor analysis (Module 18), confirmatory factor analysis (Module 19), an introduction to item response theory (IRT) (Module 20), the application of IRT to computer adaptive testing and differential item functioning (Module 21), and generalizability theory (Module 22).

New to the Second Edition

Those familiar with the first edition of this book will no doubt notice substantial changes in many of the modules presented in this second edition. Based on the feedback we received from reviewers, adopters, and users of the first edition of this book, major revisions included in this second edition comprise the division of our consideration of reliability into two separate modules (Modules 5 and 6), the separation of modules examining exploratory and confirmatory factor analysis (Modules 18 and 19), and the inclusion of a new module introducing generalizability theory (Module 22). In addition, while we no longer include a separate module on diversity issues, much of the material from that former module has been included in Modules 1 and 11 in this second edition. Throughout the book, the modules have been updated to include recent developments in measurement theory. You will also notice the addition of a new co-author, Michael Zickar, who was responsible for updating the advanced topics, including the addition of the new concluding module on generalizability theory. Finally, each module now includes an overview, best practices, case studies, exercises, and suggested further readings. Further explanation of each of these components is presented below.

Overviews

If you are hoping the overview of each module will provide an extensive and in-depth explanation of the substantive elements of each particular aspect of measurement theory, then you will certainly be disappointed. As noted earlier, our purpose is to focus on the *application* of measurement theory, not the theory itself. Thus, our intended purpose of the overviews is to provide a brief, simply stated summary of the major issues related to a particular topic in measurement theory. However, because we could not force applied case studies and exercises on students absent theory altogether, we felt it necessary to provide a bit of summary information on each major psychometric topic before launching into the applied case studies and exercises. In addition, many of the overviews include step-by-step examples of the application of measurement theory topics covered in that module. Each overview then concludes with a series of best practices, as well as practical questions intended to assess understanding of the material presented.

One of the most gratifying outcomes of the first edition of this book was hearing from instructors and students who praised the accessibility of the information provided in the overviews. We continue to hope that those new to measurement theory will find the overviews easy to read and understand. Indeed, we would be especially proud if a student conscientiously pored over a number of primary readings on a psychometric topic, then read the corresponding chapter in a typical advanced measurement textbook, and then, after reading our brief overview on the same topic, exclaimed, "Aha. So that's what all that other stuff was about!"

Best Practices

The overview of each module is immediately followed by a list of several best practices related to the topic. These best practices provide practical recommendations for ensuring appropriate application of psychometric theory.

Practical Questions

A list of practical questions is presented following each module overview. These questions can help students self-assess their understanding of the material presented in the overview.

Case Studies

Each module contains two case studies that depict typical dilemmas and difficulties faced when applying measurement theory. In many cases, we have drawn these case studies from our own applied professional experiences, as well as the trials and tribulations of our students. In some instances, the case studies summarize an exemplar from the extant psychometric literature or discuss aspects of the development of a commercially available test. Others we completely made up after hours of staring at a blank computer screen. Nonetheless, in each case study we hoped to capture the questions and doubts many psychometric novices encounter when first attempting the application of measurement theory. The case studies rarely directly answer the questions they raise. Indeed, the "questions to ponder" that follow each case study serve only to further specify the issues raised by the case study. We believe that a thoughtful consideration of these issues will better prepare students for their own application of measurement theory.

Exercises

It is our firm belief that we learn best by actually doing. Therefore, each module contains at least two exercises intended to provide students with practical experience in the application of measurement theory. Additional exercises for many modules are available on the book's website: www.routledge.com/9780415644792. The purpose of each exercise is stated in a simple objective. Some exercises are amenable to in-class administration to groups, while others are best tackled individually outside the classroom environment. Many exercises require no computer access, while a number of exercises require access to the Internet or use of statistical analysis software such as SPSS. Data sets for these exercises are available on the book's website. Appendix B presents a description of the data sets for the latter type of exercises. Exercises vary considerably in difficulty, although in no instance did we intend to include an exercise that was so difficult or so time consuming that students lost track of the relatively simple, straightforward objective.

While the vast majority of exercises require knowledge only of the material presented in that specific module, Appendix A presents a continuing exercise that incorporates many of the steps in the development of a measure of typical performance. This continuing exercise would appropriately serve as the basis of a term-long, culminating assignment for a psychometrics class.

Further Readings

For each module, we have selected a number of additional readings we think you will find useful. These sometimes include classic readings on a topic; other times, they include the latest conceptualization of the topic or chapters that nicely summarize the topic. In many cases, we have recommended those authors who made very complex material somewhat understandable to us given our own admittedly limited knowledge of a topic.

Glossary

At the back of the book, you will also find a glossary of important measurement terms. First usage of the glossary terms in the main text is in boldface type. We hope you'll find the glossary useful for defining terms presented throughout the text and in your other measurement theory–related readings. If you do not find what you are looking for, we welcome your suggestions for additional terms to add in future editions.

Web Resources

Instructor's resources are available to professors who adopt the book for use in the classroom. The website can be accessed at http://www.routledge.com/9780415644792. Instructors who adopt the book will find suggested answers to the book's questions and exercises, detailed worked solutions to the exercises, and PowerPoint slides for possible use in the classroom. In addition, both *students and instructors* can access the SPSS data sets, additional exercises, the glossary, and website references that are helpful in understanding psychometric concepts.

Acknowledgments

We would like to thank a number of individuals who provided the necessary help to put this book together. We are especially grateful to Debra Riegert for helping us to make the transition to Routledge/Taylor & Francis for the second edition of the book an easy and enjoyable process. We also thank Jennifer Mersman, Joel Wiesen, and several colleagues, who would prefer to remain anonymous, for providing the data used in several of the examples presented throughout the book.

We are also indebted to several reviewers who provided excellent recommendations for improving upon the first edition of this book: Dennis J. Devine, Indiana University–Purdue University Indianapolis; Dennis Doverspike, University of Akron; Lisa Finkelstein, Northern Illinois University; Debi Mishra, State University of New York–Binghamton; Kevin Murphy, Colorado State University; and Toni M. Somers, Wayne State University. In addition, we also appreciate the suggestions of adopters and users of the first edition of the book who e-mailed us with their suggestions for improvements. We are also very appreciative of the feedback from the reviewers who provided insightful comments on the first edition of this book: Sebastiano Fiscaro, Wayne State University; Mike Aamodt, Radford University; Keith F. Widaman, University of California at Davis; Jose Cortina, George Mason University; and additional reviewers.

We also thank our respective colleagues and students for helping to shape, and often clarify, our thoughts on challenging statistics and measurement topics. In addition, we appreciate the help of both current and former students who let us "road test" many of the exercises and case studies in this book. Last, but clearly not least, we are extremely thankful for the support and love expressed by our respective family and friends while we completed the revisions to this second edition of our book.

—Kenneth S. Shultz
San Bernardino, California
kshultz@csusb.edu

—David J. Whitney
Long Beach, California
dave.whitney@csulb.edu

—Michael J. Zickar
Bowling Green, Ohio
mzickar@bgsu.edu

Part 1
Introduction

Module 1

Introduction and Overview

Thousands of important, and sometimes life-altering, decisions are made every day. Who should we hire? Which students should be placed in accelerated or remedial programs? Which defendants should be incarcerated and which paroled? Which treatment regimen will work best for a given client? Should custody of this child be granted to the mother or the father or the grandparents? In each of these situations, a "test" may be used to help provide guidance. There are many vocal opponents to the use of standardized tests to make such decisions. However, the bottom line is that these critical decisions will ultimately be made with or without the use of test information. The question we have to ask ourselves is, "Can a better decision be made with the use of relevant test information?" In many, although not all, instances, the answer will be yes, *if* a well-developed and appropriate test is used *in combination* with other relevant, well-justified information available to the decision maker. The opposition that many individuals have to standardized tests is that they are the sole basis for making an important, sometimes life-altering, decision. Thus, it would behoove any decision maker to take full advantage of other relevant, well-justified information, where available, to make the best and most informed decision possible.

A quick point regarding "other relevant and well-justified information" is in order. What one decision maker sees as "relevant" may not seem relevant and well justified to another constituent in the testing process. For example, as one of the reviewers of the first edition of this book pointed out, a manager in an organization may be willing to use tests that demonstrate validity and reliability for selecting workers in his organization. However, he may ultimately decide to rely more heavily on what he deems to be "other relevant information" but, in fact, is simply his belief in his own biased intuition about people. To this supervisor, his intuitions are viewed as legitimate "other relevant information" beyond test scores. However, others in the testing process may not view the supervisor's intuitions as relevant. Thus, when we say that other relevant information beyond well developed and validated tests should be used when appropriate, we are not talking about information such as intuition (which should be distinguished from professional judgment, which, more often than not, is, in fact, relevant), rather we are referring to additional relevant information such as professional references, systematic background checks, structured observations, professional judgments, and the like. That is, additional information that can be well justified, as well as systematically developed, collected, and evaluated. Thus, we are not recommending collecting and using additional information beyond tests simply for the sake of doing so. Rather, any "other relevant information" that is used in addition to test information to make critical decisions should be well justified and supported by professional standards, as well as appropriate for the context for which it is being proposed.

What Makes Tests Useful

Tests can take many forms from traditional paper-and-pencil exams to portfolio assessments, job interviews, case histories, behavioral observations, computer adaptive assessments, and peer ratings—to name just a few. The common theme in all of these **assessment** procedures is that they represent a sample of behaviors from the test taker. Thus, psychological testing is similar to any science, in that a sample is taken to make inferences about a population. In this case, the sample consists of behaviors (e.g., test responses on a paper-and-pencil test or performance of physical tasks during physical **ability testing**) from a larger domain of all possible behaviors representing a construct. For example, the first test we take when we come into the world is called the APGAR test. That's right, just 1 minute into the world, we get our first test. You probably do not remember your score on your APGAR test, but our guess is your mother does, given the importance this first test has in revealing your initial physical functioning. The purpose of the APGAR test is to assess a newborn's general functioning right after birth. Table 1.1 displays the five categories that newborn infants are tested on at 1 and 5 minutes after birth: appearance, pulse, grimace, activity, and respiration (hence, the acronym APGAR). A score is obtained by summing the newborn infant's assessed value on each of the dimensions. Scores can range from 0 to 10. A score of 7–10 is considered normal. A score of 4–6 indicates that the newborn infant may require some resuscitation, while a score of 3 or less means the newborn would require immediate and intensive resuscitation. The infant is then assessed again at 5 minutes, and if his or her score is still below a 7, he or she may be assessed again at 10 minutes. If the infant's APGAR score is 7 or above 5 minutes after birth, which is typical, then no further intervention is called for. Hence, by taking a relatively small sampling of behavior, we are (or at least competent obstetrics nurses or doctors are) able to quickly, and quite accurately, assess the functioning of a newborn infant to determine if resuscitation interventions are required to get the newborn functioning properly.

The **utility** of any assessment device, however, will depend on the qualities of the test and the intended use of the test. Test information can be used for a variety

Table 1.1   The APGAR Test Scoring Table

Sign	Points		
	0	*1*	*2*
Appearance (color)	Pale or blue	Body pink, extremities blue	Pink (normal for non-Caucasians)
Pulse (heartbeat)	Not detectible	Lower than 100 bpm	Higher than 100 bpm
Grimace (reflex)	No response	Grimace	Lusty cry
Activity (muscle tone)	Flaccid	Some movement	A lot of activity
Respiration (breathing)	None	Slow, irregular	Good (crying)

of purposes, from making predictions about the likelihood that a patient will commit suicide to making personnel selection decisions by determining which entry-level workers to hire. Tests can also be used for classification purposes, as when students are designated as remedial, gifted, or somewhere in between. Tests can also be used for evaluation purposes, as in the use of a classroom test to evaluate performance of students in a given subject matter. Counseling psychologists routinely use tests to assess clients for emotional adjustment problems, or possibly for help in providing vocational counseling. Finally, tests can also be used for research-only purposes, such as when an experimenter uses a test to prescreen study participants to assign each one to an experimental condition. If the test is not used for its intended purpose, however, it will not be very useful and, in fact, may actually be harmful. As Anastasi and Urbina (1997) note, "Psychological tests are tools . . . Any tool can be an instrument of good or harm, depending on how it is used" (p. 2).

For example, most American children in grades 2–12 are required to take standardized tests on a yearly basis. These tests were initially intended for the sole purpose of assessing students' learning outcomes. Over time, however, a variety of other misuses for these tests have emerged. For instance, they are frequently used to determine school funding and, in some cases, teachers' or school administrators' "merit" pay. However, given that determining the pay levels of educational employees was not the intended use of such standardized educational tests when they were developed, they almost always serve poorly in this capacity. Thus, a test that was developed with good (i.e., appropriate) intentions can be used for inappropriate purposes, limiting the usefulness of the test. In this instance, however, not only is the test of little use in setting pay for teachers and administrators, but it may actually be causing harm by coercing teachers to "teach to the test," thereby trading long-term gains in learning for short-term increases in standardized test performance.

In addition, no matter how the test is used, it will only be useful if it meets certain psychometric and practical requirements. From a psychometric or measurement standpoint, we want to know if the test is accurate, standardized, and reliable; if it demonstrates evidence of validity; and if it is free of both measurement and predictive bias. Procedures for determining these psychometric qualities form the core of the rest of this book. From a practical standpoint, the test must be cost effective as well as relatively easy to administer and score. Reflecting on our earlier example, we would surmise that the APGAR meets most of these qualities of being practical. Trained doctors and nurses in a hospital delivery room can administer the APGAR quickly and efficiently. Our key psychometric concern in this situation may be how often different doctors and nurses are able to provide similar APGAR scores in a given situation (i.e., the **inter-rater reliability** of the APGAR).

Individual Differences

Ultimately, when it comes right down to it, those interested in applied psychological measurement are usually interested in some form of **individual differences** (i.e., how individuals differ on test scores and the underlying **traits** being measured by those tests). If there are no differences in how target individuals score on the test, then the test will have little value to us. For example, if we give a group of elite athletes the standard physical ability test given to candidates for a police officer job, there will likely be very little variability in scores, with all the athletes scoring extremely high on the test. Thus, the test data would provide little value in predicting which athletes would make good police officers. On the other hand, if we had a more typical group of job candidates who passed previous hurdles in the personnel selection process for police officer (e.g., cognitive tests, background checks, and psychological evaluations) and gave them the same physical ability test, we would see much wider variability in scores. Thus, the test would at least have the potential to be a useful predictor of job success, as we would have at least some variability in the observed test scores.

Individual differences on psychological tests can take several different forms. Typically, we look at **inter-individual differences** where we examine differences on the same construct across individuals. In such cases, the desire is usually prediction. That is, how well does the test predict some criterion of interest? For example, in the preceding scenario, we would use the physical ability test data to predict who would be successful in police work. Typically, job candidates are rank ordered based on their test scores and selected in a top-down fashion, assuming the test is indeed linearly associated with job performance. As you will see as we move further into the book, however, it is rare that any single test will be sufficient to provide a complete picture of the test taker. Thus, more often than not, several tests (or at least several decision points) are incorporated into the decision-making process.

We may also be interested in examining **intra-individual differences**. These differences can take two forms. In the first situation, we may be interested in examining a single construct within the same individual across time. In this case, we are interested in how the individual changes or matures over time. For example, there have been longitudinal studies conducted by life-span developmental psychologists that have looked at how an individual's cognitive ability and personality change over the course of his or her lifetime. In particular, these researchers are interested in studying intra-individual differences in maturation. That is, why do some individuals' scores on cognitive ability tests go up dramatically over time, while the scores of other individuals only go up a little or not at all or maybe even go down? Thus, the focus is not on group mean differences (as in inter-individual differences); rather, we are looking for different rates of change within individuals over time.

In the second form of intra-individual differences, we are interested in looking at a given individual's strengths and weaknesses across a variety of constructs, typically at one point in time. Thus, the same individual is given a variety (or **battery**) of different tests. Here we are usually interested in classifying individuals based on their strengths and weaknesses. For example, hundreds of thousands of high school students take the **Armed Services Vocational Aptitude Battery (ASVAB)** every year. The ASVAB consists of a series of 10 subtests that assess individuals' strengths and weaknesses in a wide variety of aptitudes. Those not interested in pursuing a military career can use it for career-counseling purposes, while individuals interested in military service can use it to be placed or classified within a particular branch of the armed services or career path within the military based on their relative strengths and weaknesses. The key is that the ASVAB consists of a **test battery** that allows test users to see how individuals differ in terms of the relative strength of different traits and characteristics. Hence, the ASVAB is useful for several different constituents in the testing process.

Constituents in the Testing Process

Because the decisions that result from the uses of test data are so often of great consequence, the testing process is very much a political process. Each of the **constituents** or stakeholders in the testing process will have a vested interest in the outcome, albeit for different reasons. Obviously, the **test takers** themselves have a strong vested interest in the outcome of the testing process. Because they are the ones who will be affected most by the use of the test, they tend to be most concerned with the procedural and distributive (i.e., outcome) fairness of the test and the testing process. The **test users** (those who administer, score, and use the test) may be less concerned with an individual's outcome per se, focusing more on making sure the test and testing process are as fair as possible to all test takers. They are using the test, no doubt, to help make a critical decision for both the individuals and the organization using the test. Thus, they will also be concerned with many of the psychometric issues that will be discussed throughout this book, such as reliability, validity, and test bias. The **test developer** tends to focus on providing the best possible test to the test user and test taker. This includes making sure the test is well designed and developed, in addition to being practical and effective. Test developers also need to collect and provide evidence that the test demonstrates consistency of scores (i.e., **reliability**) and that the concepts that are purported to be measured are, in fact, measured.

Thus, this book focuses on what you will need to know to be a qualified *test developer* and informed *test user*. You will learn how to develop test questions, determine the psychometric properties of a test, and evaluate test items and the entire test for potential biases. In addition, many practical issues, such as test translation, dealing with response biases, and interpreting test scores, will also be discussed. Each module includes case studies and hands-on exercises that will provide practice in thinking about and working through the many complicated psychometric processes you will learn about in the rest of the book. In addition, many modules also include step-by-step examples to walk you through the process that an applied practitioner would go through to evaluate the concepts discussed in that particular module. Thus, in short, conscientious use of this book will help you to better understand and apply the knowledge and skills you are developing as you study a wide variety of topics within advanced measurement theory.

Diversity Issues

One major purpose of testing is to assess individual differences. It is ironic, then, that a major criticism of testing is that it too often fails to consider issues of diversity. As used here, diversity issues refer to concerns that arise when testing specific populations categorized on the basis of ethnicity, gender, age, linguistic ability, or physical disability. Although test creators often attempt to use a diverse sample during test development, most tests are based on White middle-class individuals (Padilla, 2001). According to Fouad and Chan (1999),

> The most widely used tests were conceived by White psychologists working within a White mainstream culture for the purpose of assessing psychological traits in men. Yet, tests that were initially developed for men are routinely given to women, and those intended for White U.S. citizens are administered to members of minority groups or are used in other countries. (p. 32)

In essence, the primary concern in testing diverse populations is whether the psychometric properties of the test (e.g., reliability and validity) change when the test is used on a population that differs from that used during test development and standardization. The ability of a typical test to produce reliable and accurate scores for members of other diverse groups is at times suspect and, thus, is discussed in more detail in Module 11.

Testing is most pervasive in educational settings. Indeed, Haney, Madaus, and Lyons (1993) estimated that the average U.S. public school student is administered between three and eight standardized tests each year. As Samuda (1998) pointed out, however, as a group, minority children have always scored lower on standardized tests—whether the minority group was the Irish at the turn of the 20th century, southern and eastern Europeans a few decades later, or Blacks and Spanish-speaking groups later in the 20th century. Given the influence testing has in determining educational and work opportunities, the inappropriate use of tests can have serious long-term effects on individuals, groups, and American society as a whole.

Reasons for Concern

The potential reasons for differential performance across diverse groups are as different as the groups themselves, including differences in experience, beliefs, test-taking motivations, familiarity with testing, English language ability, and values. These factors may lead minorities to score considerably lower than White middle-class Americans (Padilla, 2001). If test performance is dependent on a certain degree of common experience, then tests will be problematic to the degree that all test takers do not fully share in that common experience.

Sternberg and Grigorenko (2001) argued that, to perform well on an ability test, the test taker must possess a certain test-taking expertise. If this same expertise is correlated with outcomes considered valuable in society (such as performance in school or on the job), then the test is considered useful. However, test-taking expertise may not be as highly developed for individuals in different cultures. Unfortunately, such cultural differences in test-taking expertise may obscure the true capabilities of members of a group. As an example, Sternberg and Grigorenko pointed out that while Western assessment of intelligence often emphasizes speed of mental processing, other cultures emphasize depth of mental processing, even to the extent of suspicion of work that is done too quickly. Perhaps an even more startling example used by these authors is based on a study reported by Cole, Gay, Glick, and Sharp (1971). The researchers asked adults of the Kpelle tribe in Africa to sort names of various objects. The Kpelle sorted the names functionally (e.g., banana: eat), much in the same way very young children might in the West. Reflecting unanimity of cognitive theory, however, Western tests of intellect consider functional sorting to be inferior to taxonomic sorting (e.g., banana: type of fruit). Attempts to cajole the Kpelle into sorting the names in a different manner were unsuccessful until a researcher finally asked how a stupid person might sort the names. Immediately, a member of the tribe provided a taxonomic sorting of the names. Clearly, then, cultural differences do exert important influences on the way respondents view what is "correct."

Concluding Comments

Psychological testing, when done properly, can be a tremendous benefit to society. Competently developed and implemented assessment devices can provide valuable input to the critical decisions we are faced with every day. However, poorly developed and implemented tests may, at best, be of little assistance and, in fact, may actually do more harm than good. Therefore, the rest of this book was written to help you become a more informed consumer of psychological tests, as well as to prepare future test developers in terms of the critical competencies that are needed to develop tests that will be beneficial to society and acceptable (or at least tolerable) to all testing constituents.

Best Practices

1. Keep in mind that tests are just one part of the decision-making process and should not be the sole basis for any significant decision.
2. The most appropriate assessment measure to use will depend on the type of intra- and/or inter-individual difference you wish to assess.
3. Multiple constituents exist in any testing situation. All must be considered and/or consulted during in the development, administration, and dissemination stages of the process.
4. Test users must be aware that the psychometric properties of the test can change based on the population used. Awareness of diversity issues in testing is essential.

Practical Questions

1. What specific goals do you want to achieve by taking a course in measurement?
2. What will likely be your major stake in the testing process once you finish your measurement course?
3. What alternative "test" to the APGAR could an obstetrics nurse or doctor use to assess newborn functioning? What would be the advantages and disadvantages compared to the APGAR test shown in Table 1.1?
4. Who are the major constituents or stakeholders in the psychological testing process?
5. What is the major purpose of examining inter-individual differences via test scores?
6. What are the different types of intra-individual differences?
7. What are the major purposes of the different forms of intra-individual differences in interpreting test data?
8. Can you provide examples of the uses of both inter-individual differences and intra-individual differences?

Case Studies

CASE STUDY 1.1: TESTING CONSTITUENTS AND THE STANFORD ACHIEVEMENT TEST

Professor Gilbert, an educational testing professor at a local state university, was contacted by a small school district that had decided to implement a Talented and Gifted (TAG) program for advanced students. The school district initially was going to use grade point average (GPA) as the sole basis for placement into the TAG program. However, several parents objected that the different tracks within the schools tended to grade using different standards. As a result, those students in Track A had much higher GPAs (on average) than did those in the other two tracks. Thus, those in Track A were much more likely to be placed in the TAG program if only GPA was used than were those in Tracks B and C.

Therefore, the school board decided to set up an ad hoc committee to provide recommendations to the board as to how entrance to the new TAG program would be determined. The committee was headed by Professor Gilbert (who also happened to have two sons in the school system) and included school psychologists, principals, parents, teachers, and students. The committee's initial report recommended that teacher written evaluations, test scores from the Stanford Achievement Test, and letters of recommendations be used, in addition to GPA, to determine entrance into the TAG program. As you might have guessed, the next meeting of the school board, where these recommendations were presented and discussed, was a heated affair. Professor Gilbert was suddenly beginning to ponder whether she needed to raise her consulting fees.

Questions to Ponder

1. Who are the major constituents or stakeholders in the testing process in this scenario?
2. What is Professor Gilbert's "stake" in the testing process? Does she have more than one?
3. What form of individual differences is the committee most likely to be focusing on? Why?
4. Should all of the different assessment devices be equally weighted?

CASE STUDY 1.2: DEVELOPMENT OF
A VOLUNTEER PLACEMENT TEST

A local volunteer referral agency was interested in using "tests" to place volunteer applicants in the volunteer organizations it served. In order to do so, however, the agency needed to assess each applicant to determine where his or her skills could best be used. As a first step, the director of the agency contacted a local university and found out that Professor Kottke's graduate practicum class in applied testing was in need of a community-based project. Soon thereafter, Professor Kottke and her students met with the director of the agency to determine what her needs were and how the class could help.

In the past, the agency first conducted a short 15-minute telephone interview as an initial screen for each volunteer applicant. Those applicants who appeared to be promising were asked to come in for a half-hour face-to-face interview with a member of the agency staff. If the applicant was successful at this stage, a brief background check was conducted, and the candidates who passed were placed in the first available opening. However, the agency was receiving feedback from the volunteer organizations that a large portion of the volunteers were participating for only a month or two and would then never return. In follow-up interviews with these volunteers, the most consistent reason given for not returning was that the volunteer placement was simply "not a good fit." Thus, Professor Kottke and her class were asked to improve the fit of candidates to the positions in which they were being placed. Unfortunately, Professor Kottke's 10-week course was already one-third completed, so she and her students would have to work quickly.

Questions to Ponder

1. If you were in Professor Kottke's practicum class, where would you start in the process of trying to help this agency?
2. Does this seem to be more of an inter-individual differences or intra-individual differences issue? Explain.
3. Who are the constituents in this testing process?
4. What do you think Professor Kottke and her students can realistically accomplish in the 6–7 weeks remaining in the term?

꧁ ‹o› ꧂

Exercises

EXERCISE 1.1: DIFFERENT USES FOR A GIVEN TEST

OBJECTIVE: To think critically about the wide variety of uses for a given test.

The Armed Services Vocational Aptitude Battery (ASVAB) was discussed in the module overview. Nearly one million people take this test each year, many of them high school students. The test consists of 10 different subtests measuring general science, arithmetic reasoning, word knowledge, paragraph comprehension, numerical operations, coding speed, auto and shop information, mathematics knowledge, mechanical comprehension, and electronics information. The ASVAB is used primarily to select recruits for the different branches of the armed services and then to place those individuals selected into various training programs based on their aptitude strengths and weaknesses. In fact, a subset of 100 items (called the Armed Forces Qualification Test) from the ASVAB is used by all the branches of the military to select recruits. Each branch of the military employs a slightly different cutoff score to select recruits.

Given the 10 subtests listed previously, what other purposes could the ASVAB be used for besides selection and placement (e.g., career guidance)?

EXERCISE 1.2: WHO ARE THE MAJOR CONSTITUENTS IN THE TESTING PROCESS?

OBJECTIVE: To become familiar with the major constituents in the testing process.

As noted in the overview, there are typically numerous constituents in any given testing process. These constituents may include the test takers, test developers, test users, and, more broadly, society in general. Each of these constituents will have a varying degree of interest in a given assessment device.

Who are the major test constituents with regard to the ASVAB discussed in the module overview and in Exercise 1.1? What would be the major concerns of each of these different constituents with regard to development, refinement, administration, and use of the ASVAB?

EXERCISE 1.3: TESTING AND INDIVIDUAL DIFFERENCES

OBJECTIVE: To identify the major forms of individual differences commonly assessed with psychological tests.

Most tests are administered to identify some form of individual differences. These can include inter-individual differences, intra-individual differences, or both. Again, looking at the ASVAB, what forms of inter- and intra-individual differences might be assessed with this particular test?

Further Readings

Anastasi, A., & Urbina, S. (1997). *Psychological testing* (7th ed., pp. 2–31). Upper Saddle River, NJ: Prentice Hall.

Crocker, L.M., & Algina, J. (1986). *Introduction to classical and modern test theory* (pp. 3–15). Belmont, CA: Wadsworth.

Ghiselli, E.E., Campbell, J.P., & Zedeck, S. (1981). *Measurement theory for the behavioral sciences* (pp. 9–30). New York: W.H. Freeman.

Murphy, K.R., & Davidshofer, C.O. (2005). *Psychological testing: Principles and applications* (6th ed.). Upper Saddle River, NJ: Pearson Education.

Module 2

Statistics Review for Psychological Measurement

I f you have already taken a statistics class, you probably spent a good portion of the term on statistical significance testing, learning about *t* tests, analysis of variance, and other such statistical tests. If you dreaded that part of your statistics class, you are in luck because in applied psychological measurement we typically do little in the way of statistical significance testing. Instead, we tend to focus on either descriptive statistics or estimation. For those of you who have not had an introductory statistics class or who have but are in need of a refresher, an abbreviated review follows. However, please see the Further Readings listed at the end of this module for a more detailed discussion and explanation of the statistics discussed below.

Organizing and Displaying Test Data

More often than not in applied psychological measurement, we are interested in simply describing a set of test data. For example, we may want to know how many people scored at a certain level, what the average score was for a group of test takers, or what the percentile rank equivalent is for a score of 84. Thus, we are most likely to be using univariate **descriptive statistics** to describe a set of test data. If we know the central tendency (e.g., mode, median, mean), variability or dispersion (e.g., range, interquartile range, standard deviation, variance), and shape (e.g., skew, kurtosis) of a distribution of scores, then we can completely describe that distribution (at least as far as we are concerned in applied psychological measurement). In addition, we can standardize (e.g., Z scores, stanines, percentiles) a set of test scores to help us interpret a given score relative to other scores in the distribution or to some established group norm. Before we run any "numbers," however, we are best advised to draw some graphs (e.g., histograms, stem-and-leaf plots) to get a visual picture of what is going on with our test data. As has been said, a picture is worth a thousand words. That saying definitely applies to interpreting a set of test scores with appropriate graphs, as well.

As an example, look at Table 2.1, which displays a distribution of examination scores obtained for an introductory tests and measurements class. What can we say about this distribution of scores? First, we see that we have a total of 25 scores. Next, we might notice that scores range from a low of 68 to a high of 93. In addition, we might notice that for many score values there is only one individual who obtained that score on the test. We may also notice that there is a clustering of scores in the high 80s. Looking at an individual score, say 80, we can see that two students obtained this score (see the Frequency column) and that two students represent 8% of all students (see the Percent column). We may also notice that 32% of students received a score lower than 80 (see the Cumulative Percent column). This latter figure is sometimes referred to as a score of 80 having a **percentile rank** of 32. Thus, by simply organizing the test scores into a simple frequency table as we did in Table 2.1, we can answer many questions about how the group did overall and how each individual performed on the test.

Table 2.1   Example Test Scores for a Classroom Examination With 25 Students

Test Scores	Frequency	Percent	Cumulative Percent	Z Score
68	1	4	4	−1.85
69	1	4	8	−1.73
70	1	4	12	−1.60
72	1	4	16	−1.36
73	1	4	20	−1.23
74	1	4	24	−1.11
76	1	4	28	−.86
79	1	4	32	−.48
80	2	8	40	−.36
84	1	4	44	.14
86	1	4	48	.39
87	2	8	56	.51
88	4	16	72	.64
89	1	4	76	.76
90	3	12	88	.89
91	1	4	92	1.01
92	1	4	96	1.14
93	1	4	100	1.26
Total	25			

We should also graph the data before computing any statistics. It would be common to display test data as a frequency histogram or stem-and-leaf plot. Figure 2.1a shows a histogram of the **frequency distribution** of the data in Table 2.1. Again, we see that the low score is 68 and the high score is 93. We also notice the clustering of scores at 88 and 90. In addition, we may notice that no student received a score of 71, 75, 77, 78, 81–83, or 85. Thus, there is some "wasted space" in the graph where no students obtained a given score. While all this information is useful, we could have just as easily gleaned most of this information, and more, directly from Table 2.1. Thus, did we really need to go to the trouble of creating Figure 2.1a?

Now look at Figure 2.1b. How does this graph compare to Table 2.1 and Figure 2.1a? This is called a grouped frequency histogram. It is based on the data from Table 2.1; however, scores have been logically grouped into grade categories. In this case, because we are dealing with classroom test scores, most students (as well as the professor) will likely want to know how they did "gradewise" on the test. Thus, grouping the individual scores into grade categories provides a more informative picture of how students did on the test. In addition, notice that the Y (vertical) axis now displays the percentage of scores, as opposed to the simple frequency of scores. Although using percentages instead of frequencies is not necessary for a **grouped frequency distribution**, doing so is more informative as the number of test scores increases. Also, each bar on the graph lists the actual percentage of students who received that particular grade on the test. Imagine looking at the graph without the numbers in the bars (as in

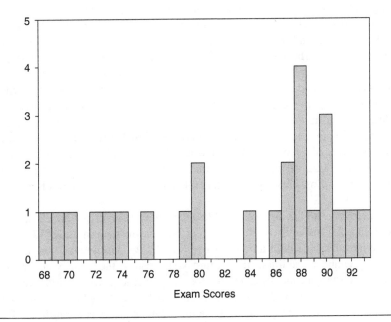

Figure 2.1a   Frequency Distribution for Exam Scores

Figure 2.1b   Grouped Frequency Distribution for Exam Scores

Figure 2.1a). Could you figure out exactly what percentage of students received an A–? It would be difficult. By the way, the change of the *Y* axis to percent and the addition of the numbers to the bars are not unique to the grouped frequency histogram. We simply added these features to this graph to highlight other ways of improving the presentation of the test data. Regardless, there are distinct advantages to using a grouped frequency histogram over an ungrouped frequency histogram, particularly when there is a wide range of test scores; several scores between the high and low score, with no individuals obtaining that score; and many individuals who took the test. There is one major disadvantage, however. Can you guess what it is? That's right, you don't know exactly how many individuals received a specific score. You only know how many students fell within a given category. For example, in the C+ grade category (without looking at Table 2.1), you do not know if the single score is a 77, 78, or 79 on the test. Looking at Table 2.1, we see that the lone individual received a 79, and there were no scores of 77 or 78. Thus, it would be wise to have both a frequency table like Table 2.1 to provide individual data *and* a grouped histogram like Figure 2.1b to allow us to obtain a general sense of what the distribution of test scores looks like.

An alternative to having both a table and a graph is to create a stem-and-leaf plot. Figure 2.2 displays the stem-and-leaf plot for the data in Table 2.1. Notice that we have retained both the ungrouped (i.e., individual) data and the grouped frequency count. In addition, if you turn your head to the right, you can get a sense of the shape of the distribution. How do you read a stem-and-leaf display? In this case, the "stem" is the 10s column (60, 70, 80, or 90), which is noted in the "Stem Width" line below the data, while the "leaf" is the 1s column (0–9). Thus,

Frequency	Stem & Leaf
2 . 00	6 . 89
4 . 00	7 . 0234
2 . 00	7 . 69
3 . 00	8 . 004
8 . 00	8 . 67788889
6 . 00	9 . 000123
Stem Width:	10 . 00
Each Leaf:	1 case(s)

Figure 2.2   Exam 1 Test Scores Stem-and-Leaf Plot

we can see that we have one score each of 68, 69, 70, 72, 73, 74, 76, and 79, but two scores of 80. We can also look in the Frequency column and see that we have two scores in the high 60s, four in the low 70s, two in the high 70s, and so on. Because we have a total of only 25 scores, each "leaf" is just one case. However, the more scores you have in your distribution, the less likely it is that each leaf will represent a single case. As a result, you may, in fact, not have individual-level data in your stem-and-leaf plot. In addition, the stem width is not always equal to 10; it depends on what you are measuring. For example, if your test scores are reaction times, then instead of the stems representing 10s, they may be 10ths or 100ths of a second. Therefore, be sure to read any stem-and-leaf plot carefully.

Univariate Descriptive Statistics

Now that we have obtained a general sense of the data by creating and looking at the frequency table and graphs such as the grouped frequency distribution and stem-and-leaf display, it would be nice to have just a couple of numbers (i.e., statistics) to summarize or describe how test scores tend to cluster (central tendency) and vary (variability or dispersion) within the sample. As noted at the beginning of the module, the three most common measures of **central tendency** are the mode, median, and mean. The **mode** represents the most frequently occurring score in the distribution. Can you determine what the mode is from looking at Table 2.1? Yes, it is a score of 88. It occurs most frequently, with four individuals obtaining this score. Often times, however, a set of scores may have more than one most frequently occurring score (i.e., mode). Such distributions are referred to as multimodal. More specifically, if it has two modes, it is referred to as bimodal; three modes, trimodal; and so on. As a result, sometimes only the highest or lowest mode may be reported for a set of test scores.

The **median** is another measure of central tendency. It is the point in the distribution where half the scores are above, and half below. Looking at Table 2.1, can you figure out the median? To do so, you would need to look at the Cumulative

Percent column until you reached 50%. Looking at Table 2.1, you will notice that it skips from 48% at a score of 86 to 56% for a score of 87. So, what is the median? Remember, the cumulative percent represents the percentage of scores at or below that level, so in this instance, the median would be a score of 87. More precise formulas for calculating the median are available in the Further Readings listed at the end of the module.

The **mean** is the most popular measure of central tendency for summarizing test data. It represents the arithmetic average of the test scores. The formula for the mean is $M = \Sigma X_i / n$, where M is the mean, ΣX_i is the sum of the individual test scores, and n is the total number of persons for whom we have test scores. Using the data from Table 2.1, we see that the sum of test scores is 2072 and n is 25; thus, $M = 2072/25 = 82.88$. Be careful when computing the sum using a frequency table such as Table 2.1. A common mistake students (and sometimes professors) make is not counting all 25 scores. For example, students may forget to sum the two scores of 80, the two scores of 87, the four scores of 88, and the three scores of 90 in this example.

Knowing how scores tend to cluster (i.e., central tendency) is important. However, just as important is how scores tend to vary or spread out from the central tendency. If you do not know how scores vary, it would be difficult to determine how discrepant a given score is from the mean. For example, is a score of 84 all that discrepant from our mean of 82.88? We really cannot answer that question until we have some sense of how scores in this distribution tend to vary. Several common measures of **variability** include the range, interquartile range, standard deviation, and variance. The **range** is simply the high score minus the low score, which, in this case, would be $93 - 68 = 25$. However, whenever there are extreme scores, it is best to trim (i.e., drop) those extreme scores before computing the range. The **interquartile range** does just that. To compute the interquartile range, one subtracts the score at the 25th percentile from the score at the 75th percentile, instead of taking the highest and lowest scores as with the range. Thus, similar to how we found the median (i.e., the 50th percentile), we look at the Cumulative Percent column in Table 2.1 until we get to 25% (a score of 76 at the 28th percentile) and then 75% (a score of 89 at the 76th percentile). Thus, the interquartile range would be $89 - 76 = 13$. As with the median we computed previously, this is a somewhat crude estimate. More precise estimates are possible and methods to compute such estimates can be found in most introductory statistics books.

One of the most common forms of summarizing variability is to compute the variance. The **variance**, like the mean, is also an average, but in this case it is the average of the squared deviation of each score from the mean. The formula for a sample variance is $S^2 = \Sigma(X_i - M)^2 / n$, where S^2 is the sample variance estimate (note that you would have to divide by $n - 1$ if you were estimating a population variance), $(X_i - M)$ is the difference between each person's test score and the mean of the test scores (i.e., the deviation score), and n is the number of persons who took the test. You might be wondering why we square the deviation score. If we do not square the deviation score, our summed deviation scores will always sum to zero, because positive deviation scores would cancel out negative deviation scores.

Therefore, by squaring the deviation scores first, we get rid of all negative values and, thus, the problem of summing to zero is alleviated. However, we create a new problem by squaring each deviation score. Can you guess what it is? In interpreting our variance estimate, we are interpreting squared test scores, not our original test scores. As a result, we typically take the square root of our variance estimate, thus returning back to the metric of original test scores. This is referred to as the **standard deviation** and labeled as S.

In our example, using the data from Table 2.1, the variance is $S^2 = 1544.64/25 = 61.79$. If we take the square root, the standard deviation will be $S = 7.86$. Thus, on average, scores tend to deviate about 7.86 points from the mean. How is this useful to us? Remember at the beginning of the module we said we could standardize our test scores in order to help us interpret the scores. One way of doing this is by converting each score to a **Z** *score*. The formula for a Z score is $Z = (X_i - M)/S$. Previously, we asked if a score of 84 is really all that different from our mean of 82.88. By converting our test score to a Z score, we can more readily answer that question. Thus, $Z = (84 - 82.88)/7.86 = .14$. Thus, a score of 84 is only a little more than one tenth of a standard deviation above the mean; not a very large difference. Notice that all the standardized Z scores for all test values have been computed in the last column of Table 2.1. The farther the score is from the mean, the larger its Z score will be. Z scores are also useful in identifying outlier cases in a set of data. A typical rule of thumb is any score more than 3 standard deviations away from the mean is considered an outlier. Can any individuals in Table 2.1 be considered outliers? Finally, Z scores also let us compare two scores that come from two different distributions, each with its own mean and standard deviation. This will be discussed in more detail later in this book.

At the beginning of this module, we said that if we knew the central tendency, variability, and shape of a distribution, we could completely describe that distribution of scores. We have discussed the two former concepts, so it is time to discuss the latter. The first measure of shape is the skew statistic. It tells us how symmetrical the distribution is. Looking at Figure 2.1a, we see that our distribution of test scores is clearly not symmetrical. Scores tend to cluster at the upper end of the distribution, and there is a bit of tail that goes off to the left. Thus, this is called a *negatively skewed distribution*. Distributions can vary in terms of both the direction of the skew (positive or negative) and the magnitude of the skew. Therefore, not surprisingly, statisticians created a skew statistic to quantify the degree of **skewness**. Similar to the variance, we look at the deviation scores, but this time we will cube the scores (i.e., take them to the third power) instead of squaring the scores. The formula is

$$Sk = [\Sigma(X_i - M)^3/n]/S^3$$

where X_i is each individual test score, M is the mean test score, n is the total number of test scores, and S^3 is the standard deviation cubed. In our example, $Sk = -.626$. A skew of zero represents a symmetrical distribution of test scores; hence, our distribution has a slight negative skew.

Kurtosis is another measure of the shape of a distribution of scores. It describes how peaked (leptokurtic) or flat (platykurtic) a distribution of scores is. If the distribution follows a relatively normal (i.e., bell-shaped) curve, then it is said to be mesokurtic. Similar to the variance and skew statistic, we again use the deviation of each score from the mean, but now we take it to the fourth power. The formula for kurtosis is

$$Ku = \{[\Sigma(X_i - M)^4/n]/S^4\} - 3$$

However, notice that, in order to have zero represent a mesokurtic distribution, we apply a correction factor of "– 3" at the end of the formula. Positive scores represent a leptokurtic (i.e., skinny or peaked) distribution, whereas negative scores represent a platykurtic (i.e., wide or flat) distribution. In our example, $Ku = -1.085$; hence, we have a slightly platykurtic distribution.

Calculating these descriptive statistics—central tendency, variance, skewness, and kurtosis—should be one of the first statistical tasks when analyzing test data. Understanding the nature of your data is important before proceeding to many of the more advanced statistical analyses that we discuss in later chapters.

Bivariate Descriptive Statistics

We may also be interested in how strongly scores on a test are associated with some criterion variable. For example, are grades on this tests and measurements exam associated with overall grade point average (GPA)? In this instance, we would use a bivariate descriptive statistic (such as the Pearson product moment correlation coefficient) to describe the strength of the relationship between test scores and GPA (i.e., the **criterion**). If the association is sufficiently strong (this is a value judgment that depends on the context), we can then use one variable to predict the other variable using regression techniques. In our haste to compute the **correlation coefficient** and regression equations, however, we must not forget about graphical techniques such as bivariate **scatterplots**. Such plots will alert us to problems that will not be evident when we only examine the correlation coefficient. For example, outliers, possible subgroups, nonlinearity, and **heteroscedasticity** (i.e., the lack of uniformity of the data points around a regression line) are best detected not with the correlation coefficient but rather with visual inspection of a scatterplot.

Data from Table 2.2 were used to create Figure 2.3. Figure 2.3 is a scatterplot that shows test scores on the X axis and GPA on the Y axis. Thus, each point on the graph represents a person's value on the test as well as his or her GPA (i.e., a **bivariate distribution**). Looking at Figure 2.3, we see that there is a very strong relationship between scores on the first examination and overall GPA. This is indicated by the positive linear relationship between the two variables. That is, as scores on the first exam get larger, so does one's overall GPA. Most data points on the scatterplot are represented by a single circle. However, notice that a few points (around a test score of 89 or 90 and an overall GPA of 3.50–4.00) have lines coming from them. Each line represents an individual who had the same combination of test score and GPA. Examining how the pairs of scores cluster around the line of the graph, we notice that most scores are fairly close to the line. There do not appear to be any bivariate outliers (extreme on both the test score and GPA). The points are also relatively uniform along the line (i.e., they exhibit **homoscedasticity**), and the relationship between test scores and GPA does appear to follow

Table 2.2   Example Test Scores and GPAs for a Classroom Examination With 25 Students

Test Score	Z Test Score	GPA	Z GPA	$\Sigma Z_1 Z_2$
68	– 1.85	2.21	–2.05	3.80
69	–1.73	2.45	–1.59	2.76
70	–1.61	2.34	–1.80	2.89
72	–1.36	2.56	–1.38	1.88
73	–1.23	2.85	–.83	1.02
74	–1.11	2.75	–1.02	1.13
76	–.86	3.10	–.36	.31
79	–.48	2.95	–.64	.31
80	–.36	3.15	–.26	.09
80	–.36	3.23	–.11	.04
84	.14	3.35	.12	.02
86	.39	3.18	–.20	–.08
87	.51	3.39	.20	.10
87	.51	3.45	.31	.16
88	.64	3.56	.52	.33
88	.64	3.53	.46	.29
88	.64	3.48	.37	.23
88	.64	3.75	.88	.56
89	.76	3.68	.75	.57
90	.89	3.85	1.07	.95
90	.89	3.88	1.13	1.00
90	.89	3.91	1.19	1.05
91	1.01	3.67	.73	.74
92	1.14	3.95	1.26	1.43
93	1.26	3.96	1.28	1.62
Total	0		0	23.22

Figure 2.3   Bivariate Scatterplot of Exam 1 Test Scores and Overall GPA

a linear trend. The graph would have to be constructed differently to discover possible subgroup differences (e.g., male vs. female students). For example, red circles could represent men, and blue circles could represent women. Then, separate regression lines could be constructed for each gender subgroup. We will discuss this issue in more detail in Module 11 when we discuss test bias and fairness.

The Pearson correlation coefficient is by far the most used statistic in all of applied psychological measurement. As you will see throughout this book or any book on **measurement theory** and testing, the Pearson correlation coefficient is used for a wide variety of purposes. For example, it is used in estimating reliability, the standard error of measurement, the standard error of prediction or estimate, validity, item analysis statistics, meta-analysis, factor analysis, utility analysis, and many other procedures conducted as part of applied psychological measurement. Therefore, if there is any one statistic you should know inside and out, it is the Pearson correlation. One simple formula (there are several more complex ones) for the Pearson correlation is

$$r_{xy} = \Sigma Z_x Z_y / n$$

where $\Sigma Z_x Z_y$ is the sum of the cross product of the two standardized variables, and n is the number of pairs of scores. Using the data from Table 2.2, $r_{xy} = 23.22/25 = .93$. A score of zero represents no relationship, and a score of 1.0 or −1.0 indicates a perfect relationship. Thus, we clearly have a rather strong relationship between test scores and GPA (the interpretation of correlation coefficients is discussed in more detail in Module 8). One problem with actually using this formula in practice is the potential for rounding error. Substantial rounding error can occur when converting raw scores to Z scores. When we used a computer to calculate the Pearson correlation coefficient, we obtained a value of .967. This may represent a substantial difference in some circumstances. Thus, in practice, the preceding formula is really a conceptual formula; it is not meant for actual calculations. If you need to calculate a correlation coefficient by hand, we would suggest using one of the computational formulas presented in any introductory statistics textbook. Better yet, let a computer do it for you.

Using univariate and bivariate descriptive statistics allows us to both interpret our test scores and evaluate the test for its usefulness in predicting certain outcomes. Typically, we give a test not so much because we are interested in what the test tells us directly, but rather in what it predicts. For example, you may have had to take the Graduate Record Examination (GRE) to get into a graduate program. Admissions officers are not interested in your GRE scores because they are obsessed with numbers, but because these scores have been shown to predict success in graduate school (or at least first-year grades). Thus, we typically are not interested in testing simply for the sake of testing; rather, we hope to use the test information to predict important outcomes. Thus, testing can be a powerful tool for decision makers if used judiciously and in combination with other relevant information. However, to justify the use of tests, we need strong statistical evidence to support our claims.

Estimation

In addition to describing a set of data, we may also be interested in estimating the underlying "true" score for individuals, which would signify what a person's score would be on a test if it was not contaminated by any types of errors (see Module 5 for more detail on this topic). Thus, with estimation, we use inferential statistics to build **confidence intervals** (CIs; e.g., 95% or 99%) around our observed test scores to estimate a population parameter. Again, using our data from Table 2.1, we know we have a sample mean of 82.88 and a standard deviation of 7.86 for a sample of 25 test scores. We would take a sample mean and, using the standard error of the mean (the standard deviation divided by the square root of the sample size), compute a 95% CI around that mean to estimate the population parameter (population mean), such as

$$CI_{.95} = \bar{X} \pm t_{.05} * S_{\bar{X}} = 82.88 \pm 2.064 * (7.86/\sqrt{25}) = 79.64 \leq \mu_x \leq 86.13 \quad (2.1)$$

where $t_{.05}$ is the tabled value for t at $\alpha = .05$, two tailed, for 24 $(n-1)$ degrees of freedom, and $S_{\bar{X}}$ is the standard error of the mean, which is equal to the sample standard deviation divided by the square root of the sample size (n). This translates into English as, "We are 95% confident that the interval of 79.64 to 86.13 includes the true population mean for the test."

We may also take an individual score and use the standard error of measurement to estimate an individual's true score. In this case, we may have an individual score of 90. We also have to know the reliability of the test; in this case, it is .88. Therefore,

$$CI_{.95} = X \pm Z_{.05} * \left(S_{\bar{x}} * \sqrt{1 - r_{xx}} \right) = 90 \pm 1.96 * \left(7.86 * \sqrt{1 - .88} \right)$$
$$= 84.63 \leq T \leq 95.37 \tag{2.2}$$

where $Z_{.05}$ is the tabled value for Z at $\alpha = .05$, two tailed (note we use Z instead of t_{df} in this case because we are looking at individual scores), $S_{\bar{x}}$ is the sample standard deviation of the test, and r_{xx} is the reliability of the test. This translates into English as, "We are 95% confident that the interval of 84.63 to 95.37 includes the true score for an individual with an obtained score of 90 on the test."

You probably noticed that the interval for estimating an individual true score is much wider than the interval for estimating the population mean of a set of scores. In both cases (the 95% CI for the population mean and the 95% CI for the true score), we are interested in the observed score only to the extent that it provides a meaningful estimate of the relevant value or population parameter of interest. Using the inferential statistic procedures of estimation allows us to do so.

Concluding Comments

Descriptive statistics play a large role in interpreting test scores. Both graphical (e.g., histograms, stem-and-leaf plots, scatterplots) and numerical (e.g., measures of central tendency, variability, and shape, as well as standardization of scores) techniques should be used to describe a set of test data fully. In particular, the Pearson product moment correlation coefficient is used in numerous procedures in psychological measurement, such as estimating reliability and validity, meta-analysis, and many other applications that you will encounter throughout the rest of this book. In addition, inferential statistics, in the form of estimation procedures (e.g., CIs), are also commonly used to interpret test data. This form of estimation can include estimating both population parameters, such as the population mean, as well as individual true scores.

Best Practices

1. A wide variety of descriptive statistics should be used in explaining and interpreting scores from psychological tests.
2. Keep in mind that the old saying, "A picture is worth a thousand words," definitely applies to interpreting test scores. So, use lots of univariate (e.g., histograms) and bivariate (e.g., scatterplots) techniques when describing data from psychological tests.
3. Proper estimation procedures (e.g., 95% CIs) go a long way in depicting the confidence we can have in our observed test scores.

Practical Questions

1. Are descriptive statistics or inferential statistics used more in applied psychological measurement?
2. Why are we more likely to use estimation rather than statistical significance testing in applied psychological measurement?
3. How do descriptive statistics and standardized scores allow us to interpret a set of test scores? Why?
4. What are the advantages of using a scatterplot in addition to the Pearson product moment correlation?
5. What does a 95% CI of the mean tell us? How about a 99% CI for an individual score?

Case Studies

CASE STUDY 2.1: DESCRIPTIVE STATISTICS FOR AN INTRODUCTORY PSYCHOLOGICAL STATISTICS TEST

Professor Ullman had just given the first examination in her introductory psychological statistics class. She passed the results on to Rudy, one of her graduate teaching assistants, so that he could "make sense" of the scores. After entering the scores into the computer, Rudy calculated some descriptive statistics. He first calculated the mean and standard deviation. The mean seemed a little low (68 out of 100), and the standard deviation seemed high (28). Therefore, he decided to go back and look at a histogram of the raw scores. Rudy was expecting to see something close to a **normal distribution** of scores. He had always learned that scores on cognitive ability and knowledge tests tend to approximate a normal distribution. Instead, the histogram for the first statistics test seemed to show just the opposite. The distribution of scores was basically a U-shaped distribution. That is, there were a bunch of students in the A and high-B range and then a bunch of students in the low-D and F range, with very few in between.

Rudy wasn't sure what to do next. He wanted to show Professor Ullman that he knew the statistics and measurement material, but why was he getting the strange looking distribution? The course was set up with a 50-student lecture section and two 25-student lab sections. Rudy taught the morning lab session, and Lisa taught the afternoon session. "I wonder how the scores for the two lab sections compare?" Rudy thought. Rudy also remembered that on the first day of the lab session students filled out several questionnaires. There were a couple of personality questionnaires, an attitude toward statistics measure, and demographic data, including GPA, year in school, whether the student had transferred from a junior college, gender, ethnicity, and similar items. Could those somehow be useful in understanding what was going on with the test data? Rudy decided he had better present his preliminary results to Professor Ullman and see what she had to say.

Questions to Ponder

1. What additional descriptive statistics should Rudy have run to try to make sense of the exam data?
2. How could Rudy have used the additional questionnaire data to help make sense of the test scores?
3. What statistics could Rudy calculate to determine if there really were any "significant differences" between the two laboratory sections?
4. Professor Ullman has taught the undergraduate statistics class many times. Would it make sense to go back and compare this term's results on the first exam to previous classes' performance on exam 1? Why or why not?
5. What graphical or visual data displays of the data would be appropriate in this situation?
6. Would it be helpful to estimate any population parameters in this situation?
7. Would it make sense to estimate any true scores in this situation?

CASE STUDY 2.2: CHOOSING AND
INTERPRETING A CLINICAL TEST

Megan, a second-year clinical psychology graduate student, had just gotten her first assignment in her graduate internship placement in the Community Counseling Center (CCC). Dr. Chavez had given her a set of two standardized psychological tests that she was to administer to a CCC client who was referred by a judge from the county's family court system. The client had a history of verbally abusing his wife and children. In addition, he had threatened physical harm against his family on numerous occasions. Fortunately, however, he had never actually followed through on his verbal threats of physical violence. Given the client's history, the judge wanted to refer the client for anger management treatment. In order for the client to qualify for the court-ordered treatment, however, he had to score "sufficiently high" on at least one of two psychological tests. Ultimately, it was up to Dr. Chavez and Megan to determine if he had scored sufficiently high on the tests and to make a recommendation to the judge as to whether the client should be referred to the anger management treatment program.

Megan administered the two psychological tests to the client. She then scored the tests. As it turned out, for both tests the client had fallen just a point or two below the cutoff set by the court to be considered "sufficiently high" to warrant participation in the court-ordered anger management treatment program. However, Megan had just completed her graduate measurement course the term before. She knew that a test taker's observed score is only an estimate of his or her true underlying level on the construct being measured. To her, it seemed wrong to take the test at "face value" in that there is always measurement error associated with any psychological test. What about the other information in this client's history? Feeling a little frustrated, Megan thought it was time to discuss the case further with Dr. Chavez.

Questions to Ponder

1. What statistics should Megan calculate to obtain an estimate of the client's underlying true score on the psychological measures?
2. If you were Megan, what other information would you want to know about the tests in order to make the best decision possible?
3. Should the nature of the offense have any impact on how Megan determines if the client is "sufficiently high" on the psychological measures? If yes, how so? If no, why not?
4. How should (or could) the other information in the client's file be combined with the test data to make a recommendation to the court?

﹌﹩﹢﹢﹩﹌

Exercises

PROLOGUE: The Equal Employment Opportunity Commission (EEOC) has received a complaint about our current Mechanical Comprehension (MC) test from a former job applicant (a female minority) who applied and was rejected for our engineering assistant position. As you know, we are in the process of replacing our current MC test with a new one. The EEOC analyst assigned to our case will be here to meet with us in 1 hour, so we had better have some answers by then. Use the data set "Mechanical Comprehension.sav" described in Appendix B to complete the following exercises.

EXERCISE 2.1: COMPUTING DESCRIPTIVE STATISTICS

OBJECTIVE: To practice computing and interpreting descriptive statistics on test data.

1. What descriptive information can we provide to the EEOC regarding the current MC test being used? How about the proposed one?

2. Create appropriate graphs to describe the current and proposed MC tests.
3. Compute appropriate measures of central tendency, variability, and shape for the current and proposed MC tests.
4. Create standardized Z scores for both the current and the proposed MC tests.

EXERCISE 2.2: COMPUTING BIVARIATE STATISTICS

OBJECTIVE: To practice computing and interpreting bivariate inferential statistics.

1. Is the current test related to any other demographic information such as age, education level, or work experience? How about the proposed test?
2. The complainant (with ID #450) is suggesting that the test is biased/unfair. What was her score? What is your best guess of her "true" score? How does her score compare to the scores of the other applicants? To the scores of other female applicants? To the scores of other minority applicants? (Look at this in terms of both the current and the proposed test.)

Further Readings

Crocker, L.M., & Algina, J. (1986). *Introduction to classical and modern test theory* (pp. 16–42). Belmont, CA: Wadsworth.
Ghiselli, E.E., Campbell, J.P., & Zedeck, S. (1981). *Measurement theory for the behavioral sciences* (pp. 31–58). New York: W.H. Freeman.
Murphy, K.R., & Davidshofer, C.O. (2005). *Psychological testing: Principles and applications* (6th ed.). Upper Saddle River, NJ: Pearson Education.
In addition, most introductory (psychological) statistics books will provide a more detailed description of the descriptive statistics discussed in this module, although not as specific to psychological testing as the preceding references.

Module 3

Psychological Scaling

"**M**easurement essentially is concerned with the methods used to provide quantitative descriptions of the extent to which individuals manifest or possess specified characteristics" (Ghiselli, Campbell, & Zedeck, 1981, p. 2). "Measurement is the assigning of numbers to individuals in a systematic way as a means of representing properties of the individuals" (Allen & Yen, 2001, p. 2). "'Measurement' consists of rules for assigning symbols to objects so as to (1) represent quantities of attributes numerically (scaling) or (2) define whether the objects fall in the same or different categories with respect to a given attribute (classification)" (Nunnally & Bernstein, 1994, p. 3).

No matter which popular definition of the term **measurement** you choose, several underlying themes emerge. First, we need to be able to quantify the attribute of interest. That is, we need to have numbers to designate how much (or little) of an attribute an individual possesses. Second, we must be able to quantify our attribute of interest in a consistent and systematic way (i.e., standardization). That is, we need to make sure that if someone else wants to replicate our measurement process, it is systematic enough that meaningful replication is possible. Finally, we must remember that we are measuring attributes of individuals (or objects), not the individuals per se. This last point is particularly important when performing high-stakes testing or when dealing with sensitive subject matter. For example, if we disqualify a job candidate because he or she scored below the established cutoff on a pre-employment drug test, we want to make sure that the person is not labeled as a drug addict. Our tests are not perfect, and whenever we set a cutoff on a test, we may be making an error by designating someone as above or below the cutoff. In the previous example, we may be mistakenly classifying someone as a drug abuser when, in fact, he or she is not.

Levels of Measurement

As the definition of Nunnally and Bernstein (1994) suggests, by systematically measuring the attribute of interest we can either classify or scale individuals with regard to the attribute of interest. Whether we engage in classification or scaling depends in large part on the level of measurement used to assess our construct. For example, if our attribute is measured on a nominal scale of measurement, then we can only classify individuals as falling into one or another mutually exclusive category. This is because the different categories (e.g., men vs. women) represent only qualitative differences. Say, for example, we are measuring the demographic variable of racial/ethnic identity. An individual can fall into one (or more!) of several possible categories. Hence, we are simply classifying individuals based on self-identified race/ethnicity. Even if we tell the computer that Caucasians should be coded 0, Africans/African Americans 1, Hispanics/Latinos 2, Asians/Asian Americans 3, and so on, that does not mean that these values have any quantitative meaning. They are simply labels for our self-identified racial/ethnic categories.

For example, the first author once had an undergraduate student working on a research project with him. She was asked to enter some data and run a few Pearson correlation coefficients. The student came back very excited that she had found a significant relationship between race and our outcome variable of interest (something akin to job performance). Race had a coding scheme similar to that described above. When the student was asked to interpret the correlation coefficient, she looked dumbfounded, as well she should, because the correlation coefficient was not interpretable in this situation, because the variable race was measured at the nominal level.

On the other hand, we may have a variable such as temperature that we can quantify in a variety of ways. Assume that we had 10 objects and wanted to determine the temperature of each one. If we did not have a thermometer, we could simply touch each one, assuming they were not too hot or too cold, and then rank order the objects based on how hot or cold they felt to the touch. This, of course, is assuming that the objects were all made of material with similar heat transference properties (e.g., metal transfers heat, or cold, much better than does wood). This would represent an ordinal scale of measurement where objects are simply rank ordered. You would not know how much hotter one object is than another, but you would know that A is hotter than B, if A is ranked higher than B. Is the ordinal level of measurement sufficient? In some cases, it is. For example, if you want to draw a bath for your child, do you need to know the exact temperature? Not really; you just need to be careful not to scald or chill your child.

Alternatively, we may find a thermometer that measures temperature in degrees Celsius and use it to measure the temperature of the 10 items. This device uses an **interval scale** of measurement because we have equal intervals between degrees on the scale. However, the zero point on the scale is arbitrary; 0°C represents the point at which water freezes at sea level. That is, zero on the scale does not represent "true zero," which in this case would mean a complete absence of heat.

However, if we were to use a thermometer that used the Kelvin scale, we would be using a **ratio scale** of measurement, because zero on the Kelvin scale does represent true zero (i.e., no heat).

When we measure our construct of interest at the nominal (i.e., qualitative) level of measurement, we can only classify objects into categories. As a result, we are very limited in the types of data manipulations and statistical analyses we can perform on the data. Referring to the previous module on descriptive statistics, we could compute frequency counts or determine the modal response (i.e., category), but not much else. However, if we were at least able to rank order our objects based on the degree to which they possess our construct of interest (i.e., we have **quantitative** data), then we could actually scale our construct. In addition, higher levels of measurement allow for more in-depth statistical analyses. With ordinal data, for example, we can compute statistics such as the median, range, and inter-quartile range. When we have interval-level data, we can calculate statistics such as means, standard deviations, variances, and the various statistics of shape (e.g., skew and kurtosis). With interval-level data, it is important to know the shape of the distribution, as different-shaped distributions imply different interpretations for statistics such as the mean and standard deviation.

Unidimensional Scaling Models

In psychological measurement, we are typically most interested in **scaling** some characteristic, trait, or **ability** of a person. That is, we want to know how much of an attribute of interest a given person possesses. This will allow us to estimate the degree of inter-individual and intra-individual differences (as discussed in Module 1) among the respondents on the attribute of interest. This measurement process is usually referred to as **psychometrics** or *psychological measurement*. However, we can also scale the stimuli that we give to individuals, as well as the responses that individuals provide. Scaling of stimuli and responses is typically referred to as *psychological scaling*. Scaling of stimuli is more prominent in the area of psychophysics or sensory/perception psychology that focuses on physical phenomena and whose roots date back to mid-19th-century Germany. It was not until the 1920s that Thurstone began to apply the same scaling principles to scaling psychological attitudes. In addition, we can attempt to scale several factors at once. This can get very tricky, however. So, more often than not, we hold one factor constant (e.g., responses), collapse across a second factor (e.g., stimuli), and then scale the third factor (e.g., individuals).

For example, say we administered a 25-item measure of social anxiety to a group of schoolchildren. We would typically assume that all children are interpreting the response scale (e.g., a scale of 1–7) for each question in the same way (i.e., responses are constant), although not necessarily responding with the same value. If they did all respond with exactly the same value, then we would have no variability, and thus the scale would be of little interest to us, because it would have no predictive value. Next, we would collapse across stimuli (i.e., compute a total score for the 25 items). As a result, we would be left with scaling children on the construct of social anxiety.

Many issues (besides which factor we are scaling) arise when performing a scaling study. One important factor is who we select to participate in our study. When we scale people (*psychometrics*), we typically obtain a random sample of individuals from the population that we wish to generalize. In our preceding example, we would want a random sample of school-aged children so that our results generalize to all school-aged children. Conversely, when we scale stimuli (*psychological scaling*), we do not want a random sample of individuals. Rather, the sample of individuals we select should be purposefully and carefully selected based on their respective expertise on the construct being scaled. That is, they should all be **subject matter experts (SMEs)**. In our preceding example, we would want experts on the measurement of social anxiety, particularly as it relates to children in school settings, to serve as our SMEs. Such SMEs would likely include individuals with degrees and expertise in clinical, school, developmental, counseling, or personality psychology.

Another difference between psychometrics and psychological scaling is that with psychometrics we ask our participants to provide their individual feelings, **attitudes**, and/or personal ratings toward a particular topic. In doing so, we will be able to determine how individuals differ on our construct of interest. With psychological scaling, however, we typically ask participants (i.e., SMEs) to provide their professional judgment of the particular stimuli, regardless of their personal feelings or attitudes toward the topic or stimulus. This may include ratings of how well different stimuli represent the construct and at what level of intensity the construct is represented. Thus, with psychometrics, you would sum across items (i.e., stimuli) within an individual respondent in order to obtain his or her score on the construct. With psychological scaling, however, the researcher would sum across raters (SMEs) within a given stimulus (e.g., question) in order to obtain ratings of each stimulus. Once the researcher was confident that each stimulus did, in fact, tap into the construct and had some estimate of the level at which it did so, only then should the researcher feel confident in presenting the now scaled stimuli to a random sample of relevant participants for psychometric purposes.

The third category of responses, which we said we typically hold constant, also needs to be identified. That is, we have to decide in what fashion we will have subjects respond to our stimuli. Such response options may include requiring our participants to make comparative judgments (e.g., which is more important, A or B?), subjective evaluations (e.g., strongly agree to strongly disagree), or an absolute judgment (e.g., how hot is this object?). Different response formats may well influence how we write and edit our stimuli. In addition, they may also influence how we evaluate the quality or the accuracy of the response. For example, with absolute judgments, we may have a standard of comparison, especially if subjects are being asked to rate physical characteristics such as weight, height, or intensity of sound or light. With attitudes and psychological constructs, such standards are hard to come by.

There are a few options (e.g., Guttman's Scalogram and Coomb's unfolding technique) for simultaneously scaling people and stimuli, but more often than not, we scale only one dimension at a time. However, we must scale our stimuli first (or seek a well-established measure) before we can have confidence in scaling individuals on the stimuli. Advanced texts such as Nunnally and Bernstein (1994), Ghiselli et al. (1981), and Crocker and Algina (1986) all provide detailed descriptions of different scaling methods for scaling stimuli and response data at a variety of different levels of measurement. We refer you to these advanced texts for more detailed explanations. In the following discussion, we will provide only a general overview of the major unidimensional scaling techniques.

We can scale stimuli at a variety of different measurement levels. At the nominal level of measurement, we have a variety of sorting techniques. In this case, SMEs are asked to sort the stimuli into different categories based on some dimension. For example, our SMEs with expertise in the social anxiety of school-aged children might be asked to sort a variety of questions according to whether the items are measuring school-related social anxiety or not. In doing so, we are able to determine which items to remove and which to keep for further analyses when our goal is to measure school-related social anxiety.

At the ordinal level of measurement, we have the Q-sort method, paired comparisons, Guttman's Scalogram, Coomb's unfolding technique, and a variety of rating scales. The major task of SMEs is to rank order items from highest to lowest, or from weakest to strongest. Again, our SMEs with expertise in school-related social anxiety might be asked to sort a variety of questions. However, instead of a simple "yes" and "no" sorting, in terms of whether the questions measure social anxiety or not, the SMEs might be asked to sort the items in terms of the extent to which they measure social anxiety. So, for example, an item that states "I tend to feel anxious when I am at school" would likely get a higher ranking than an item that states "I tend to have few friends at school." While both items may be tapping into social anxiety, the first item is clearly more directly assessing school-related social anxiety.

At the interval level of measurement, we have direct estimation, the method of bisection, and Thurstone's methods of comparative and categorical judgments. With these methods, SMEs are asked not only to rank order items but also to actually help determine the magnitude of the differences among items. With Thurstone's method of comparative judgment, SMEs compare every possible pair of stimuli and select the item within the pair that is the better item for assessing the construct. Thurstone's method of categorical judgment, while less tedious for SMEs when there are many stimuli to assess in that they simply rate each stimulus (not each pair of stimuli), does require more cognitive energy for each rating provided. This is because the SME must now estimate the actual value of the stimulus.

Multidimensional Scaling Models

With unidimensional scaling, as described previously, subjects are asked to respond to stimuli with regard to a particular dimension. For example, a consumer psychologist might ask subjects how they would rate the "value" of a particular consumer product. With **multidimensional scaling (MDS)**, however, subjects are typically asked to give just their general impression or broad rating of similarities or differences among stimuli. For example, subjects might be asked to compare several different types of products and simply rate which are similar or which they prefer the best overall. Subsequent analyses, using Euclidean spatial models, would "map" the products in multidimensional space. The different multiple dimensions would then be "discovered" or "extracted" with multivariate statistical techniques, thus establishing which dimensions the consumer is using to distinguish the products. MDS can be particularly useful when subjects are unable to articulate why they like a stimulus, yet they are confident that they prefer one stimulus to another.

A Step-by-Step Scaling Example

Let us now work through our earlier example on school-related social anxiety in school-aged children from start to finish. What would be the first step in conducting a study where you wanted to develop a measure to assess school-related social anxiety in school-aged children? Well, our first step is to make sure we have a clear definition of what we mean by our construct of school-related social anxiety. Everyone who hears this term may have a slightly different impression of what we would like to assess. Therefore, we need to be able to present our SMEs with a single definition of what we are trying to assess when we talk about this construct. In this case, we will start with the following definition: "School-related social anxiety refers to the uneasiness school-aged children experience when they are in school-related social settings, but that may not be manifested in nonschool social settings such as at home or with friends outside of school. Such uneasiness may include feelings of isolation, physical stressors, and other such psychological and physical symptoms." Okay, it is not perfect, but it is a start. What next? Now we need to start developing items to assess our construct. Who should do that? Ah, yes, our infamous SMEs. Who should serve as SMEs in this instance and how many do we need? We stated earlier that, ideally, we would want to use school psychologists, clinical psychologists, counseling psychologists, developmental psychologists, and/or personality theorists. It may be difficult, however, to convince such individuals to participate in the item generation stage of the study. Therefore, it may be more practical and realistic for you, the researcher, and some colleagues and/or research assistants to generate potential items and then reserve the SMEs to provide actual ratings on the items you generate.

How many items do we need? Unfortunately, there is no easy answer to this question. The best response is, "The more the better." Ideally, you would want to generate at least twice as many items as you hope to have on your final scale. Therefore, if you want a 25-item scale of school-related social anxiety, you should generate at least 50 items. Now that we have our 50 or more items, it is time to bring in our SMEs. Again, how many SMEs do we need? Ideally, it would be nice to have "lots" of them; in reality, we may be lucky to get four or five. At a minimum, you need to have more than two in order to obtain variability estimates. Any number beyond two will be advantageous, within reason of course. This is also the step where we need to select one of the scaling models. Remember, these "models" are simply standardized procedures that will allow us to attach meaningful numbers to the responses our subjects will ultimately provide. Thus, we need not get too anxious (pardon the pun) over which method we choose to scale social anxiety. One prominent scaling procedure, which we touched on briefly, is Likert scaling, so we will use that.

Before we jump into scaling our stimuli, however, we need to know what type of responses we want our subjects to provide. In fact, this would probably be good to know as we are writing our questions. Remember, we pointed out earlier that these might include evaluative judgments, degree of agreement, frequency of occurrence, and so on. Which one we choose is probably not as critical as the fact that all of our items are consistent with the response scale we choose. For example, we do not want to mix questions with statements. In this case, we will go with the degree of agreement format, because this is common with Likert-type scales. With most **Likert scales**, we usually have a four- or five-option response scale ranging from strongly agree to strongly disagree (e.g., 1 = Strongly Disagree, 2 = Disagree, 3 = Undecided, 4 = Agree, and 5 = Strongly Agree). With an odd number of scale values, we have an undecided or neutral option in the middle. With an even number of scale values, we force the respondent to agree or disagree (sometimes called a forced format or choice scale). So should we use four or five options? It is mostly a matter of preference; be aware, however, that which one you choose can affect the interpretation of your scores.

So far, we have defined our construct, generated items, and decided on a response scale. Now it is time to let our SMEs loose on the items. Remember, the SMEs are providing their professional judgment as to how well each item represents the construct or to what degree it represents the construct, regardless of their personal feelings. Once we have the SME ratings, how do we use these to decide which items to retain? Well, we could compute statistics for each item such as means and variances. Specifically, if the mean for a given item is relatively high and the variance relatively low, then we would retain that item. Unfortunately, there are no hard-and-fast rules for what constitutes a high mean and low variability. However, if the ratings for a given item do not differ much, then the SMEs are being consistent in their ratings, which is a good thing, but from a psychometric standpoint, too little variability leaves us unable to compute certain statistics (i.e., correlation coefficients). A high average rating would also indicate that the item should be retained. Ultimately, which items to keep and which to remove is a professional judgment call. However, in practical terms, remember you wanted a 25-item scale. So why not choose the top 25 items in terms of their mean and variance? Some of these items may, of course, still require further editing before being implemented.

Finally, you are ready to administer your newly developed Likert scale to actual subjects. How many subjects do you need? For the psychometric portion of the study (estimating reliability and validity, as discussed later in the book), again the answer is, "The more the better." Realistically, though, we need to have enough for our statistics to be meaningful. That usually means at least 100 respondents. For evaluating research questions and hypotheses, many factors come into play in determining appropriate sample size. In that instance, most researchers now conduct power and/or precision analyses to determine the most desirable sample size for their particular situation.

An individual's score on the scale will be the sum or mean of his or her responses to the 25 items. Remember that you may have some items that have reverse meaning (e.g., they were really assessing social calmness, not social anxiety). These items will need to be reverse scored. That is, what was a 1 is now a 5, a 2 becomes a 4, 3 stays 3, 4 becomes 2, and 5 becomes 1. This reverse scoring of reversed items should be done before the summated total score is obtained. Now that you have created and evaluated your school-related social anxiety scale, you are ready to carry out the psychometric studies that we discuss in Modules 5 through 8.

Concluding Comments

We began by looking at several definitions of measurement and examining the key elements of psychological measurement. Next, we discussed the different levels of measurement that our psychological scales can assess. Then, we talked about key issues distinguishing psychometrics from psychological scaling. We next provided an overview to the different unidimensional scaling models and how they relate to the different levels of measurement. Finally, we worked through a realistic step-by-step example of what an applied scaling project might look like. We also briefly touched on MDS. In the final analysis, the key is first to have confidence in your stimuli and responses and then move on to scale individuals. This is the crux of the psychometric process, which is the topic of the remainder of this book.

Best Practices

1. Knowing the level of measurement of your psychological test data is key to making sure you conduct the appropriate analyses and interpret the test score properly.
2. It is important to properly scale items before we try to scale individuals.
3. While true MDS is somewhat complex, it is important to make sure we understand how we are measuring items, responses, and individuals.

Practical Questions

1. What is the difference between scaling and classification?
2. What is the difference between psychometrics and psychological scaling?
3. Why do you think it is so difficult to scale more than one dimension (i.e., people, stimuli, and responses) at once?
4. Why is it important to know the level of measurement of our data before we begin the scaling process?
5. How would we scale multiple dimensions at one time?

Case Studies

CASE STUDY 3.1: SCALING STUDY IN CONSUMER PSYCHOLOGY

Benjamin, a college senior who had a dual major in psychology and marketing, decided he wanted to complete his undergraduate honors thesis in the area of consumer psychology. Specifically, he was interested in determining how well young children were able to recall a series of visual-only (e.g., magazine advertisements), auditory-only (e.g., radio commercials), and combined visual- and auditory- (e.g., television commercials) advertisements for Lego building toys. He had learned in his undergraduate tests and measurements class that most of the time we were interested in looking at individual differences within our subjects. In this case, would it be who was able to remember one type of advertisement better than another? That didn't really seem to be the issue of major concern here. Why would advertisers be interested in the type of preadolescent who remembered one type of advertisement better than others his age? Maybe it would allow advertisers to target their product to specific children (e.g., those who watch PBS programming vs. those who watch network or cable programming).

On second thought, Benjamin wondered whether the real issue was which method of advertising was most likely to be remembered by a "typical" child. If so, it seemed as if he should really be more interested in scaling different types of advertising modalities (i.e., stimuli) than in scaling subjects. By doing so, advertisers could determine which modalities would produce the best recall and thus how to most effectively spend their advertising dollars. As Benjamin thought some more, he began to wonder if it was the response that was really of most interest. That is, who cares if the child recalls the advertisement or not; isn't the bigger issue whether the child (or his or her parents) actually buys the toy (i.e., their response)? Maybe he needed to scale the responses children have to the different modes of advertisement, not the subjects or stimuli. Suddenly, it all seemed rather confusing. So, it was off to his advisor's office to get some advice and direction.

Questions to Ponder

1. What type of scaling should Benjamin be most concerned with? Subject, stimulus, or response? Why?
2. Who should Benjamin get to serve as participants for his study?
3. Would he be better served with a random sample of children or with a relatively homogeneous group of subject matter experts (SMEs) for his scaling study?

4. What level of measurement data is Benjamin dealing with?
5. Will Benjamin actually have to do several scaling projects to get the information he needs?

CASE STUDY 3.2: A CONSULTING PROJECT ON PERFORMANCE ASSESSMENT

Amanda, a graduate student who had just completed her first year in an industrial and organizational psychology PhD program, was excited because she had just gotten her first consulting job. She was to develop a performance appraisal form to assess workers in her uncle's small domestic cleaning service. There were a total of 15 "maids" and two office supervisors. Her uncle wanted to know which maids should receive a pay raise and how much he should give each of them. He wanted to make sure, however, that their raises were performance based. So, he contracted with Amanda to create an easy-to-use performance appraisal form that he and his two office supervisors could use to assess each maid and, ultimately, use that information to determine the size of the raise for each maid.

Amanda first conducted a literature search to see if she could find an existing performance assessment form that would fit the bill. While some existing forms looked like they might work, it seemed like no matter which one she chose, she would have to make some significant modifications. She also noticed that different forms used different points of reference. For example, some performance appraisal forms used an absolute scale (e.g., below standard . . . at standard . . . above standard), while others used a relative scale (e.g., below average . . . average . . . above average). Some used a paired comparison technique. That is, who is the better performer? Maid A or Maid B? Maid A or Maid C? Also, some scales had three categories or anchors, others five, some seven, and one was on a scale of 1–100. There was even one that had no numbers or words at all; it was simply a series of faces ranging from a deep frown to a very big grin. A bit overwhelmed and a little unsure of how to proceed, Amanda decided to seek the advice of the professor who would be teaching her performance appraisal class the following semester.

Questions to Ponder

1. What difference (if any) does it make if Amanda uses an absolute or a relative rating scale?
2. Should Amanda just develop her own scale or try to use an existing measure?

3. What issues should Amanda be concerned with if she modifies an existing scale?
4. Is Amanda more interested in scaling responses, stimuli, or subjects? Explain.
5. Who should serve as the raters in this case? The supervisors? Her uncle? The respective clients?
6. Would the decision in terms of who will serve as raters affect which type of scale is used (e.g., relative vs. absolute vs. paired comparison)?

⊸•⊶•⊷

Exercises

EXERCISE 3.1: CONDUCTING A SCALING STUDY

OBJECTIVE: To provide practice in conducting a scaling study.

Outline a scaling study similar to the example that is provided at the end of the overview section of the module. Select a construct (other than school-related social anxiety) and answer the following questions:

1. What is the definition of your construct?
2. Who is going to generate items to measure the construct? How many items do they need to generate? Why?
3. What scaling model would be most appropriate for your example?
4. Who is going to serve as SMEs to rate the items?
5. On what basis are you going to select the items to keep for the final version of your scale?
6. Who are going to serve as subjects for your study? How many subjects do you need?

EXERCISE 3.2: SCALING ITEMS

OBJECTIVE: To practice scaling items.

Using the data from the "Bus Driver.sav" data set described in Appendix B, scale the 10 task items on the three dimensions of "Frequency," "Relative Time Spent," and "Importance." Use Table 3.1 to fill in the mean task ratings across the three dimensions. In order for an item to be "retained" for further consideration, the task must, on average, be carried out at least "regularly" (i.e., 3.0 or higher) in

Table 3.1   Summary of Task Ratings

Task Number	Average Frequency Rating (≥ 3.0)	Average Relative Time Spent Rating (≥ 2.5)	Average Importance Rating (≥ 4.0)
1			
2			
3			
4			
5			
6			
7			
8			
9			
10			

terms of frequency, fall between "little" and "moderate" (i.e., 2.5 or higher) in terms of relative time spent, and be rated as "very important" (i.e., 4.0 or higher) in terms of importance. Given these criteria, which of the 10 tasks meet all three of these criteria and, thus, should be retained?

Further Readings

Crocker, L.M., & Algina, J. (1986). *Introduction to classical and modern test theory* (pp. 45–66). Belmont, CA: Wadsworth.

Ghiselli, E.E., Campbell, J.P., & Zedeck, S. (1981). *Measurement theory for the behavioral sciences* (pp. 391–420). New York: W.H. Freeman.

Guildford, J.P. (1954). *Psychometric methods*. New York: McGraw-Hill.

Nunnally, J.C., & Bernstein, I.H. (1994). *Psychometric theory* (3rd ed., pp. 31–82). New York: McGraw-Hill.

Torgerson, W.S. (1958). *Theory and methods of scaling*. New York: Wiley.

van der Ven, A.H.G.S. (1980). *Introduction to scaling*. New York: Wiley.

Module 4

Test Preparation and Specification

In developing a test from scratch, it might seem that we would begin the process by writing items. However, test development begins much earlier than item writing. Indeed, a number of issues must be carefully considered before creating even a single test item. This module presents these issues as a number of steps to be conducted during the early phases of test development. These steps, if fully embraced, will facilitate the writing of items and help ensure the development of a quality test. In many ways, the steps we take in developing a test prior to item writing are analogous to the steps a good researcher takes in preparation for conducting a study. Before conducting a study, the researcher must first define the objective of the investigation, determine the intended population to which he or she would like to generalize the results of the study, select an appropriate research methodology, and consider the appropriate analysis once data is collected. In the realm of testing, the test author must consider a set of related issues prior to item writing.

Step 1: Specify the Type of Measure

Tests can be categorized into measures of maximal performance and measures of typical performance. Measures of maximal performance refer to **aptitude tests** or **achievement tests**, including classroom exams and personnel selection tests. Such measures are intended to assess an individual's all-out effort. Typically, each item on these tests has a known correct answer. Measures of typical performance, on the other hand, include personality and interest inventories as well as attitude scales. Items on these measures are considered to have no single "correct" response.

While the test development process for these types of measures differs, this module identifies many of the developmental steps that these measures share in common. Additional discussion of the development of tests of maximal performance is presented in Module 12, while the development of measures of typical performance is further discussed in Module 15.

Step 2: Define the Domain of the Test

Defining the domain you intend to assess is perhaps the single most important step in the test development process. Clear specification of the domain to be assessed determines the limits the test is intended to have and is essential for evaluating the content validity of the test. On first blush, providing a definition for the domain or construct may seem easy. After all, you know what you want to measure, right? Or do you? Various researchers define even familiar constructs such as "intelligence" very differently. If you are creating the test, you get to choose the definition that you believe is most appropriate. However, it is important that other experts can express agreement with your definition.

Some pundits suggest that any good definition of a construct will be relatively brief, perhaps no longer than a couple of sentences. However, there are a multitude of issues to consider in developing the definition. The answers to each of the following questions will have a huge impact on exactly how the construct will be defined.

Step 2a: What Is the Intended Context of the Test?

Is the test intended to assess some trait that applies to all people and is somewhat constant across every context? If so, then this should be specified in the definition. An alternative approach is to measure the trait relative to a specific context. For example, although conscientiousness is identified as one of the Big Five personality dimensions, a person may be conscientious at work, but not so conscientious in the performance of household chores. Thus, we would likely develop a very different scale if we were assessing one's general level of conscientiousness across contexts than if we were merely interested in conscientiousness related to the work environment. By limiting the domain to the context in which we are specifically interested, we will likely reduce the amount of error associated with the test, thus increasing the internal consistency reliability. Recent research in personality testing has found that specifying a specific context in items using so-called frame-of-reference tags can increase validity by reducing both variability between people and within-person inconsistency (Lievens, De Corte, & Schollaert, 2008). As an added benefit, test takers might perceive the more specific measure as possessing greater face validity than does a more general instrument measuring a broader domain.

Step 2b: How Is the Construct to Be Measured Different From Related Constructs?

What is assumed in this question is that you first identify related constructs. Once identified, it is essential to distinguish differences between your construct and related constructs. This will ensure that, once you begin developing items, your test items will not unintentionally stray beyond the limited context to which your test applies. Identification of related but distinct concepts will be important again later on if you choose to collect validity evidence for the newly developed measure using a construct validation approach.

Step 2c: What Is the Dimensionality of the Construct?

Many constructs are fairly broad in nature but are themselves composed of several related components that must be measured to assess the construct fully. Political conservatism, for instance, is a multidimensional construct. Under the general rubric of political conservatism, one might want to develop specific subscales assessing the dimensions of social, economic, and ecological conservatism. In identifying the dimensionality of a construct, we help ensure that the entire construct is fully assessed.

Step 2d: How Much Emphasis Should Be Placed on Each Dimension or Facet of the Construct?

In identifying that a construct is multidimensional or multifaceted, it becomes imperative to consider how much weight each dimension or facet should have in the final scale. Are all dimensions or facets equally important, or are some more important than others? The number of items per dimension or facet should reflect these decisions.

Step 3: Determine Whether a Closed-Ended or Open-Ended Item Format Will Be Used

Should the measure be composed of items that are open ended, as with interview questionnaires, essay exams, and projective (i.e., ambiguous stimuli) tests, or should a limited number of response options be provided for each item, as is the case for multiple-choice exams and scales utilizing Likert-type response options?

Closed-ended items minimize the expertise required for test administration, and responses are far easier to analyze than is typically the case for responses to open-ended items. Because closed-ended items present the response options to test takers, however, they do not allow respondents to clarify their answers. Further, the presence of response options may suggest answers that respondents would not have otherwise considered.

In contrast, test takers can qualify their answers to open-ended items by elaborating upon their responses. Responses tend to reveal that which is most salient to the examinee, and responses are uninfluenced by response options. However, responses to open-ended items can be repetitive and often provide irrelevant information. Not only must the test administrator be more highly trained than is the case for administration of most closed-ended measures, but individual differences in respondents' abilities to articulate their responses are likely to play a much greater role in testing with open-ended items. Perhaps the greatest concern with open-ended items is the increased difficulty in reliably coding and scoring responses. Indeed, when constructing knowledge tests, developers often consider the relative difficulty in creating good multiple-choice questions against the ease of scoring such exams, versus the relative ease of creating good essay questions against the more burdensome scoring of such written exams.

Step 4: Determine the Item Format

Once a decision has been made to use open-ended items, closed-ended items, or some combination of both, the test developer must further choose the type of item format. For an open-ended measure, would a written-response format be acceptable, or would additional information be obtained if respondents provided verbal responses? If closed-ended items are to be employed, should multiple-choice, true-false, matching, Likert-scale, or some other closed-ended item format be used?

Once an item format has been selected, additional issues may arise. For example, with multiple-choice items, should each item have four response options, five, or more? Even more thought is required when a Likert-type scale is to be used. Appropriate scale anchors must be determined based on what the respondent is expected to indicate. Agreement with items is typically assessed using anchors ranging from strongly disagree to strongly agree. Frequency is often assessed using anchors ranging from never to always. Many evaluative measures pose statements that are rated using a scale ranging from poor to excellent. Additional Likert-type response options include anchors portraying varying degrees of importance or approval. Thus, it is important for the test construction specialist to have a clear understanding of the different types of possible item format options, as well as their advantages and disadvantages.

Step 5: Determine Whether the Exam Will Be Administered Individually or in a Group Setting

Time and resource constraints play a large role in making this determination. While group administration generally offers the benefits of greater cost savings and ease of scoring, individual administration of tests allows us to clarify both the items and the test taker's responses, when necessary.

Step 6: Determine the Appropriate Test Length

The inclusion of many high-quality test items allows for better assessment of a testing domain and helps to improve a test's internal consistency reliability by reducing error variance (see Module 5). In many cases, however, considerable time constraints preclude the possibility of a very lengthy exam. Further, a lengthy exam can lead to test-taker fatigue and reduced test-taking motivation. These issues must be considered in relation to the item format and number of items that can be administered. In determining a test's appropriate length, a balance must be struck between practical concerns, such as time constraints, and equally important concerns with the psychometric properties of a test, including reliability. Do keep in mind, however, that because many items are often discarded during the test development process, it is worthwhile to produce as many items as possible in the early stages of test development.

Step 7: Determine the Appropriate Difficulty Level of Items That Will Compose the Test

The difficulty of items is dependent on the ability of the sample population tested under classical test theory assumptions. Therefore, it is important to have a clear idea of the abilities of potential test takers when developing items to ensure that they are appropriately difficult for this population. For tests of maximal performance, item difficulty can be determined based on the percentage of test takers who get the item correct. Module 13 provides additional information on the process to be employed for item analysis. However, our concerns with item difficulty can be broadened somewhat to apply to measures of typical performance. Identifying the likely population of test takers can assist test developers in creating items that are at the proper level of readability. Items that are written at a level beyond the likely educational attainment of the targeted population of test takers will increase error variance in responses, leading to a less reliable test.

Concluding Comments

While the concepts presented in this module are not difficult, they are extremely important to successful test development. Though a novice test developer may be tempted to skip past the steps discussed in this module in order to start writing items sooner, such an action will only complicate the process of test development. Careful consideration of the issues presented in this module will help make item writing easier, and will have an enormously beneficial impact on the appearance and quality of the finished product.

Best Practices

1. Research the content domain thoroughly before writing a single test item.
2. Specify, in writing, the definition of the content domain or construct to be assessed.

Practical Questions

1. Why do measures that claim to assess the same construct sometimes appear so vastly different from one another?
2. Some measures of a particular construct are better than others. Discuss what you believe to be the three most important issues that should be considered prior to item writing that may affect the quality of the final measure.
3. To what extent is it likely that two different measures of the same construct that employ the use of distinct item formats will provide similar results?
4. What practical constraints often play a large role in the determination of test specifications?
5. If you were assigned to develop a new measure for a personality construct, what sources might you seek to better inform yourself about the construct prior to defining the construct?

Case Studies

CASE STUDY 4.1: DEVISING A MEASURE OF JOB SATISFACTION

As new interns in the human resource department at SAVECO, Juan and Barbara were excited to receive their first major assignment. The president of the company had just asked them to assess the job satisfaction of the company's 210-person workforce. After returning to a shared office, Barbara was quick to provide the first suggestion: "I think we should work on developing an open-ended questionnaire that we could use to interview employees about their level of satisfaction."

Juan thought for a moment and said, "I'm not so sure. That sounds like a lot of work, not only in developing the interview questions but also in summarizing the results across employees. I think we should develop a number of opinion statements related to job satisfaction. For each statement, we could ask employees to indicate the degree to which they agree or disagree."

"I don't know if that would work," argued Barbara. "I think the use of open-ended questions presented in an interview format would better capture exactly *what* people are and are not happy about with their jobs, as well as provide some indication as to *why* they feel the way they do. By determining what influences job satisfaction, we might be able to implement some organizational changes to increase job satisfaction."

"Is *why* the employees are happy relevant?" queried Juan. "Our assignment is to determine the degree to which SAVECO's employees are satisfied, not to determine why they are happy or not."

Barbara frowned. "I'm not so certain about that. Just knowing the degree of job satisfaction of the workforce seems silly. I think we need to include some assessment of what influences job satisfaction."

"Well," interjected Juan, "maybe we should be even more concerned with which aspects of their work employees are satisfied. Isn't it possible that employees are satisfied with some aspects of their jobs at SAVECO and dissatisfied with other parts of their jobs? For example, can't employees be happy with their supervisor but dissatisfied with their pay?"

"You are right there," Barbara agreed. "Perhaps we need to think this through a bit more before getting started."

Questions to Ponder

1. As an alternative to developing a new measure of job satisfaction, Juan and Barbara might have considered obtaining an existing measure for use at SAVECO. What advantages and disadvantages might there be to (a) using a preexisting measure versus (b) creating a new measure of job satisfaction?
2. Is job satisfaction a one-dimensional or a multidimensional construct? How might the answer to this question impact the development of the job satisfaction measure?
3. How might the item format chosen to measure job satisfaction impact the following?

   a. Administration of the measure
   b. Analysis of the data
   c. Findings of the investigation

4. How might the development of clear test specifications help Barbara and Juan avoid their conflict?
5. What sources of additional information regarding the measurement of job satisfaction might Juan and Barbara seek prior to developing test items?

CASE STUDY 4.2: ISSUES IN DEVELOPING A STATISTICS EXAM

The time had come, at last. After countless years as a student, Janie had been teaching her first undergraduate college course—an introductory statistics course—for nearly 5 weeks. Now the time had finally arrived to create her very first exam. Sure, she'd had plenty of experience on the test-taker side of the table, but now it was her turn to create a test of her own. She had serious criticisms of some of the tests her own professors had administered to her over the years, and she was determined to do better. Janie wanted to ensure that the statistics test was fair by ensuring that the test assessed knowledge proportionate to what was covered in the course. The only trouble was that determining what was actually covered in the course was a little trickier than she had thought it would be.

Because she had only lectured on the first four chapters of the textbook, she thought she would have a fairly clearly defined domain. The material covered so far included (a) a general introduction to statistics; (b) a chapter on frequency distributions that emphasized the interpretation and development of graphs and tables; (c) a chapter on measures of central tendency, including the mean, median, and mode; and, finally, (d) a chapter on measures of variability, including the range, standard deviation, and variance. The latter two chapters seemed more important than either of the first two chapters. Janie wondered whether it would be best to create more items on these latter chapters, or if students might expect that each chapter would be tested equally. Her stomach began to be tied into knots when she thought about the prospect of having to create a lot of items from the first chapter, which seemed to provide little information of any real substance.

Suddenly, another thought came to her. The test really shouldn't be drawn just from the assigned textbook readings. She recognized that the course content was actually composed of three elements: content that had been presented during lecture only, content that had been part of the assigned textbook readings only, and, finally, content that had been presented in both her lecture and the assigned readings. Each of these components of course content was important, although she recognized an implicit pecking order of importance of the material: The material that she lectured on and was presented in the readings was most crucial to a good understanding of course concepts, while material presented only in lecture would likely come next in importance, and the content that was presented only in the assigned readings was somewhat less important.

Janie was also concerned about the types of items she should use in testing. On the one hand, she wanted to ensure that students could apply their learning through the use of computational problems, but, on the other hand, she felt that introductory statistics should emphasize understanding of these foundational concepts above anything else. How, then, could she ensure not only that she covered the domain appropriately but also that the right types of items were used to assess exactly the type of learning she hoped to promote? This question was no easier to answer when Janie realized that students would have only about 50 minutes to complete the test.

One thing seemed certain—she was quickly developing a greater respect for the professors who had constructed all those exams she had taken throughout the years.

Questions to Ponder

1. Describe the first few steps you would take in defining the **content domain** that would constitute Janie's statistics exam.
2. Would you recommend that Janie write the same number of items for each of the textbook chapters? Why or why not?
3. What percentage of items should be written for each of the following?

   a. Content presented both in readings and in lecture
   b. Content presented in lecture only
   c. Content presented in the assigned readings only

   On what basis are you making your recommendations?

4. What types of items should Janie use to assess student learning in the statistics class? Should all of the course content be assessed using the same item format?

Exercises

EXERCISE 4.1: DEFINING A PERSONALITY TRAIT

OBJECTIVE: To gain practice in defining a construct as a part of test specification.

There are a large number of personality differences that to date have little or no means of assessment. While some of these constructs are well defined, others suffer the disgrace of poor construct definition. Following is a list of words and phrases that describe propensities that can differ across individuals. Select one of the following constructs and develop a clear definition that could serve as the first step toward the operationalization of the construct. Be sure to specify the (a) context and (b) dimensionality of the construct as well as its (c) relationship to, and differentiation from, related constructs.

List of Possible Constructs

1. Jealousy
2. Patience
3. Impulsiveness
4. Street smarts
5. Empathy
6. Selfishness

EXERCISE 4.2: TEST SPECIFICATIONS FOR A MEASURE
OF POTENTIAL FOR VIOLENCE

OBJECTIVE: To illustrate how the purpose of testing influences test specifications.

Assume that you are currently working as a(n)

   a. clinical psychologist for a local parole board,
   b. industrial/organizational psychologist for the U.S. Postal Service, or
   c. school psychologist for a local high school.

You've recently been asked to create a test to measure "Potential for Violence." Provide a response for each of the following questions related to the test preparation and specification. Be sure to provide a convincing rationale for each response (questions taken from Cohen & Swerdlik, 2002).

   1. How would you define the purpose of the test?
   2. In what ways will the intended purpose of the test influence your definition of the test?
   3. Are there alternatives to developing a new test?
   4. What content will the test cover?
   5. What is the test's intended dimensionality?
   6. What is the ideal format for the test?
   7. Who will the test be administered to?
   8. What type of responses will be required of test takers?
   9. Should more than one form of the test be developed?
   10. Who will administer the test?
   11. What special training will be required of test users for administering or interpreting the test?
   12. How long will the test take to administer?
   13. How many items will compose the test?
   14. What is the intended difficulty level of the test?
   15. How will meaning be attributed to scores on the test?
   16. What benefits will result from use of the test?
   17. What potential harm could result from use of the test?

EXERCISE 4.3: COMPARING TWO MEASURES
OF THE SAME CONSTRUCT

OBJECTIVE: To illustrate the potential impact that test specifications can have on the development of measures of the same construct.

For this exercise, identify two different measures of the same construct. For example, you could identify two different measures of the personality construct agreeableness. Also, obtain the test manual for each measure, if at all possible.

(*Note:* Many colleges and universities have test banks in their libraries, psychology department, and/or education departments. These test banks may contain many commercially available tests and test manuals.)

After obtaining the two different measures (and test manuals) of the construct, carefully inspect each before answering the following questions:

1. Did both test developers define the construct in the same way? (Be sure to review Step 2 in the module overview before answering this question.) If not, identify the differences in the definitions of the construct used by the test developers.
2. Did each measure use open-ended items, closed-ended items, or both?
3. Which item formats were used in each measure of the construct?
4. Is each measure intended to be individually administered, or can it be administered in a group setting?
5. Are the measures of similar length?
6. What is the intended population of each test? Does the difficulty of the items appear appropriate for this population?
7. Based on your responses to questions 1–6, do you feel one of the two measures might be a better measure of the construct? Explain whether you believe each test developer's decisions regarding test specifications were appropriate for each measure of the construct.

Further Readings

Downing, S.M. (2006). Twelve steps for effective test development. In S.M. Downing & T.M. Haladyna (Eds.), *Handbook of test development* (pp. 3–25). Mahwah, NJ: Lawrence Erlbaum.

Ebel, R.L. (1982). Proposed solutions to two problems of test construction. *Journal of Educational Measurement, 19,* 267–278.

Lievens, F., De Corte, W., & Schollaert, E. (2008). A closer look at the frame-of-reference effect in personality scale scores and validity. *Journal of Applied Psychology, 93,* 268–279.

Millman, J., & Greene, J. (1989). The specification and development of tests of achievement and ability. In R.L. Linn (Ed.), *Educational measurement* (3rd ed., pp. 335–366). New York: American Council on Education/Macmillan.

Part 2
Reliability, Validity, and Test Bias

Module 5

Reliability Overview

Classical Test Theory

Among automobile manufacturers, Toyota has a reputation for producing reliable, though not flashy, vehicles. Its reputation for reliability sets it apart from some other manufacturers. Indeed, a recent inquiry into *Kelley Blue Book* values for a 10-year-old Toyota Camry with 100,000 miles showed that the Camry's value retained approximately 44% of its original manufacturer's suggested retail price, compared to a mere 22% for similar sedans produced by some competitors. No doubt Toyota's reputation for reliability plays a significant role in the determination of resale value.

Applied to measurement, reliability is just as important. Reliability can be defined as the degree to which measures are free from error and yield consistent results (Peter, 1979). Any phenomenon we decide to "measure" in the social sciences and education, whether it is a physical or mental characteristic, will inevitably contain some error. For example, you can step on the same scale three consecutive times to weigh yourself and get three slightly different readings. To deal with this, you might take the average of the three weight measures as the best estimate of your current weight. In most field settings, however, we do not have the luxury of administering our measurement instrument multiple times. We get one shot at it, and we had better obtain the most accurate estimate possible with that one administration. Therefore, if we have at least some measurement error in estimating a physical characteristic such as weight, a construct that everyone pretty much agrees on, then imagine how much error is associated with a controversial phenomenon we might want to measure, such as intelligence. With classical psychometric true score theory, we can stop "imagining" how much error there is in our measurements and start estimating it.

Classical test theory (CTT) states that our observed score (X) is equal to the sum of our true score, or true underlying ability (T), plus the measurement error (E) associated with estimating our observed scores, or

$$X = T + E$$

The observed score (X) is the score the test taker receives on the single administration of the test. The true score (T) is the score we would obtain if we were to take the average score of an infinite number of independent test administrations for that individual. Of course, in practice, one cannot administer a test continuously to the same person. Rather, we typically get only one chance to administer a test to a test taker. In CTT, an individual's true score is tied to the particular test administered. If a different test measuring the same construct was administered, the test taker would be expected to have a different true score on that test. This is a major point of contrast with item response theory, which is neither sample nor test dependent (see Module 20).

Due to the amount of error (E) associated with the test, each observed score often deviates from the corresponding true score. While several assumptions are made about the relationship among observed scores, true scores, and error components (see Allen & Yen, 2001; Crocker & Algina, 1986), a foundational principal behind the assumptions of CTT is that error is random. As such, the mean of error scores is zero. Since the Graduate Record Examination, for example, is not a perfectly reliable test, one's observed score (e.g., the score reported back from the Educational Testing Service) can be either higher or lower than his or her true score. It is not uncommon for a student to feel that some random error depressed his or her observed score. In truth, it is just as likely that random error increased his or her observed score! If we could wipe your memory of the test you were just administered (think *Men in Black*) and then administer the same test to you an infinite number of times, each time wiping your memory of the previous administration, the mean of the error scores would sum to zero. Thus, your true score would equal the mean of your observed scores. Another important assumption of CTT is that true scores are uncorrelated with error scores. Since error is considered random in CTT, one would expect that true scores would be uncorrelated with error scores. But, what about systematic errors, such as discrimination in testing, intentional response distortion, and changes due to learning over time? Quite simply, systematic errors are not considered errors in CTT.

Across people, variability in observed scores is equal to true score variance plus error variance, or

$$\sigma^2_{observed} = \sigma^2_{true} + \sigma^2_{error}$$

We use **reliability coefficients** to estimate both true and error variance associated with our observed test scores. Theoretically speaking, the reliability estimate is the ratio of the true score variance to the total variance:

$$r_{xx} = \frac{\sigma^2_{true}}{\sigma^2_{observed}} = \frac{\sigma^2_{true}}{\sigma^2_{true} + \sigma^2_{error}}$$

where r_{xx} is the reliability, σ^2_{true} is the true score variance, $\sigma^2_{observed}$ is the total score variance, and σ^2_{error} is the error variance. Conceptually, then, reliability is the fraction of observed score variance that is due to true score variance. Of course, we will never be able to directly estimate either the true score or its variance; hence, this particular formula serves merely as a heuristic for understanding the components of reliability. However, the variance equation above can be rewritten as

$$\sigma^2_{true} = \sigma^2_{observed} - \sigma^2_{error}$$

and then plugged into the reliability formula. Since error variance can be estimated, we can produce a practical formula to estimate reliability:

$$r_{xx} = \frac{\sigma^2_{observed} - \sigma^2_{error}}{\sigma^2_{observed}}$$

CTT estimates only one type of error at a time. As a result, there are different types of reliability, each focusing on different sources of error. Further discussion of the estimation of reliability is presented in Module 6. However, the focus on only a single type of error at any given time might be considered a limitation of CTT. Module 22 presents generalizability theory, which considers estimations for simultaneously occurring measurement error.

Interpreting the Size of the Reliability Coefficient

Reliability is perfect when there is no measurement error. In this ideal case, each individual's observed scores would equal his or her true score, and all differences between observed scores would reflect actual differences in true scores. At the other end of the spectrum, if a test has zero reliability, the measurement assesses only random error. In such a case, observed scores would be meaningless, as they would merely reflect measurement error. In most cases, measurements in the social sciences and education fall somewhere between these two extremes (though we would hope somewhere much closer to perfect reliability than zero reliability!). In such a case, the differences between observed scores are due to both differences in true scores and error variance. How much reliability is considered acceptable for a psychometric test? The general rule is that a reliability coefficient of .70 or greater is desired. This conventional value indicates that observed scores could reflect 30% measurement error and still be considered quite acceptable. However, how the test is to be used matters quite a lot. Testing conducted for applied purposes typically demands higher reliability. If a doctor was trying to determine whether a patient needed brain surgery, the doctor would certainly not be confident in a test that contained 30% error in measurement! Likewise, scales used in some psychological research might be acceptable even if they don't achieve the desired reliability of .70. However, it should be kept in mind that when correlating a measure with low reliability with any other measure, the resulting correlation will be reduced (i.e., attenuated).

Reliability and Test Length

Imagine the following scenario: As a rabid sports fan, your favorite college or professional team has made it to the league finals. Congratulations! If you know in your heart that your team is the superior team, would you prefer a single championship game (as is the case for the Super Bowl in the National Football League [NFL]) or a series (such as the best of seven games played in Major League Baseball's World Series)? If you were certain your team was superior, you'd be better off taking the best of seven games series option. Why? We all know that strange things can happen in any single game. The ball can take a funny bounce, a star can have an uncharacteristically bad game, and so forth. Indeed, in the NFL, a common saying is that on any given Sunday, any team can win. In a series, though, we'd expect that the superior team should eventually win the majority of the games.

In measurement, all else being equal, longer tests have better reliability. Each item composing a test can be viewed as a separate, parallel test. Most students would wisely want to avoid a one-item test. However, with many items, we become more confident that the resulting observed score more closely approximately one's true score. Intuitively, students understand that the greater the number of items on the test, the more measurement errors will tend to cancel each other out. Thus, longer tests have greater reliability.

The relationship between test length and reliability is due to the relationship between true score variance and error variance. If the number of items on a test is doubled, for example, true score variance increases fourfold. At the same time, error variance is only doubled when the number of items on a test is doubled. Given the relative increase of true score variance to error variance, reliability increases with longer tests.

The relationship between test length and reliability is illustrated by the **Spearman-Brown prophecy formula**. This formula can be used to estimate the "new" reliability of a measure if it is increased (or decreased) in length.

$$r_{XX'n} = \frac{nr_{XX'}}{1+(n-1)r_{XX'}}$$

where $r_{XX'n}$ is the Spearman-Brown corrected reliability estimate, n is the factor by which we want to increase the test, and $r_{XX'}$ is the original reliability estimate. If we wanted to estimate the new reliability of a test after doubling the items on the original test (such as by increasing a 10-item test to a total of 20 items), then n would be 2. If we wanted to estimate the new reliability of a test after tripling the items on the original test (such as increasing a 20-item test to a total of 60 items), then n would be 3. An important caveat is that the formula assumes that the new items are similar to the original items in terms of content, difficulty, correlation with other items, and item variance. If the items added to the test are of much poorer quality than the original items, the actual reliability of the longer test will be less than the formula would predict.

Concluding Comments

There will always be some degree of error when we try to measure something. Measurements of physical characteristics, however, tend to have less measurement error than measurements of psychological phenomena. Therefore, it is critical that we accurately estimate the amount of error in psychological measures. In CTT, observed scores are recognized as resulting from both true scores and random error. Reliability is conceived as a ratio of the amount of true score variance relative to total test variance. The simplicity of CTT is one of its strengths. However, more modern conceptions of testing, including item response theory (see Module 20) and generalizability theory (see Module 22), explicate the complex nature of psychological and educational measurement more fully and completely.

Best Practices

1. CTT is a highly useful, though limited, framework for understanding test reliability. CTT posits that an individual's observed score on a test is a combination of the individual's true score on the measure and random error.
2. The desired magnitude of a reliability estimate depends upon the purpose of the testing. For research uses, a reliability estimate of .70 may be considered acceptable. For some applied purposes, much higher reliability is desired.
3. Longer tests are generally more reliable than shorter tests. The Spearman-Brown formula can be used to estimate the reliability of a test that is increased or decreased in length by a specific factor.

Practical Questions

1. Why is reliability important in psychological and educational testing?
2. In your own words, explain the concept of a true score.
3. What are some of the major assumptions of CTT?
4. What are some of the limitations of CTT?
5. How is reliability defined in terms of CTT?
6. Under what conditions might we want a very high reliability coefficient?
7. Under what conditions might we accept a low reliability coefficient for a psychological measure?
8. Why are longer tests generally more reliable than shorter tests? What conditions must be met for this to be true?
9. How much can we shorten an existing measure and still maintain adequate reliability? (See Case Study 5.2.)

Case Studies

CASE STUDY 5.1: SHOULD STUDENTS HAVE A CHOICE AMONG ITEMS?

Caleb knew he had to pay a visit to Dr. Zavala, the instructor of his psychometrics course. Caleb's grade on the first exam was, shall we say, less than impressive. While his performance on the multiple-choice section was nothing spectacular, the brief essay section of the exam had really tripped him up. Caleb had received only 5 out of 10 points on the first essay question, and 6 out of 10 points on the second and third essay questions.

When Caleb walked up to his instructor's office, he was happy to see the door was open and no other students were in the office. Dr. Zavala had been willing to go over the exam with Caleb, question by question. Unfortunately, Caleb was unable to detect any particular pattern in the multiple-choice items that he'd gotten wrong. He certainly had missed quite a few, but it did not seem that the items he'd gotten wrong were all from the same chapter or lecture. Rather, the items he'd gotten wrong were from content throughout the topics covered in the course. Caleb did have one major question for the instructor when it came to the essay questions.

"Dr. Zavala, how come you don't provide several options for the essay questions? My history professor allows us to choose three out of five essay questions."

"I'd like you to tell me, Caleb," replied the professor. "The primary reason I don't like to offer an option between essay questions has to do with reliability, and classical test theory. Given what we've discussed in class, can you hazard a guess as to why I don't like to provide a choice between questions?"

Caleb thought for a few minutes before responding. "I understand that my actual test score is called an observed score, and that is due to my true score plus error."

"Correct," interjected Dr. Zavala.

"So are you saying that my score is due to error?" asked Caleb.

"Well, in part" chuckled Dr. Zavala. "But that is true for just about every test. What I want you to do is focus on the true score. It's because of the true score that I don't provide students a choice between test questions."

Caleb responded, "I know that the true score is my theoretical expected number of items correct on the test. Basically, if I took the test an infinite number of times, it would be the average of my observed scores. Although a true score is what we really want to measure, the observed score on any one administration of the test is only an approximation of the true score because of the error on the test."

Dr. Zavala smiled. "You know more than your exam grade might indicate. You just revealed what I was trying to get at."

Caleb looked confused. "I did?"

"You stated the true score is your expected number of items correct *on that test*. So, if . . ."

Caleb cut him off. "Oh, I get it. If you provided a choice between items, there would actually be different tests, depending upon which items a student chose."

"Exactly," responded Dr. Zavala, "and your true score would actually differ, depending upon which items you chose. I'll admit that giving students options on which test questions to answer can raise their grades. But that's not the purpose of testing. I also believe there is a certain content domain that I want to ensure students master. I then pick items that assess that entire content domain. I don't want students picking items from just part of that content. I want to make sure that all students in your class are tested on the same measure, so I don't provide students an option between items."

Questions to Ponder

1. Caleb was unable to detect any pattern in the content of the multiple-choice items the he had gotten wrong. Does this challenge the reliability of the test in any way?
2. Explain why Caleb's performance on the essay items might provide some small evidence of reliability for the exam.
3. Caleb appears to have a good understanding of the concept of a true score. How would you define error according to CTT?
4. Explain why, according to CTT, a student's true score might differ depending upon which items among several alternatives the student answered.
5. How convincing is Dr. Zavala's argument for not allowing students to choose among several alternative items? Explain your opinion.

CASE STUDY 5.2: LENGTHENING AND SHORTENING PSYCHOLOGICAL SCALES

Sheila was frustrated. Although she was happy with both the topic and the constructs she had chosen to examine in her senior honors thesis, she had hit several roadblocks in determining what measures to use to assess each variable in her proposed study. Now that she had finally identified useful measures to include in her survey, she was concerned that her response rate would suffer because of the rather impressive length of the survey. Reasoning that individuals in the sample population she hoped to use were unlikely to spend more than a few minutes voluntarily responding to a survey, Sheila considered her options. First, she could eliminate one or more variables. This would make her study simpler and would have the added benefit of reducing the length of the survey. Sheila rejected this option, however, because she felt each variable she had identified was necessary to adequately address her research questions. Second, she considered just mailing the survey to a larger number of people in order to get an adequate number to respond to the lengthy survey. Sheila quickly rejected this option as well. She certainly didn't want to pay for the additional copying and mailing costs. She was also concerned that a lengthy survey would further reduce the possibility of obtaining a sample that was representative of the population. Perhaps those individuals who would not respond to a long survey would be very different from the actual respondents.

Suddenly, a grin spread across Sheila's face. "Couldn't I shorten the survey by reducing the number of items used to assess some of the variables?" she thought. Some of the scales she had selected to measure variables were relatively short, while scales to measure other variables were quite long. Some of the scales were publisher-owned measures and thus copyrighted. Others were nonproprietary scales both created and used by researchers. Recognizing the reluctance of publishers to allow unnecessary changes to their scales, Sheila considered the nonproprietary measures. The scale intended to assess optimism was not only nonproprietary but also very long: 66 items. A scale assessing dogmatism was also nonproprietary and, at 50 items, also seemed long. Sheila quickly decided that these would be good scales to target for reduction of the number of items.

In class, Sheila had learned that the Spearman-Brown prophecy formula could be used to estimate the reliability of a scale if the scale was doubled in length. Her instructor also explained that the same formula could be used for either increasing or decreasing the number of items by a certain factor. Sheila knew from her research that the typical internal consistency reliability finding for her optimism scale was .85, and for the dogmatism scale, it was .90. Because she wanted to reduce the number of items administered for each scale, she knew the resulting reliability estimates would be lower. But how much lower? Sheila considered reducing the number of items in both scales by one half. Because she was reducing the number of items, the number of times she was increasing the scale was equal to one half, or .5. She used this information to compute the Spearman-Brown reliability estimate as follows in Table 5.1:

Table 5.1   Optimism and Dogmatism Tests

Optimism Test	Dogmatism Test
$r_{XX'n} = \dfrac{nr_{XX'}}{1+(n-1)r_{XX'}}$ $= \dfrac{.5(.85)}{1+(.5-1).85}$ $= .74$	$r_{XX'n} = \dfrac{nr_{XX'}}{1+(n-1)r_{XX'}}$ $= \dfrac{.5(.90)}{1+(.5-1).90}$ $= .82$

In considering these results, Sheila thought she'd be satisfied with an internal consistency reliability estimate of .82 for the dogmatism scale, but she was concerned that too much error would be included in estimates of optimism if the internal consistency reliability estimate were merely .74.

Undeterred, Sheila decided to estimate the reliability if only onethird of the optimism items were removed. If onethird of the items were dropped, twothirds (or .67) of the original items would remain. Therefore, the Spearman-Brown prophecy estimate could be computed as follows in Figure 5.1:

$$r_{XX'n} = \frac{nr_{XX'}}{1+(n-1)r_{XX'}}$$
$$= \frac{.67(.85)}{1+(.67-1).85}$$
$$= .79$$

Figure 5.1   Optimism Test

Sheila decided that this reliability would be acceptable for her study. In order to complete her work, Sheila randomly selected 25 (50%) of the items from the dogmatism scale and 44 (67%) of the items from the optimism scale. She was confident that although her survey form was now shorter, the reliability of the individual variables would be acceptable.

Questions to Ponder

1. Do you think an $r_{xx'} = .74$ for the optimism scale would be acceptable or unacceptable for the purpose described above? Explain.
2. Should Sheila have randomly selected which items to keep and which to delete? What other options did she have?
3. How else might Sheila maintain her reliability levels yet still maintain (or increase) the number of usable responses she obtains?
4. Why do you think Sheila is using .80 as her lower acceptable bound for reliability?

Exercises

EXERCISE 5.1: IDENTIFYING CTT COMPONENTS

OBJECTIVE: Correctly identify each component of CTT.

Mark each of the following as observed score (X), true score (T), or error (E)

1. During a timed, 2-hour exam, both of Celia's mechanical pencils ran out of lead, causing her temporary distress and a loss of several minutes of precious time.
2. After completing an online measure, Shana was informed that she was in the 73rd percentile of extraversion.
3. Despite not knowing the content, Tomás provided totally lucky guesses to three out of five multiple-choice questions on a recent Business Ethics quiz.
4. After dedicating his life to science, Jerry repeatedly took the same 20-item IQ test every month for 15 years. A researcher then averaged Jerry's IQ scores to derive an overall score.
5. Jeff gloated that the score on his Early Elementary Education final exam was five points higher than Stephanie's score.

EXERCISE 5.2: EXAMINING THE EFFECTS OF THE
SPEARMAN-BROWN PROPHECY FORMULA

OBJECTIVE: To practice using the Spearman-Brown prophecy formula for estimating reliability levels.

Using the Spearman-Brown prophecy formula provided in Case Study 5.2, estimate Sheila's reliability for the dogmatism scale if she used only one third of the number of original items. Is this an "acceptable level" of reliability? Why or why not?

Further Readings

Allen, M.J., & Yen, W.M. (2001). *Introduction to measurement theory.* Long Grove, IL: Waveland Press.

Schmidt, F.L., & Hunter, J.E. (1996). Measurement error in psychological research: Lessons from 26 research scenarios. *Psychological Methods, 1,* 199–223.

Traub, R.E. (1994). *Reliability for the social sciences: Theory and application.* Thousand Oaks, CA: Sage.

Module 6

Estimating Reliability

In Module 5, we stated that in classical test theory, reliability is a ratio of true score variance relative to total test variance. The more that observed scores reflect true score variance rather than error variance, the more reliable the measure. The less that observed scores reflect true score variance, the more that observed scores reflect error variance, and the less reliable the measure. When estimating reliability, however, it is essential to recognize that the differing methods for computing reliability consider different sources of error.

Sources of Measurement Error

In a classic text, Magnusson (1967) pointed out various factors that can influence the reliability estimate of a measure. Magnusson identified measurement errors, lack of agreement between parallel measurements of true scores, fluctuation in true scores, and memory effects. Subsequently, we borrow Magnusson's notation system to identify each of these individual sources of error.

Measurement errors occur when true scores remain the same, but observed scores differ from one test to another. These errors include administration of the test, guessing, and scoring. Any variability in test administration procedures ($\sigma^2_{e(\text{adm})}$), including changes in the way instructions are provided, the environment in which test administration occurs, the administrator, and even the other test takers, can introduce random sources of measurement error. Guessing ($\sigma^2_{e(\text{g})}$) results in getting items correct on one test administration that would not necessarily be correct on a second administration. As anyone who has been asked to score examines can tell you, scoring ($\sigma^2_{e(\text{subj})}$) can result in random error, as well. The more subjective the scoring procedures, the more likely errors in scoring will occur. Though subjectively scored items such as essays tend to have more scoring errors, even objective items (e.g., multiple choice) are subject to scoring errors.

In devising a measure of a particular construct, the test developer is thought to choose from a universe of possible test items. In assessing the reliability of the measure, it is possible to consider how equivalent scores obtained on the test are to scores on a second measure composed of different items intended to measure the same construct. The degree to which these parallel tests produce identical scores is a measure of reliability. In this case, we'd hope that for any individual test taker, the true score on one measure is the same as the true score on the parallel measure. However, the degree to which the true scores are not identical across the two measures would be error ($\sigma^2_{true(equ)}$). Therefore, in the resulting reliability estimate, the differences in true scores on the two measures (i.e., true score variance) would in this case be a source of error variance and would decrease the reliability coefficient.

True scores can also change over time ($\sigma^2_{true(fl)}$). Indeed, a goal of many research studies is to effect some sort of change by applying an experimental manipulation. In terms of reliability, however, consistency is key, not change. If the true score variance changes over time, this fluctuation in true scores is considered a source of error, which would underestimate the reliability.

Finally, memory effects ($\sigma^2_{e(m)}$) can also impact reliability but have the opposite effect of overestimating reliability. If true scores don't change over time, but test takers remember what answers they provided the first time a test was administered and, thus, provide the same responses a second time, the estimated reliability will appear better than it is in reality.

In Module 5, we noted

$$\sigma^2_{observed} = \sigma^2_{true} + \sigma^2_{error}$$

Considering all possible sources of error identified by Magnusson, one might rewrite the equation as

$$\sigma^2_{observed} = \sigma^2_{true} + \sigma^2_{e(adm)} + \sigma^2_{e(g)} + \sigma^2_{e(subj)} + \sigma^2_{true(equ)} + \sigma^2_{true(fl)} + \sigma^2_{e(m)}$$

Types of Reliability

The various types of reliability differ in which sources of error are emphasized. In **test-retest reliability**, the focus is on consistency of test scores over time. When examining test-retest reliability, the conceptual formula for observed score variance is as follows:

$$\sigma^2_{observed} = \sigma^2_{true} + \sigma^2_{e(adm)} + \sigma^2_{e(g)} + \sigma^2_{e(subj)} + \sigma^2_{true(fl)} + \sigma^2_{e(m)}$$

For most reliability estimates, we compute a Pearson product moment correlation (correlation coefficient for short) or some other appropriate estimate (e.g.,

Spearman correlation if we have ordinal data) to estimate the reliability of our measurement scale. For test-retest reliability, we calculate the correlation coefficient between a test given at time 1 and the same test given at some later point. In examining the above conceptual formula, it is clear that test-retest reliability emphasizes errors associated with changes in the examinees, such as memory effects, true score fluctuation, and guessing. If the time period is too short between administrations of the test, memory effects are likely to overestimate the reliability. If the time period between test administrations is longer, there is an increased chance that the true score will change, thus leading to an underestimate of the reliability of the measure. There are also other error sources that can impact the estimate of test-retest reliability, including variability in scoring and administration procedures.

In **parallel forms reliability**, the reliability coefficient provides an estimate of equivalence of two versions of the same test. For test versions to be considered parallel in classical test theory, the two versions must measure the same construct, be composed of the same type of items (e.g., multiple choice, short answer, true/false, etc.), and have the same number of items. In order for the tests to be considered parallel, they must have the same true score and the same error variance for populations of examinees. Therefore, we'd expect the two test versions to also have the same observed score means and variances. The conceptual formula for observed score variability in parallel forms reliability is

$$\sigma^2_{observed} = \sigma^2_{true} + \sigma^2_{T(equ)} + \sigma^2_{e(adm)} + \sigma^2_{e(g)} + \sigma^2_{e(subj)} + \sigma^2_{true(fl)}$$

While many possible sources of error might influence the parallel forms reliability estimate, of particular interest is the degree to which the two forms of the test are equivalent. If the true scores differ substantially, the parallel forms reliability estimate will be lowered. With alternate forms reliability, we administer examinees one form of the test and then give them the second form of the test. Because we do not have to worry about the individuals remembering their answers, the intervening time between testing sessions does not need to be as long as with test-retest reliability estimates. In fact, the two testing sessions may even occur on the same day. From a practical standpoint, this may be ideal, in that examinees may be unwilling or simply fail to return for a second testing session. As you have probably surmised, the biggest disadvantage of the alternate forms method is that you need to develop two versions of the test. It is hard enough to develop one psychometrically sound form of a test; now you have to create two! Is it possible to just look at content sampling within a single test? Yes.

It's possible to consider any single test as being composed of two parallel halves. By dividing a test into two halves, we could derive an estimate of **internal consistency** reliability. For example, a 20-item measure could be divided into two 10-item tests by considering all even-numbered items to be part of one measure and all odd-numbered items to be part of a second measure. The degree to which these halves are equivalent could be determined in the same way as described above to examine parallel forms reliability. The primary advantages of internal consistency reliability estimates are that there is no need to create two separate tests, and the measure is administered just once to examinees. When considering a *split-half reliability* estimate of internal consistency, there are two concerns. First, dividing a test in half actually reduces the reliability of the test as a whole because it reduces the total number of items that compose the test by half (see Module 5). Fortunately, the Spearman-Brown prophecy formula discussed in Module 5 can be used to correct that issue. A second concern is that there are many ways to divide the items composing a measure into two separate halves. In addition to comparing odd-numbered items to even-numbered items, it is also possible to compare scores on the first 10 items with scores on the second 10 items. If we simply correlate the first half with the second half, however, we may get a spuriously low reliability estimate, due to fatigue effects. In addition, many cognitive ability tests become progressively harder as you go along. As a result, correlating the first half of the test with the second half of the test may be misleading. There are, of course, many additional ways to split a test into two separate halves. Unfortunately, each method may yield a slightly different reliability estimate than the previous method used. Therefore, a more common method for computing the internal consistency reliability is the alpha reliability estimate. **Coefficient alpha**, or Cronbach's alpha, is the average of all possible split-half reliabilities. As a result, the formula for computing alpha is a little more involved than a simple bivariate correlation coefficient:

$$\alpha = \frac{k}{k-1}\left(1 - \frac{\Sigma \sigma_i^2}{\sigma_x^2}\right)$$

where α is the estimate of the alpha coefficient, k is the number of items on the test, σ_i^2 is the variance of item i, and σ_x^2 is the total variance of the test.

All other things being equal, the more items you have on your test (k), the higher your alpha coefficient will be. Hence, one way to increase the reliability of your test is to increase the number of items on the test. In addition, the alpha coefficient will also increase if we increase the variability of each item. Removing items with very little variability from a test and replacing them with higher-variability items will actually increase the test's alpha coefficient.

How does one interpret the coefficient alpha? Actually, the interpretation is very similar to that of the other reliability estimates based on correlation coefficients. Zero indicates no reliability (i.e., all measurement error). A value of 1, on the other hand, indicates perfect reliability (i.e., no measurement error). Thus, the common standard of a reliability estimate of at least .70 or higher holds for alpha, as well.

Two precautions should be kept in mind when interpreting alpha reliability estimates. First, many students and practitioners often refer to coefficient alpha as "the" estimate of reliability. As should be clear by now, coefficient alpha is but one estimate of reliability that focuses on just one form of measurement error. Therefore, if you are interested in other forms of measurement error, you will need to compute additional reliability estimates. Second, as Cortina (1993) and Schmitt (1996) pointed out, one common misconception of alpha among naive researchers is that coefficient alpha is an indication of the unidimensionality of a test. If you have a large enough set of items, you will have a high alpha coefficient, but this does not mean that your test is unidimensional. The measurement of job satisfaction can serve as a good example of this phenomenon. Most job satisfaction scales measure several different facets of job satisfaction, such as satisfaction with one's job, supervisor, pay, advancement opportunities, and so on. However, the scales can also be combined to create an overall job satisfaction score. Clearly, this overall job satisfaction score is not unidimensional. Because the overall score is typically based on a large number of items, however, the overall scale's alpha coefficient will be large. As a result, it is important for researchers to remember that an alpha coefficient only measures one form of measurement error and is an indication of internal consistency, not unidimensionality.

Inter-rater reliability examines the relationship between scores provided by different raters observing the same phenomenon. This occurs, for example, in Olympic gymnastics when raters from different countries provide ratings of an athlete's performance. If we limit our comparison to just two of those raters, an inter-rater reliability coefficient could be computed by correlating the first rater's rating with the second rater's rating for each of the phenomena (in this case, gymnasts) rated. Conceptually, the observed score variance for inter-rater reliability would be as follows:

$$\sigma^2_{observed} = \sigma^2_{true} + \sigma^2_{e\,(adm)} + \sigma^2_{e\,(subj)} + \sigma^2_{true(equ)} + \sigma^2_{e\,(m)}$$

Although each of these components can contribute to observed score variance, the primary focus in on the error in scoring.

While an inter-rater reliability coefficient will attest to the degree of consistency between the two raters, an inter-rater reliability coefficient does not indicate the degree to which two raters agree in their ratings. For example, if rater A consistently provides ratings 10 points below those provided by rater B, the two raters would have perfect inter-rater reliability, though they would never have agreed on a single rating!

If you are interested in examining the degree to which two raters agree in their ratings, an estimate of inter-rater agreement can be computed using a statistic such as Cohen's kappa. To compute kappa, you would need to set up a cross-tabulation of ratings given by raters, similar to a chi-square contingency table. For example, you might have a group of parents, both the mother and the father (your two raters), rate their children on the children's temperament (e.g., 1 = easygoing, 2 = anxious, 3 = neither). You would want to then determine if the parents agree in terms of their respective perceptions (and ratings) of their children's temperaments. To compute the **kappa statistic**, you would need to set up a 2 (raters) × 3 (temperament rating) contingency table of the parents' ratings. Then you would compute the kappa statistic as follows:

$$k = \frac{(O_a - E_a)}{(N - E_a)}$$

where k is the kappa statistic, O_a is the observed count of agreement (typically reported in the diagonal of the table), E_a is the expected count of agreement, and N is the total number of respondent pairs. Thus, Cohen's kappa represents the

Table 6.1   Sources of Error and Their Associated Reliability Statistics

Source of Error	Reliability Coefficient	Reliability Estimate	Statistic
Change in Examinees	Stability	Test/retest	r_{12}
Content Sampling	Equivalence	Parallel forms	$r_{xx'}$
Content Sampling	Internal consistency	Split-half Alpha	r_{x1x2} α
Inter-rater	Rater consistency	Inter-rater agreement	R_{r1r2} kappa

proportion of agreement among raters after chance agreement has been factored out. In this case, 0 represents chance ratings, while a score of 1 represents perfect agreement. But what about values of kappa between these extremes? How high a level of kappa can be considered acceptable? Unfortunately, the answer is not straightforward, because the magnitude of kappa is dependent on factors beyond just the agreement between raters. Several somewhat arbitrary guidelines for the interpretation of kappa have been proposed. Fleiss suggested that values below .40 can be considered poor, values between .40 and .75 are fair to good, and kappas above .75 can be considered excellent. Landis and Koch (1977) suggested that kappas from .21 to .40 can be considered fair; from .41 to .60, moderate; between .61 and .80, substantial; and greater than .80, nearly perfect. (*Note:* Exercise 6.2 provides data for computing Cohen's kappa.)

As with many statistics, however, kappa has not been without its critics (e.g., Maclure & Willett, 1987). One criticism is that kappa is not a good estimate of effect size. Although it will give a pretty good estimate of whether the observed ratings are significantly different from chance (an inferential statistic), using kappa as an estimate of the actual degree of agreement (i.e., as an effect size estimate) should be done cautiously, as the statistic assumes that the raters are independent. In our preceding example, it is highly unlikely that the parents will provide independent ratings. Thus, when it can be reasonably assumed that raters are not independent, you would be better off using other estimates of rater agreement, such as the intra-class correlation coefficient.

Thus, we see that there are many forms of reliability, each of which estimates a different source of measurement error. Table 6.1 presents a summary of each of these reliability estimates.

What Do We Do With the Reliability Estimates Now That We Have Them?

You are probably asking yourself, "Now that we have an estimate of reliability, what do we do with it?" First, we will need to report our reliability estimate(s) in any manuscripts (e.g., **technical manuals**, conference papers, and articles) that we write. Second, if we have followed sound basic test construction principles, someone who scores high on our test is likely to be higher on the underlying trait than is someone who scores low on our test. Often, this general ranking is all we are really looking for—who is "highest" on a given measure. However, if we want to know how much error is associated with a given test score (such as when we set standards or cutoff scores), we can use our reliability estimate to calculate the **standard error of measurement**, or *SEM*. If we have the reliability estimate and the sample standard deviation, computing the *SEM* allows us to determine the confidence interval (CI) around our observed score so that we can estimate (with a certain level of confidence) someone's underlying true score,

$$SEM = S_x \sqrt{1 - r_{xx}}$$

where S_x is the sample standard deviation and r_{xx} is the reliability estimate.
EXAMPLE: $X = 100$, $S_x = 10$, $r_{xx} = .71$

$$SEM = 10\sqrt{1 - .71} = 10(.5385) = 5.38$$
$$95\% \text{ CI} = X \pm 1.96 * SEM = 100 \pm 1.96 * (5.38)$$
$$= 100 \pm 10.54 = 89.46 \leq T \leq 110.54$$

where X is our test score, 1.96 is the critical z value associated with the 95% CI, *SEM* is the standard error of measurement value, and T is our estimated underlying true score value.

You can see from the preceding formula that as our test becomes more reliable, our CI becomes narrower. For example, if we increase the reliability of our test to .80, the *SEM* in the previous example becomes 4.47, and thus the 95% CI narrows to $91.24 \leq T \leq 108.76$. We could even reverse the formula and figure out how reliable our test needs to be if we want a certain width CI for a test with a given standard deviation. For example, if we want to be 95% confident that a given true score is within 5 points (*SEM* = 2.5, plus or minus in either direction) of someone's observed score, then we would have to have a test with a reliability of .9375:

$$SEM = S_x \sqrt{1 - r_{xx}}$$

becomes

$$1 - \left[\frac{SEM}{S_x} \right]^2 = 1 - \left[\frac{2.5}{10} \right]^2 = 1 - .0625 = .9375$$

Concluding Comments

There will always be some degree of error when we try to measure something. Physical characteristics, however, tend to have less measurement error than do psychological phenomena. Therefore, it is critical that we accurately estimate the amount of error associated with any measure, in particular, psychological measures. To estimate the measurement error, we have to first decide what form of error we are most interested in estimating. Once we do that, we can choose an appropriate reliability estimate (see Table 6.1) to estimate the reliability. We can then use the reliability estimate to build CIs around our observed scores to estimate the underlying true scores. In doing so, we will have much more confidence in the interpretation of our measurement instruments.

Best Practices

1. Different types of reliability emphasize different sources of measurement error. Consider the most relevant sources of error when choosing which type(s) of reliability should be reported.
2. Report inter-rater reliability when considering consistency across two raters, but report inter-rater agreement when the focus is on the degree to which the raters reported the same exact score.
3. Recognize the difference between a reliability coefficient and standard error of measurement. A reliability coefficient is the correlation between the scores of test takers on two independent replications of the measurement process. Reliability refers to the degree to which test scores are free from measurement error for a given group of test takers. The *SEM* uses reliability information to indicate the amount of error associated with the estimate of an individual's true score. Therefore, the *SEM* estimates how much a test-taker's observed score might vary over repeated administrations of the test.

Practical Questions

1. What are the different sources of error that can be assessed with classical test theory reliability analysis?
2. Which sources of error are of primary concern in test-retest reliability? In parallel forms and internal consistency reliability? In inter-rater reliability?
3. Which sources of error tend to decrease the reliability of a measure? Which source of error tends to lead to an overestimate of the reliability of a measure?
4. How is Cohen's kappa different from the other forms of reliability?
5. Why are some authors (e.g., Cortina, 1993; Schmitt, 1996) cautious about the interpretation of coefficient alpha?

Case Studies

CASE STUDY 6.1: DON'T FORGET TO REVERSE SCORE

It didn't make sense. It just didn't. How could the reliability be so low? Chad scratched his head and thought. Chad had agreed to help analyze the data from his graduate advisor's most recent study. Although entering the data into a computer database had not been exciting, it had been relatively easy. Once he had entered each research participant's responses, he spot-checked a few cases to ensure accuracy. He then conducted frequency analyses on each variable to ensure that there were no out-of-bounds responders. In fact, he'd found two cases in which he had incorrectly entered the data. He could tell because items that were responded to on a five-point Likert-type rating scale had reported scores of 12 and 35, respectively. Sure enough, he'd just made a typo when entering the data. Everything else looked fine.

Or so he thought, until he decided to examine the reliability of one of the scales. Chad's advisor, Dr. John Colman, was primarily interested in troubled adolescents and, over the last several years, had investigated adolescent attitudes toward alcoholic beverages. The same measure of adolescent attitudes toward alcohol was routinely used in this research. Respondents indicated on a scale of 1–5 how strongly they agreed with each of the 12 items. Internal consistency reliability estimates for the scale were consistently good, typically around .80. However, not this time, apparently. In computing the reliability estimate for the data he'd just entered, Chad found that alpha was estimated to be –.39.

Chad couldn't remember ever hearing of a negative internal consistency reliability estimate. In addition, he couldn't explain why the scale would have such a different reliability on this sample than it had with the many samples his advisor had previously used. His first thought was that he might have entered the data incorrectly—but he knew he hadn't. After all, he'd checked the data carefully to ensure that the computer data file matched exactly what was on the original surveys. So what could be the problem?

In examining the item-total correlations for each item on the scale, Chad noticed that several items correlated negatively with a composite of the remaining items. Chad grabbed the original survey and reexamined the 12 items that composed the scale of adolescent attitudes toward alcohol. Each item certainly seemed to measure the intended construct. Chad was about to give up and go report the problem to his advisor when he noticed something. Although each of the 12 items measured attitudes toward alcohol, agreement to 8 of the items would be indicative of acceptance of alcohol use. In contrast, agreement to the other 4 items would be indicative of a rejection of alcohol use. That was it. He'd correctly entered the data from the surveys into the computer data file but had forgotten to recode the reverse-coded items. Because his advisor wanted high scores to be indicative of an acceptance of the use of alcohol, Chad decided he'd recode the 4 reverse-coded items. To do this, he used the recode command of his statistics program to recode all responses of "5" into "1," "4" into "2," "2" into "4," and "1" into "5." He did this for each of the 4 reverse-coded items. Holding his breath, he again computed the alpha. This time, the reliability estimate was $\alpha = .79$, and all of the item-total correlations were positive. Satisfied that he'd been able to resolve the problem on his own, Chad made a mental note to always recode the appropriate items once the entire data file had been completed.

Questions to Ponder

1. In terms of Table 6.1, what type of reliability coefficient did Chad estimate? What source of error is being estimated?
2. Did Chad make the right interpretation of his negative reliability estimate? What else might cause a negative reliability estimate?
3. In practice, how does one know which items to recode and which to keep the same?
4. Both positively and negatively worded items are frequently included on tests. Assuming you recode the negatively worded items before you run your reliability analysis, will the inclusion of negatively worded items affect the test's internal consistency reliability estimate?

CASE STUDY 6.2: CHOOSING AMONG TYPES OF RELIABILITY

Olivia and Gavin had been studying for their upcoming psychometrics midterm for more than an hour, but the past few minutes had been less than productive. While the two thought they both had a good understanding of the various types of reliability, they just couldn't agree on when each measure should be used.

"Let's say we were going to test military officers to determine who might be the best fit for a promotion. Which form of reliability would we be most concerned with?" asked Gavin.

Lauren thought for a brief moment before responding, "Assuming there were a lot of officers to test, I'd bet the most serious concern would be with the officers sharing information about the test with others. Since test security would be a big concern, they'd want to develop more than one form of the test, but they'd want to be certain that each form was equivalent. I'd say, then, that parallel forms reliability would be the type of reliability they'd be concerned with."

"That's what I was thinking," said Gavin, "but when is coefficient alpha going to be used?"

Olivia was ready for that, "I think coefficient alpha is likely to be a major consideration when we want to ensure that the items on the test are highly interrelated. That's a primary concern whenever we have paper and pencil-based measures of psychological constructs like intelligence, extraversion, or even job satisfaction."

"You always know everything," said Gavin, "That's why I like studying with you. You are so darned conscientious."

"I wish I did," said Olivia, "but I am having a hard time coming up with an example of when to use test-retest reliability."

"Actually," said Gavin, "I think you just helped me come up with an example. Your conscientiousness, like any other personality variable, is supposed to be pretty stable, right? So our measures of those variables should be, too."

Olivia beamed, "Right. So if our measure of a personality construct like conscientiousness yields about the same score over repeated administrations, then we'd feel more confident about the measure."

"Exactly," stated Gavin. "Ready to move on to the next topic?"

Olivia glanced at her watch and frowned. "I wish I could, but I've got to go. I promised Dr. Warren I'd help him judge the student research poster competition this afternoon."

"Alright," said a clearly disappointed Gavin, "but I sure hope you and Dr. Warren have good inter-rater reliability!"

Questions to Ponder

1. Why is coefficient alpha such a commonly reported reliability estimate in psychology and education?

2. Provide additional examples of instances in which each type of reliability (test-retest, parallel forms, internal consistency, and inter-rater reliability) might be used.
3. In judging the reliability of judges' ratings of a student research competition, would we be satisfied with inter-rater reliability as computed by a correlation coefficient, or would computation of kappa be necessary?
4. Are there times when we might be interested in obtaining more than one type of reliability? Explain by providing an example.

Exercises

EXERCISE 6.1: COMPUTING TEST-RETEST, ALPHA, AND PARALLEL FORMS OF RELIABILITY VIA COMPUTER

OBJECTIVE: To practice calculating different types of reliability.

Using the data set "Reliability.sav" (see the variable list in Appendix B), perform the reliability analyses outlined below. The scales provided here include a depression scale (14 items, V1–V14), a life satisfaction scale (10 items, V15–V24), a reasons-a-person-retired scale (10 items, V25–V34), a scale with regard to good things about retirement (8 items, V35–V42), and a scale with regard to bad things about retirement (6 items, V43–V48). For your assignment (be sure to do an ocular analysis of all items first, checking for outliers, missing data, etc., before jumping into the reliability analyses):

1. Perform alpha, split-half, and parallel forms reliability analyses for each of the five scales. How do the three different types of reliability compare for each scale listed above? Is one form of reliability more appropriate than another? Discuss for each scale. (*Note:* You may wish to put your results in table form for easy comparison.)
2. Using alpha reliability, with item and scale information, what items should be included in the final versions of each scale in order to maximize the alpha reliability for that scale? (*Note:* You will need to examine the item-total correlations. In addition, once an item is removed, you will need to repeat the process until a final scale is decided upon.)
3. For the life satisfaction and depression scales, determine if the alpha reliabilities are different for men and women (SEX). If yes, do you have any guesses why? (*Note:* This requires using the "split file" option in SPSS or comparable options in other statistics programs.)

EXERCISE 6.2: ESTIMATING AGREEMENT COEFFICIENTS
(COHEN'S KAPPA)

OBJECTIVE: To practice calculating the Cohen's kappa estimate of rater agreement.

Assume you wanted to determine the degree of inter-rater agreement between two forensic psychologists who were each rating 100 potential parolees in terms of their potential for committing additional violent crimes. In general, sociopaths are more likely to commit additional violent crimes than are depressed or normal individuals. Therefore, each psychologist rated each of the 100 potential parolees on a scale of 1–3 in terms of their primary personality category (1 = sociopath, 2 = depressed, 3 = normal). The following results were obtained:

Table 6.2   Comparisons Between Forensic Psychologists A and B

		Forensic Psychologist A		
Forensic Psychologist B		Personality 1	Personality 2	Personality 3
	Personality 1	44	5	1
	Personality 2	7	20	3
	Personality 3	9	5	6

Using the data in Table 6.2 and the formula for kappa presented in the module overview, determine the level of agreement between the raters.

Further Readings

Cortina, J.M. (1993). What is coefficient alpha? An examination of theory and applications. *Journal of Applied Psychology, 78,* 98–104.

Maclure, M., & Willett, W.C. (1987). Misinterpretation and misuse of the kappa statistic. *American Journal of Epidemiology, 126,* 161–169.

Schmitt, N. (1996). Uses and abuses of coefficient alpha. *Psychological Assessment, 8,* 350–353.

Module 7

Content Validity

An Important Note

A popular definition of validity is whether a test measures what it is intended to measure. More accurately, the process of validation does not seek to determine whether the test itself is valid, but rather whether the inferences and conclusions that are made on the basis of test scores are valid (Murphy & Davidshofer, 2001). The traditional concept of validity considered several seemingly independent strategies for establishing the validity of a test, including content validation, criterion-related validation, and construct validation. Today, we recognize that all evidence examined in relation to the inferences and conclusions of test scores contributes to the same process: validation. Although we recognize validity as a unified construct, Modules 7, 8, and 9 each provide a discussion of the issues involved in the various traditional approaches to validation.

The Role of Expert Judgment

Content validation is initially a central concern of the test developer. Once the test is developed, the evaluation of content validity is performed by a rational inspection of the completed test by subject matter experts (SMEs). Any single test intended to assess a construct can be potentially composed of an infinite number of items that assess that particular domain. Unfortunately, not a single test taker would ever be able to answer an infinite number of items. Therefore, the test developer must create a limited number of items to assess the domain—these are the items that actually compose the test. If we have some subset of an infinite number of possible items, it is possible that the items that compose the test may not be representative of the entire domain the test was intended to assess. Thus, once a test is developed, SMEs can evaluate the representativeness of the measure for its intended content domain.

The selection of appropriate SMEs is a crucial step of the content validation process. Borden and Sharf (2007) point out that legal disputes over the content validity of a measure often result in the qualifications of SMEs being challenged. Therefore, the expertise of those selected to evaluate the representativeness of a measure must able to be justified to the satisfaction of others. In the context of validating personnel selection measures, Buster, Roth, and Bobko (2005) recommend that the SME sample be composed of satisfactory (or better) performing job incumbents and supervisors, and that the sample possess good ethnic and gender diversity. The SME sample should also be composed of individuals who are representative of the various work assignments, geographical locations, and other functional areas of the job. Finally, Buster et al. recommend that probationary employees be excluded from the SME sample.

The importance of clearly defining a content domain cannot be emphasized enough. During test development, the definition of the content domain determines which items should be written and selected for inclusion in the test. Later, during the content validation process, SMEs use the definition of the content domain as a basis for judging the degree to which the test has approximated its intended purpose. In Module 4, we pointed out the importance of adequately defining the domain. Here we see why such a clear specification of the intent of the test is necessary.

Even with the best intentions, however, defining the content domain for some constructs is simply easier than it is for others. Namely, it is easier to describe the content domain of academic achievement and job knowledge than it is to describe the content domains for constructs with less clearly defined boundaries, such as ability and personality. Abstract content domains may defy simple description, making it difficult or impossible to determine whether test items are contained within a particular domain. Content validation is, therefore, most appropriate for domains that can be concretely described and defined.

Content Validity: A Simple Example

Consider the case in which an instructor develops a midterm exam based on the reading assignments of Chapters 1–6 of the course's textbook. If the midterm exam is composed in such a way that 75% of the questions on the exam come directly from Chapter 5, we might question the **content validity** of the test. Did the exam representatively sample from the entire domain (as defined by Chapters 1–6)? If 75% of the items on the test originate from a single chapter, it is unlikely that the items that compose the exam are a representative sample of the entire testing domain. Indeed, important topics in Chapters 1–4 and Chapter 6 are likely to have been omitted from the exam. Likewise, topics in Chapter 5 are probably overrepresented. Therefore, the test would be considered to have problems in regard to content validity. However, who would be appropriate judges of the content validity of this exam? Certainly, the students would vocally express their opinions. SMEs, such as other instructors of the same course, might be even more useful for providing some indication of the content validity of the exam.

Examination of the content validity of a test relies on accurately defining the domain that the test is intended to assess and then making some judgment as to the sufficiency with which that domain has been assessed. The items that compose the test must be a representative sample of the domain. That does not mean that all content areas within a domain need to be assessed equally. Rather, more important topics should be assessed proportionately to their relative importance to other topics in the domain.

Formalizing Content Validity With the Content Validity Ratio

Although a correlation coefficient is not used to assess content validity, several approaches have been suggested to help quantify content validity through the summary of raters' judgments. For example, Lawshe (1975) proposed the **content validity ratio (CVR)**. In assessing the CVR, a panel of SMEs is asked to examine each item on a test. For each item, each SME rates whether the item is "essential," "useful," or "not necessary" to the operationalization of the construct. Across raters, the CVR for an item is determined as follows:

$$CVR = \frac{n_e - \frac{N}{2}}{\frac{N}{2}}$$

where n_e is the number of SMEs rating the item as essential, and N is the total number of SMEs making a rating.

Acceptable Size of the CVR

The CVR can range from +1 to −1 for a particular item, with higher scores indicating greater content validity for the item. A CVR of 0 indicates that half the SMEs rated the item as essential. Any positive value indicates that more than half of the SMEs rated the item as essential. Items that are deemed to have too low a CVR value would be deleted from the test before administration. But what exactly is a low CVR value? Lawshe (1975) suggested that appropriate CVR values would exceed statistical levels of chance. To operationalize this suggestion, Lawshe (1975) recommended consideration of critical values based on a table composed by Lowell Schipper. While Lawshe (1975) claimed that the table of CVR critical values was based on a one-tailed significance test with alpha = .05, Wilson, Pan, and Schumsky (2012) pointed out that this table more closely approximates a binomial at alpha = .05, two-tailed, or alpha = .025, one tailed. Thus, Lawshe's recommended table of CVR critical values is a very conservative approach for determining which test items should be retained. Because the CVR value is dependent on the number of SMEs in the sample, a minimally statistically significant

CVR value will be highly dependent on the number of SMEs used to provide ratings. For example, Lawshe concluded that a CVR value of .29 would be fine when 40 SMEs were used, a CVR of .51 would be sufficient with 14 SMEs, but a CVR of at least .99 would be necessary with 7 or fewer SMEs. Obviously, following Lawshe's recommendations strictly would require a substantial number of SMEs. Note that, in practice, positive CVR values that are considerably lower in magnitude than required using Lawshe's criterion have sometimes been used as the basis to argue for evidence of content validity when a relatively small number of SMEs are used to provide ratings (e.g., Schmitt & Ostroff, 1986).

A CVR Computational Example

Let's try a computational example. Consider the case in which a test developer has developed a 30-item job knowledge test. Wanting to know the CVR of each item, our test developer asks 12 job incumbents to act as SMEs and rate each item on a three-point scale. The degree to which each item is an essential element of job knowledge is rated on a scale with anchors ranging from 0 (not necessary) to 1 (useful) to 2 (essential). Item 14 on the 30-item scale receives nine ratings of "essential," two ratings of "useful," and one rating of "not necessary." What is the CVR of item 14?

$$R = \frac{n_e - \dfrac{N}{2}}{\dfrac{N}{2}} = \frac{9 - \dfrac{12}{2}}{\dfrac{12}{2}} = \frac{9-6}{6} = \frac{3}{6} = .50$$

Although 9 out of the 12 SMEs provided a rating of "essential," the CVR value is only .50. According to Lawshe, when 12 SMEs are used, a CVR of at least .56 would be required to retain the item. Thus, item 14 would be discarded (unless additional SMEs could be found to rate the item, in which case the CVR could be recomputed).

The Content Validity Index

It is important to note that the CVR provides an item-level analysis of validity, while our concern is often with the validity of the test as a whole. To determine an index of the content validity for the test as a whole, the mean CVR across all retained items is computed, resulting in the **content validity index (CVI)**. It should be noted that reliance on the CVI alone could be problematic in determining the validity of a test. After all, consider the example discussed earlier in which an instructor developed a midterm exam that was heavily weighted on a single chapter from the textbook. Individually, each item might receive a high CVR rating. By computing the average CVR rating across all retained items, we would determine that our test's CVI was impressively high. However, few would claim that the test was truly content valid, because it fails to assess many important aspects of the entire domain tested. Therefore, Lammlein (1987, as cited in DuBois & DuBois, 2000) suggested that it is important to obtain additional judgments from the SMEs regarding whether the number of items proportionately represents the relative importance of each knowledge category the test is intended to measure.

A Second Approach to Formalizing Content Validity

Barrett (1992, 1996) proposed quantifying content validity through use of a content validation form (CVF). Developed to assess whether a personnel selection test met the requirements of the Uniform Guidelines, this approach employs a series of 18 questions posed to SMEs. Each question assesses one of three aspects of the test: (a) the test as a whole, (b) an item-by-item analysis, and (c) symptoms of questionable tests. Questions regarding the test as a whole include judgments on the need for and appropriateness of the test (e.g., Have the applicants had access to education, training, or experience necessary to prepare them to take the test?). The item-by-item analysis assesses each item individually (e.g., Is the wanted answer correct?). Finally, symptoms of questionable tests pose questions that are not crucial to establishing content validity, but that are characteristic indicators of a test that is content valid (e.g., Can competent practitioners pass the test?).

Face Validity

Content validity is based on judgment, particularly the judgment of SMEs. However, test takers themselves often make judgments as to whether the test appears valid. Such judgments are referred to as **face validity**. This judgment is based less on the technical components of content validity and more on what "looks" valid (Anastasi & Urbina, 1997). While the veracity of the content validity judgments typically relies heavily on the competence of the SMEs, Bornstein (1996) asserted that face validity is an essential element in understanding the concept of validity. Further, research has indicated that test takers' perceptions regarding a test, including perceptions of face validity, can have an important impact on test-taking motivation and performance (Chan, Schmitt, DeShon, & Clause, 1997). Therefore, the judgments of both SMEs and test takers should be taken into consideration in any assessment of the content validity evidence for a test.

Concluding Comments

The content approach to test validation is one of several traditional validation strategies that involve examining inferences about test construction (Tenopyr, 1977). The content approach relies heavily on expert judgments of whether test items representatively sample the entire content domain. The selection of appropriate test experts (i.e., SMEs) is key to ensuring a proper assessment of content validity. Despite criticisms of the usefulness of content validation (e.g., Fitzpatrick, 1983; Murphy, 2009), expert evaluation of psychological and educational tests remains an important, popular, and legally defensible method of providing validity evidence.

Best Practices

1. Develop a clear, complete definition of the content domain prior to test administration.
2. Select a diverse sample of SMEs that have undeniable knowledge of the content domain.

Practical Questions

1. Validity is a unified construct. In what ways does content validity provide validity evidence?
2. Would it be more appropriate to adopt a content validation approach to examine a final exam in a personality psychology course or to examine a measure of conscientiousness? Explain.
3. The content approach to test validation relies heavily on expert judgment. Discuss the degree to which you feel it is appropriate to rely on judgment to provide evidence of validity.
4. Would content validity alone provide sufficient evidence of validity for (a) an employment exam, (b) an extraversion inventory, and (c) a test to determine the need for major surgery? In each case, provide an argument for your reasoning.
5. Does face validity establish content validity? Explain your answer.
6. What could a student do if he or she thought a classroom exam was not content valid?
7. What could an instructor do if a student asserted that a classroom exam was not content valid?
8. Consider a test or inventory of your choosing. If you wanted to examine the content validity of this measure, how would you go about choosing experts to provide judgments?
9. Is quantifying content validity through the use of the CVI, CVF, or other similar method necessary to establishing content validity? Explain.
10. Imagine the case in which 14 SMEs were asked to provide CVR ratings for a five-item test. Compute the CVR for each of the items based on the ratings shown in Table 7.1.
11. Given that 14 SMEs were used to provide the ratings in question 10, which items do you feel have received a CVR so low that you would recommend deleting the item? Justify your response.
12. What is the CVI for the five-item test in question 10 prior to deletion of any items due to low CVR?

Table 7.1   Sample CVR Ratings for Five Items

Item	Not Necessary	Useful	Essential
1	1	3	10
2	6	6	2
3	0	0	14
4	0	2	12
5	0	5	9

Case Studies

CASE STUDY 7.1: WHAT IS SUFFICIENT CONTENT VALIDATION?

In her years of experience as a clinical therapist, Juanita had come to suspect that some of her clients seemed to share a common trait. Specifically, a significant portion of her clients expressed great loneliness. Juanita found that different therapeutic approaches had varying success with these clients, depending on the degree of loneliness experienced. To help match the correct therapeutic approach to the client, Juanita sought a self-report paper-and-pencil scale of loneliness. Unfortunately, she was unable to locate a scale with established reliability and validity. Undaunted, Juanita began development of a paper-and-pencil measure that would assess the degree of loneliness experienced by the respondent.

Juanita began by reading scientific journals and book chapters on the construct of loneliness. Based on her understanding of the research and her own clinical experience, Juanita defined the trait of loneliness as a persistent, painful awareness of not being connected to others. Juanita then used her knowledge of test construction to develop a measure of 33 items intended to assess the trait of loneliness.

Upon completion of the development of her scale, Juanita wondered whether her new creation was indeed content valid. Therefore, before administering the scale to any clients, she asked four other experienced therapists to scrutinize the items. Each of these clinicians provided positive assurance that the scale seemed to capture the concept of loneliness quite well. Satisfied, Juanita set out to begin using her scale.

Questions to Ponder

1. Are Juanita's efforts sufficient to provide evidence of content validity? Explain.
2. To what degree does Juanita's purpose for the test influence your response to question 1?

3. What additional sources might Juanita seek to help define the trait of loneliness?
4. Is Juanita's choice of individuals to serve as SMEs appropriate? Explain.
5. Has Juanita used an appropriate number of SMEs? Explain.
6. How might Juanita identify other SMEs who would be useful in the content validation of her scale?
7. Is it possible that 33 items could capture the complexity of a construct such as the trait of loneliness?

CASE STUDY 7.2: CONTENT VALIDATION OF A PERSONNEL SELECTION INSTRUMENT

Reflecting for a moment on the results of his ambitious undertaking, Lester smiled. His boss at the Testing and Personnel Services Division of a large midwestern city had assigned him the task of validating the selection test for the job of Supervisor—Children's Social Worker only 2 weeks ago, and he had just completed the task. Lester was quite satisfied with the method he'd used to validate the test, and he was happier still with the results of the effort.

Upon his first inspection of the newly created test, the 145 items seemed to make sense for assessing the behavioral dimensions identified in the job description—knowledge of federal and state laws related to child welfare, supervisory skills, skill in data analytic techniques, skill in reading comprehension, and so on. Still, Lester knew little about the job of a social work supervisor. However, he did have access to the city's database that contained the names of individuals who actually held this position. Through repeated efforts, Lester was able to persuade seven long-time incumbents in the position of Supervisor—Children's Social Worker to serve as expert raters for assessing the content validity of the new test.

Lester arranged for each of the seven SMEs to attend a 1-day session. At the beginning of the day, Lester carefully explained the importance of assessing the content validity of the test, and then he explained the process that was to be used to review each item on the test. Each rater was to make several independent judgments about each and every item on the test. Specifically, SMEs were asked to consider several dimensions of item QUALITY, including (a) the appropriate level of difficulty, (b) the plausibility of item distracters, and (c) the veracity of the answer key. Each SME was then asked to indicate whether he or she was satisfied with all three of these indicators of quality or not satisfied, if any one of the three characteristics needed improvement. If the latter choice was indicated, the SME was asked to provide additional comments for how the item might be improved.

In addition to the QUALITY rating for an item, each SME provided a second rating based on RELEVANCE. For the relevance ratings, each SME was asked to rate the extent to which the knowledge area or ability assessed by the item was essential to correctly performing the critical functions of the job of Supervisor—Children's Social Worker. SMEs rated each item as 2 (Essential), 1 (Useful, but not essential), or 0 (Not useful).

Lester then used both the QUALITY and RELEVANCE ratings to determine which items might be kept in the test and which might be deleted or revised. Specifically, Lester decided that items would be retained if the QUALITY rating was "satisfied" by at least 57% of the raters (i.e., four of the seven SMEs) and if the mean RELEVANCE rating for that particular item was at least 1.5. Using these criteria, Lester eliminated 30 items from the original test. The resulting content-validated test retained 115 items.

As a final step, Lester computed the CVR for each of the retained 115 items based on the SMEs' RELEVANCE ratings. Once the CVR was computed for each item, he then computed the mean CVR across all 115 of the retained items. It was this result that pleased Lester the most—the mean CVR score was .78. Reflecting on his work, Lester began to wonder whether now was a good time to ask his boss for a raise.

Questions to Ponder

1. Would seven SMEs serve as a sufficient number of expert raters to provide adequate evidence of content validity for this employment selection test? Why or why not?
2. Do the criteria Lester used for inclusion of an item seem appropriate? Defend your response.
3. Why would Lester be happy with a mean CVR rating of .78?
4. What other validation strategies might Lester have employed? What additional information would be needed to adopt a different validation strategy?

Exercises

EXERCISE 7.1: IDENTIFYING SMEs

OBJECTIVE: To gain practice identifying appropriate samples to provide content validation ratings.

For each of the following tests, identify two different samples of people who would have the expertise to serve as SMEs for providing judgments regarding the content validity of the test:

1. A knowledge test of local residential electrical codes
2. A measure of political predisposition along the liberalism/conservatism continuum
3. A midterm exam for a high school algebra course
4. A structured interview used to select salespersons
5. A survey of the electorate's preferences for major political office in the upcoming election

EXERCISE 7.2: ENSURING REPRESENTATIVE ASSESSMENT OF TEST DIMENSIONS

OBJECTIVE: To consider the relative importance of various dimensions of a test.

Given the limited number of items that can be included on a test or inventory, test developers must often make difficult decisions regarding the proportion of items that can be used to assess each dimension of a construct. For each of the following multidimensional tests, determine the proportion of items you would choose to assess each of the specified dimensions. For each test, ensure that the total proportion of items sums to 100% across dimensions. Justify your determination for each test.

1. A knowledge test of local residential electrical codes assesses knowledge of (a) municipal, (b) county, and (c) state electrical codes.
2. A midterm exam for a high school algebra course assesses each of the following topics:

   a. Working with variables
   b. Solving equations
   c. Solving word problems
   d. Polynomial operations
   e. Factoring polynomials
   f. Quadratic equations
   g. Graphing linear equations
   h. Inequalities

3. A structured interview used to select salespersons is intended to assess each of the following characteristics of the applicant:

   a. Ability to communicate verbally
   b. Planning and organization
   c. Persuasiveness
   d. Anxiety in social situations

4. A measure of religiosity is composed of the following dimensions:

   a. Religious beliefs
   b. Religious practices

c. Religious knowledge
d. Religious feelings (mystical experiences, sense of well-being, etc.)
e. Religious effects on personal behaviors

EXERCISE 7.3: DETERMINING THE CVI OF A MEASURE OF UNDERGRADUATE ACADEMIC WORK ETHIC

OBJECTIVE: To gain experience obtaining and computing content validity ratings.

INSTRUCTIONS: Below you will find a description of a measure intended to assess the construct Undergraduate Academic Work Ethic. Following this brief description are the items initially written to compose the scale.

For this exercise, choose an appropriate sample of at least 10 individuals to act as SMEs for this scale. Ask these SMEs to familiarize themselves with the proposed dimensions of the scale. Then ask each SME to rate each item on the scale as "essential," "useful," or "not necessary." Remind the SMEs that negatively worded items can be just as useful in assessing the construct as positively worded items. Finally, provide a response for each of the following:

1. Compute the CVR for each item on the scale.
2. Compute the CVI for the entire set of 20 items that make up the initial scale.
3. Based on statistical significance, Lawshe (1975) recommended that with 10 raters the CVR should be at least .62 to retain an item. Which items would be deleted using this criterion?
4. If the items identified in the preceding item were deleted, what would be the CVI of the remaining items?

The Undergraduate Academic Work Ethic Measure

The Undergraduate Academic Work Ethic scale is a 20-item measure of the academic work ethic of undergraduate college students. Undergraduate academic work ethic is defined as an undergraduate student's academic work habits, including the following:

a. Class-related attendance and participation
b. Study habits
c. Procrastination tendencies
d. Dedication to schoolwork
e. Academic honesty

Respondents are asked to indicate the degree to which they agree with each item using a five-point Likert-type scale ranging from 1 (Strongly Disagree) to 5 (Strongly Agree).

1. I make an effort to come to every class, even when I don't feel like attending.
2. I am NOT overly concerned with being in class at the beginning of the lecture.
3. I enjoy participating in class discussions.
4. I would go to my professor's office hours if I needed help in the class.
5. When working in a group, I rarely attend all the group meetings.
6. When writing a paper, I usually wait until the last minute to start it.
7. I usually do NOT procrastinate when it comes to my homework.
8. I have a tendency to cram for tests.
9. I do the least amount of work required in order to pass.
10. I consider myself to have good time management skills when it comes to my schoolwork.
11. I rarely take advantage of extra-credit opportunities.
12. I would turn down an appealing offer to go out if I had to study.
13. During finals week, I rarely have any free time because I am so busy studying.
14. If I don't understand something in class, I will ask the professor or a classmate to explain it.
15. It would NOT bother me to receive a poor grade in a course.
16. I try to be one of the top-ranked students in the class.
17. Doing well in school is NOT a priority in my life.
18. I set high academic goals for myself.
19. I would cheat on a test if I knew I could get away with it.
20. I would allow a classmate to copy my homework.

Further Readings

Burns, R.S. (1996). Content validity, face validity, and quantitative face validity. In R.S. Barrett (Ed.), *Fair employment strategies in human resource management* (pp. 38–46). Westport, CT: Quorum Books/Greenwood.

Messick, S. (1995b). Validity of psychological assessment: Validation of inferences from persons' responses and performances as scientific inquiry into score meaning. *American Psychologist, 50,* 741–749.

Murphy, K.R. (2009). Content validity is useful for many things, but validity isn't one of them. *Industrial and Organizational Psychology: Perspectives on Science and Practice, 2,* 453–464. [See also numerous responses to this article in the same volume.]

Tenopyr, M.L. (1977). Content-construct confusion. *Personnel Psychology, 30,* 47–54.

Module 8

Criterion-Related Validation

If the purpose of validation is to examine whether the inferences and conclusions based on test scores are defensible, just how does the criterion-related approach provide this information? The answer is relatively straightforward. The criterion-related approach to test validation involves examining the empirical relationship between scores on a test and a criterion of interest, typically by use of a correlation coefficient. The appropriate choice of a criterion will depend on what inferences we hope to make. Thus, in determining the validity of a college entrance exam, we would desire a criterion of college success. In determining the validity of an employment selection exam, we would want a criterion of successful job performance. Moreover, in examining the success of a new type of psychiatric therapy, we would select a criterion that captured psychological health.

When examining the relationship between test scores and criterion scores, the choice of a relevant, psychometrically sound criterion is crucial. Typically, there are several criteria that might be considered. For example, within the extant literature reporting typical criterion-related validities of various employment tests, criteria have included subjective measures such as supervisor ratings, co-worker ratings, client ratings, and self-ratings, as well as objective measures including quantity of items produced, number of sales, attendance, and even training success.

In everyday language, it is common to inquire *whether* a test is valid. Criterion-related validation strategies remind us to inquire about *what* exactly the test is valid *for*. In fact, test scores may validly predict scores on one criterion, but not another. For example, intelligence may serve as a good **predictor** of college grade point average, but it may be a poor predictor of morality.

Criterion-Related Validation Research Designs

Three research designs can be employed in the examination of **criterion-related validity**. Although these designs differ in the order in which test scores and criterion scores are collected, a more important issue revolves around the selection of the sample used in the validation study. **Predictive validity** studies correlate test scores at one time with criterion scores collected at some future date. Here, the desire is to examine how well test scores predict future criterion scores. Predictive criterion-related research designs typically utilize less restricted samples than other criterion-related designs, including random samples in some cases. **Concurrent validity** studies collect test and criterion scores at about the same time. Because there is no lag in time between collection of test scores and collection of criterion scores, the validity of the test can be determined much more quickly than is the case for most predictive designs. However, because the sample is typically predetermined (i.e., limited to those individuals for whom we can immediately collect criterion data) in concurrent criterion-related research, the sample on which the validation study is conducted is rarely randomly selected. In fact, concurrent validity samples are usually conducted on samples of existing participants, a sample that is definitely not randomly sampled. A third research design that can be used for criterion-related validation is somewhat less well known: **postdictive validity** designs. With postdictive designs, criterion scores are collected prior to obtaining test scores. As is the case for the concurrent design, postdictive criterion-related validation studies use a predetermined sample. In this case, the sample is limited to those individuals for whom we already have criterion data.

Independent of the research design, examining the empirical relationship between the test and the criterion provides validity evidence. However, the design of the study often has important implications for the possible conclusions that can be drawn from the data. With concurrent criterion-related validity, for example, we are interested in how well test scores are indicative of one's current standing on a criterion. Because individuals can change considerably over time due to a number of factors, the concurrent and postdictive research designs are not as well suited to prediction of future criterion performance as the predictive criterion-related approach.

Examples of Criterion-Related Validation

Industrial/organizational psychologists frequently use criterion-related validity to demonstrate the job relatedness of a proposed employment selection test. A predictive criterion-related validity approach would require the administration of an experimental selection test to job applicants. Selection of new employees is then made either completely randomly or on some basis unrelated to scores on the experimental selection test. Those applicants who are hired are then provided an adequate amount of time to learn the new job—perhaps 6 months to a year. At the end of this time period, criterion information is collected, such as supervisor ratings of employee performance. A correlation between scores on the experimental selection test and the job performance criterion provides the estimate of predictive criterion-related validity.

An estimate of the concurrent criterion-related validity for a new selection test is typically derived by administering the experimental selection test to current employees. Simultaneously, job performance criterion scores are obtained for these individuals. A correlation between scores on the experimental selection test and the job performance criterion provides the estimate of concurrent criterion-related validity.

A postdictive design to examine the criterion-related validity of an employment test might be conducted to examine whether a newly developed test of conscientiousness might relate to employees' absenteeism records (i.e., a job performance criterion). The measure of conscientiousness would be administered to employees. The absenteeism record for each of these same employees would be accessed for some specified amount of time, such as the last 2-year period. A correlation between scores on the measure of conscientiousness and absenteeism would provide the estimate of the postdictive criterion-related validity.

Although the concurrent and postdictive approaches have the obvious advantage of requiring considerably less time to evaluate the experimental selection test than does the predictive approach, two concerns must be considered. First, samples in concurrent and postdictive criterion-related research designs often have restricted variance on variables of interest. For example, in employment studies, people with poor job performance are often terminated early in their careers. These individuals would thus not be included in a concurrent criterion-related validity study, leading to restriction in range. Second, with concurrent and postdictive research designs, concern has been raised about the degree to which the sample used to validate the test (e.g., current employees) differs from the population the test is actually intended for (e.g., job applicants). For example, job applicants would be much more motivated to use an impression management response strategy on a job selection test than would current employees. Interestingly, however, research provides evidence that the validity estimates yielded by predictive and concurrent designs are often nearly identical (Barrett, Phillips, & Alexander, 1981; Schmitt, Gooding, Noe, & Kirsch, 1984). Even so, we must also be aware of legal concerns, at least in the realm of employment testing. According to the Uniform Guidelines on Employee Selection Procedures ("Section 60-3," 1978), criterion-related validity studies must ensure that the sample used in the validation is representative of the applicants in the relevant labor market. This emphasis on representativeness is pertinent to the sample's composition in terms of race, sex, and ethnicity.

Interpreting the Validity Coefficient

Because the criterion-related approach to validation correlates test scores with criterion scores, an easily interpretable measure of effect size is provided that will range from −1 to 0 to +1. Because most tests are constructed such that higher scores on the test are intended to be associated with higher scores on a criterion (e.g., we typically assert the relationship between intelligence and performance, not stupidity and performance), a **validity coefficient** will typically range from 0 to 1. Still, many individuals are surprised to learn that the magnitude of a validity coefficient rarely exceeds .50. While the purpose of testing will determine what magnitude of correlation will be considered sufficient for a given situation, Cohen's (1988) suggestions for the interpretation of the magnitude of correlation-based effect sizes might be useful. Cohen suggested that correlations of .1 are small, .3 are moderate, and .5 can be considered large. It is important to keep in mind that even relatively small validity coefficients can improve prediction significantly over random selection.

A criterion-related validity estimate can be used to determine the percentage of variance accounted for in the criterion by use of the predictor. The **coefficient of determination** is a simple formula to compute:

$$r_{xy}^2 * 100\%$$

where r_{xy} is the validity coefficient.

As an example, a validity coefficient of $r_{xy} = .4$ would indicate that, by using our test, we could account for 16% of the variability in the criterion. In the case of a selection exam with a validity of $r_{xy} = .4$, we would be able to predict 16% of the variability in job performance by using the test in our selection system. Of course, that would also mean that $100\% - 16\% = 84\%$ of the variability in the criterion remained unexplained. Although we could add more tests to increase our prediction of the criterion, that solution is not without its problems (see Module 17).

Attenuation and Inflation of Observed Validity Coefficients

Although it is easy to grasp a basic understanding of the criterion-related approach to test validation, a number of issues should be considered when employing use of this validation strategy. The magnitude of an observed validity coefficient can be affected by a number of factors. These problems are discussed below, along with suggested corrections that may provide a more accurate (and often larger) criterion-related validity estimate.

Inadequate Sample Size

Due to convenience or practical limitations, criterion-related validation studies often employ use of samples that are too small. Because of sampling error, criterion-related validation studies that employ very small samples may produce spurious results regarding the estimated magnitude of the population correlation. Further, because statistical power relies heavily on sample size, use of an inadequate sample size often results in a failure to detect an authentic relationship between the test and the criterion in the population. Such a finding may lead to the unnecessary rejection of the use of the test under consideration.

The clear recommendation to avoid these problems is simple, if not always practical: increase the size of the sample used in the criterion-related validation study.

How large should the sample be? Schmidt, Hunter, and Urry (1976) suggested use of sample sizes in excess of 200 individuals for criterion-related validation studies. Unfortunately, samples of this size are not always possible to obtain. What other options exist? The concept of *synthetic validity* suggests that the validity of a test can be generalized from one context to another similar context (Guion, 1965; Lawshe, 1952). For example, a small organization may wish to use a selection test to hire a new office assistant. Because the organization currently employs only eight office assistants, a full-blown criterion-related validation study would be out of the question. However, through job analysis the small organization might successfully identify a number of job duties that are performed by its office assistants that are similar to those job duties performed by office assistants in larger organizations. Employment tests that are highly related to job performance for office assistants in the larger organizations should validly predict the job performance of office assistants in the small organization as well. Further, meta-analytic reports of the relationship between predictors and a specific criterion could also be sought out to determine the feasibility of use of a predictor (see Module 10).

Criterion Contamination

Another concern in criterion-related validation is **criterion contamination**. Criterion contamination is present when a criterion measure includes aspects unrelated to the intended criterion construct. Put another way, criterion contamination occurs when the criterion measure is affected by construct-irrelevant factors that are not part of the criterion construct (Messick, 1989). Criterion contamination often results in an inflated observed validity coefficient. A common source of criterion contamination occurs when an individual with knowledge of test scores also assigns criterion scores.

Many organizations employ the use of assessment centers in which employees participate in a number of exercises intended to assess management potential. Indeed, many organizations have used these assessment center scores as a basis for determining future promotion. Criterion contamination would result if the organization later decided to examine the relationship between assessment center scores and promotion. Obviously, a strong positive correlation would exist because the assessment center scores were used as the basis for determining who would be promoted and who would not.

The problem of criterion contamination can only be addressed through appropriate measurement of the criterion and by minimizing construct-irrelevant variance in the measurement of both the predictor and the criterion.

Attenuation Due to Unreliability

Because a test is judged based on its relationship to a criterion in criterion-related validation, we had better ensure that the criterion itself is appropriate and is measured accurately. All too often, however, this is not the case. A criterion-related validity coefficient will be attenuated (i.e., reduced) if the criterion is not perfectly reliable. As a result, we might erroneously conclude that our test fails to demonstrate criterion-related validity. Unfortunately, most psychological constructs—including criteria—are measured with some amount of error (see Module 5). Because our focus in validation is the test, we can ethically perform a statistical correction for unreliability in the criterion (Spearman, 1904) in order to provide a more accurate assessment of the validity of the test:

$$r_{xyc} = \frac{r_{xy}}{\sqrt{r_{yy}}}$$

where r_{xyc} is the validity of the test, corrected for unreliability in the criterion; r_{xy} is the original observed validity of the test; and r_{yy} is the reliability of the criterion.

For example, let us consider the case in which a measure of general cognitive ability was being considered for use in hiring retail sales clerks at a popular clothing store. A consultant conducted a concurrent criterion-related validation study and correlated job incumbent scores on the cognitive ability test with supervisor ratings of job performance. The consultant determined that cognitive ability was indeed related to supervisor ratings of job performance, $r_{xy} = .37$. However, the consultant was able to determine that the reliability of supervisor ratings of job performance was only .70. What would be the validity of the test of cognitive ability following correction of the criterion due to unreliability?

$$r_{xyc} = \frac{r_{xy}}{\sqrt{r_{yy}}} = \frac{.37}{\sqrt{.70}} = \frac{.37}{.84} = .44$$

Obviously, the validity coefficient is more impressive following **correction for attenuation** due to unreliability in the criterion.

Note that *mathematically* we could also correct for attenuation due to unreliability in the test at the same time we correct for attenuation in the criterion. This can be done by slightly modifying the preceding formula

$$r_{xyc'} = \frac{r_{xy}}{\sqrt{r_{xx}r_{yy}}}$$

where $r_{xyc'}$ is the validity of the test, corrected for unreliability in the test and the criterion, and r_{xx} is the reliability of the test.

If the consultant decided to further correct for unreliability in the test, we could extend the preceding example. Assuming the reliability of cognitive ability scores on this test was found to be .88, we could perform the following analysis:

$$r_{xyc'} = \frac{r_{xy}}{\sqrt{r_{xx}r_{yy}}} = \frac{.37}{\sqrt{.88(.70)}} = \frac{.37}{\sqrt{.62}} = \frac{.37}{.79} = .47$$

Correction for attenuation due to unreliability in both the criterion and the predictor would further increase our estimate of criterion-related validity.

Unfortunately, this last analysis should *not* be performed to provide an estimate of the validity of our test, because the error associated with unreliability in our predictor will be present whenever we administer the test. If, on the other hand, we wish to know the true population correlation between our test and our criterion (as is often the case in meta-analysis), then correction for unreliability in both the predictor and the criterion is ethically permissible. In addition, using this formula can help motivate test takers to develop predictor tests with increased reliability by showing them the potential increase in validity that could be obtained.

Restriction of Range

Restriction of range is another important concern with criterion-related validation. The variability in test scores in our sample may be considerably smaller than that in the actual population. Unfortunately, it is typically the case that when we reduce the variability in test scores, we reduce the magnitude of the observed correlation. We would then erroneously conclude that our test is less valid than it actually is. This, in fact, is a major concern when using concurrent criterion-related validity rather than predictive designs. Fortunately, there is a formula (Pearson, 1903) to statistically correct for the effects of restriction of range in the test, assuming we can estimate the variability of scores in the population:

$$r_{xyu} = \frac{r_{xy}\dfrac{S_u}{S_r}}{\sqrt{1 - r_{xy}^2 + r_{xy}^2 \dfrac{S_u^2}{S_r^2}}}$$

where r_{xyu} is the unrestricted validity, r_{xy} is the obtained validity, S_u is the population (i.e., unrestricted) predictor standard deviation, and S_r is the restricted predictor standard deviation.

As an example, let us once again consider the case described previously, in which a consultant has determined that the criterion-related validity estimate of a cognitive ability test for predicting the job performance of retail sales clerks is $r_{xy} = .44$ (following correction for attenuation due to unreliability in the criterion). However, this consultant learns that the standard deviation of cognitive ability test scores among job incumbents is only $S_r = 9$, whereas the standard deviation of cognitive ability test scores among applicants for the position of clerk in this retail store is $S_u = 13$. Here, there is clear evidence that score variability in the job incumbent sample is restricted in comparison to the variability of scores among applicants. Thus, we would expect that our unrestricted validity estimate would be greater than our current estimate of .44. Let us work through the example:

$$r_{xyu} = \frac{r_{xy}\dfrac{S_u}{S_r}}{\sqrt{1-r_{xy}^2+r_{xy}^2\dfrac{S_u^2}{S_r^2}}} = \frac{.44\dfrac{13}{9}}{\sqrt{1-(.44)^2+(.44)^2\dfrac{13^2}{9^2}}} = \frac{.44(1.44)}{\sqrt{1-.19+.19\dfrac{169}{81}}}$$

$$= \frac{.63}{\sqrt{1-.19+.19(2.09)}} = \frac{.63}{\sqrt{1-.19+.40}} = \frac{.63}{1.10} = .57$$

Thus, after the additional correction of attenuation due to restriction in range of the predictor, we find that the criterion-related validity of our test of cognitive ability is quite impressive. One challenge with restriction of range corrections is that it is often difficult to obtain good estimates of what variance would be in an unrestricted sample; oftentimes, it is important to consult previous studies for realistic estimates of this term.

Additional Considerations

The criterion-related approach to test validation discussed in this module assumes that we consider the sample of test takers as a single group. Sometimes, however, we might be concerned about whether a test is valid for one subgroup of our sample and not for another. The subgroups can be determined on the basis of whatever is relevant to the researcher, including those based on age, sex, or ethnicity. *Differential validity* examines whether there exist separate test validities for these groups. This topic is considered in Module 11.

Further, our discussion in this module has been limited to the case in which we are examining the relationship between a criterion and a single test. Module 17 addresses additional concerns that arise when more than one predictor is utilized in relation to a criterion.

Concluding Comments

The criterion-related approach to validation attempts to provide evidence of the accuracy of test scores by empirically relating test scores to scores on a chosen criterion. Despite the seemingly simplistic nature of this endeavor, a number of issues must be considered regarding the research design, the sample, and the criterion employed.

Best Practices

1. When conducting criterion-related validation, choose the most relevant criterion, not necessarily the most easily measured.

2. Attempt criterion-related validation only if the sample is sufficiently large (perhaps 200 or more) to provide a stable validity estimate.
3. Correct for artifacts that may lower the estimated criterion-related validity estimate.

Practical Questions

1. How does the criterion-related approach to test validation help provide evidence of the accuracy of the conclusions and inferences drawn from test scores?
2. What are the differences among predictive, concurrent, and postdictive criterion-related validation designs?
3. What concerns might you have in using a concurrent or postdictive criterion-related validation design?
4. The various criterion-related validity research designs might not be equally appropriate for a given situation. For each of the following criterion-related validity designs, provide an example situation in which that design might be used:

   a. Predictive
   b. Concurrent
   c. Postdictive

5. What factors would you consider to ensure that you have an appropriate criterion?
6. What factors might attenuate an observed correlation between test scores and criterion scores? Explain.
7. What might inflate an observed correlation between test scores and criterion scores? Explain.
8. For each of the following, explain how the correction formula provides a more accurate estimate of the true relationship between the predictor and the criterion:

   a. Correction for unreliability in the criterion
   b. Correction for range restriction in the predictor

9. Although it is empirically possible to correct for attenuation due to unreliability in a predictor, this is a violation of ethics if we intend to use the predictor for applied purposes. Explain why we can ethically correct for unreliability in the criterion but cannot ethically correct for unreliability in a predictor.
10. How could a small organization determine which selection tests might be appropriate for use in selection of new employees?

Case Studies

CASE STUDY 8.1: USING MECHANICAL ABILITY TO PREDICT JOB PERFORMANCE

"This will be a cinch," Cecilia had thought when she first received the assignment to conduct a criterion-related validity study. She'd been a human resource (HR) specialist at Joyco for only 3 weeks, and she relished the thought of tackling her first major project independently. In fact, she had jumped at the opportunity when her boss asked her to conduct a criterion-related validation study to determine whether a newly created test of mechanical ability would be useful in selecting production workers. She thought it would be relatively easy to collect test scores and correlate them with some measure of job performance. Only slowly did she realize how much thought and hard work would actually be required to complete the task properly.

She soon realized that the first major issue she'd have to tackle would be identifying an appropriate criterion. Clearly, job performance was appropriate, but how should job performance be measured? Supervisors formally appraised each production worker's performance annually, and the HR office seemed pleased with the quality of the process. Still, Cecilia knew the supervisor ratings were far from perfect assessments of an employee's job performance.

Cecilia's thoughts suddenly leaped to another concern—when her boss had asked her to determine the criterion-related validity of the new test, she had provided a 2-week deadline. Such a tight deadline clearly precluded use of a predictive design. Unfortunately, the current production workers were likely very different from job applicants. In comparison to applicants, current production workers tended to be older, they were more similar to one another ethnically, and they also had much more job experience. Given the timeline provided by her boss, however, Cecilia thought that it was the current production workers that she'd need to use to validate the proposed selection tests.

Undeterred, Cecilia went ahead with the project. Cecilia administered the new mechanical ability test to a sample of Joyco's production workers. In an effort to ensure that she had done a complete job, Cecilia also collected information on everything she thought *might* be relevant. Nonetheless, she knew she had collected an impressive amount of information regarding the new test of mechanical ability and the criterion, including the following:

Sample size for the validation study = N = 178 job incumbents
Observed validity = r_{xy} = .24

Reliability of the new mechanical ability test = r_{xx} = .85
Reliability of supervisor ratings of job performance = r_{yy} = .78
Standard deviation of mechanical ability tests scores for current employee sample = 9
Standard deviation of mechanical ability test scores for applicant sample = 14

Although the completion deadline was quickly approaching, Cecilia still had a ways to go before producing an accurate criterion-related validity estimate for the new mechanical ability test. Cecilia slumped back into her chair. "This is definitely going to take some work," she thought.

Questions to Ponder

1. What research design did Cecilia use to conduct her criterion-related validation study? What was the major determinant of this decision?
2. Why might Cecilia have preferred another research design for her criterion-related validation study?
3. Would Cecilia have to be concerned with criterion contamination in conducting this validation study? Explain.
4. Identify three alternate criteria that Cecilia might have used to assess job performance, rather than supervisor ratings. What concerns do you have with each possible criterion?
5. Given the sample used to validate the proposed selection tests, which correction formulas would be most important to use?
6. Given the data that Cecilia collected, compute each of the following:

   a. Correction for attenuation in the criterion
   b. Correction for predictor range restriction (*Note:* Use the corrected validity estimate from part a.)

7. Examining the corrected validity coefficient produced in question 6b, how impressed would you be with this test of mechanical ability for use in selection of new employees? Would you recommend use of the test? Explain.

CASE STUDY 8.2: AN INVESTIGATION OF STUDENT
DROPOUT RATES

Principal Andrew Dickerson of Mountain Central High School had a hunch. Actually, it was more like a strong suspicion. At nearly 15%, the student dropout rate in his high school was well above the statewide average. Upon assuming his position, Principal Dickerson had pledged that he would change things for the better. Although he knew it would be impossible to eliminate dropouts altogether, he intended to do everything in his power to curb the problem. To begin, he intended to identify factors that put students most at risk for dropping out. The usual socioeconomic factors helped identify some individuals who might be at risk for dropping out, but combined, these factors accounted for only a modest amount of the variance in dropout rates at his school.

In reviewing the academic files of the six latest students to drop out, Principal Dickerson noticed that most of these students had experienced behavioral problems in the very early years of their formal education. Principal Dickerson began to wonder whether this was also true of other students who had dropped out of high school. He knew enough about research methods to acknowledge that you couldn't conclude anything on the basis of such a small sample. Further, he felt it was necessary to examine the files of those students who hadn't dropped out of school, in order to determine their record of discipline in early education as well.

Principal Dickerson decided to examine a sample of all students who had entered his high school in the years 2006–2010. This 5-year block would provide him with a total sample of about 1500 students who entered as freshmen. Because the dropout rate at his school averaged roughly 15% during this time period, he knew that about 225 of these students dropped out of school without graduating. Committed to thoroughly testing his hunch, Principal Dickerson assigned three members of his staff to scan the grade school academic records of all 1500 students who had entered Mountain Central High School between 2006 and 2010. These staff members were told to inspect each student's grade school records and to record the number of behavioral problems noted while the student was in grades 1 through 5. Principal Dickerson planned to correlate these records of behavioral problems with whether or not the students graduated. Given the vast amount of work involved, Principal Dickerson sure hoped his hunch was right.

Questions to Ponder

1. Why must we examine those individuals who graduated from high school if our real concern is with those students who dropped out of high school?
2. What type of criterion-related validity design did Principal Dickerson employ? Explain.
3. Principal Dickerson developed his hunch after reviewing the files of six recent dropouts. Would the files of six dropouts be sufficient to identify a potentially useful trend that should be followed up with an empirical

investigation? What minimum number of files do you feel could be used to initially form a hypothesis worthy of empirical testing?

4. What other methods might Principal Dickerson have employed to identify possible correlates of high school dropout rates?

5. Principal Dickerson is planning to investigate the relationship between early education behavioral problems and high school dropout rate. If the study reveals a significant relationship between these variables, how might this information be used to combat the problem of high school dropouts?

꧁ꙮ꧂

Exercises

EXERCISE 8.1: IDENTIFYING POSSIBLE PREDICTORS AND CRITERIA

OBJECTIVE: To gain practice identifying relevant predictors and criteria for validation.

For each of the criteria presented in items 1–3, identify at least two psychological or cognitive measures that might serve as useful predictors in a criterion-related validation study.

1. Grades in an educational psychology doctoral program
2. A medical student's "bedside manner" as a doctor
3. Success in a retail sales position

For each of the scenarios presented in items 4–6, recommend at least two relevant, practical measures that could serve as criteria.

4. A state in the Southeast would like to determine the usefulness of requiring road tests for drivers older than 70 years of age.
5. A supervisor wishes to determine the job performance of her factory workers.
6. A researcher wishes to determine whether regular consumption of a certain vitamin supplement influences cardiovascular health in men aged 50–75.

EXERCISE 8.2: DETECTING VALID PREDICTORS

OBJECTIVE: To gain experience identifying valid predictors in a data set.

PROLOGUE: The data set "Bus Driver.sav" (see Appendix B) contains a number of variables that assess job performance. Because several independent measures

Table 8.1   Potential Predictors of Bus Drivers' Job Performance

Possible Predictors	
Variable Name	Description
so_hpi	Hogan Personality Inventory service orientation subscale
st_hpi	Hogan Personality Inventory stress tolerance subscale
r_hpi	Hogan Personality Inventory reliability (e.g., integrity) subscale
age	Age of bus driver, in years
sex	Sex of bus driver, coded 0 = male, 1= female
tenure	Tenure on the job, in years
Job Performance Measures	
Variable Name	Description
sickdays	Number of sick personal days in last year
srti	Number of self-reported traffic incidents in last year
drivetst	Score on driving performance test
pescore	Overall performance evaluation score

are also included in this data set, we might be tempted to identify variables that might be useful for predicting the performance of future bus drivers. Following in Table 8.1 are descriptions of several potential predictors and measures of bus driver job performance.

Use the data set "Bus Driver.sav" to correlate the possible predictors with the job performance measures and then answer the following questions. (*Note:* For this exercise, examine the predictors individually using correlation. An opportunity to examine combinations of these predictors using multiple regression is provided in Exercise 17.1.)

1. Overall, how highly are the possible predictors intercorrelated?
2. Overall, how highly are the job performance measures intercorrelated?
3. Overall, how useful would the personality measures be in predicting job performance?
4. Overall, how useful would the demographic variables be in predicting job performance?
5. Inspecting only the significant correlations, interpret the findings for tenure across the job performance criteria.

6. If you were examining the validity of a set of variables that you hoped to use for prediction, and you found validity coefficients similar to those in this analysis, what would you do?

EXERCISE 8.3: PREDICTING SALES JOB PERFORMANCE USING ZERO-ORDER CORRELATIONS

OBJECTIVE: To practice computation of a validity coefficient using statistical software.

PROLOGUE: A sales manager hoping to improve the selection process for the position of product sales compiled the data file "Sales.sav" (see Appendix B). The manager administered several tests to her current employees and also collected basic demographic information. Simultaneously, the manager collected performance data in the form of quantity of products sold by each employee in the past month. Table 8.2 shows the variables in the data file, which include the following:

Table 8.2   Potential Predictors of Salespersons' Job Performance

Variable Name	Description
sex	Sex of employee, coded 0 = female, 1 = male
ethnic	Ethnicity of employee, coded 0 = Caucasian, 1 = African American
w1–w50	Each indicates the employee's score on a separate item on the test of cognitive ability, coded 0 = incorrect, 1 = correct
cogab	Employee's total cognitive ability score
sde	Employee's score on a test assessing one's level of self-deception
impress	Employee's score on a test of impression management
selling	Number of products employee sold in the past month

1. What type of validation study is the manager conducting? Explain.
2. Examining the zero-order correlations, what variables are significantly related to selling?
3. What percentage of variance in selling is accounted for by impression management?
4. If impression management were measured with an $\alpha = .80$, what would be the validity estimate of this variable following correction for attenuation due to unreliability?
5. Cognitive ability has little relationship to performance in these employees.

   a. Is this finding likely due to poor reliability in the measure of cognitive ability? Explain.

    b. Is this finding likely due to very poor reliability in the measure of "selling"? Explain.

    c. Even if cognitive ability were highly related to selling, what other information provided in this data set would make you wary of using cognitive ability for selection of new employees?

Further Readings

Barrett, G.V., Phillips, J.S., & Alexander, R.A. (1981). Concurrent and predictive validity designs: A critical reanalysis. *Journal of Applied Psychology, 66,* 1–6.

Johnson, J.W., Steel, P., Scherbaum, C.A., Hoffman, C.A., Jeaneret, P.R., & Foster, J. (2010). Validation is like motor oil: Synthetic is better. *Industrial and Organizational Psychology: Perspectives on Science and Practice, 3,* 305–328.

Schmidt, F.L., & Hunter, J.E. (1980). The future of criterion-related validity. *Personnel Psychology, 33,* 41–60.

Section 60-3, Uniform Guidelines on Employee Selection Procedures, 43 Fed. Reg. 38295 (August 25, 1978).

Sussmann, M. (1986). The validity of validity: An analysis of validation study designs. *Journal of Applied Psychology, 71,* 461–468.

Module 9

Construct Validity

In the introduction to Module 7, we noted that the contemporary conception of validation includes any evidence examining the accuracy of the inferences and conclusions drawn from test scores. While the evidence provided by the content- and criterion-related methods discussed in the earlier modules is relatively narrow in scope, construct validation might be considered a more comprehensive umbrella approach that subsumes all validation approaches. The construct approach first and foremost recognizes that psychological constructs are abstract theoretical conceptions. Unlike concrete constructs such as distance or weight, psychological constructs such as empathy, intelligence, and greed are not directly measureable. Rather, we observe and measure behaviors to provide evidence of these latent constructs. However, even experts can differ on their definition of a construct. Therefore, test developers must be sure to carefully define their construct as a necessary first step in the test development process (see Module 4: "Test Preparation and Specification").

Part of defining a construct is identifying other constructs that would be theoretically related to the construct and that would be theoretically distinct. In other words, we specify a theory regarding our construct. This theory defines our construct, and it specifies our expectations regarding the relationships between our construct and other constructs, between our construct and other measures (i.e., tests), and between our measure of the construct and other measures. Cronbach and Meehl (1955) referred to this as a *nomological network*. The explication of this theory allows for both empirical investigation and rational discussion of the theory's inferences. Such undertakings are the work of construct validation.

As an example, let's imagine that we have recently developed a measure of the construct of affective empathy. In developing our paper and pencil measure, we appropriately began with an explicit definition: Affective empathy refers to the ability to express appropriate emotional responses to match the emotional experience of another individual. By specifying a nomological network, we would make inferences about the expected relationships between our construct and others, between the construct and our measure, and between our measure and measures of other constructs. We might begin by trying to identify other constructs that should be theoretically related to the construct of affective empathy. For example, affective empathy should be theoretically related to the personality trait agreeableness. Likewise, we might want to consider constructs that are unrelated to affective empathy. Affective empathy might be argued to be unrelated to openness to experience. In order to examine whether these expected relationships are found with our measure, we could correlate scores on our newly developed measure of affective empathy with scores on the NEO Personality Inventory (NEO-PI) measure of agreeableness, as well as scores on the NEO-PI measure of openness to experience. If scores on our affective empathy measure correlated highly with scores on the agreeableness measure, we'd have garnered **convergent validity** evidence. If, as expected, scores on our affective empathy measure showed little relationship to scores on the measure of openness to experience, we'd have garnered evidence of **discriminant validity**. Obviously, no single study will ever provide irrefutable validation evidence. Rather, each study might provide evidence about the accuracy of one (or a very limited number) of the inferences in the nomological network.

Multitrait-Multimethod Matrices

One concern with assessing the convergent validity between measures of constructs is that researchers frequently use similar methods to assess both variables. Common method variance (CMV) refers to a problem in which correlations between constructs are artificially inflated because the data were obtained using the same method of data collection for each variable. Thus, CMV results in correlations between measures due not to some underlying relationship between constructs (i.e., traits), but rather to the use of the same method of measurement in each of our tests. In psychology, our concern is often with the overuse of self-report data collection procedures. For example, a personality researcher may employ use of Likert-type rating scales to assess a number of self-report variables in a study. Because the same method of measurement (e.g., Likert-type self-report rating scales) is used to assess each of these variables, observed correlations between variables may be inflated due to the tendency of research participants to respond similarly across items assessed in this manner. CMV, therefore, would be a potential concern when examining convergent and discriminant validity because correlations between measures may be inflated by the use of the same measurement method. Thus, CMV may lead a researcher to erroneously conclude that he or she has support for convergent validity, or a lack of discriminant validity.

In proposing the concept of a **multitrait-multimethod (MTMM) matrix**, Campbell and Fiske (1959) introduced a method for examining the expected patterns of relationships between measures while also examining the possible influence of CMV. While today confirmatory factor analysis (CFA) is more commonly used to detect the influence of CMV, the MTMM approach is very useful for developing a conceptual understanding of the identification of CMV. Using an MTMM matrix, we can systematically assess the relationships between two or more constructs (i.e., traits), each of which is measured using two or more methods. Data are collected from a single sample of individuals. The MTMM matrix is the resulting correlation matrix between all pairs of measures.

Evidence of convergent validity for a measure of interest is provided in an MTMM matrix when our measure of a trait of interest correlates highly with traits that are theoretically similar to it (regardless of the methods used to assess these other traits). Evidence of discriminant validity occurs when our measure of a trait of interest has a low correlation with traits that are theoretically dissimilar from it (again, regardless of the methods used to assess these other traits).

An MTMM matrix is capable of examining the degree to which CMV influences the observed correlations between variables. To build an MTMM matrix, multiple methods (e.g., self-reports, peer ratings, observations) of assessment must be used to assess each included trait. To produce evidence of construct validity in this way, the pattern of correlations within an MTMM matrix must provide evidence that our measure of a trait of interest correlates higher with theoretically similar constructs that are measured by different methods than our measure of interest correlates with measures of theoretically dissimilar constructs, whether measured using the same method of measurement or not. When variables that are theoretically distinct but measured using the same method are found to correlate highly, we would suspect the influence of CMV.

Let us consider a brief, concrete (albeit fabricated) illustration, based on the earlier example. Let us assume that we administered several scales and obtained the following correlations:

Table 9.1   Potential Correlation Coefficients for NEO PI Extraversion and Conscientiousness Scales, as well as Locus of Control Scale

	NEO PI Agreeableness (self-report)	NEO PI Agreeableness (peer report)	NEO PI Openness to Experience (self-report)	NEO PI Openness to Experience (peer report)
Affective Empathy (self-report)	.62	.51	.35	.18

Here, scores on the newly created affective empathy measure and NEO PI Agreeableness scales represent theoretically similar constructs. Theory would indicate that scores on these measures should be positively, substantially correlated. The NEO PI Openness to Experience subscale is theoretically dissimilar from our conception of affective empathy. Our expectation, therefore, would be that scores on these measures would be unrelated (i.e., have near zero correlations).

The data in Table 9.1 were collected using two different methods. Affective empathy, agreeableness, and openness experience were all measured using self-report. Additionally, both agreeableness and openness to experience were measured a second time by peer report. The researcher asked peers to complete the NEO PI Agreeableness and Openness to Experience subscales as they saw the target individual (the person completing the self-report scales).

Inspection of these scores suggests evidence of convergent validity. Affective empathy scores do, in fact, substantially correlate with scores on the NEO PI Agreeableness subscales, whether measured by self-report or by peers. There is also evidence of discriminant validity, in that scores on the scale assessing affective empathy correlate less highly with either of the methods used to assess openness to experience. Note that the correlation between scores on affective empathy and the self-report measure of openness to experience are moderate, however. This unexpected correlation between variables may be attributable to CMV. Indeed, since the correlation of affective empathy and openness to experience is quite a bit larger when both variables are assessed using the same measurement method (i.e., self-report), the most likely explanation is CMV. For a fuller explanation and some practice with a MTMM, see the website exercises associated with this module.

Although visual inspection of an MTMM matrix provides some evidence of the construct validity of a measure, researchers have found that intuitive interpretations of these matrices can yield erroneous conclusions (Cole, 1987). Today, CFA is the preferred method for examining the convergent and discriminant validity of MTMM matrices (e.g., Schmitt & Stults, 1986; Widaman, 1985). CFA is discussed in Module 19.

Additional Aspects of Construct Validation

In their classic article, Cronbach and Meehl (1955) recognized that construct validation was much more than the examination of convergent and discriminant validity evidence. They also proposed various studies to examine evidence regarding the **construct validity** of test scores, including the following:

> *Studies of group differences:* If two groups are expected to differ on a construct, do they indeed differ as expected? Storholm, Fisher, Napper, Reynolds, and Halkitis (2011) provided construct validation evidence in this way for their self-report Compulsive Sexual Behavior Inventory (CSBI). In their sample of nearly 500 individuals, participants who scored higher on the CSBI, indicating greater involvement in compulsive sexual behavior, were more likely to have been diagnosed with gonorrhea or syphilis.
>
> *Studies of internal structure:* If a test is put forth as measuring a particular construct, then the items on the test should generally be interrelated. Thus, analysis of the internal consistency of items, such as coefficient alpha, can provide evidence of construct validation.

Studies of the stability of test scores: We would expect measures of enduring traits to remain stable over time, whereas measures of other constructs are expected to change over time, such as following an intervention or experimental treatment. Construct validation evidence can be garnered based on whether test scores reflect the expected stability (or lack thereof) over time. Hahn, Gottschling, and Spinath (2012), for example, provided validity evidence for a 15-item measure of the Big Five personality dimensions by demonstrating the temporary stability of scores over an 18-month period.

Studies of process: Unfortunately, differences in test scores are sometimes determined by more than just the construct the researcher intended to assess. A test intended to assess one's mathematical ability may unintentionally assess one's verbal ability, for example, if many of the items involve word problems. Examination of the process by which a test taker derives a response may thus provide important evidence challenging the construct validity of a test. Zappe (2010) used a think-aloud procedure to examine the equivalence of multiple forms of a test assessing legal case reading and reasoning. Zappe concluded that the think-aloud procedure, by which participants verbalize their interpretation of what the items are assessing, was a wise investment for ensuring the equivalency between test forms.

A Contemporary Conception of Construct Validation

It may have occurred to you that Cronbach and Meehl's (1955) assertions regarding construct validation can be applied to all test validation efforts. Indeed, contemporary thinking on validation views any evidence regarding the interpretation of test scores as construct validation (Messick, 1995b). This includes each of the types of research studies suggested by Cronbach and Meehl, as well as the validation efforts we previously referred to as content validation and criterion-related validation. After all, each of these validation strategies is intended to do the same thing: provide "a compelling argument that the available evidence justifies the test interpretation and use" (Messick, 1995b, p. 744).

In the development of such an argument, we should carefully consider exactly what threats exist to construct validity (Messick, 1995b). The first threat, *construct underrepresentation*, refers to measurement that fails to capture the full dimensionality of the intended construct. Thus, construct underrepresentation occurs when important elements of the construct are not measured by the test. The second major threat to construct validity is *construct-irrelevant variance*. This refers to the measurement of reliable variance that is not part of the construct of interest. That is, something is measured by the test that is not part of the intended construct. Construct-irrelevant variance can include the measurement of other constructs, or the assessment of method variance. Unfortunately, both construct underrepresentation and construct-irrelevant variance may be committed simultaneously whenever measuring a construct. Thus, as Messick pointed out, validation is concerned with examining the extent to which our measurement both underrepresents the intended construct *and* assesses construct-irrelevant variance.

If all validation efforts can be viewed as providing construct validation evidence, then we have developed a *unified* vision of test validation. As Messick (1995b) cautioned, however, there are many important, and often entangled, issues related to construct validation. To increase awareness of these many issues, Messick distinguished six important aspects of construct validity. Each of these aspects is briefly presented below.

> *Content:* The content aspect of construct validity specifies the boundaries of the construct domain to be assessed. It is concerned with both the relevance and the representativeness of the measure. In this way, the content aspect is reminiscent of the issues presented in Module 7 on content validation.

> *Substantive:* The substantive aspect of construct validity expands on the concerns of the content aspect by suggesting the need to include "empirical evidence of response consistencies or performance regularities reflective of domain processes" (Messick, 1995b, p. 745). In the assessment of the construct, assessment tasks should be included that are relevant to the construct domain, and the processes required to respond to these assessment tasks should be empirically examined.

> *Structural:* The structural aspect reminds us of the importance of ensuring that the construct domain determines the rational development of construct-relevant scoring criteria and scoring rubrics. This aspect of construct validity emphasizes the importance of score comparability across different tasks and different settings.

> *Generalizability:* The generalizability aspect of construct validity asserts that the meaning of the test scores should not be limited merely to the sample of tasks that constitute the test, but rather should be generalizable to the construct domain intended to be assessed. Evidence regarding the generalizability of test scores would help determine the boundaries of the meaning of the test scores.

> *External:* The external aspect of construct validity refers to the empirical relationships between the test scores and scores on other measures. The external aspect examines whether the empirical relationships between test scores and other measures is consistent with our expectations. This aspect includes the elements of convergent and discriminant validity, as well as criterion-related validity.

> *Consequential:* The consequential aspect of construct validity is perhaps the most unique contribution of Messick's aspects of construct validity. Messick encourages the examination of evidence regarding the consequences of score interpretation. What are the intended as well as unintended societal impacts and consequences of testing? Messick recommended that such examination be conducted not only in the short term but also over

longer periods of time. The primary concern is to ensure that any negative consequences of test usage are unrelated to sources of test invalidity.

Concluding Comments

The concept of validation has evolved substantially over time. Landy's (1986) seminal article titled "Stamp Collecting versus Science: Validation as Hypothesis Testing" pointed out that in the past, a certain "type" of validity was all too often viewed as appropriate or inappropriate for a particular situation. Today, we recognize that validation concerns any and all evidence regarding the meaningfulness of test scores. Rather than examining various "types" of validity, we now recognize that the interpretation and use of test scores requires an ongoing process of validation. Many issues related to the meaning of test scores have been routinely ignored by researchers and test developers. The contemporary conceptualization of construct validity promotes awareness of many of these long-neglected issues.

Best Practices

1. Psychological and educational measures assess latent constructs. Examination of validity, therefore, requires a clear specification of the expected relationships between the construct of interest and other constructs.
2. Relationships between variables measured using the same measurement method (e.g., self-reports assessed at a single period in time completed by the same individual using the same response scale across measures) can be inflated or deflated due to the influence of CMV. Avoidance of research designs that are susceptible to CMV is recommended.
3. Recognize that no single study can ever prove the validity of test scores. Validation is an ongoing process.

Practical Questions

1. The unified view of test validation regards all aspects of validation as reaching for the same goal. What is the overall goal of test validation?
2. Explain why a thorough understanding of the construct measured is essential to the validation process.
3. What did Cronbach and Meehl (1955) mean by the term "nomological network"?
4. Can reliability estimates be used to provide evidence of the construct validity of test scores? Explain.
5. Explain how a researcher could conduct a "study of process" to provide evidence of the construct validity of test scores.

6. Identify two established measures that could be used (other than those discussed previously) to examine the convergent validity of the affective empathy scale discussed above. Identify two established measures that could be used to examine the discriminant validity of the affective empathy measure.

7. Why is CMV a concern in construct validation studies that involve correlation matrices?

8. Correlations between what elements of an MTMM matrix would provide the best assessment of CMV?

9. How does use of an MTMM matrix provide evidence of the construct validity of test scores?

10. Messick (1995b) identified six aspects of construct validation. Choose any three of these aspects to discuss how Messick's conceptualization has extended your awareness of the meaning of construct validation.

Case Studies

CASE STUDY 9.1: LOCATING A MEASURE OF EMOTIONAL INTELLIGENCE

Ever since learning about the concept in her psychology class, Khatera had known that she would complete her thesis on the construct of emotional intelligence. Since her initial introduction to the term, she learned that emotional intelligence represented a complex construct consisting of multiple dimensions, including self-awareness, empathy, and an ability to manage emotions. Khatera was proud that, despite the complexity of the construct, she was among the first students in her entire graduate class to clearly specify her research hypotheses. Further, Khatera secretly reveled in her advisor's praise for developing such a great research idea and for doing it so quickly.

There was just one problem. Because the construct of emotional intelligence was relatively new, few measures had been developed to assess the construct. Further, those that were commercially available were unaffordable, at least on a graduate student's salary. The vast majority of research on the topic, however, seemed to use one of these commercially available measures of emotional intelligence. Khatera had spent a considerable amount of time investigating ways to measure emotional intelligence at little or no cost to her, and she was beginning to fear that she'd soon face a difficult decision: either pay a considerable amount of money for commercially available measures of emotional intelligence or abandon her thesis idea altogether and start from scratch.

Just yesterday, however, she'd gotten a lucky break. In reviewing research articles, she stumbled across one article that used a measure of emotional intelligence she hadn't heard of before. Much to her glee, Khatera discovered that the items of the scale were actually printed in the article itself. Khatera sent an e-mail to the author of the article and was ecstatic to receive an immediate response from the author giving her permission to use the scale.

Unfortunately, Khatera's thesis advisor, Dr. Jennifer Bachelor, seemed far less enthusiastic about the newly discovered scale of emotional intelligence. Indeed, Dr. Bachelor insisted that Khatera produce some evidence of the psychometric properties of the scale before using it in her thesis research. Determined not to delay progress on her thesis any longer, Khatera set out to find that evidence. If she closed her eyes, she could almost see her name emblazoned on the spine of her bound thesis.

Questions to Ponder

1. What role should cost play in determining an appropriate measure for research?
2. Why would Dr. Bachelor be skeptical of the scale of emotional intelligence that Khatera found?
3. What information in the article should Khatera search for to help address some of her advisor's concerns?
4. What other steps could Khatera take to gather information regarding the validity of the newly found scale of emotional intelligence?
5. What evidence of validity for a measure is most frequently provided by (a) publishers of commercially available tests and (b) authors of research scales?
6. What validity evidence would you consider sufficient to use in an important research study such as a graduate thesis?

CASE STUDY 9.2: EXPLAINING THE CONCEPT OF VALIDITY

DiAnn wasn't too surprised to see Edgar arrive shortly after her office hours began. The material recently presented by the instructor in the psychological testing course for which she served as the graduate teaching assistant was challenging for many of the students in the class. "How can I help you, Edgar?" she inquired.

Edgar, his usual affable persona replaced by a serious tone, replied, "I can't get this topic of validity. I knew I'd better come in and see you after I threw the textbook down in frustration."

"Wow, I'm glad you did. What seems to be the trouble?" DiAnn asked.

"Well, in class I thought I understood the definition of validity. *Validity refers to whether the test measures what it purports to measure.* Fine. But after class, the more I read the textbook's explanation of validity, the more I got confused."

Interrupting, DiAnn asked, "How so?"

Edgar was ready. "I was reading about content validity, criterion-related validity, and construct validity. Are these all related? Or are they different? Initially, as I was reading, there seemed to be three distinct types of validity. But then it seemed that I couldn't tell the difference among the three."

DiAnn smiled. "Perhaps you are smarter than you give yourself credit for Edgar. In many ways, you are correct." As DiAnn explained what she meant by her rather cryptic initial response, Edgar began to feel more and more comfortable with the material.

Questions to Ponder

1. In what ways does "content validity" provide evidence of the meaningfulness of test scores?
2. In what ways does "criterion-related validity" provide evidence of the meaningfulness of test scores?
3. Is Edgar's concern over not being able to distinguish among the various validation strategies warranted? Explain.
4. Explain why the trinitarian view of validity (content, criterion-related, construct) indicates an insufficient view of validation.
5. Explain how Messick's (1995b) aspects of construct validation incorporate each of the following "outdated" terms under the umbrella of construct validity:

   a. Content validity
   b. Criterion-related validity
   c. Convergent and discriminant validity

Exercises

EXERCISE 9.1: IDENTIFYING MEASURES FOR CONSTRUCT VALIDATION

OBJECTIVE: To gain experience in identifying relevant measures for examining convergent and discriminant validity.

PROLOGUE: Imagine that you have recently developed the following construct measures. For each of these newly developed instruments, identify two actual measures that could be used to examine the new instrument's convergent validity and two actual measures that could be used to examine the new instrument's discriminant validity. When possible, propose measures that use different methods of measurement (e.g., self-report for one proposed measure and observer ratings for the other measure).

1. A newly developed paper-and-pencil intelligence test intended to assess academic giftedness among sixth graders
2. An interview evaluating an adult's personal integrity
3. A self-report form assessing one's interpersonal assertiveness
4. A peer rating form measuring an individual's general optimism
5. A supervisor's rating form of an employee's career achievement motivation

EXERCISE 9.2: EXAMINING ELEMENTS OF A NOMOLOGICAL NETWORK

OBJECTIVE: To determine whether empirical evidence provides support for expected relationships between measures.

An industrial/organizational psychologist developed a personality-based measure to assess the integrity of potential job applicants. The measure she developed was intended to mask the purpose of the test from test takers. To examine the validity of the personality-based integrity measure, the psychologist administered the measure to a group of $N = 255$ individuals. She also administered two additional measures to this same group of individuals: an overt measure of integrity, in which individuals were queried about their actual involvement in theft and dishonest behaviors, and a measure of general cognitive ability. The data are presented in the data file "Nomonet.sav" (see Appendix B).

1. What is the expected pattern of relationships among these three measures? Explain.
2. Is there evidence of convergent validity for the personality-based integrity measure?
3. Is there evidence of discriminant validity for the personality-based integrity measure?
4. Based on the results obtained, can the psychologist claim that she has established the construct validity of the measure? Explain.

Further Readings

Cronbach, L.J., & Meehl, P.E. (1955). Construct validity in psychological tests. *Psychological Bulletin, 52,* 281–302.

Eid, M. (2000). A multitrait-multimethod model with minimal assumptions. *Psychometrika, 65,* 241–261.

Kehoe, J.F., & Murphy, K.R. (2010). Current concepts of validity, validation, and generalizability. In. J.L. Farr & N.T. Tippins (Eds.), *Handbook of employee selection* (pp. 99–123). New York: Routledge/Taylor & Francis Group.

Landy, F.J. (1986). Stamp collecting versus science: Validation as hypothesis testing. *American Psychologist, 41,* 1183–1192.

Messick, S. (1995a). Standards of validity and the validity of standards in performance assessment. *Educational Measurement: Issues and Practice, 14,* 5–8.

Module 10

Validity Generalization and Psychometric Meta-Analysis

S chmidt and Hunter (2001) discussed the myth of the "perfect study." That is, if we could somehow get a large enough sample with perfectly reliable and valid measures, then we could definitively answer the key and nagging questions plaguing the social and behavioral sciences. Although some large-scale studies have been conducted with thousands of participants, most individual empirical studies, particularly in psychology, tend to average in the hundreds (or fewer) of participants, not thousands. As a result, sampling error is a major source of error in estimating population relationships and parameters within any given empirical investigation. In addition, a variety of factors (i.e., methodological artifacts), such as unreliable measures, restriction of range, and artificial dichotomization of continuous variables, are an undeniable part of any individual empirical investigation. In the end, such artifacts cloud our observed relationships and ultimately our ability to estimate population relationships based on sample data. Therefore, it is simply unrealistic to believe that any single study is going to be able to definitively explain the complex relationships found among key variables in the social and behavioral sciences. So, what is a budding social and behavioral scientist to do?

Well, if we could somehow cull individual empirical studies examining similar phenomenon conducted by different researchers, we could drastically reduce the effects of sampling error. In addition, if we could somehow correct for the artifacts noted previously (e.g., unreliability, restriction of range), we could also reduce the effects of these sources of error and as a result would have much better estimates of our population parameters. Up until the late 1970s, however, most reviews of the extant empirical research on a given topic were narrative in fashion. The inevitable conclusion of almost every narrative review seemed to be that the empirical research was contradictory and inconclusive and as a result more research was needed. As granting agencies and policymakers became more frustrated with consistently predictable inconclusive findings, researchers in the social and behavioral sciences began to seek ways to quantify the cumulative findings in a given research area. In the mid- to late 1970s, several researchers (e.g., Glass, 1976; Schmidt & Hunter, 1977) proposed analytic procedures that would allow researchers interested in summarizing a body of empirical literature to do so in a quantitative fashion. Thus, the concept of **meta-analysis** (the analysis of analyses) was born— or at least "discovered" by social and behavioral scientists.

Validity Generalization

Early work on quantitatively summarizing previous empirical studies by Schmidt and Hunter (1977) focused specifically on criterion-related validity coefficients (as discussed in Module 8), examining how cognitive ability tests, for example, could predict job or training performance for a variety of jobs across organizations. That is, they were interested in generalizing empirical validity estimates from one situation to another. The conventional wisdom up to that point in time was that all validity coefficients were situation specific (i.e., the situational specificity hypothesis), meaning that validity coefficients were expected to differ from one situation or organization to another due to differences in jobs and/or the context of the job. However, Schmidt and Hunter demonstrated that most of the differences that were observed in empirical criterion-related validity estimates from one job or organization to another were simply the result of sampling error and other artifacts such as unreliable measures and restriction of range. Obtaining a weighted (based on sample size) average validity coefficient and correcting the weighted estimate for sampling error was recommended by Schmidt and Hunter as a more precise way of estimating validity coefficients. Correcting for only sampling error associated with studies is known as performing a "bare bones" **validity generalization** (VG) study. Such studies provide stronger and more realistic estimates of the average observed validity coefficients across studies than is possible in any single study.

In addition, if other corrections beyond sampling error are also made (e.g., for unreliability or restriction of range), then this is referred to as psychometric VG. Performing these additional corrections for psychometric shortcomings in the studies used to compute the VG estimates allows researchers to better estimate the latent relationships among constructs. Thus, performing these additional (psychometric) corrections allows researchers to move beyond simply documenting observed relationships to formulating and testing relationships among latent constructs. If, subsequent to making the additional corrections, substantial variability in the observed validity coefficients was still unaccounted for, a search for potential moderators would be initiated. What constitutes "substantial variability" remaining? Schmidt and Hunter used the 75% rule. That is, if sampling error and various other **statistical artifacts** account for less than 75% of the variability in observed validity coefficients, nonartifact (true) variability likely exists and so moderator analyses should be performed. Such moderators might include the type of organization or job, when the study was conducted, the type of criterion used in the validation study, and so forth.

From VG to Psychometric Meta-Analysis

Schmidt and Hunter (1977) soon realized, however, that their procedures could be applied not just to validity coefficients but also to any estimate of association (or effect size) between key variables. Hence, they (Hunter, Schmidt, & Jackson, 1982) independently proposed a much broader set of procedures similar to the meta-analytic strategies of Glass, McGaw, and Smith (1981). The first of two major goals of most meta-analyses is to obtain the most accurate and best possible point estimate of the population effect size. For example, if you wanted to know the relationship between the Premarital Compatibility Index (PCI) (X) and how long couples stay married (Y), you would need to obtain all available correlation coefficients between these two variables from previous empirical studies. You would then compute a weighted-average observed correlation (validity coefficient) across all studies obtained. This weighted-average statistic would be your point estimate of the population correlation (ρ_{xy}) between the compatibility index and the length of marriage. Other statistical indexes (e.g., t, Z, and d) can also be used within the same meta-analytic study, and formulas are available to convert such estimates from one statistic to another so that all the studies will be on the same metric. For example:

$$\text{For } t_{df} : r = \sqrt{\frac{t^2}{t^2 + df}} \text{ or for } Z : r = \sqrt{\frac{z^2}{N}} \text{ or for } \chi^2 : r = \sqrt{\frac{\chi^2}{N}}$$

where t is the obtained Student t statistic, df represents the degrees of freedom associated with that t statistic, z is the obtained Z statistic, N is the sample size, and χ^2 is the obtained chi-square statistic. Formulas are also available for the standardized difference (d) statistic and the F statistic. Scores in various formats can also be converted to a common standardized difference (d) statistic when one is more interested in group differences as opposed to simple bivariate associations as with the r statistic.

Your next question, hopefully, is, "So how good is this point estimate?" Hence, the second key goal of most meta-analytic procedures is to determine the variability around the estimated effect size, or what is commonly called a confidence interval (CI). The CI tells us how much confidence we have in the population parameter we estimated initially. Sometimes, however, we are more interested not in the population parameter but rather in the value we would obtain if we were to conduct the study again. To answer this question, we would instead calculate a credibility interval (CRI). To obtain either the CI or the CRI, we would need to know the standard error of the average correlation coefficient. This statistic will be presented later.

Conducting a Meta-Analysis

Schmitt and Klimoski (1991) presented a flowchart of seven steps to be carried out in conducting a meta-analysis (see Table 10.1). Before we even begin any meta-analytic work, however, we must clearly and precisely identify what it is we hope to accomplish by conducting a meta-analysis. Continuing with our earlier example, it may be to determine how useful the PCI is in predicting marriage longevity. Once this is clear, the first step is to compile a list of relevant published and unpublished studies using a variety of sources and computerized search options. Next, we must then read all of the papers obtained and formulate hypotheses about potential **moderator variables**. For example, maybe the age of the couple, whether it is their first marriage, or their religious beliefs could all serve as potential moderators. Third, we need to develop a coding scheme and rules of inclusion and exclusion of studies. Should, for example, only studies that used version 1 of the PCI be included? Fourth, we need to train those who will be doing the coding, and after coding a few studies, we should check for inter-coder consistency. Once we are satisfied that the raters are consistent (and accurate), then step 5 is to code all studies pulling out the key data (e.g., sample size, effect size) to conduct our meta-analysis, as well as essential information regarding potential moderators. In step 6, we actually analyze the data. Finally, in step 7, we draw appropriate conclusions about the effect of interest and potential moderators.

Although, at first glance, the process of conducting a meta-analysis may seem straightforward, Wanous, Sullivan, and Malinak (1989) noted numerous judgment calls that need to be made in the process of conducting a meta-analysis. The judgment calls start at the very beginning when we must first define the domain of research to be studied. They continue through establishing the criteria for deciding which studies to include, how to search for them, and how studies are ultimately selected for inclusion. The judgment calls continue when we must decide which

Table 10.1   Flowchart for Meta-Analysis

Source: Adapted by permission from Schmitt, N., & Klimoski, R. (1991). *Research methods in human resource management.* Cincinnati, OH: Southwest.

data to extract, how to code the data, whether to group similar variables, the actual calculations to perform, and the subsequent search for moderators. How these judgment calls go can dramatically impact what gets studied, how it gets studied, and the interpretation of the resulting analyses. Thus, if nothing else, one needs to be detailed and explicit in reporting any meta-analytic procedures.

A Step-by-Step Meta-Analysis Example[1]

Previous research has indicated that the age at which individuals retire affects their subsequent retirement satisfaction and adjustment (e.g., Kim & Moen, 2001; Shultz, Morton, & Weckerle, 1998). As a result, it would be informative to know what factors seem to be predictive of the age at which individuals retire. Beehr (1986), however, suggested that individuals first have certain preferences regarding retirement, which, in turn, influence their intentions with regard to retirement. It is these intentions that ultimately lead to actual retirement decisions. Thus, to understand the retirement process, one must first understand the prospective preferences and intentions toward retirement that older individuals have, not simply document (in a retrospective fashion) the actual retirement age and its predictors. Therefore, Shultz and Taylor (2001) set out to perform a meta-analysis of the predictors of planned retirement age.

Shultz and Taylor's (2001) first task was to compile a list of relevant studies that had examined the factors that predict planned retirement age (see Table 10.1). Therefore, Shultz and Taylor performed an extensive review of the interdisciplinary research literature on the predictors of planned retirement age using several electronic database search engines, including the AgeLine database, EBSCOhost, ERIC, General Science Abstracts, Humanities Abstracts, JSTOR, PsycINFO, ScienceDirect, Sociological Abstracts, and Wilson Omnifile. In addition, they performed a manual search of relevant journals (*The Gerontologist, International Journal of Aging and Human Development, Journals of Gerontology, Journal of Vocational Behavior, Personnel Psychology, Psychology and Aging,* and *Research on Aging*) from 1980 to 2000 and reviewed the reference sections of review articles and book chapters to locate relevant empirical studies reporting correlation coefficients (i.e., effect size estimates) between a variety of potential predictors and planned retirement age. Studies that did not measure planned retirement age and/or did not report zero-order bivariate correlation coefficients were excluded.

As is unfortunately true of many meta-analytic studies, the vast majority of the empirical studies did not provide individual effect size estimates (e.g., bivariate correlation coefficients or t, F, or χ^2 values that could be converted to correlation coefficients) in the papers themselves. Instead, most papers, particularly the older studies, reported only results of multivariate analyses (e.g., logistic regression coefficients, beta-weights in hierarchical ordinary least squares regressions). In all, 16 different studies (one study had two samples) that provided individual effect size estimates were coded for the variables that are hypothesized to influence planned retirement age. Because of the small number of studies, no specific moderator hypotheses were put forth. Cohen's kappa statistic, which measures inter-rater agreement (see Module 6), was computed to examine the degree to which raters coded the information from the studies in the same way. Somewhat surprisingly, perfect agreement was obtained regarding which variables were measured in each of the coded studies.

Meta-Analytical Procedure and Results

The bivariate correlation coefficients were subjected to the meta-analytic procedures outlined in Hunter and Schmidt (1990) using the MetaWin 16 meta-analysis program. Study correlation coefficients were weighted by sample size, and corrections were made for sampling error and, when data were available, for measurement error (i.e., unreliability in the predictor and/or criterion variables) using the artifact distribution method (Hunter & Schmidt, 1990).

Table 10.2 summarizes the number of studies (k); the pooled sample size (N); the unweighted-average effect size (r_{ave}); the sample weighted-average effect size (r_{wa}); the corrected sample weighted-average effect size (r_{wc}), which has been corrected for unreliability of the predictor and/or criterion variable when the information was available; the percentage of variance attributable to sampling error; and, finally, the 95% CI for the uncorrected sample weighted-average effect size estimate indicating whether the estimated population correlation coefficients are significantly different from zero. Thus, Table 10.2 summarizes the results obtained for the predictors of planned retirement age. Only predictor variables with effect size estimates from at least two different studies with different authors were included (see Exercise 10.2 for an example of how to compute by hand many of the statistics reported in Table 10.2).

As can be seen in Table 10.2, the weighted-average effect size estimates are generally small. In fact, sex had an unweighted-average correlation of zero. Age was clearly the strongest predictor of planned retirement age, with a weighted-average correlation of .29 (considered a moderate effect size). Education (.21), expected retirement adjustment (−.17), and job satisfaction (.13) demonstrated small to medium effect sizes. All others variables estimated were below .10.

Interpretation of Meta-Analysis Results and Limitations

The major goal of the meta-analytic study described here was to summarize the relationships among a number of variables (including demographic, financial, health, psychosocial, and organizational) that have a suggested and/or demonstrated association with planned retirement age. The limited evidence that was summarized supports past research that indicates that age is a strong predictor of anticipated retirement age, and that education level, household income, job satisfaction, and expected retirement adjustment are also predictive, albeit less so than age, of planned age of retirement.

These results serve as a starting point for both larger-scale meta-analytic investigations on the topic and future theoretical model-testing studies. As for future, large-scale meta-analyses, it may be difficult to obtain correlation coefficients from studies carried out decades ago and to track down unpublished conference

Table 10.2   Meta-Analysis of the Correlates of Planned Retirement Age (from Shultz & Taylor, 2001)

| Factor | k | N | Average Correlations | | | % Total Variance | 95% CI | |
			r_{ave}	r_{wa}	r_{wc}		Lower Bound	Upper Bound
Demographics								
Age	10	4039	.3285	.2927	.3103	13.59	.2645	.3210
Education	6	3154	.1417	.2087	.2087	57.50	.1753	.2421
Sex	5	1391	.0000	−.0068	−.0068	28.74	−.0595	.0458
Financial								
Pay satisfaction	4	821	−.0050	.0017	.0020	100+	−.0669	.0703
Household income	4	1039	−.1425	−.0984	−.0984	9.80	−.1587	−.0381
Health								
Self-rated health	5	1244	.0100	−.0040	−.0054	23.80	−.0597	.0517
Health satisfaction	4	690	.0100	.0302	.0337	64.52	−.0446	.1049
Psychosocial								
Job satisfaction	9	5307	.1322	.1346	.1563	81.84	.1081	.1610
Expected ret. adj.	2	475	−.1350	−.1669	−.1968	32.73	−.2545	−.0793

Note: k = the number of studies, N = the pooled sample size, r_{ave} = the average correlation coefficient without correction or weighting, r_{wa} = the uncorrected sample weighted-average correlation coefficient, r_{wc} = the sample weighted-average correlation coefficient corrected for unreliability of measurement, and % Total Variance = the percentage of total variance in the effect sizes that is accounted for by sampling error only. CIs were computed from weighted-average correlation coefficients (uncorrected).

papers and technical reports on the topic. Continued diligence in obtaining such information may prove fruitful in the end; not only will more reliable and stable estimates of population values of central tendency and dispersion be obtained, but if the estimates do, in fact, demonstrate heterogeneity, then moderators can also be assessed. In terms of future model-testing studies, while most effect sizes were considered small in the Shultz and Taylor (2001) study, they may still prove useful in future theory testing as they provide the best quantitative summary of past studies. Also, as more variables are assessed, the total variance accounted for should increase as well.

Several major limitations with regard to the Shultz and Taylor (2001) study should be mentioned. First, it was disappointing how few empirical studies report the effect size estimates (e.g., bivariate correlation coefficients) needed to complete a meta-analysis in this area. Dozens of published studies were conducted up to that time looking at the predictors of planned retirement age, retirement intentions, and the actual retirement decision. Most, however, reported only multivariate results and not the basic descriptive statistics of individual effect sizes needed for meta-analyses. For example, an earlier qualitative review of the area by Doering, Rhodes, and Schuster (1983) turned up 34 studies that examined a variety of predictors of the retirement decision-making process. However, only 3 of the 34 studies reviewed by Doering et al. reported bivariate correlation coefficients (or similar effect size estimates), with most reporting results of multivariate analysis of variance, logistic regression, or discriminant function analyses. Consequently, the results of Shultz and Taylor's (2001) attempted meta-analysis are limited in their generalizability to a broad range of studies.

Second, because of the small number of studies, moderator analyses were not attempted. As indicated in Table 10.2, however, only two of the nine estimated relationships exceeded Hunter and Schmidt's (1990) 75% criterion. That is, sampling error accounted for more than 75% of the variance in observed effect size estimates in fewer than one quarter of the relationships examined. Therefore, if these relationships hold for large samples of effect sizes, moderator analyses should be conducted in future meta-analytic studies in order to determine what factors, beyond sampling error and other psychometric artifacts, account for the observed differences in empirical effect size estimates across studies.

Concluding Comments

No single study will ever be able to definitively answer the meaningful and complex questions typically addressed in social and behavioral science research. However, meta-analytic procedures allow us to cull data from numerous studies on a given topic, thus drastically reducing sampling error. In addition, most meta-analytic procedures also allow for correction of a variety of study artifacts, thus further helping to clarify the relationships we study in the social and behavioral sciences. However, as noted in the example study provided, the process of conducting a meta-analysis can be a daunting one, with many judgment calls along the way, sometimes with little reward.

Best Practices

1. When conducting psychometric meta-analysis, realize that garbage in will equal garbage out (i.e., meta-analysis will not turn a series of poor studies into a definitive answer).
2. Be sure to clearly define the population to which you are interested in generalizing your results. This is just one of many judgment calls that will need to be made during the meta-analysis process.

3. Realize that psychometric meta-analysis is simply another tool to add to your methodological toolbox. It will not be a panacea for a series of ill-conceived and ill-conducted studies.
4. Document, in detail, all steps completed during your meta-analysis study.

Practical Questions

1. Assume you wanted to carry out a meta-analysis to determine how effective typing software is in improving typing speed and accuracy. What is the best way to get started in conducting such a meta-analysis?
2. Most papers and books on meta-analysis say that one should include both published and unpublished studies on a given topic. How does one go about getting unpublished studies?
3. How do you decide which studies to include or exclude? What information to code?
4. Can a single person conduct a meta-analysis, or does it take a team of researchers? Why?
5. There are several options with regard to which analytical approach to use. How do you decide which one to use?
6. How do you decide which moderators to examine?

Case Studies

CASE STUDY 10.1: THE REALITIES OF CONDUCTING A META-ANALYSIS

Raul, a second-year master's student, was very excited that his thesis committee had just approved his proposal to conduct a meta-analysis looking at what predicts employees' satisfaction with their supervisor. His committee wisely suggested that he focus on only three key predictors of supervisor satisfaction: the managerial style of the supervisor, the perceived competence of the supervisor, and the degree of warmth exhibited by the supervisor. Raul was excited in that he was the first master's student in his program ever approved to conduct a meta-analysis for his thesis. In addition, he was glad he didn't have to go beg other students to fill out a lengthy questionnaire to collect his data or have to go out to organizations to collect data. Raul figured that all he had to do was "go find" the data that were already out there and (re)analyze them.

In Raul's original search of the literature for his thesis proposal using PsychLit, he obtained almost a thousand "hits" on the words "supervisor satisfaction," so he figured it would be just a matter of narrowing it down a little. However, as Raul began to examine the abstracts of these papers, he realized that a large number of them were not empirical studies. In fact, most were short articles in popular magazines on how to increase one's satisfaction with one's supervisor. So, after days, and then weeks, of sifting through abstracts, he was finally able to narrow down his list to 150 or so articles in the past 40 years that were empirical investigations of supervisor satisfaction.

Upon closer inspection, however, he realized that fewer than half the studies investigated managerial style, perceived competence, and warmth in relation to employees' current supervisor satisfaction. Well, that didn't seem so bad. In fact, he was relieved he had a more manageable number of articles to work with. As he delved further into the studies, however, it seemed that every study was using a different measure of supervisor satisfaction. The same seemed to be true for managerial style and the perceived competence measures. About the only consistently measured variable seemed to be the perceived warmth of the supervisor. In addition, most of the studies conducted prior to 1980 reported multivariate results (e.g., R^2) but didn't provide actual correlation coefficients—the exact "data" he needed for his study. Frustrated and a bit overwhelmed, Raul decided it was time to go see his thesis advisor for some help.

Questions to Ponder

1. What other databases or outlets should Raul have used to obtain a more complete set of studies on supervisor satisfaction?
2. If you were Raul, what criteria would you use to decide which studies to include and which to exclude?
3. How should Raul go about deciding which factors in the studies to code to investigate possible moderators later on?
4. Is it possible for Raul to use the studies that don't provide correlations? What are his options?
5. How many studies do you think Raul will ultimately need in order to satisfy his thesis committee? In order to obtain "accurate" results?

CASE STUDY 10.2: HOW TO CONDUCT A META-ANALYSIS

Ming-Yu, a new PhD student, was just given her first assignment as a graduate research assistant for Professor Riggs. Professor Riggs was a quantitative psychologist who studied the effects of sport fishing on a variety of psychological outcomes. Ming-Yu was to take a stack of 60 studies obtained by the previous research assistant for a meta-analytic study examining the varying effects of lake (e.g., bass), stream (e.g., trout), and deep-sea (e.g., marlin) fishing on stress levels of the participants. She was asked to "code" each study, and when she was done with that, she was to enter the relevant data and "analyze them."

Ming-Yu had never fished in her life, so she did not have a clue as to what she should be coding in the studies. Undaunted, however, she read each study and eventually was able to come up with what she thought was a reasonable coding scheme. She then coded each study and extracted the relevant data to be entered into the meta-analysis program. She coded for year of study, size of sample, type of journal, type of design, and reported effect size. She also pulled out the relevant information to examine possible moderators. For example, she looked at where the fishing took place (river vs. lake/ocean) and the type of rod used (cheap vs. expensive). Thus, her next assignment was to enter the data and begin the preliminary analyses. However, Professor Riggs, being a quantitative psychologist, had six different meta-analysis programs. She tried to contact Professor Riggs to see which program he wanted her to use, but he was not available, as he was out doing "field work" on his next fishing study. So, it was up to her to select an appropriate software option, enter the data, and obtain initial results.

Ultimately, she chose one of the more popular meta-analysis programs and carried out the initial analysis. The preliminary analysis, however, seemed to indicate that the type of fishing made very little difference in the stress levels of participants. However, Professor Riggs had spent nearly his entire career demonstrating the superior stress-reducing effects of stream fishing over other types of fishing. Ming-Yu was not looking forward to her next meeting with Professor Riggs.

Questions to Ponder

1. If you were Ming-Yu, would you have coded for any other variables?
2. What factors should Ming-Yu have considered in choosing which software package to use to analyze the data?
3. What do you think could have led to Ming-Yu getting results contradictory to the results Professor Riggs had found in most of his individual studies?
4. Should Ming-Yu have "updated" the previous literature search? If so, how?
5. Because Ming-Yu didn't find any difference, does she need to conduct moderator analyses?

❧ ⟨o⟩ ❧

Exercises

EXERCISE 10.1: OUTLINING A META-ANALYTIC STUDY

OBJECTIVE: To practice outlining a meta-analytic study.

Individually or in small groups of three to five, students will select a topic on which to perform a meta-analysis. They will then outline, in detail, the steps to be taken if they were to actually carry out this study. In particular, they need to address the stages of meta-analysis outlined by Schmitt and Klimoski (1991) in Table 10.1. For example:

- Where can we find studies on this topic?
- How do we locate unpublished studies?
- What moderator hypotheses might be appropriate for this topic?
- How should we code studies? Who should code the studies?
- How will we assess inter-coder accuracy?
- What statistical artifacts should be corrected for when running the studies?

EXERCISE 10.2: ALBEMARLE SUPREME COURT CASE

OBJECTIVE: To calculate meta-analytic estimates by hand.

BACKGROUND: In Table 10.3, you will find data from the *Albemarle Paper Company v. Moody* (1975) Supreme Court case. The case involved looking at the use of meta-analysis (more specifically, VG) to "validate" several tests across a series of jobs. Albemarle lost the case, not because it used meta-analysis, but rather because it failed to perform adequate job analyses to show that the jobs were sufficiently similar and required comparable knowledge, skills, and abilities to apply the tests for all jobs investigated (really more of an issue of transportability). In addition, Albemarle's initial validation efforts were criticized because of the use of only older, experienced White male workers (the new job applicants were younger, largely inexperienced, and more ethnically and gender diverse) and the use of deficient job performance measures.

ASSIGNMENT: Table 10.3 displays the data for the Beta, W-A, and W-B tests that the Albemarle Paper Company used for personnel selection purposes for a variety of jobs. An example of how to perform a "bare bones" meta-analysis for the Beta exam is provided. Perform similar analyses for the W-A and W-B exams. Specifically, calculate the weighted average r, the s_r^2, and the σ_e^2, and perform an χ^2 analysis for each exam. Also, determine the percentage of total variance accounted for by sampling error and the 90% credibility and 95% CIs for both scales/exams.

Table 10.3   Data for Exercise 10.2

			Test	
Job Group	N	Beta	W-A	W-B
Caustic Operator	8	.25	1.00	.47
CE Recovery Operator	12	.64	.32	.17
Wood Yard	14	.00	1.00	.72
Technical Services	12	.50	.75	.64
B Paper Mill	16	.00	.50	.34
B Paper Mill	8	−.50	.00	.00
B Paper Mill	21	.43	.81	.60
Wood Yard	6	.76	−.25	1.00
Pulp Mill	8	.50	.80	.76
Power Plant	12	.34	.75	.66
			Beta Test Example	
Job Group	N	r	N*r	N*(r − r̄)²
Caustic Operator	8	.25	2.00	.0098
CE Recovery Operator	12	.64	7.68	1.5123
Wood Yard	14	.00	.00	1.1372
Technical Services	12	.50	6.00	.5547
B Paper Mill	16	.00	.00	1.2996
B Paper Mill	8	−.50	−4.00	4.9298
B Paper Mill	21	.43	9.03	.4415
Wood Yard	6	.76	4.56	1.3538
Pulp Mill	8	.50	4.00	.3698
Power Plant	12	.34	4.08	.0363
Total	117		33.35	11.6447

$$\bar{r} = \frac{\sum Nr}{\sum N} = \frac{33.35}{117} = .2850 \quad K = \text{number of studies(here 10)}$$

$$s_r^2 = \frac{\sum\left[N(r - \bar{r})^2\right]}{\sum N} = \frac{11.6447}{117} = .0995 \qquad \sigma_e^2 = \frac{(1 - \bar{r}^2)^2 k}{\sum N} = \frac{(.8441)(10)}{117} = .0721$$

$$\sigma_\rho = \sqrt{s_r^2 - \sigma_e^2} = \sqrt{.0995 - .0721} = .1655 \quad \chi_9^2 = \frac{Ns_r^2}{(1 - \bar{r}^2)^2} = \frac{(117)(.0995)}{.8441} = 13.8ns$$

$$\text{Percentage of variance accounted for by sampling error} = \frac{\sigma_2^2}{s_r^2} = \frac{.0721}{.0995} = 72.5\%$$

$$95\% \text{ Confidence Interval} = \bar{r} \pm Z_{\alpha/2} * \frac{\sigma_e}{\sqrt{k}} = .2850 \pm 1.96 * \frac{\sqrt{.0721}}{\sqrt{10}} = .119 \le \rho \le .451$$

$$90\% \text{ Credibility Interval} = \bar{r} \pm Z_{\alpha/2} * \sigma_\rho = .2850 \pm 1.645 * .1655 = .0128 \le \bar{r} \le .5572$$

Provide a brief, less than one typed page or so, interpretation and explanation of what all of this means.

Further Readings

Lipsey, M.W., & Wilson, D.B. (2001). *Practical meta-analysis.* Thousand Oaks, CA: Sage.

Murphy, K.R., & Newman, D.A. (2003). The past, present, and future of validity generalization. In K.R. Murphy (Ed.), *Validity generalization: A critical review* (pp. 403–424). New York: Routledge Academic Press.

Rothstein, H.R., McDaniel, M.A., & Borenstein, M. (2002). Meta-analysis: A review of quantitative cumulation methods. In F. Drasgow & N. Schmitt (Eds.), *Measuring and analyzing behavior in organizations: Advances in measurement and data analysis.* San Francisco, CA: Jossey-Bass.

Schmidt, F.L., & Hunter, J.E. (2001). Meta-analysis. In N. Anderson, D.S. Ones, H.K. Sinangil, & C. Viswesvaran (Eds.), *Handbook of industrial, work and organizational psychology* (Vol. 1, pp. 51–70). Thousand Oaks, CA: Sage.

Schmitt, N., & Klimoski, R. (1991). *Research methods in human resource management* (pp. 403–426). Cincinnati, OH: Southwest.

Note

1. This example is based in part (and very loosely) on a meta-analysis conducted by Shultz and Taylor (2001). Please note that several creative liberties have been taken for pedagogical purposes.

Module 11

Test Bias, Unfairness, and Equivalence

As we noted in Module 1, applied psychological testing is as much a political process as it is a psychometric one. Not surprisingly, then, accusations of test bias and unfairness surface on a predictable basis whenever a test is used to make an important decision affecting people's lives. Some laypeople have used the terms *test bias* and *test fairness* interchangeably. However, a series of articles from the professional testing literature of the late 1960s and early 1970s clearly distinguish the two concepts. Test **bias** is a technical psychometric issue that focuses on statistical prediction, whereas test **fairness** is a sociopolitical issue that focuses on test outcomes. The concept of test bias has been operationalized in several ways (including differences in subgroup test means or validity coefficients); however, the consensus definition or current standard is what is known as the Cleary model (AERA/APA/NCME, 1999; Aguinis, Culpepper, & Pierce, 2010). Namely, one determines if a test has differential prediction for one group versus another by means of moderated multiple regression (MMR) analysis. Specifically, we are looking for possible subgroup differences in either regression slopes or Y intercepts. It is up to us, as evaluators of the test, to determine what subgroups are relevant. However, it is most common to examine so-called "protected" subgroups of test takers. These are typically demographically determined subgroups that receive protection by law. Thus, test bias is most commonly examined in subgroups formed on such factors as age, sex, or ethnicity.

Establishing Test Bias

As an example, we may use a test to predict which clinical patients are most likely to commit suicide. We may find that the test is a very good predictor of suicide for young (younger than 18 years old) and old (older than 70 years old) patients, but not a very good predictor for those in between (see Figure 11.1). As a result,

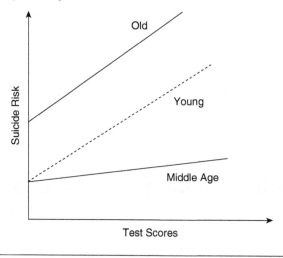

Figure 11.1   Hypothetical Regression Lines for Three Age Groups

the two extreme age groups may have a different slope from the middle age group when we try to predict suicide risk based on the test score. In addition, although the two extreme age groups may have approximately the same slope, they may have very different Y intercepts. For example, younger clients who obtain a test score of zero may have a much lower predicted likelihood of committing suicide (i.e., a lower Y intercept) than elderly clients, yet the rate of increase in the likelihood of committing suicide (i.e., the slope) is approximately equal (see Figure 11.1 for an illustration of these biases).

To demonstrate intercept and slope bias empirically in our preceding example, we would first enter the test score and age group variables into a multiple regression prediction equation to predict suicide risk. If the **regression coefficient** for the age group variable were significant, possible **intercept bias** would be indicated. To test for possible **slope bias**, the interaction between age group and test performance (i.e., their cross product) would be entered in the second step of the regression equation. If the regression coefficient for the interaction term were significant, that would indicate possible slope bias.

There is typically little evidence of test bias in terms of slope bias in most applied settings. When a particular group scores lower on average on the test, they also tend to score lower on average on the criterion, resulting more often in intercept bias rather than slope bias. For example, in Figure 11.1, the young group scored lower on average on the test than the old group; however, the young test takers also have a lower predicted chance of committing suicide. Thus, the real problem would come in if we used a common (i.e., single) regression line for the young group and the old group. If, in fact, a single regression equation were used for both groups, for any given score on the test we would overpredict the risk of suicide in young clients, while underpredicting the risk of suicide in older patients. Thus, we must make sure that subgroup differences are not present before a test is administered.

Sackett, Laczo, and Lippe (2003) revisited the issue of test bias (or what they referred to as differential prediction), focusing on the so-called omitted-variable problem. That is, they wanted to see if omitting a variable from the analysis that was related to the criterion and the grouping variable, but not the other predictor (i.e., the test scores), caused the predictor variable to appear to be biased against certain subgroups when, in fact, it was not. Sackett et al. provided convincing evidence for the need to search for such omitted variables using data from the U.S. Army's Project A. They were able to show that a personality test of conscientiousness appeared to be biased against African Americans when it was the only variable used to predict job performance. However, when the Armed Services Vocational Aptitude Battery, a cognitive test, was also added to the prediction equation, the test was no longer biased. Thus, researchers must be continually aware of potential omitted variables that may be the "real culprits" in terms of test bias.

Test Fairness

The concept of test fairness, unlike test bias, is not a psychometric concept. It is a sociopolitical concept. As a result, there tends to be little consensus in regard to what constitutes test (un)fairness. In some ways, then, test fairness is similar to beauty—it tends to be "in the eye of the beholder." As a result, two individuals can take the same test, at the same time, under identical circumstances, yet one may claim the test is unfair while the other thinks it completely fair. Many accusations of test unfairness really stem from the testing process rather than the test per se. For example, some individuals may be allowed extra time or provided clues or assistance during the exam while other are not afforded such advantages. Thus, an important first step to heading off complaints of test unfairness is to standardize the testing process to every extent possible. That is, everyone is treated exactly the same, unless, of course, an individual requests and is granted a "reasonable accommodation" under laws such as the Americans with Disabilities Act (ADA). We discuss such instances at the end of this module.

Even if you are able to completely standardize the testing process, however, some individuals (i.e., stakeholders in the testing process) may still claim unfairness. For example, a parent who desperately wants his or her child to be admitted to a highly selective private school may claim unfairness if the child does not obtain a high enough score to be admitted into the school. In the vast majority of cases, it is the individual who does not obtain the favorable outcome as a result of using the test who is most likely to complain that the test is unfair. Thus, most accusations of unfairness tend to be more about the outcome of the testing process than the test per se. As a result, much of the debate that occurred in the professional literature in the late 1960s and early 1970s revolved around how best to define the outcomes of testing.

Figure 11.2 displays four quadrants (or possible outcomes) when a test is given and a cutoff score is set. Quadrant A would represent a correct decision (i.e., a positive hit). The persons falling in this quadrant passed the test and are subsequently successful on the criterion (e.g., job performance). Similarly, Quadrant C also represents a correct decision (i.e., a negative hit). Quadrant C individuals failed the test but also would be unsuccessful on the criterion. Quadrants A and C together thus represent the **hit rate**. In Quadrant B, however, these individuals passed the test but would not be successful on the outcome. These individuals represent a decision error, and thus they are labeled **false positives**. Quadrant D individuals were unsuccessful on the test but would have been successful on the criterion. These individuals are referred to as **false negatives**. Minority group members are often overrepresented in Quadrant D. You will notice that as the cutoff score is moved to the right (e.g., it is more difficult to pass the test) the size of Quadrants C and D grows much larger in comparison to that of Quadrants A and B. If we have a situation where having a large number of false positives (Quadrant B individuals) would be particularly detrimental, then moving the cutoff score higher to reduce Quadrant B may be justified. For example, who wants a surgeon who might be a false positive (i.e., Quadrant B individual)?

In reference to the professional testing debate of the late 1960s and early 1970s mentioned earlier, several models were put forth regarding how the outcomes should be distributed in order for the test to be considered "fair." For example, advocates of the **constant ratio model** argued that there should be a *constant ratio* for each subgroup in terms of who is "successful" (on the criterion) and who passes the test. That is, the ratio $(A + D)/(A + B)$ in Figure 11.2 should be the same for all subgroups (e.g., men vs. women, or Caucasian vs. African American vs. Hispanic vs. Asian).

Alternatively, others argued that the *conditional probability* of the proportion of individuals selected versus those who would be successful on the criterion should be the same for each subgroup. That is, the ratio of $A/(A + D)$ in Figure 11.2 should be the same for all subgroups. Another argument put forth suggested that there should be an *equal probability* of the proportion selected versus those who pass the test for each subgroup. That is, the ratio of $A/(A + B)$ in Figure 11.2

Figure 11.2   Distinguishing Different Forms of Test Unfairness

should be the same for all subgroups. Finally, some argued that a *culture-free* test would have an equal **selection ratio** for each group. That is, the ratio of $(A + B)/(A + B + C + D)$ in Figure 11.2 should be the same for all subgroups.

Many other possibilities exist; however, the common thread through all the definitions debated in the professional literature was that, in order for the test to be "fair," the outcomes (however variously defined) should be approximately the same for each subgroup. However, the only way to obtain most of these comparable outcomes is to have different cutoff scores and/or performance standards for each subgroup. The Civil Rights Act of 1991, however, prohibits differential treatment of different subgroups. Thus, the test fairness debate has been somewhat of a moot issue in recent years within the professional testing arena. However, as you might imagine, the test fairness debate has not ebbed in the practice setting. Tests are still being used to make life-altering decisions, and as a result, test fairness continues to be a hot issue.

A Step-by-Step Example of Estimating Test Bias

As noted previously, Sackett et al. (2003) initially found that a measure of conscientiousness was biased against African Americans when predicting job performance. Once a cognitive ability test was added into the regression equation, however, the conscientiousness test was no longer biased against African Americans. Saad and Sackett (2002) found gender differences on the conscientiousness variable as well. Therefore, we decided to look closer at the conscientiousness construct to see whether there might be gender differences in using conscientiousness to predict a few different outcomes. Using data from Mersman and Shultz (1998), with a sample size of approximately 320 subjects, we found women ($N = 221$, $M = 6.78$, $s = 1.02$) to have significantly higher conscientiousness scores (using Saucier's, 1994, Mini-Markers measure of the Big Five personality constructs) than men ($N = 91$, $M = 6.48$, $s = .97$) for a sample of working students ($t_{(310)} = 2.46$, $p = .015$, $\eta^2 = .019$). Thus, the two groups do differ in their level of conscientiousness, with women scoring significantly higher on conscientiousness.

As noted earlier, mean differences on a test typically are not considered an indication of test bias in and of themselves. Instead, we need to determine if the mean differences are associated with differential prediction of a criterion variable. Another factor looked at in the study by Mersman and Shultz (1998) was whether the subjects engaged in socially desirable responding. That is, do subjects tend to provide answers that are viewed as more socially acceptable than their "honest" answers? In the Mersman-Shultz data set, the conscientiousness scores and the social desirability scores correlated at .405. That is, those who scored high on conscientiousness also tended to score high on social desirability. Therefore, while conscientiousness is typically considered a good thing (e.g., being dependable and trustworthy), responding in a socially desirable way is considered a bad thing in that the respondents who have high social desirability scores may not be providing completely accurate or truthful answers.

If we were to try to predict social desirability based on the conscientiousness scores, given we know that they are associated, we would want to know whether there is any bias in doing so. As already noted, women scored significantly higher on conscientiousness than men. They also scored higher on the social desirability scale, although these differences were not statistically significant. To determine test bias, however, we must move beyond looking at mean differences and instead look at differences in prediction. Examining Figure 11.3, we can see that the slopes and intercepts appear to be the same for men and women when using conscientiousness scores to predict scores on the social desirability measure. In fact, the regression equation for men when using conscientiousness to predict social desirability was $\hat{Y} = 87.31 + 10.39*$Conscientiousness, whereas the regression equation for women was $\hat{Y} = 87.24 + 10.57*$Conscientiousness. As you can see, the slopes (10.39 vs. 10.57, difference = .18) and intercepts (87.31 vs. 87.24, difference =.07) are virtually the same. In addition, when conscientiousness and gender were used in a prediction equation to predict social desirability, only the conscientiousness regression weight was significant (another indication of a lack of intercept bias). The addition of the cross-product term between conscientiousness and gender (i.e., MMR) did not significantly improve the prediction equation. This lack of significance demonstrates a lack of slope bias.

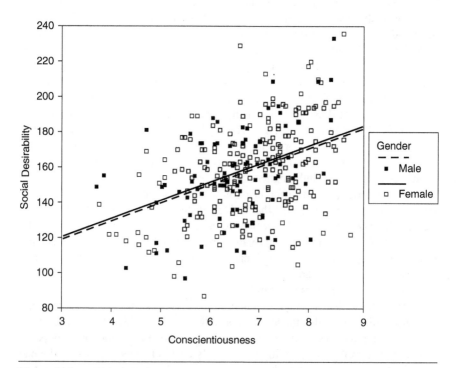

Figure 11.3   Actual Regression Lines Demonstrating a Lack of Both Intercept and Slope Bias

Next, we wanted to see if conscientiousness was related to intellect (sometimes referred to as "openness to experience"), another measure of the Big Five personality traits. In fact, conscientiousness and intellect correlate at .286. Thus, we wanted to determine if there is any bias in using conscientiousness to predict intellect. Remember, women scored significantly higher than men on conscientiousness; however, men ($N = 91$, $M = 6.74$, $s = 1.17$) scored significantly higher than women ($N = 225$, $M = 6.37$, $s = 1.16$) on the intellect scale ($t_{(310)} = -2.54$, $p = .012$, $\eta^2 = .020$). Looking at Figure 11.4, it appears we may have intercept bias, but probably no slope bias. The regression equation for women using conscientiousness to predict intellect was $\hat{Y} = 3.98 + .35*\text{Conscientiousness}$, whereas the regression equation for men was $\hat{Y} = 4.28 + .38*\text{Conscientiousness}$. Thus, we see a difference of .30 in the Y intercepts, but only .03 in the slopes.

We must be careful, however, not to overinterpret the differences in slopes, intercepts, or both, as they are based on unstandardized regression values. Thus, the size of the observed differences is highly dependent on the scale used to measure both the predictor and the criterion variables. Therefore, we again need to compute an MMR, adding in conscientiousness and gender in the first step and their cross product in the second step. As anticipated, gender was a significant predictor of intellect in the first step, thus indicating intercept bias. However, there was not a significant increase in prediction when the cross product of conscientiousness and gender was added into the regression equation in the second step, thus

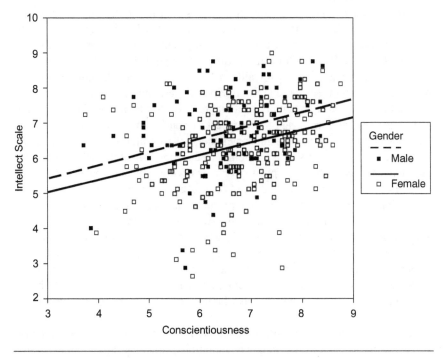

Figure 11.4   Actual Regression Lines Showing No Slope but Intercept Bias

demonstrating a lack of slope bias. As noted earlier, instances of slope bias are relatively rare. In fact, we were unable to find any demonstration of slope bias in the data set of Mersman and Shultz (1998).

Test Equivalence

Issues of diversity are clearly important considerations in testing; however, the appropriate methods for addressing these concerns are significantly less clear (Frisby, 1998). One commonly encountered problem is how to administer a test developed in English to a non–English-speaking sample. **Back translation** refers to tests that have been translated by bilingual individuals from English to the target language, and then retranslated back into English by other bilingual individuals. The idea is that if the retranslated English version of the test is highly similar to the original English version, then the target language test version must be acceptable. Unfortunately, this process falls far short of ensuring equivalent test versions (Sperber, Devellis, & Boehlecke, 1994).

A number of ways of conceptualizing test equivalence have been proposed (e.g., Lonner, 1990; Marsella & Kameoka, 1989; Steenkamp & Baumgartner, 1998). Lonner (1990), for example, identified four issues to consider regarding equivalence of tests that are translated for use in a culture other than that in which it was initially developed.

Content equivalence refers to whether items are relevant to the new group of test takers. In 1972, Robert Williams created the Black Intelligence Test of Cultural Homogeneity, or BITCH. This test is composed of words, terms, and expressions particular to Black culture at that time. An example item is, "If a judge finds you guilty of holding wood [in California], what's the most he can give you?" A member of any other ethnic group is virtually certain to perform poorly on the test. Williams's point was that many of the items on commonly used tests of intelligence are similarly irrelevant for members of non-White groups.

Conceptual equivalence examines whether, across cultures, the same meaning is attached to the terms used in the items. To describe something as "wicked," for example, can have either very positive or very negative attributions, depending on the audience. Conceptual equivalence is concerned with the degree to which test takers share a common understanding of the terms used in the items.

An examination of *functional equivalence* determines the degree to which behavioral assessments function similarly across cultures. Interest inventories are often used to illustrate this form of equivalence. In the United States, for example, there exists an expectation that career choice is a personal decision. Thus, the assessment of career interests is quite popular. Such inventories would be far less useful in societies in which one's family largely determines the career one pursues.

Reid (1995) pointed out a second example relevant to functional equivalence. Whereas Americans have a negative connotation of the concept of "dependency," the high value placed on interdependence in Japanese society leads to positive regard for the concept of dependency. Given the cross-cultural differences in understanding of the concept, use of American measures of dependency would be inappropriate for use in a Japanese population.

Scalar equivalence assesses the degree to which different cultural groups produce similar means and standard deviations of scores. Clearly, this form of equivalence is difficult to obtain given true between-group differences. Fouad and Chan (1999) recommended interpretation of an individual's score on a psychological test within the cultural context of the test taker, rather than in comparison to a mainstream norm.

Testing Individuals with Disabilities

Issues of test equivalence can also be raised when testing individuals with disabilities. While the validity of test scores may change when a test is adapted for an individual with a disability, failing to adapt the test for a disability will likely be even more detrimental to the validity and interpretation of test scores. The ADA requires test administrators to provide individuals with disabilities a reasonable **accommodation**. Exam administrators are encouraged to provide test takers with a description of each test well in advance of test administration, in order to allow test takers with disabilities the opportunity to request a needed accommodation. Unfortunately, it is virtually impossible to provide guidelines as to exactly what accommodations or test adaptations will be necessary to ensure test equivalence across all possible disabilities. Therefore, in practice, decisions regarding what constitutes a reasonable accommodation are determined on a case-by-case basis. Ways in which tests might be adapted, or in which an accommodation might be provided, include increasing the amount of time given to take the test, increasing the font size used on the test, translation into Braille, verbal administration of a test, allowing verbal responses to test items, and so on.

In Module 12, we introduce the Wonderlic Classic Cognitive Ability Test (WCCAT) as a measure of cognitive ability. This test is composed of 50 constructed-response items administered with a 12-minute time limit. The WCCAT test manual suggests a number of possible test accommodations for individuals with specified disabilities (Wonderlic Inc., 2002). For example, in testing individuals with learning disabilities, the WCCAT is initially administered by means of the usual timed procedure. The WCCAT is then administered a second time, but the individual is allowed to complete the exam without a time limit. The number of items correct on each of the two test administrations is then compared. If the difference in number of items correct between the two administrations is less than nine, the test administrator is encouraged to use the test taker's original timed score as representative of the test taker's ability. Using the regular test administration procedure, an individual's test score is determined simply by summing the number of items correct. On the other hand, if the difference between the two testing administrations is nine points or more, then the untimed administration is thought to serve as a better representation of the learning-disabled individual's ability. In this latter case, the individual's test score is determined by subtracting a value of six from the number of items the individual answered correctly on the untimed administration of the test. While the recommendations of the WCCAT test manual suggest that this accommodation is reasonable, some test administrators may take issue with this recommended adjustment. For example, a test administrator may be concerned with the impact of practice effects on test performance when using this accommodation, particularly given the likely brief interval between testing and retesting.

The WCCAT is also available in a Braille version. This version is administered untimed, and the test score is again determined by subtracting a value of six from the number of items correct.

Levels of Accommodation

Styers and Shultz (2009) suggested that researchers typically categorize accommodations into three levels. Level I accommodations, called "Change in Medium" accommodations, present disabled individuals with the same test items presented to other test takers, but the items are presented in a different manner, such as by providing a reader or a Braille version of a test to a blind individual. Level II accommodations, "Time Limits," provide additional time for individuals with disabilities when completing power tests. Level III, or "Change in Content," accommodations include item revision, deletion of items on the test, and change in item format. Any modification of typical administration procedures should be noted in the reporting of test scores.

It is important to note that accommodations should not be provided if the disability is directly relevant to the construct being assessed. For example, sign language interpretation should not be provided for a test assessing hearing ability. Professional judgment plays an important role in determining whether, and to what degree, a reasonable accommodation is necessary.

Concluding Comments

Test bias and test fairness are separate, although potentially related, concepts. Test bias (also referred to as prediction bias) is a technical psychometric issue that can be investigated empirically through procedures such as MMR. Slope bias tends to be relatively rare, whereas intercept bias is somewhat more common.

However, researchers must be aware of potential omitted variables that can change one's conclusions regarding test bias. In addition, researchers must also investigate possible criterion problems (i.e., maybe it is not the test but the criterion being used), differing sample size issues (i.e., we tend to have drastically smaller sample sizes for minority groups), and also the influence of individual items versus the entire test (to be discussed in more detail in Module 21). In addition, MMR analysis assumes homogeneity of error variances. If this assumption is not met, alternative procedures should be used to estimate slope and/or intercept biases. Finally, it should be noted that we have focused in this overview on test bias in terms of bias in prediction. Test bias can also be conceptualized in terms of bias of measurement. That is, our test is actually measuring a different trait than we said it was. Test bias in the form of bias in measurement will be discussed in Module 21.

Test fairness, conversely, is more of a sociopolitical concept. As a result, there is no standardized way of determining if a test is fair or not. We presented several conceptual models for defining test fairness; however, many others are possible. Standardizing the testing process and treating everyone the same can, however, go a long way toward heading off claims of test unfairness. In the end, though, adequately addressing test unfairness would require treating different subgroups differently on either the test or the criterion variable. This is unacceptable in many instances, and, as a result, you may well be left to search for another test that does not demonstrate test unfairness.

Finally, test users must be aware that the psychometric properties of a test may change when used on a population different from that for which the test was originally developed. Concerns with testing diverse populations, whether in terms of sex, race, different cultures, or those with mental and physical disabilities, remain at the forefront of debate in American society. This area of testing is currently experiencing significant theoretical and empirical development that will no doubt greatly improve our understanding of the true meaning of test scores and their equivalence across various groups.

Best Practices

1. Test bias, unfairness, and equivalence are distinct concepts that should be dealt with in their own right.
2. MMR is still the most common analytic strategy for determining predictive test bias.
3. Recent Monte Carlo simulations indicate that both intercept and slope bias may be more prevalent in pre-employment testing than previous thought.
4. Test accommodations need to be made on a case-by-case basis.

Practical Questions

1. Based on the data in Figure 11.1, what would have happened if we had used a common regression line to predict suicide risk in all three age groups?
2. Assuming we did use the same regression line for all three groups, which group would be most likely to raise claims of test bias? Unfairness?
3. How does one go about narrowing down the seemingly endless list of potential "omitted variables" in moderated regression analysis used to determine test bias?
4. Why do you think that intercept bias is much more common than slope bias?

5. What other factors (besides a truly biased test or an omitted variable) might be falsely suggesting test bias when, in fact, the test is not biased?
6. Which stakeholders in the testing process (see Module 1) are responsible for determining whether test bias actually exists or not?
7. Can a test that is determined to be biased still be a fair test? Alternatively, can a test that is determined to be unfair still be an unbiased test?
8. Describe the process of back translation. Why is back translation insufficient to guarantee equivalence?
9. Provide an example of each of the four types of test equivalence identified by Lonner (1990).
10. If you had recently translated a test into a different cultural context, how would you assess each of the four types of equivalence?
11. What factors should be considered when determining whether a requested test accommodation is reasonable?

Case Studies

CASE STUDY 11.1: ESTIMATING TEST BIAS IN A PHYSICAL ABILITY TEST

Larry had just completed his master's degree in industrial and organizational (I/O) psychology and obtained his first job with the human resources department of a large local school district. The school district had just had an EEOC (Equal Employment Opportunity Commission) complaint filed against it regarding its physical ability test used to select School Security Officers (SSOs). In particular, both women and older (i.e., those age 40 and older) applicants had complained that the dynamometer test (a test of hand grip strength) was biased against both groups. Therefore, one of Larry's first projects was to determine if, in fact, the dynamometer test was biased against these two groups.

Fortunately for Larry, the school district tested a very large number of applicants each year for the SSO job. In addition, because the dynamometer test had been used for almost two decades, he had data going back almost 20 years and, thus, had a sufficiently large sample of female and older job candidates who had subsequently been hired, thus allowing him to examine for possible test bias on sex and age. Looking back on his notes from his graduate applied psychological measurement class, Larry remembered that he had to perform an MMR analysis to examine for possible test bias. Larry first looked at possible test bias based on gender by entering all the dynamometer test scores in the database for those who had been hired and the gender variable (0 = women, 1 = men) into the regression equation to predict those who successfully completed a 12-month probationary period. Both the dynamometer and the gender variables had significant regression coefficients (i.e., they significantly predicted who passed probation). Therefore, in a second step, Larry entered the interaction term (i.e., gender × test score) into the regression equation. Lo and behold, the regression coefficient for the interaction term was also significant in predicting who successfully completed probation.

Next, Larry reran the multiple regression equation. This time, however, Larry entered the dynamometer test score and age (less than age 40 = 0, age 40 and older = 1) in the first step to predict successful completion of probation. Again, both regression weights were significantly related to who completed probation. However, when Larry entered the interaction term (test score × dichotomous age group) in step 2 of the regression equation, the regression coefficient for the interaction term was not significant. Now, it was time to sit down and look at the results more carefully and try to figure out what was going on with this dynamometer test.

Questions to Ponder

1. Does there appear to be any test bias in terms of gender? If so, what kind of predictor bias seems to be evident?
2. Does there appear to be any test bias in terms of age? If so, what kind of predictor bias seems to be evident?
3. If you were Larry, what omitted variables would you investigate? Would you look for different potential omitted variables for gender and age? Why or why not?
4. What other factors besides the omitted-variable concern might be impacting Larry's results?
5. Would drawing a scatterplot (similar to Figures 11.3 and 11.4) help in determining what is happening with the data, or is the MMR analysis sufficient?
6. Does the criterion variable that Larry used (i.e., whether a new hire passed probation) make a difference in whether we are likely to find test bias?

CASE STUDY 11.2: BIAS IN MEASURING ACTIVITIES OF DAILY LIVING

Joelle, a life span developmental psychology graduate student, recently completed an internship at an adult day care facility. The majority of the facility's clientele were elderly individuals who were living with their adult children and needed assistance with their activities of daily living (ADLs;

i.e., eating, toileting, ambulating, bathing). The adult children typically worked during the day and could not afford a full-time home nurse. In addition, most adult children were concerned that even if they could afford a home nurse, the inability of their parent to interact with others their own age would lead to a feeling of social isolation and eventually to depression. Therefore, while most of these elderly individuals used walkers or were in wheelchairs, they were still able to get around somewhat and interact with others their own age at the facility. However, at some point in the near future, most of the clients would probably have to be referred to a full-time care facility (i.e., a nursing home).

In the past, each decision to refer a client to a full-time care facility was made on a case-by-case basis. However, a major determinant of whether a client was referred to a full-time care facility was how he or she scored on the standardized ADL scale. This scale measured how much difficulty (from 1 = none at all to 7 = a great extent) the client had performing personal functions such as bathing, ambulating, and eating. Those who scored beyond an established cutoff score were typically referred to nursing homes. However, the adult day care facility had received several complaints from the adult children of several clients that the test was somehow unfair or biased against minority clients. To the adult children, it appeared that minority clients were much more likely to be referred to a nursing home than were Caucasian clients. Therefore, the director of the center, knowing that Joelle had just completed an applied psychometrics course, asked her if she could somehow "determine" if, in fact, the ADL test was biased or unfair to minority clients. Joelle was unsure of where to start. She knew that the predictor was the ADL test, but what was the criterion? In addition, the adult day care facility wasn't all that big and hadn't been using the ADL test all that long, so there weren't many data available on who had and had not been referred, particularly for minority clients. A little unsure of where to even start, Joelle decided that it was time to e-mail her psychometrics professor to see if he had any suggestions for her.

Questions to Ponder

1. If you were Joelle, where would you start? What key factors would you want to consider?
2. What information would you want to know from the test publisher or from reviews conducted of the test?
3. Does this appear to be more of a test bias or test fairness issue? Why?
4. If Joelle wanted to examine for test bias, what data would she need?
5. Which of the models of test fairness presented in the module overview would be most applicable here? Why?
6. Assuming Joelle actually found the test to be "unfair," what could she do to make the test fair?

〜⋯〜

Exercises

EXERCISE 11.1: EXAMINING TEST BIAS

OBJECTIVE: To practice computing moderated multiple regression (MMR) analyses and drawing scatterplots to examine test bias issues.

Using the data set of Mersman and Shultz (1998) ("Personality.sav" in Appendix B), recreate the results presented in Figures 11.3 and 11.4. In addition, recreate the regression equations presented in the module overview. Finally, run the MMR procedure for both the social desirability and the intellect criterion variables. What are your final regression equations? (*Note:* Be sure to use the honest condition responses when computing these regressions, i.e., conmean1 and intmean1.)

EXERCISE 11.2: EXAMINING DIFFERENT MODELS OF TEST BIAS/FAIRNESS (EEOC REQUEST FOR INFORMATION AND ANALYSIS—PART 2)

OBJECTIVE: To practice running and interpreting data to investigate several forms of test bias.

BACKGROUND: In Exercise 2.1, you performed some analyses for two mechanical comprehension (MC) tests in regard to an EEOC complaint using the "Mechanical Comprehension.sav" data set (see Appendix B for a description of the data). Well, they're back. The EEOC is requesting additional information/ analyses regarding the complaint about our current MC test from a former job applicant (an older [more than 40 years of age] female minority, case ID # 450) for a clerical position. As you might remember, we are in the process of replacing our current MC test with a new one. The EEOC analyst assigned to our case will be here to meet with me tomorrow, so we had better have some answers by then. Specifically, they want us to look for test bias in our current MC measure using the four "models" outlined in Arvey and Faley (1988). Are any of these present and to what extent? (You probably should review your previous notes and analyses from Exercise 2.1 first if you have completed that exercise.)

1. **Model I: *Mean difference between subgroups*** (described on pp. 122–123 of Arvey & Faley, 1988). Specifically, examine the group differences between minority and majority group applicants. Also, examine the differences between male and female applicants. Test these group means for statistical significance using independent groups *t* tests. What did you find?
2. **Model II: *Difference in validities*** (described on pp. 123–130 of Arvey & Faley, 1988). Specifically, compute the criterion-related validity coefficients separately for majority and minority groups and also for men and women.

Perform separate analyses using both the current and the proposed MC tests as the predictor variables, respectively, and the job performance ratings as the criterion variable.

3. **Model III:** *Difference in regression lines* (described on pp. 130–138 of Arvey & Faley, 1988, and pp. 274–275 of Crocker & Algina, 1986). Specifically, compute separate regression analyses for men and women, as well as for minority and majority groups. Use the same predictor and criterion variables as in Model II. To perform the MMR, however, you will also need to enter the demographic term (i.e., minority or sex) as well as the cross product of the demographic term and the appropriate MC test into the regression equation. In addition, create four scatterplots, one each for both the current and the proposed MC test as well as for sex and ethnicity. Be sure to plot separate regression lines for the respective demographic groups.

4. **Model IV:** *Thorndike's "quota" model* (described on pp. 138–141 of Arvey & Faley, 1988). To perform this analysis, you will have to set a cutoff on both the MC test and the job performance rating (similar to Figure 11.2). We recommend using the median value for the job performance measure (i.e., a 50% base rate) to make things a little easier. Now adjust the cutoffs for the MC exams for each group in order meet the requirements of the model. This model is similar to the equal probability model discussed in the module overview (i.e., the proportion $A/[A + B]$ is the same for each group). What final cutoffs should be used for each group on each of the two MC tests in order to meet the requirements of the model?

5. Are there any other analyses that we should carry out to be comprehensive and fully prepared?

Further Readings

Aguinis, H., Culpepper, S.A., & Pierce, C.A. (2010). Revival of test bias research in pre-employment testing. *Journal of Applied Psychology, 95,* 648–680.

Arnold, B.R., & Matus, Y.E. (2000). Test translation and cultural equivalence methodologies for use with diverse populations. In I. Cuellar & F.A. Paniagua (Eds.), *Handbook of multicultural mental health: Assessment and treatment of diverse populations* (pp. 121–136). San Diego, CA: Academic Press.

Arvey, R.D., & Faley, R.H. (1988). *Fairness in selecting employees* (2nd ed.). New York: Addison-Wesley.

Berk, R.A. (Ed.). (1982). *Handbook of methods for detecting test bias.* Baltimore: Johns Hopkins University Press.

Camilli, G., & Shepard, L.A. (1994). *Methods for identifying biased test items.* Thousand Oaks, CA: Sage.

Part 3
Practical Issues in Test Construction

Module 12

Developing Tests of Maximal Performance

Given that students are administered possibly hundreds of tests throughout their academic careers, it should not be surprising to find that most students equate the term "testing" with educational assessment. This module is concerned with the development of the sorts of psychological tests with which students are most familiar—tests of knowledge, achievement, and ability. What distinguishes these tests from other psychological measures (such as those discussed in Module 15) is that tests of maximal performance are intended to assess an individual's performance at his or her maximum level of effort (Cronbach, 1970). Further, the items that constitute tests of maximal performance typically have a single correct answer.

Despite their familiarity with taking these types of tests, few students have considered the process that is required to develop tests of maximal performance. Unfortunately, it may also be true that, in many cases, little thought actually did go into the development of these tests. Module 4 discusses the preparatory steps required to develop any psychological test—it would be a good idea to review these steps before proceeding with the current module.

Getting Started

Initially, the developer of a test of maximal performance must clearly specify the domain the test is intended to assess. In developing a classroom knowledge test, this is likely to be a fairly straightforward process. The domain is often limited by the reading assignments, lectures, and class discussions. Still, the relative weighting or emphasis on various topics must be determined. For the development of a job knowledge test, however, specification of the domain may be considerably more complex. For example, for the job of human resource worker, what exactly does "Knowledge of Equal Employment Opportunity (EEO) law" mean? Does this include knowledge of executive orders and court decisions, or is it limited to legislation? Would the test assess knowledge at the federal level only, or should state and local statutes also be assessed? These issues need to be specified in order to guide subsequent item writing, as well as to serve as a basis for evaluating the test once initial development is complete. Hopefully, you recognize that these issues relate to the content aspect of test validation.

Speed Versus Power Tests

An important issue for the construction of tests of maximal performance is whether the test will be a pure speed test, a pure power test, or some combination of both. Tests can differ in the emphasis on time provided for completion during administration. Pure **speed tests** provide a large number of relatively easy items. How someone performs is determined by the number of items that can be completed in a relatively short period of time. Alternatively, **power tests** provide an ample amount of time for completion. Here, how someone performs is assumed to result from differences in understanding or ability. Many tests use some combination of both speed and power. The Wonderlic Classic Cognitive Ability Test (Wonderlic Inc., 2002), for example, is a measure of cognitive ability often used in personnel selection. Test takers are provided exactly 12 minutes to complete the 50 items that constitute the test. Although the time provided is brief, it is unlikely that many test takers would get all items correct even if given an unlimited amount of time to complete the test.

Murphy and Davidshofer (2001) pointed out that computation of an internal consistency method for estimating reliability is inappropriate for speed tests. Because any items that are completed by a test taker on a pure speed test are likely to be correct, and all items that are not completed are necessarily incorrect, an internal consistency reliability estimate will be greatly inflated. Indeed, such a value is likely to approach 1.0. Test-retest or equivalent forms are more appropriate methods to assess reliability of pure speed tests (Crocker & Algina, 1986).

Level of Cognitive Objective

The items that constitute a test can assess various cognitive objectives. While some items are intended to assess whether a test taker has retained basic facts, others are intended to assess a test taker's ability to perform more complex tasks, such as developing rational arguments based on evaluation of information. Bloom (1956) proposed a useful taxonomy for categorizing the level of abstraction assessed by test items. Bloom's taxonomy includes the following six levels, ordered in terms of increasing abstraction.

- *Knowledge:* These items are the most concrete and include memorization of fact. Key words may include define, list, and name.

- *Comprehension:* These items assess understanding and interpretation of information. Key words may include summarize, discuss, and distinguish.
- *Application:* These items measure the test taker's ability to use information to solve novel problems. Key words may include apply, demonstrate, and calculate.
- *Analysis:* These items assess the test taker's ability to see patterns and organize components of a whole. Key words may include analyze, order, and classify.
- *Synthesis:* These items assess the test taker's ability to draw appropriate conclusions from information and to use old ideas to create new ones. Key words may include generalize, combine, and create.
- *Evaluation:* These items at the highest level of abstraction require test takers to compare and discriminate between ideas. Test takers are required to substantiate their choices based on rational argument. Key words may include assess, convince, and recommend.

Anderson and Krathwohl (2001) proposed revisions to Bloom's taxonomy. Chief among the modifications in the revised Bloom's taxonomy was to reverse the ordering of the last two categories and to change the labels for the levels of abstraction from nouns to verbs. The cognitive process dimension of the revised Bloom's taxonomy is composed of the following six levels, presented in increasing level of cognitive abstraction: remembering, understanding, applying, analyzing, evaluating, and creating. Anderson and Krathwohl's framework also included a second dimension composed of four categories of knowledge to be learned: factual, conceptual, procedural, and metacognitive knowledge. A taxonomy table is constructed by crossing the knowledge categories on a vertical axis and the cognitive process levels on a horizontal axis (see Table 12.1). A specific learning objective can be classified by the intersection between the corresponding levels of the cognitive process dimension and the knowledge dimension. For example, the objective "Students will formulate research questions to test theory" would be analyzed in terms of both the knowledge and cognitive process dimensions.

Table 12.1   Example Taxonomy Table

	Cognitive Process Dimension					
Knowledge Dimension	*Remembering*	*Understanding*	*Applying*	*Analyzing*	*Evaluating*	*Creating*
Factual Knowledge						
Conceptual Knowledge						X
Procedural Knowledge						
Metacognitive Knowledge						

The type of knowledge assessed by this objective would be *conceptual knowledge*, which includes knowledge of theories. The cognitive process required to formulate research questions would be *creating*. Therefore, an X is placed in the corresponding cell of the taxonomy table in Table 12.1. Similar mapping of each objective in a course would provide a quick overview of the focus of the learning objectives.

Whether assessing the appropriate focus of the learning objectives for an entire course or merely examining the level of cognitive abstraction assessed by the items composing a test, Bloom's taxonomy and the revision by Anderson and Krathwohl (2001) provide useful frameworks for gaining better insight into our learning and assessment strategies.

Item Format

The test specifications for tests of maximal performance must consider the appropriate format for items. Constructed-response (i.e., closed-ended) items include multiple-choice, true-false, and matching. These items provide test takers with a number of possible options from which to select the correct choice. Free-response (i.e., open-ended) items, including short-answer and essay items, require test takers to provide an answer varying in length from a few words to several pages. Free-response items may also require the solution of mathematical or other problems in which no set of possible solutions is provided. Although constructed-response options have been criticized in some educational quarters (e.g., Resnick & Resnick, 1992; Wiggens, 1989), it is important to recognize that both constructed- and free-response item formats have benefits and shortcomings.

For tests of maximal performance, free-response items are generally easier to create than constructed-response items. Some test developers prefer free-response items because they more readily allow for the testing of higher-order cognitive objectives. Because test takers produce their own response, free-response items also allow test takers to provide evidence of the depth of their knowledge. Although free-response items assessing maximal performance are relatively easy to create, they can be difficult and time-consuming to score. A certain degree of subjectivity is hard to avoid in scoring the responses of test takers. Further, because free-response items frequently take greater time to administer, these tests typically contain fewer items than their constructed-response counterparts. The inclusion of fewer items raises concerns over whether the test assesses a truly representative sample of the entire content domain. Another practical concern is whether test takers interpret the free-response items in the way the test developer intended. Invariably, some test takers fail to focus their response on the question asked. Finally, a test taker's language ability may have a significant influence on his or her responses to free-response items. The degree to which language ability is an important component of the testing domain must be considered.

Maximal performance tests composed of constructed-response items are typically easy to score objectively. These tests are therefore suitable for administration whenever a large number of individuals will be tested. Further, these tests can include a large number of items, which provides a more representative assessment of the content domain. However, constructed-response items can be much more difficult to construct than free-response items, particularly if the test developer's goal is to assess higher-order cognitive objectives. Constructed-response items that are poorly written can be either unintentionally difficult, as is the case with the inclusion of double negatives in item stems, or too easy, when either the item stem or a previous item suggests the correct response. Due in part to the difficulty of constructing quality constructed-response items, test developers are likely to retain items for administration to additional groups of test takers. Such practices raise concerns with test security.

It is wrong to decry the perceived weaknesses of one format while trumpeting the virtues of another format as appropriate for all testing situations. However, choice of item format is an important consideration, as it will impact a variety of factors, including the level of knowledge assessment, the test's efficiency of assessment, objectivity of scoring, and even the strategies employed by examinees in preparation for the test. The test developer must carefully consider the intent of the testing and carefully select an item format (or combination of item formats) useful for that purpose.

Item Writing

Once the test specifications are complete, item writing can begin. Many sources provide recommendations regarding the construction of specific item formats. Following are brief descriptions of several specific item formats and a sample of item-writing recommendations taken from Ebel and Frisbie (1986), McKeachie (1994), Tuckman (1988), and Wiersma and Jurs (1990). These or other similar sources should be consulted for more complete recommendations on item writing.

True-False Items

True-false items require a test taker to determine whether a statement is valid. These items tend to be easily created and require little time to administer. Unfortunately, the apparent simplicity of creating true-false items makes these items popular with unskilled test developers. Further, because each item has only two possible response options (i.e., true or false), item discrimination is often low. Tips for writing quality true-false items include the following:

- Express the item as clearly, concisely, and simply as possible.
- Assess only important knowledge; avoid assessment of trivia.
- Create items that assess understanding—not just memory.
- Avoid double negatives.
- Use more false statements than true statements in the test.
- Word the item so that superficial logic suggests a wrong answer.

- Ensure that the intended correct answer is obvious only to those who have good command of the knowledge being tested.
- Make the wrong answer consistent with a popular misconception or a popular belief irrelevant to the question.

Matching Items

Matching items typically present a number of stems in one column and response options in a separate column. These items are useful for determining whether a test taker can distinguish between similar ideas, facts, or concepts. Because of the required brevity of matching items, they typically assess lower-order cognitive objectives, thus encouraging rote memorization. Tips for writing quality matching items include the following:

- Denote each item stem with a number, and each possible response option with a letter.
- Choose item stems and response options that demonstrate the test taker's ability to distinguish between similar things.
- Keep response options short.
- Provide additional plausible response options to avoid a "process of elimination" approach.
- Provide clear instructions regarding what the test taker is intended to do. For example, specify whether response options can be used more than once.

Multiple-Choice Items

Multiple-choice items are used extensively in many testing contexts; thus, test takers are very familiar with this testing format. Multiple-choice items present a statement or question in an item stem, followed by a choice among several possible response options. These items can be used to assess both lower- and higher-order cognitive objectives, although greater expertise is required to develop the latter. Tips for writing quality multiple-choice *item stems* include the following:

- Make sure that items assess important, significant ideas.
- Pose a question (or statement) that has a definitive answer.
- Avoid giveaways as to the correct answer.
- When using a negative in the item stem (e.g., not), use capitalization or underlining to ensure that the word is read.
- Consider using two sentences in the stem, one to present necessary background information, and one to ask the question.
- Use gender and ethnicity in an inclusive fashion. Alternate between "she" and "he." Proper names should reflect ethnic diversity.

Tips for writing quality *response options* for multiple-choice items include the following:

- Place words that appear in every response option in the stem.
- Arrange response options in a logical order.

- Include plausible distracters.
- Include some true statements in the distracters that do not correctly answer the question posed in the stem.
- Ensure that response options are parallel—that is, of approximately equal length and of equal complexity.
- Write brief response options, rather than long ones.
- Across the test, ensure that the correct response is balanced roughly equally across the possible response options (i.e., A, B, C, D, and E).
- Create distracters that include familiar-sounding phrases that would be attractive to those with only superficial knowledge.
- Avoid use of "all of the above." Once a test taker has determined that at least two response options are correct, the correct response must be "all of the above."
- Use "none of the above" only if this is sometimes the correct response option. Further, avoid the common mistake of including the option "none of the above" only in items for which it is the correct response.
- Avoid use of "A & C"–type response options. While item difficulty increases, item discrimination does not improve.

Short-Answer and Essay Items

Short-answer and essay items are free-response items that are typically used to assess higher-order cognitive objectives. These items differ in the length of response required. Tips for *writing* quality short-answer and essay items include the following:

- Ask only questions that produce responses that can be verified as better than other responses.
- Provide terminology in the questions that limit and clarify the required response.
- Provide multiple specific questions rather than a very limited number of long questions.
- Do not provide test takers a choice among several questions. This, in effect, is providing different exams to different students. The equivalency of alternative essay items is highly suspect.
- Specify the number of points for each part of an essay item.
- Test each item by writing an ideal answer prior to administration.

The following tips are provided to help improve the quality of *scoring* short-answer and essay items:

- When you are familiar with the test takers, ask test takers to record a confidential code rather than names on the test.
- Develop a set of criteria for the scoring of each item.
- Read several responses before assigning grades.
- Select papers to serve as excellent, good, nominal, and poor models of the standards by which you are grading.
- Assign global, holistic grades to each question rather than multiple grades on such elements as content, originality, grammar, and organization.

Test-Wise Test Takers

Item-writing recommendations are intended to clarify the item for test takers, avoid unnecessary assessment of language capabilities, assist in ensuring good test psychometrics, and ward against test-wiseness. Test-wiseness refers to the ability to answer items correctly based not on knowledge of the subject matter tested, but rather on clues presented by the item itself or elsewhere in the test. A classic example is the recommendation that if you have no idea as to the correct answer on a multiple-choice item, simply select the longest response option. You may notice in the lists of sample recommendations given previously that some tips are intended to "trip up" those who would seek to practice their test-wise skills on the test.

The Process of Item Modification

The remaining steps in the development of a maximal performance test include (a) having subject matter experts (SMEs) review the items, (b) pretesting the items, and (c) making any necessary modifications. For large-scale applications, SMEs are asked to provide confirmation that items assess the intended construct. When SMEs question the relevance of an item, it is dropped from further consideration. Pretesting is often initially conducted on a small sample to determine whether items are interpreted as intended. This is then followed by large-scale piloting that allows the examination of the test's factor structure and internal consistency reliability, along with computation of item statistics. In classroom settings, these steps are typically undertaken less formally. The instructor will often attempt to critically evaluate any newly written items. Another instructor or a teaching assistant may also be asked to provide feedback. Unfortunately, classroom exams are rarely pretested. Rather, students themselves typically serve as both the pilot and the implementation sample. Of course, once the test is administered, those items with poor item statistics (see Module 13) can be subsequently discarded.

Concluding Comments

Creation of a test of maximal performance proceeds through a series of important steps. Prior to development of test items, the test developer must make a number of important decisions regarding the test's content, item format, test length, and so on. A number of recommendations exist for the development of good items. Once initially developed, pretesting, examination by experts, and other steps should be taken to modify items prior to administration.

The construction of a knowledge test is a deliberate process intended to ensure the reliability and validity of the test. However, what may not be quite as obvious in this module is that test developers must make a large number of choices throughout this process. It is this considerable flexibility that allows test developers to engage their creative juices as well.

Best Practices

1. The development of maximal performance tests relies heavily on test specifications.
2. Quality items result from a deliberate and painstaking writing process. Assess important concepts only, not trivial information. Avoid common pitfalls in item writing.
3. The purpose of the testing should influence the choice of items at various levels of cognitive abstraction. Avoid assessing only lower levels of abstraction unless that is the objective of the learning experience.

Practical Questions

1. Why is test-wiseness a problem in tests of maximal performance?
2. What do you think of intentionally incorporating test-wise characteristics into item distracters? Defend your position.
3. What are the advantages and disadvantages of constructed-response items?
4. What are the advantages and disadvantages of free-response items?
5. Why shouldn't use of "all of the above" be included in multiple-choice response options?
6. Why shouldn't test takers be given a choice among several different essay items?
7. Why are multiple short-answer items preferable to one long essay question?
8. Why is pretesting of items important in test construction?
9. In what ways does the revised Bloom's taxonomy differ from the original?
10. Who would be appropriate to fulfill the role of SME for a test designed to assess knowledge of the following?

    a. Twelfth-grade mathematics
    b. Modern automotive repair
    c. American pop culture

Case Studies

CASE STUDY 12.1: ESSAY SCORING AND WRITING ABILITY

Jaime was rightly proud of the midterm exam he created for the course in which he served as teaching assistant, PSY 451: Introduction to Forensic Psychology. The instructor, Dr. Dan Kellemen, had asked him to create a free-response test that could be completed within the 1.5-hour class session.

Jaime had given a lot of thought to proper test construction techniques in the creation of the test. He carefully went over the topics Dr. Kellemen wanted covered, and he considered the relative importance of these various topics. Jaime considered a variety of free-response options for the test but, in the end, decided to modify Dr. Kellemen's usual approach of two to three essay questions. Similar to the midterm exam Dr. Kellemen had used the previous semester, Jaime's test was organized around three large "questions." However, Jaime used these broad questions only to introduce the topic and to help students focus on the subitems that followed. Under each of the three broad questions, Jaime created between three and four subitems labeled a, b, c, and so on. It was the responses to these items that were to be graded for the exam. Following each of these subitems, Jaime recorded the number of points that a student could possibly receive for that item. Items on more important topics received a higher number of points. Overall, the exam contained 10 items.

Before showing the test to Dr. Kellemen, Jaime produced responses to each item to ensure that the questions were, in fact, answerable. Based on this exercise, Jaime had to revise a couple of the items. Much to Jaime's delight, Dr. Kellemen had been noticeably impressed with the quality of the exam and had not made a single modification. During the administration of the exam, a few students asked for the usual types of clarification, but no one indicated any major difficulties in understanding the items on the exam. Now that the students had completed their midterm, Jaime's next responsibility was to score it.

When it came to scoring, Jaime was once again a man with a plan. To be fair to everyone, he had asked students to record only their student identification numbers on their blue books, rather than their names. He also planned on scoring every student's response to the first item, before scoring even a single response to the second item. Jaime also decided to assign a single, holistic score to each item, rather than assigning separate scores based on content, clarity, originality, and so forth. Even so, Jaime was surprised how long it took to score all of the exams in the class.

Back in class the next day, Jaime was excited to return the exams to the students. It was, in many ways, the final step in the life span of his first exam. Later that day during office hours, he received a visit from Juan, a student in the class. Juan demanded to know why he received a much lower score than another student who, he claimed, had provided similar correct answers. As evidence, Juan produced both his own and another student's blue books. On question after question, the content of each response was similar, yet Jaime had given the other student a higher score. "How could that be?" Jaime nearly wondered aloud. Stalling, Jaime informed Juan that he'd examine both blue books and would provide a decision at the next class session.

In reviewing both blue books more carefully, Jaime realized that he had to agree with Juan on one point—both blue books contained similar quality of information in response to the items. However, Juan's responses were characterized by poor grammar, spelling, and a general lack of organization. Still, the answers were there, if one searched for them sufficiently. "What role should writing ability play in determination of this grade?" wondered Jaime. On the one hand, it seemed irrelevant to knowledge of forensics. On the other hand, wouldn't clear communication play a major role in the job of forensic psychologist? Luckily, perhaps, he was "just" the TA—he'd need to seek the advice of Dr. Kellemen on this one.

Questions to Ponder

1. Jaime followed a number of recommended steps for test development. For each of the following, explain how it assists in the development of a quality test of maximal performance:

   a. Consideration of the various weighting of topics
   b. Consideration of appropriate response formats
   c. Creation of subitems, rather than fewer, larger essay questions
   d. Specification of the number of points assigned to an item
   e. Creation of ideal responses to items prior to test administration

2. Jaime also followed a number of recommended steps to score this essay test. For each of the following, explain how it helps improve reliability:

   a. Recording of student identification numbers rather than names on blue books
   b. Scoring one item at a time for all respondents, before proceeding to the next item
   c. Using holistic scores for an item, rather than using multiple sub-scores for an item

3. Jaime unwittingly included writing ability in his scoring. Is writing ability an appropriate test component for a university class in forensic psychology? Explain.

CASE STUDY 12.2: EASY MONEY?

"It'll be easy money." So said the director of faculty development, when trying to convince Dr. Patricia Lonergan to present a brief overview on test development to a group of interested faculty. She'd earn $200 for delivering a 2-hour lecture. The words still rang in her ears. "It'll be easy money." So then, what could have gone so wrong?

Patricia had taught a graduate-level course in test construction for several years, but she knew it would be a challenge to condense a semester's worth of material into a 2-hour faculty seminar. Recognizing that most faculty were interested primarily in how to improve the development of their own tests, Patricia decided to limit her lecture to a quick overview of the concepts of reliability and validity, followed by a lengthy discussion of item-writing tips, and ending with simple procedures for computing item statistics.

Though she had lectured many times before on these subjects, Patricia realized she was more than a little anxious about presenting before a group of her peers. She had only been out of graduate school for 3 years, and she knew that her colleagues at her university had reputations as great teachers. Perhaps it was for this reason that she decided to bring along a lengthy handout that would help the faculty participants remember her main points. Reflecting back on the experience, Patricia was grateful that she'd brought the handout—otherwise, most of her points would never have been heard at all.

The talk had gotten off to a fairly good start. The conference room in which she gave the presentation was surprisingly full—nearly 20 faculty members were in attendance, most of whom she had never met. These faculty members seemed to follow most of what she reviewed about the importance of developing reliable and valid exams. Most of the participants nodded in agreement to her points, and she noticed that several jotted down a few notes. Somewhat disappointingly, however, no one seemed to contribute his or her own thoughts about these topics.

Then came what Patricia considered the "meat" of her presentation—a discussion of item-writing tips. In referring to the handout, she asked the faculty participants to alternate taking turns reading aloud the recommendations for writing the first type of items she planned on discussing, multiple-choice questions. A few tips were read. Then Patricia noticed that, simultaneously, several faculty members raised their hands to contribute to the discussion. "Great," thought Patricia, "now we'll get some insights into people's own approaches to creation of these items." But no. Instead, that's when things started to go terribly wrong.

Patricia first selected a faculty member from the philosophy department. Clearing his throat, he asked, "Why should we waste our time discussing these so-called objective items. Everyone knows they serve no good academic purpose." A professor across from him concurred, saying, "Unless we abandon our dependence on these types of items, we'll never prepare our students for the real world. Life doesn't provide multiple-choice options." Looking at Patricia, a third faculty member accusatorily asked,

"If you call these constructed-response items 'objective,' what does that say about your opinion of essays? Are you saying they are subjective?" Several other faculty members added their own comments in support of these individuals.

Just when Patricia was trying to formulate a response—any response—several other faculty members began taking issue with the comments of their colleagues. "I'm tired of this rhetoric about the importance of testing through writing," quipped a member of the chemistry department. Actually, now that Patricia thought about it, he hadn't used the word "rhetoric," but something a bit more colorful. At any rate, several other faculty members then chimed in their agreement with the chemist. A few complained about the large size of their classes and the perceived difficulty in using free-response exams. The next few minutes were something of a blur to her. Suffice it to say, however, that a heated discussion erupted, and little of her talk went as planned. Try as she might, her colleagues seemed a lot more interested in airing their opinions about the appropriateness of certain item formats rather than her recommendations for writing better test items.

Returning to her office, Patricia reflected once more on those words that had got her into this in the first place. "It'll be easy money."

Questions to Ponder

1. Do certain item formats prepare students for the "real world" better than others? Why or why not?
2. What are likely some of the arguments put forth by those who reject constructed-response testing in universities? To what degree do you feel these arguments are valid?
3. In a university setting, why might some departments likely champion free-response item formats while other departments prefer constructed-response formats?
4. What role does politics play in the choice of adoption of item formats in a college classroom?
5. What role should practical concerns (such as class size) play in the determination of item formats?
6. Can constructed-response items assess higher-level cognitive objectives?
7. What item formats do you prefer to be tested with? Why?
8. Based on your own personal experience and observations, in what ways does the choice of item format influence student test preparation?

Exercises

EXERCISE 12.1: DETERMINATION OF TEST COMPOSITION

OBJECTIVE: To gain practice developing test specifications for knowledge tests.

In developing knowledge tests, many important decisions must be made to ensure that test objectives are achieved. Although unlimited time and resources might allow for creation of a near-perfect knowledge test, almost all exams must be developed with practical considerations in mind. For each of the tests described below, complete the following:

A. Determine the item format.
    Select one or more item formats that will appropriately measure the test objectives.
B. Determine the number of points per format.
    Assuming the test will be scored out of 100 points, determine the total number of points that will be used for each item format chosen. For example, if you choose to create a test with multiple-choice and essay questions, assign the total number of points to be assessed by multiple-choice format and the total number of points to be assessed by essay format. (*Note:* The total number of points must sum to 100.)
C. Determine the number of items per format and the number of points per item for each format.
    For each item format selected, determine the number of items that will be written. The number of points assigned to each individual item (within a particular format) will be determined by dividing the number of points for this item format by the number of items using this format.
D. Provide justification.
    Explain and justify why you believe your decisions will lead to the development of a practical, reliable, and content-valid exam.

1. Test Description:
    Midterm exam for an entry-level statistics course for the behavioral sciences
    Number of students: 30
    Class period: 60 minutes, plus 40-minute lab
    Students would be expected to:

    • Summarize, display, and interpret sets of data.
    • Understand the logic of statistical analysis, probability, and hypothesis testing.
    • Conduct descriptive statistical analyses and probability problems with the use of a calculator.

2. Test Description:
    Final exam for an introductory psychology course
    Number of students: 200
    Class period: 1.5 hours
    Students would be expected to:

    - Define basic psychological terminology.
    - Comprehend the role of research in the field of psychology.
    - Understand major psychological theories and research findings.
    - Identify leading contributors to the field of psychology.
    - Critically apply the principles and theories of psychology to contemporary daily life.

3. Test Description:
    Final exam in a college-level history course titled History of Western Civilization
    Number of students: 25
    Class period: 3 hours
    Students would be expected to:

    - Demonstrate factual knowledge of the history of Western civilization.
    - Understand how various conditions, social structures, and ideas shape the development of society.
    - Identify the historical roots of current practices and debates.

4. Test Description:
    Final exam for a graduate-level educational measurement course
    Number of students: 12
    Class period: 3 hours
    Students would be expected to:

    - Discuss the purposes, utility, and limitations of various psychometric concepts.
    - Compare and contrast classical test theory with item response theory.
    - Identify and compute appropriate psychometrics for a given testing situation.

EXERCISE 12.2: WRITING ITEMS TO ASSESS KNOWLEDGE

OBJECTIVE: To develop high-quality items to assess knowledge of a specific domain.

Students sometimes complain that items on a test are vague, exceedingly difficult, or even unrelated to the topics presented in the course. Here's your opportunity to see what it's like to create those items yourself.

For this exercise, you will develop a knowledge test that contains a minimum of 25 constructed-response (e.g., matching, multiple-choice, and true-false) items and 3 short-answer essay items. In completing this exercise, heed the following instructions:

A. Carefully define the domain that you are seeking to test.

   • Perhaps consider a course that you have recently taken or a course for which you may have served as a teaching assistant. However, any domain of knowledge that can be clearly defined is acceptable, from knowledge of basic photography to knowledge of plot and character development on the *Buffy the Vampire Slayer* television series.

B. For the constructed-response items, choose a format (or formats) that is appropriate to assess the level of abstraction for the domain you are assessing.

   • Justify your selection of each item format chosen.

C. Attempt to write items that will representatively sample the entire content domain.
D. Avoid all common pitfalls in item writing.
E. Identify the appropriate response to each constructed-response item.

Further Readings

Krathwohl, D.R. (2002). A revision of Bloom's taxonomy: An overview. *Theory into Practice, 41,* 212–218.

Ory, J.C., & Ryan, K.E. (1993). *Tips for improving testing and grading.* Newbury Park, CA: Sage.

Osterlind, S.J. (1998). *Constructing test items: Multiple-choice, constructed-response, performance, and other formats.* Boston: Kluwer.

Rodriguez, M.C. (2002). Choosing an item format. In G. Tindal & T.M. Haladyna (Eds.), *Large-scale assessment programs for all students: Validity, technical adequacy, and implementation* (pp. 213–231). Mahwah, NJ: Erlbaum.

Module 13

Classical Test Theory Item Analysis

I n Module 12, we discussed how best to construct maximal performance (i.e., knowledge) tests. After you put in hours and hours (if not days and days or weeks and weeks) constructing such a test, the day will finally come when you actually have to give the test to someone. Once you administer the test to a designated group of test takers, you will want to evaluate it. That is, you will want to know if the test worked the way you hoped it would and if it is accomplishing what you set out to accomplish. If the test is not up to your high standards, are you going to simply throw out the entire test? We hope not. Instead, you will want to determine which specific items may be causing problems by performing an **item analysis**. You can then eliminate and/or replace the lackluster items or, better yet, revise and reuse the problematic items. Think about it, you just spent a lot of time and painstaking effort writing items to create your test, so you do not want to be throwing out items needlessly or, worse yet, indiscriminately. Thus, the questions become "Which items do I keep unchanged?" "Which do I throw out?" "Which do I try to salvage with some well-placed revisions?" The answers can be found in your favorite classical test theory item analysis statistics.

Item Difficulty

Once you have the data following administration of your test, you will want to look at two key statistics. The first is the *item response distribution*. In particular, you will want to know how difficult the group of test takers found each item to be (i.e., the **item difficulty**). This statistic is typically referred to as the *p value* (for percentage correct), indicating what percentage of test takers answered a given item correctly. Although ideally we strive to obtain an average *p* value of 50%

correct to maximize the variability of the entire test and thus the reliability, in practice, issues such as guessing on multiple-choice items and the political challenge of having more than half the students failing a class usually prohibit such a low average p value. The typical range of p values for educational and employment knowledge tests is somewhere between approximately 50% and 90% correct per item. In particular, we want to have easier items at the beginning of the test in order to allow the test taker to get "warmed up." However, if our p value is too extreme (i.e., near 0%, all test takers answering it incorrectly; or 100%, all answering it correctly), then that item is of little use to us because the lack of variability results in minimal differentiation among test takers. It should be noted, however, that these are assumptions under **classical test theory (CTT)** models. Modern test theory models (i.e., item response theory, IRT) make somewhat different assumptions (see Module 20 for a discussion of the differing assumptions between CTT and IRT).

We must keep in mind, however, that an item is not good or bad in and of itself; rather, the real question is whether it is helping us to differentiate among test takers from a particular population. Therefore, for example, you may have a job knowledge question that all senior computer programmers could easily answer, but only about 70% of entry-level computer programmers could answer. Hence, that item might serve us well in an employment exam to select entry-level computer programmers but would be of little use to us in the promotional exam for senior computer programmer.

Item Discrimination

Our second key item analysis statistic is an index of item discriminability. Analogous to the concept of reliability being a necessary but not sufficient condition for validity, variability in a group of test takers is a necessary but not sufficient condition for **item discrimination**. That is, we want to obtain items that allow us to discriminate, in the psychometric, not legal, sense, among test takers. However, if test takers do not vary in their responses, then the item will be of little use to us. For example, if we are using a test we developed to decide which students should be placed in remedial reading classes versus normal classes versus accelerated classes, then we need to have a test—more specifically, test items—that allow us to differentiate these three levels of students. The more precise our need to discriminate among test takers, the more items of varying difficulty we will need to make those fine distinctions. In addition, each item should predict some internal (e.g., total test score) or, on rare occasion, external (e.g., grade point average, GPA) criterion of interest. These are evaluated with item discrimination statistics.

There are several item discrimination indexes we can compute. One of the earliest and most basic approaches was to examine contrasting groups. Here we break the test takers into the highest-scoring onethird, the middle onethird, and the lowest-scoring onethird of the distribution of scores. Alternatively, some item analysis programs compare the upper and lower 27% of the distribution of test takers. We then examine each item to see what percentage of each extreme group correctly answered a particular item and compute the difference between those two percentages. We hope that the upper group will answer the item correctly more often than will the lower group. Hence, we are looking for positive difference scores. In fact, we are basically doing the same thing we did with item difficulty (i.e., looking at p values), the difference being that we are now examining them within each of these extreme subgroups. Although this approach provides only a crude estimate of item discrimination, it does provide some valuable information. For example, assume we see that the overall p value for an item is about 70%. At first blush, that might appear to be a good item. If we looked at contrasting groups, however, we might notice that only 50% of the top-scoring group answered the item correctly, while 90% of the bottom-scoring group answered the item correctly. Clearly, this is an item we would want to look at more closely, in that those who did worse on the test overall are actually doing better on this particular item. The downside of this procedure is that we end up ignoring a significant portion of test scores in the middle of the test score distribution. Why not use the entire set of test scores? That is exactly what our next set of item analysis statistics does.

More precise and complete indicators of item discrimination are the biserial and point-biserial correlation coefficients, which compute the relation between how the test takers answered a given item (i.e., correct or incorrect) and overall test score. Thus, these indexes use all the available test data to compute an index of discrimination. These indexes are typically referred to as the *item-total correlations*. Ideally, we hope to have a positive and strong (i.e., close to 1.0) item-total correlation. In practice, a positive low-to-moderate (i.e., .20–.50) correlation typically suffices as an indicator of an acceptable item. Of the two factors, direction and strength, direction is the more critical concern. A positive item-total correlation (assuming the items are scored 0 for incorrect and 1 for correct) would indicate that those who correctly answer a particular item also tend to do well on the test overall. This is what we are hoping for. Conversely, a negative item-total correlation would indicate that those test takers who answer a particular item correctly tend to do worse on the test overall. That would not be a good thing. We do not want items that the knowledgeable test takers answer incorrectly, while those lacking in sufficient knowledge of the subject matter answer them correctly. Thus, a negative item-total correlation would be an indication that something is problematic with a given item. This would require going back and examining the item carefully. Maybe this is a "trick" question where one of the nonkeyed alternatives (distracters) is being selected more frequently by the more knowledgeable test takers. Thus, simply replacing that one distracter may be enough of a revision to remedy the problem.

In addition, we need to have acceptable test-taker-to-item ratios in order to obtain stable item-total correlation coefficients. Ideally, we would like to have at least 5–10 test takers per item. However, in many situations (e.g., the classroom), this ratio is rarely achieved. Thus, we have to work with whatever data we have.

We also need to be cautious in computing item-total correlations when the number of items on the test is small (e.g., less than 20). This is because the total test score includes the item we are correlating it with. Thus, the fewer the number of items on the test, the more weight that item will have in the computation of the total test score. Crocker and Algina (1986) provided a correction formula that can be used when the number of items on the test is small. When the number of items is larger, there is no need for such a correction.

You are probably asking yourself what the difference is between the biserial correlation and the point-biserial correlation. The **point-biserial correlation coefficient** is an index of the association (a Pearson product moment correlation coefficient) between the dichotomous item response and the overall test score. Thus, it is an index of how well the item differentiates candidates in terms of the knowledge or trait being measured by the test. The biserial correlation coefficient, however, corrects for the often-artificial dichotomy created by scoring an item as correct or incorrect. That is, all those test takers who answer an item correctly most likely do not have the exact same level of knowledge or trait being measured by the test. Similarly, all those who answer the item incorrectly are not equally deficient in the knowledge or trait. Thus, there is an underlying continuum of knowledge or trait, assumed to be normally distributed, that is measured by each item on the test. However, this continuum is masked to a large extent by dichotomizing the item. The biserial correlation corrects for this artifact. As a result, the biserial correlation is always somewhat larger than the point-biserial correlation. The difference between the two values for any item becomes more extreme as the *p* value becomes more extreme (see Crocker & Algina, 1986, pp. 315–320, for a more detailed discussion of the difference between the two indexes). Linear polytomous (i.e., ordinal) item scoring more directly addresses the problem of artificially dichotomizing item scores by providing partial credit for "incorrect" alternatives based on how "reasonable" the alternative response options are. Linear polytomous scoring, however, requires specialty software that is much harder to come by than CTT item analysis software for dichotomously scored tests (Shultz, 1995).

We may also correlate each item with some external criterion instead of the total test score. For example, early development of biographical data (i.e., biodata) used in employment situations correlated how job applicants performed on a given item with an external criterion of interest. A classic example is that during World War II there was a question on a biographical data form that asked fighter pilot trainees if they had ever built model airplanes that flew as a child. According to lore, this item was the single best predictor of how many "kills" (i.e., enemy planes shot down) a fighter pilot had. However, you might have surmised that if all the items are selected based on their level of association with their respective criteria, then it is unlikely that you will have an internally consistent test. As a result, using item-criterion correlations as the primary basis for constructing tests is less common today (see Case Study 15.1 for another interesting example).

Norm-Referenced Versus Criterion-Referenced Tests

Up to this point, we have assumed that we are interested primarily in **norm-referenced testing**. That is, we want to be able to maximally differentiate among test takers, and we want to determine where test takers fall within a particular normative population. Thus, we want average p values close to .50 in order to maximize the variability and thus increase the reliability of our test. This is the case in many employment situations, for example, where we have more applicants than openings, and we need to narrow down our potential employee pool. Hence, being able to differentiate among test takers is a key concern, and thus we wish to maximize the variability among test takers.

Alternatively, in educational and professional licensing scenarios, the goal is not to maximize variability among test takers. Instead, we are interested in determining if the test takers have achieved a certain level of competence. Thus, content validity of the test is of paramount importance. In these scenarios, item discrimination statistics are of little use. Item difficulty statistics, on the other hand, may be of use in evaluating test items. However, the goal in using item difficulty statistics is not to maximize variance among test takers. Instead, the primary objective is to assess if the test takers have achieved a given level of competence (as in a professional licensing exam) and/or whether the primary objectives of an instructional process were successfully conveyed (i.e., the effectiveness of classroom instruction). However, a problem is that we may not know why a p value is low. It could be that the instructor did not cover the educational objective assessed by a given item, or it may be that the students were not paying attention when it was covered or the objective was confused with another concept or the item itself is technically flawed. Thus, more detective work is needed to assess *why* a given item is not performing as expected when we are interested in **criterion-referenced testing** as opposed to norm-referenced testing.

This additional detective work might include examining the difference between p values for items given before (pretest) and after (posttest) instruction. In addition, we might enlist subject matter experts to review our items to see if the troublesome items are indeed assessing our objective and doing so appropriately. We may also conduct focus groups with some test takers after they take the test to determine why they selected the responses they did. Doing so may allow for immediate remedial instruction or, at the very least, improve future instruction and evaluation. Also, more recently, many instructors have begun to use "real-time" assessment during instruction where they present questions during a class session and students respond using educational technology such as individual response pads (i.e., clickers). Thus, even in very large classroom settings (100 students or more), students can provide the instructor with instant feedback on whether the material just covered is being comprehended by a majority of students or whether additional class time should be spent explaining and discussing the key concepts. Such formative assessment (i.e., obtaining real-time responses during instruction that provides feedback to adjust ongoing learning and instruction to improve student achievement), once restricted to small classrooms, can now be carried out even in large lecture halls with the help of increasingly sophisticated educational technology!

Overall Test Statistics

In addition to analyzing each individual test item, test developers and users need to evaluate the overall test statistics as well. For example, what is the average p value across the entire test? How about the average item-total correlation? What is the alpha reliability of the test? The variability? The minimum and maximum values? The standard error of measurement? The shape (i.e., skewness and kurtosis) of the distribution of exam scores? Such statistics can prove valuable in making revisions to the test. While they may not help in revising specific items, they will provide hints on where to focus your revision efforts. For example, if the average p value on a classroom test is only 55% correct, you will want to determine if revising particularly attractive item distracter alternatives might make them less attractive and thus increase the average p value on the test. Alternatively, you may notice that the test is highly negatively skewed and leptokurtic (i.e., very peaked). That is, test takers are concentrated at the upper end of the score distribution, with only a few doing poorly. Thus, you may want to look at the distracters that no one is choosing for the high p-value items and make those distracters somewhat more attractive in order to lower the average p value, thus reducing the skewness of the test.

A Step-by-Step Example of an Item Analysis

Table 13.1 displays eight items taken from a test recently administered to students in an undergraduate tests and measurements class. There were actually 74 items on the test, and 35 students took the test. The values presented in Table 13.2 are based on all 74 items and 35 students, even though only eight items are displayed in the table. Remember we stated earlier that ideally we would want 5–10 test takers per item. In this case, we have a little more than two items per test taker. Obviously, the ratio of items to students leaves a lot to be desired. Thus, we must be cautious not to read too much into the statistics we obtained from our CTT item analysis. It would be foolish, however, to simply ignore valuable test item analysis statistics because we failed to reach some ideal ratio of test takers to items. Basically, we have to work with whatever we have. Welcome to the reality of classroom testing.

   Table 13.2 displays the item analysis statistics generated from a commercially available item analysis program (ITEMAN for Windows, Version 3.5, Assessment Systems Corp.). The ITEMAN program provides several important pieces of item analysis information. In the first column is the "sequence number." This number matches the number of the corresponding question in Table 13.1. In the second

Table 13.1   Example of Undergraduate Tests and Measurements Exam Questions

---

1. Testing is to assessment as _____ is to _____.

   A. blood test:physical exam   C. mechanic:automobile

   B. blood test:X-ray   D. selection:placement

2. In everyday practice, responsibility for appropriate test administration, scoring, and interpretation lies with

   A. test users.   C. elected representatives.

   B. test developers.   D. test publishers.

3. Which of the following best describes norms?

   A. They give meaning to a behavior sample.

   B. They provide a parallel form for comparison.

   C. They indicate whether a test is reliable.

   D. They tell whether a distribution of scores is normally distributed.

4. Which is true of a psychologist who is relying on a single test score to make an important decision about an individual? The psychologist is

   A. acting responsibly if the test is reliable and valid for the purpose for which it is being used.

   B. violating a basic guideline in psychological assessment.

   C. utilizing a case-study approach to assessment.

   D. acting in a perfectly legal and ethical way.

5. Of the following, which best characterizes what "validity" refers to?

   A. How a test is used   C. How a scale is scaled

   B. How a test is scored   D. How a test is normed

6. Much of 19th-century psychological measurement focused on

   A. intelligence.   C. sensory abilities.

   B. ethics and values.   D. personality traits.

7. Which of the following is the most important reason why translating a test into another language is not recommended?

   A. It can be extremely costly.

   B. It can be extremely time consuming.

   C. Meanings and difficulty levels of the items may change.

   D. Precise translation is never possible.

8. Test-retest reliability estimates would be least appropriate for

   A. intelligence tests.

   B. tests that measure moment-to-moment mood.

   C. academic achievement tests on topics such as ancient history.

   D. tests that measure art aptitude.

Table 13.2 Item Analysis Results for Example Tests and Measurements Questions

		Item Statistics					Alternative Statistics			
								Endorsing		
Seq. No.	Scale Item	Prop. Correct	Disc. Index	Point Biser.	Alt.	Prop. Total	Low	High	Point Biser.	Key
1	0–1	.51	.48	.38	A	.51	.22	.70	.38	*
					B	.03	.00	.00	−.08	
					C	.17	.22	.00	−.26	
					D	.29	.56	.30	−.17	
					Other	.00	.00	.00		
2	0–3	.86	.44	.52	A	.86	.56	1.00	.52	*
					B	.14	.44	.00	−.52	
					C	.00	.00	.00		
					D	.00	.00	.00		
					Other	.00	.00	.00		
3	0–4	.14	−.12	.00	A	.14	.22	.10	.00	*
	CHECK THE KEY				B	.80	.67	.90	.09	?
	A was specified, but B works better				C	.03	.00	.00	.05	
					D	.03	.11	.00	−.26	
					Other	.00	.00	.00		
4	0–9	.54	.47	.36	A	.46	.67	.20	−.36	
					B	.54	.33	.80	.36	*
					C	.00	.00	.00		
					D	.00	.00	.00		
					Other	.00	.00	.00		
5	0–11	.71	.44	.42	A	.71	.56	1.00	.42	*
					B	.06	.00	.00	−.08	
					C	.11	.33	.00	−.37	
					D	.11	.11	.00	−.17	
					Other	.00	.00	.00		
6	0–13	.23	.50	.56	A	.49	.78	.40	−.31	
					B	.03	.11	.00	−.20	
					C	.23	.00	.50	.56	*
					D	.26	.11	.10	−.11	
					Other	.00	.00	.00		

Table 13.2   (*Continued*)

Seq. No.	Scale Item	Prop. Correct	Disc. Index	Point Biser.	Alt.	Prop. Total	Low	High	Point Biser.	Key
		Item Statistics					*Alternative Statistics*			
							Endorsing			
7	0–22	.69	−.09	−.11	A	.00	.00	.00		
	CHECK THE KEY				B	.00	.00	.00		
					C	.69	.89	.80	−.11	*
	C was specified, but D works better				D	.31	.11	.20	.11	?
					Other	.00	.00	.00		
8	0–48	.89	.33	.44	A	.06	.22	.00	−.43	
					B	.89	.67	1.00	.44	*
					C	.03	.00	.00	−.08	
					D	.03	.11	.00	-.18	
					Other	.00	.00	.00		

Test statistics:	
Number of items	74
Number of examinees	35
Mean	39.74
Variance	72.48
Standard deviation	8.51
Skew	.27
Kurtosis	−.34
Minimum	24.00
Maximum	59.00
Median	40.00
Alpha	.81
SEM	3.75
Mean p	.54
Mean item-total	.26
Mean biserial	.35
Max score (low)	34
N (low group)	9
Min score (high)	44
N (high group)	10

column is the "scale-item" number. This feature allows you to look at subtests within the overall test. Here we did not have any subtests, so the first number for all items is zero. The number after the dash is the number of the question from the original test. For example, the fifth question listed here was actually question 11 on the complete 74-item version of the test.

The next three columns provide the item analysis statistics for the keyed response. Column 3 displays the item difficulty statistic of proportion correct. For example, for sequence item 1, just over half the students answered this item correctly, while 54% answered question 4 correctly. While these p values are ideal from a variability standpoint, they are at the lower end of the acceptable range for a classroom test, for two reasons. First, these items are from a four-option multiple-choice test, so by answering randomly, the student has a 25% probability of getting the item correct just by chance. Therefore, we would expect p values even for ideal items to be somewhat higher than 50%. Second, this is more of a criterion-referenced test than a norm-referenced test. Therefore, we would expect (hope) that the typical p value would be higher than 50%, indicating that a larger portion of the students have learned the material.

Items 2, 5, 7, and 8 have p values between .69 and .89. These are much more typical of the level of difficulty instructors should strive for in creating classroom tests. However, we still need to examine the item discrimination indexes before we can put our stamp of approval on these items. At the other end of the difficulty continuum, only 14% of students answered question 3 correctly, while only 23% answered question 6 correctly. Both of these items need to be examined carefully to determine how they may be revised or edited to make them easier. Again, because the focus is more on criterion-referenced than norm-referenced standards, we may also investigate whether the item was covered in class or somehow caused confusion among the students. Thus, based on the item difficulty statistics, at least initially, it appears that items 2, 5, 7, and 8 are acceptable. Items 1 and 4 are somewhat low but may serve to balance out some other easier items (with 90% plus p values) on the test. Items 3 and 6 will command the bulk of our attention as they have extremely low p values.

Column 4 displays the discrimination index: Disc. Index = $P_{High} - P_{Low}$, where P_{High} is the percentage of students in the highest 27% of the score distribution who answered the item correctly, while P_{Low} is the percentage of students in the lowest 27% of the score distribution who answered the item correctly. Hence, the discrimination index values in Table 13.2 represent the difference in p values for these two groups. As noted earlier, we want a discrimination index that is moderate to large and positive. All but items 3 and 7 appear to meet these criteria. Hence, we would want to look at items 3 and 7 more closely. In fact, note that the ITEMAN program prints a message to "CHECK THE KEY __ was specified, but __ works better," indicating that an alternative option has a higher discrimination index, point-biserial value, or both than the keyed option. Remember that a disadvantage of the discrimination index is that it ignores the middle 46% of the distribution of test scores. Thus, we should also examine column 5, which displays the point-biserial correlation coefficient. Again, we are seeking moderate to large, as well as positive, point-biserial correlation coefficients. In this case, the point-biserial correlation appears to confirm the results of the discrimination index. That is, items 3 and 7 should be examined more closely, given that the former has a point-biserial correlation coefficient of zero and the latter is negative. Thus, the item difficulty statistics lead us to focus on items 3 and 6, whereas the item discrimination indexes suggest we focus on items 3 and 7. In order to do so, we must next look at the response alternative statistics in columns 7 through 10.

First, let us turn our attention to the most offending question, item 3. It has an extremely low p value (.14) and a small negative discrimination index. Inspecting column 7, we see that most individuals (80%) chose option B (option A was the keyed response). Looking at Table 13.1, item 3 dealt with the issue of norms. Thinking back as the instructor, we might remember that we talked about z scores and norms on the same day. As a result, students may have assumed that, similar to z scores, norms "provide a parallel form for comparison." Is this question salvageable? Possibly, by simply replacing option B with another option—for example, "They provide evidence of content validity,"—fewer individuals will choose option B in favor of the keyed response, option A.

The second troublesome item is item 6. The p value for item 6 was very low (.23); however, the two discrimination indexes are quite favorable. What is going on here? It appears that option A (which 49% of students chose) was too attractive. Looking at Table 13.1, we see that this item dealt with the topic of historical issues in measurement. We may find out from asking students afterward that they chose option A because many of them read the question too quickly, and when they read "19th century," they thought 1900s instead of 1800s. Therefore, replacing the "19th century" with "1800s" in the stem of the question may well be all that is needed to raise the p value for this item.

The third item of concern is item 7. Although almost 70% of the students answered this item correctly, those students actually did worse on the test overall (i.e., they had a negative item-total correlation). Looking at the alternative statistics in Table 13.2, we see that no students chose alternative A or B. The keyed answer was option C, which 69% chose, while 31% selected option D. In addition, those who did choose option D also did better on the test overall. Looking at Table 13.1, we see that this item dealt with translating a test into another language. It may have been that the stem uses the term "translating" and option D uses "translation." Hence, changing option D to something such as "It is difficult to accommodate different dialects in other languages" may make it less attractive to the high scorers. In addition, you would want to make options A and B at least a little more attractive. Removing the term "extremely" from options A and B would make them somewhat more attractive. A student who is "test-wise" will know that terms such as "extremely" are more likely to be used in distracters than in keyed alternatives.

Finally, it was noted earlier that it is wise to look at not only individual item statistics but also statistics for the entire test. Several informative statistics were obtained for this 74-item test, and they can be found at the end of Table 13.2. First, the average p value was .54. That is probably too low a figure for a classroom examination. However, from a practical standpoint, we would rather have a test that is a little too hard than too easy. It would be difficult to justify taking points away from the test takers under the rationale that the test was too easy, but few test takers will complain about a hard test having bonus points added. The mean point-biserial correlation of .26, while a little low, is positive. The alpha reliability for the test was .81. While this is clearly an acceptable level of reliability, this may be due to simply having 74 items on the test. It is unlikely that the 74 items represent a single trait or dimension. The distribution of test scores was also positively skewed (skew = .27) and somewhat flat (i.e., platykurtic, kurtosis = −0.35). Most classroom tests tend to have a slight negative skew or close-to-normal distribution. Thus, the positive skew in this sample is yet another indication that the test is probably too hard and the items with lower p values are in need of revision.

Concluding Comments

We need to examine both item difficulty and item discrimination indexes to determine whether we should keep an item as is, revise it, or throw it out. In addition, examining the overall test statistics will provide guidance on which items to focus our efforts. In order to have confidence in our statistics, we need to have adequate sample sizes, both in terms of absolute numbers (e.g., more than 25 respondents) and in terms of respondent-to-item ratios (ideally at least 5–10 respondents per item). In most instances, at least minor revisions will be required to the stem, the alternative responses, or both. For example, your item difficulty index might be .70, and your item discrimination index .50. Both would indicate a useful item. However, inspection of the item analysis might indicate that none of the test takers chose option B. Hence, you would want to revise or replace option B to make it more attractive, especially to those with little knowledge of the concept being examined. Thus, every attempt should be made to revise an item before it is tossed out. In the end, you should have very few instances where an entire item needs to be thrown out. Instead, a few well-placed revisions (sometimes a single word change) can go a long way in improving the quality and usefulness of future uses of the revised items.

Best Practices

1. Be sure to interpret item difficulty, item discrimination, and overall test statistics based on the context of the testing situation (i.e., norm referenced vs. criterion referenced).
2. Increasingly, best practices in educational environments include "real-time" formative assessment, such as the use of student response pads (i.e., clickers) in order to improve both instruction and student learning, even in large classroom settings that previously made formative assessment impractical.
3. Every attempt should be made to revise an item before you summarily delete it because of poor item analysis statistics.

4. Polytomous scoring of test items (i.e., weighting each response rather than simply dichotomizing responses as 1 = correct and 0 = incorrect) provides much more information from each item and thus results in needing fewer items on the test.

Practical Questions

1. What is the difference between an item difficulty index and an item discrimination index?
2. How do you know whether to calculate the discrimination index (which contrasts extreme groups), the biserial correlation, or the point-biserial correlation coefficient as your item discrimination statistic?
3. How do you decide which external criterion to use when computing an item-criterion index?
4. Is there ever a time when a .25 p value is good? How about a 1.00 p value?
5. Will your criteria for evaluating your item difficulty and discrimination indexes change if a test is norm referenced versus criterion referenced?
6. Will your criteria for evaluating your item difficulty and discrimination indexes change as the format of the item changes (e.g., true-false; three-, four-, or five-option multiple choice; Likert scaling)?
7. Oftentimes in a classroom environment, you might have more students (respondents) than you have items. Does this pose a problem for interpreting your item analysis statistics?
8. What corrections, if any, might you make to items 1, 2, 4, 5, and 8 based on the information provided in Table 13.2?

Case Studies

CASE STUDY 13.1: ITEM ANALYSIS IN AN APPLIED SETTING

Andrew, a third-year graduate student, was enrolled in a PhD program in quantitative psychology. He had recently obtained a highly competitive summer internship with a Fortune 500 company in its employment testing section. As one of his first assignments, his new supervisor asked Andrew to review the item analysis statistics for a short 25-item timed test of **general mental ability (GMA)** that the company administers to thousands of job candidates every year. Test scoring is conducted and processed within four regional centers (East, South, West, and Midwest). Therefore, before combining all the regions, Andrew decided to first examine the item statistics within each region by each of five broad job classifications (i.e., administrative/professional, clerical, skilled craft, semiskilled, and unskilled/laborer).

After completing and reviewing the initial set of item analyses, Andrew noticed an interesting pattern. The first 10 items had very good item analysis statistics for the clerical and semiskilled positions, but not very good statistics for the other job classifications. In particular, he noticed that an extremely high percentage (more than 98%) of the administrative/professional candidates and 88% of the skilled craft candidates answered the first 10 questions correctly, whereas very few (less than 10%) of the unskilled/laborer job candidates answered the first 10 questions correctly. As a result, the item discrimination indexes for these job classes were near zero. For items 11–19, the item analysis statistics were still favorable for the administrative/professional candidates and unskilled/laborer candidates but were much more favorable for the skilled craft candidates. Finally, for items 20–25, the item analysis statistics were favorable for the administrative/professional candidates, but very few of the other candidates were even able to attempt these items. As a result, their p values were extremely low, and their item discrimination indexes were near zero. To top it all off, this pattern seemed to hold for three of the four regions, but the Midwestern region seemed to be getting very different results. In particular, the unskilled and semiskilled job candidates appeared to be doing significantly better on the early items than did their counterparts in other regions of the country. Somewhat perplexed, it seemed time for Andrew to discuss things with his new supervisor.

Questions to Ponder

1. What might explain the pattern of results that Andrew observed for the different job classifications?
2. Given the differing results by job classification, should the same test still be used for all the job classifications? What key issues should Andrew consider?
3. What might be unique about the unskilled and semiskilled job candidates in the Midwest as compared to their counterparts in the West, South, and East?
4. What do you think would have happened if Andrew had not separated the data by job classification and region?
5. Andrew focused primarily on the difficulty index. What other item-level statistics should he compute? What unique information would they provide?

CASE STUDY 13.2: ITEM ANALYSIS FOR AN OUTCOMES ASSESSMENT MEASURE

Linda, a second-year master's student, had agreed to help out the department of psychology with its outcomes assessment process. In exchange for her work on the project, the department chair agreed to let Linda use some of the data collected for the outcomes assessment project for her master's thesis. Linda had decided to investigate whether students' attitudes toward statistics were related to performance on a comprehensive statistics exam. Therefore, Linda needed to construct a 100-item statistical knowledge test. She gathered old exams, study guides, and items from professors in the department who taught undergraduate and graduate statistics classes.

Table 13.3   Item Analysis Results for the First 5 Items of a 100-Item Statistics Knowledge Test

	Item Statistics				Alternative Statistics			
Quest. No.	Prop. Correct	Biser.	Point Biser.	Alt.	Prop. Endorsing	Biser.	PointBiser.	Key
1	.381	.238	.187	A	.238	−.106	−.077	
				B	.143	−.227	−.146	
				C	.381	.238	.187	*
				D	.238	−.022	−.016	
2	.667	.353	.272	A	.238	−.615	−.447	
				B	.000	.000	.000	
				C	.095	.366	.211	
				D	.667	.353	.272	*
3	.143	.238	.153	A	.810	−.392	−.271	
				B	.143	.238	.153	*
				C	.048	.533	.248	
				D	.000	.000	.000	
4	.857	.614	.396	A	.857	.614	.396	*
				B	.095	−.770	−.444	
				C	.048	−.084	−.039	
				D	.000	.000	.000	
5	1.000	.000	.000	A	.000	.000	.000	
				B	1.000	.000	.000	*
				C	.000	.000	.000	
				D	.000	.000	.000	

She went through piles of statistics books, study guides, and test banks of test items to draft items for the test. Some professors had even agreed to write items for her.

After several months of pulling together items and going through multiple revisions from the department outcomes assessment committee, Linda was finally ready to pilot test her assessment device. She was able to get 21 current graduate students in the program to take her 100-item statistics knowledge test. Some of the items seemed to be working for her, whereas others clearly needed revision. Table 13.3 displays the item analysis results for the first five items from her assessment device. Answer the questions that follow, based on the item analysis results reported in Table 13.3.

Questions to Ponder

1. How did students seem to do based on the five items presented in Table 13.3?
2. Based only on the information presented in Table 13.3, what revisions should Linda make to each item?
3. Do you have a concern that Linda had 100 items but only 21 subjects? What problems might this cause in interpreting her item analysis results?
4. Why do you think .000s are printed for all the entries in item 5, as well as for some options in the other items?
5. Which item would you say is the "best" item? Why?
6. Are there any items that Linda should simply throw out (i.e., they are just not worth spending the time revising)?
7. What additional information would be helpful in evaluating the test items?
8. Is there a problem with using graduate students during the pilot-testing phase if the test will eventually be used as an outcomes assessment device for undergraduates?

꒓ ꒐ ꒒

Exercises

EXERCISE 13.1: ITEM ANALYSIS OF AN
ORGANIZATIONAL BEHAVIOR TEST

OBJECTIVE: To practice evaluating items using item analysis statistics.

Selected items (13 to be exact) from a 50-item multiple-choice test given to an undergraduate organizational behavior class are presented in Table 13.4. Look through the test to get a sense of the item types and content and then proceed to the actual assignment outlined below. (*Note:* You will need to have access to the Internet to complete this assignment.)

Assignment

Part 1—Working alone or in small teams, perform an item analysis of the data at the end of Table 13.4. You will do this by going to http://www.hr-software.net/cgi/ ItemAnalysis.cgi. Once at the website, enter the data at the end of Table 13.4 in the boxes as appropriate and select "compute" (i.e., run the program). The results will come up on the screen. You should have access to a printer at this point because you cannot "save" the output (at least as far as we can tell). Once the output is printed, you are ready for Part 2 (the fun stuff).

Part 2—Working alone, interpret the results of your item analysis. That is, go through each item and see what the statistics (e.g., proportion correct, biserial correlations, and point-biserial correlations) look like for each item and each response option for each item. Discuss if the item is "okay" (i.e., no recommended changes) or if changes are needed to improve the item. As you might guess, there should be very few (if any) questions that are without room for improvement. Perhaps a single option needs to be reworded or the stem needs wording changes. Perhaps the item as a whole is just too complex for an undergraduate class and should be thrown out. However, this option should be extremely rare, given how difficult it is to come up with sufficient questions. Therefore, what you need to do is (1) discuss what should be done to improve the item/question (e.g., reword the stem, reword a distracter) and (2) discuss why you think that should be done,

Table 13.4   Questions and Data for Exercise 13.1

Organizational Behavior Questions

General Instructions: There are two parts to Exam I. In part I, there are 50 multiple-choice questions worth 1 point each (50 points, part I). In part II, you will complete 5 of 6 short-answer essay questions worth 5 points each (25 points, part II). Therefore, work at a steady pace and do not spend too much time on any given question.

Multiple-Choice Instructions: Read each question carefully. Mark your answers on the answer sheet provided.

Name: _____ Date: _____

1. Joe doesn't like his job very much but does it quite well. By contrast, Sam likes his job a great deal but doesn't do it very well. To help explain the underlying reasons why this might occur at the individual level of analysis, an OB scientist would be most likely to conduct research that

   A. attempts to prove Theory X and disprove Theory Y.

   *B. measures Joe and Sam's individual behavior and attitudes.

   C. examines the interpersonal dynamics between Joe and Sam.

   D. focuses on the structure of the organization within which Joe and Sam work.

(Continued)

Table 13.4   (*Continued*)

---

2. You are working as an assistant to an OB scientist on a research project. She is trying to find out when people are motivated by pay and when they are motivated by recognition. By examining the connection between motivation and incentives, she appears to be using which one of the following approaches in her research?

  A. the open-systems approach

  B. the human resources approach

  C. the Hawthorne approach

 *D. the contingency approach

3. A proponent of scientific management is most likely to be interested in

  A. treating people in a humane way.

  B. using the contingency approach.

  C. conceiving of people using an open-systems perspective.

 *D. learning ways to improve productivity on the job.

4. The Hawthorne studies were important because they

  A. provided support for scientific management.

  B. demonstrated that human behavior in organizational settings is highly predictable.

 *C. called attention to the complex factors that influence behavior in organizational settings.

  D. established that the study of human behavior was not particularly relevant in organizational settings.

(9) 5. Suppose an OB scientist wants to learn how the employees of a certain company responded to a massive downsizing plan that was recently implemented. To find out, he or she conducts careful interviews with many of the different people involved and then summarizes the results in a narrative account describing all the details. This scientist appears to be using

  A. participant observation.

 *B. the case method.

  C. survey research.

  D. the experimental method.

(10) 6. Once we form a favorable impression of someone, we tend to see that person in favorable terms. This is known as

  A. the similar-to-me effect.

  B. the attribution effect.

 *C. the halo effect.

  D. a stereotype.

(14) 7. Suppose an army major inspects his troops' barracks on the average of once a month, although at no predetermined times. The major could be said to be using a _____ schedule of reinforcement.

  A. fixed ratio

(*Continued*)

    *B. variable interval

    C. fixed interval

    D. variable ratio

(22) 8. Personality exerts strong influences on behavior in

    A. personal life more than in organizations.

    B. organizations more than in personal life.

    C. situations in which external forces encourage certain actions.

    *D. situations where external pressures to behave a certain way are not strong.

(25) 9. Compared to Maslow's need hierarchy theory, Alderfer's ERG theory

    *A. is less restrictive.

    B. is more poorly supported by existing research.

    C. proposes a higher number of needs.

    D. all of the above

(27) 10. To help strengthen employee commitment to goals, an organization should

    A. provide feedback about performance.

    B. set very difficult goals.

    *C. involve employees in the goal-setting process.

    D. provide monetary incentives along with specific goals.

(33) 11. Which of the following is not a technique typically used to assess people's satisfaction with their jobs?

    A. critical incidents

    B. interviews

    C. questionnaires

    *D. participant observation

(34) 12. According to Herzberg's two-factor motivator-hygiene theory, which of the following factors is most likely to be associated with job satisfaction?

    A. high pay

    B. pleasant working conditions

    *C. opportunities for promotion

    D. social relations with coworkers

(45) 13. We see a co-worker totally screw up a major project. If we perceive that this is an unusual (unstable) behavior and that this event was due to external pressures (an external locus of control), we are likely to attribute our colleague's actions to

    *A. bad luck.

    B. a difficult task.

    C. a lack of effort.

    D. a lack of ability

(*Continued*)

Table 13.4   (*Continued*)

ANSWER KEY: 2443232413431
NUMBER OF ITEMS:13
RESPONSES OFFSET BY: 3
NUMBER OF ALTERNATIVES: 4444444444444
RESPONSES:
01 2413334313144
02 4443212333411
03 2443334313144
04 4143344314123
05 2443331413431
06 2223234431131
07 4213133413422
08 4243332411122
09 2343233211133
10 2443332413432
11 2443234413431
12 2243322313432

Note: Column 3 should be left blank for all subjects. Once the data are entered at the website, go to the top left of the page and click on "compute." The resulting data output should look similar to that provided in the module overview.

based on the information from the item analysis and your general understanding of good item writing and editing principles discussed in Module 12. Please annotate your item analysis printout directly and hand it in with your critique of the test (one to two pages).

EXERCISE 13.2: ITEM ANALYSIS OF A TESTS AND MEASUREMENTS CLASS EXAMINATION

OBJECTIVE: To re-create the item analysis results found in the step-by-step example in the module overview.

Working alone or in small teams, perform an item analysis of the data at the end of Table 13.5. The data from Table 13.5 are also available at the book's website http://www.routledge.com/9780415644792 or from your instructor, allowing you

Table 13.5 Data for Step-by-Step Example

Key AAAAAABCBCAACCBDCDDBCCBBCAABBBDBCCBAACCBACABBABDBCDBBBBCBCAABAAAACBADCCBDC

Number of items: 74

Items off set by: 03

No. of Alts 444444444444444444444444444444444444444444444444444444444444444444444444

01 DABBCAADADADAAACBAADDDACABABBBDBBCDAAAACDACACADADBBCCCBBAAABAAABCAACDCAABBDD

02 CAAAAABDACADDDBACBDCBCAEBAAACBADBCDADACDBDAADBCBDACDABAACABAABDAACCDABBBBD

03 CDABAAACBCAAACCDCDDCBDDBADABABBBDDAADBAACBCCABBBBDCDBBDCDCCAABBBACBCABBBDD

04 DDAAABBDACAAACBACDCAADDCDADABBBBDBAAABBCABAAAACADBDADDABDBCBAADBACDADADABDDD

05 A - AAAACBDDACCBACDCDACDDACAADDDDADABBCABADABBBDACADABBDDAAABADACDDACCBDD

06 ADABBABDBBCACACBACDCDADBDDADABABDDDCAAACDABAACBDBADCDBBBCCBAABBAACCDBCCDDD

07 ADABAAAACBDAADCBBCDDDACCBBCAABBAADDABABBCCCCAABBBAAADADBBBCBCAABDDACBDBDBBDD

08 BCABBABAACBCDACCCDDBCBDCCCABBCBBABBBDBCBAAAACBACABBABACCABBCACDAAABBAACCDDACDCD

09 ADABACADACABDCBACDCAACBDBCABBBBDBCBAAAACBACABBABACCABBCACDAAABBAACCDDACDCD

10 CAABCADCBDCAACDDCDDCACDCDDBAAAADDBAAABACABCCADBADAAADCABACBAAADBAAACDCBCCACD

11 AAABAADCACABCCCBCCCBDBBCCABBCBBDCAADCCBACADBABDADCBBDBBDDAADBAABBACCBDDC

12 CAABAAABADABDABABBBDBCDDCAABBBADACBBACABDAABBBCDACDBAAACDAAADBAACDBDCBDDC

13 ADABBABDACDAADBCBDCDBDBDBCAABCCDBAAACBACBABACBDBDCCAABABABDADBCAACACDBBDDD

14 AAABACBDADAAACCCCDAABCBBCAAABBBDBCADDACCBACBBBDBDBABDBADBAABAAAACBADABBCD

15 ACBBABDDACCAACBABDCDBCBDBDBDAABAADBADAAADCADBCCACDAADBDBCCBADBADDCBABDDCBBBDA

16 CCABAABCBDBAACCDCDCCBDCBDDAABBBDCADACDACCADCCBAADDBCBADDAADCAACACDCBDDD

17 ADABABBCBCACACBACBCCBCABCDDAAABCACBDAACBDBAABDBBBCACBAAABBACCAACBADD

18 DDAAAADDADCAACBACADDACBDDABBABACDADABACDDBAAABCBADBDBABCBADBCCBADBCABBBDCBBBDD

19 DAABBABDBBCADCBACDDDADDDCAABABDCDCDBACDCACACBDBDACDDBAACBBAACBACBAAABDDD

(*Continued*)

Table 13.5   (*Continued*)

20	ABABAABDBAAACCBDCDCCBCABCADABBBBCADAACABAAABBABDACDBBBBCBAADBDBACBACBBBDD
21	ACBBAABAACACDBBACDDBCCDDCAABBCBAAADDCDBADADBDDADBDDCBBAABCAACBCACBABC
22	ACABACADBCAADCBBCDDDBCDDCAAAABCDDACACADCBBAADBDBDDABBABCBBAAABDBACBCDCBDDD
23	DAABAABCBCAAAABDCDBDCDCAAABCDBCDABACDDCAABBBDDCDBBBACBBAABABDCBCDABBDD
24	AAABACDCACDACCBACDDDBDDDBAABBAADDDAAACDBCAADBDBDDBABCABADBAAACDDCCCDDD
25	DCABAAADBCAAACBBDCDACDDCCAAABDDBADBDACDBACACBDBDDCBBBDACCBAABAAACDADCCDDD
26	DABDAADDADDBDABACDDACCCADBBDCBBBAADADCAAACADAABDCCDBCAADABCDAABBBDADCDBCD
27	DAABBABABCAAACBACACDCBDCDDDBABABCDADADACCBCDADBDBACDDCABCDBAABDBACDDDCBDDD
28	DAAAAABCBCAACCBDCDBDADCDCCAABBBBCCBAACCAADABBABDACBBBBCBBAABAAACBADCBADD
29	AAACACACBDAAABBACDCCACDBCAAABDBDBDAADACCAAAABBCBDACBBBAACBCADBCBDDCBDDD
30	AAABAAAABDAACCBACDCDACDBCCABACDBCCABACDBCDABACDBCBCBCAABBAACBBBCCDDD
31	AAABAABABCAAACBACBDDACDBBCAABBBDBACBAACABDCADBABABCDBBBBCDAAABBAACBADCCDDD
32	AAABAAADBCAACCBBCADDBCCDDCAABBBADCAABACCBDDABBABDACDBBBBDCDCBABCAACADDABDDD
33	CDBBACADBCAAADBADADCBCCDABBACACDBDCBACDCCBDDACCCACBDBABAAADDADBDBBBCDACBBBD
34	DDABAABAADAABBCCCDDDACDADDBAACDBAACABDCDAABACCBAADDBBBCABADCDAACCDDABDDC
35	AAABAADAADAACCCDCDCDDBAABBBCDBCCBAACCBACABBCBDBCBDBBDBCDAAABABACBBBCDDC

Note: Column 3 should be left blank for all subjects. Once the data is entered at the website, go to the top left of the page and click on "compute." The resulting data output should look similar to that provided in the module overview.

to cut and paste the data into the appropriate box at http://www.hr-software.net/cgi/ItemAnalysis.cgi. Once at the website, enter (or cut and paste) the data in Table 13.5 in the boxes as appropriate and select "compute" (i.e., run the program). The results will come up on the screen. Next, see if you get the same results as were presented in Table 13.2.

Further Readings

Crocker, L.M., & Algina, J. (1986). *Introduction to classical and modern test theory* (pp. 311–338). Belmont, CA: Wadsworth.

Haladyna, T.M. (1999). *Developing and validating multiple-choice test items* (2nd ed.). Mahwah, NJ: Erlbaum.

Hogan, T.P. (2013). *Psychological testing: A practical introduction* (3rd ed.). Hoboken, NJ: Wiley.

Johnson, R.L., Penny, J.A., & Gordon, B. (2009). *Assessing performance: Designing, scoring, and validating performance tests.* New York: The Guildford Press.

Module 14

Scoring Tests

U p to this point in the book, we have focused on proper techniques for developing and evaluating tests. We have talked about establishing evidence for the reliability and validity of our tests. We have even talked about performing item analyses to evaluate individual items on a test. Essentially, we have been recommending that you perform certain analyses to make sure you would have confidence in any decisions that resulted from use of the test. At some point, however, you will have to do something with the test. That is, as noted in Module 1, you are most likely administering the test to help you make an important decision. As a result, you will have to score the test and most likely set a cutoff or pass point for the test to decide who "passes" and who "fails." Subsequently, we present several of the more common methods for scoring tests, thus allowing us to actually use our test data to help us make important, even life-altering, psychometrically sound decisions with confidence.

Berk (1986) presented a self-described "consumer's guide" to setting pass points on criterion-referenced tests. He presented a continuum from purely judgmental procedures to purely empirical procedures. At the purely judgmental end of the continuum are procedures that rely heavily on the use of opinions from subject matter experts (SMEs) such as the Angoff, Ebel, and Nedelsky methods of setting passing scores. These procedures are often used in setting **cutoff scores** for employment knowledge testing as well as professional licensing exams where those scoring above the cutoff score qualify for the job or appropriate license.

Judgmental Methods

The most common judgmental method of setting passing scores is the Angoff method. The Angoff method of setting passing scores asks SMEs to determine the probability (0%–100%) of a "minimally competent person" (MCP) answering a given multiple-choice item correctly. These probabilities are averaged across SMEs for each item and then summed across all items to determine the final cut-off score. For example, on a five-item test, several SMEs may assign probabilities of passing for the five items that average to .70, .75, .80, .85, and .90, respectively, for each of the five items. Summing these average probabilities across the five items gives us a cutoff score of four out of five (or 80%) for this example. Thus, one of the reasons for the popularity of the Angoff method is its simplicity.

For the Nedelsky method, all SMEs examine each multiple-choice question and decide which alternatives an MCP could eliminate (e.g., option D really isn't feasible). As a result, for a four-option (one correct response and three distracters) multiple-choice question, the only values possible are 25% if no distracters can be eliminated, 33% if one distracter can be eliminated, 50% if two distracters can be eliminated, or 100% if all three distracters can be eliminated. Again, these ratings (or judgments) are averaged across all SMEs for each question and then summed across items in order to set the pass point.

A third, more involved, method is the Ebel method. For the Ebel method, the SMEs set up a 3 × 4 table. Across the top of the table is the difficulty level of each item (easy, moderate, and difficult), and down the side is the relevance of each item (essential, important, acceptable, and questionable). Then, similar to the previous two methods, the SMEs determine the likelihood that an MCP would correctly answer items that fall within each of the 12 cells in the 3 × 4 table. For example, the minimally competent test taker should have a very high probability of answering an easy and essential item correctly, whereas such a person would have a very low probability of getting a questionable and difficult item correct. Once this classification table is complete, all items on the test are placed into one of the 12 cells in the 3 × 4 table. Then, the number of items in the cell is multiplied by the probability of answering the items in the cell correctly, and the totals for each cell are then summed across all 12 cells to establish the pass point. Note that when there are few items on the test, there may be some cells that have no items. In addition, from a content validity standpoint, we would hope to have more es-sential and important items than those rated merely as acceptable or, worse yet, questionable. Thus, the distribution of items across cells can vary dramatically from test to test.

A persistent problem with these three judgmental methods of setting cutoff scores is how the MCP is defined. While all the individuals performing the scoring are SMEs, they may not be using the same standard or have the same ideal person in mind when they think of an MCP. Maurer and Alexander (1992) provided some helpful hints on how to deal with this issue. For example, the SMEs could discuss, as a group, what constitutes an MCP and develop a com-mon written description. SMEs would then have the written description to refer to when they make their independent ratings. In addition, if the MCP refers to someone who is applying for a certain job or licensing in a particular occupa-tion, detailed job analysis information could be used to develop the written MCP description.

Once the MCP is adequately defined, frame-of-reference training could be provided to SMEs. Such training allows SMEs to rate a series of items that have predetermined standards in terms of the probability of success for MCPs on such items. A facilitator can then discuss any discrepancies that occur between the sample ratings provided by SMEs during the training and the predetermined standards. Alternatively, SMEs could be provided with actual item analysis statistics (e.g., *p* values) to give them a sense of the difficulty of the item for all test takers. This would then provide some context for providing item ratings with regard to the MCPs. No matter which procedures are used to improve the definition and ratings of MCPs, it must be remembered that SMEs are selected because they are experts. Thus, we expect them to share and use their respective expertise when making their ratings. Therefore, we must be careful not to be too prescriptive in the rating process provided to SMEs. Hopefully, we have selected a diverse group of SMEs in terms of sex, age, race, experience, specialty, geographical location, and other relevant characteristics. As such, differences in the conceptualization of the MCP may be inevitable and even desirable, to some extent.

Maurer and Alexander (1992) also suggested adding several procedural and psychometric techniques to the standard judgmental methods, thus allowing one to assess the quality of the ratings provided by SMEs. A procedural technique would be the inclusion of bogus items in the test. These might include items that could easily be answered by all respondents or by none at all. Thus, the SMEs who rated such items with other than 0% and 100%, respectively, may be providing questionable responses for other items as well.

An example psychometric technique to assess the quality of SME ratings would include identifying idiosyncratic raters by looking at rater-total correlations, which are analogous to the item-total correlations discussed in Module 13. Such correlations will allow you to identify SMEs whose ratings are out of line with the other SMEs. Of course, such correlations do not tell us why the aberrant SMEs' ratings are out of line with those of the other SMEs. It could be due to a variety of factors, including flawed reasoning, inattentiveness, or a host of other reasons. The question, of course, becomes what to do with such aberrant ratings. Should they be deleted? Given less weight? Maurer and Alexander (1992) suggested other, more advanced and complicated psychometric techniques, such as item response theory and **generalizability theory**, to assess the quality of SME ratings. Please consult their paper for a complete discussion of these and other similar techniques for improving and evaluating Angoff ratings in particular.

Judgmental/Empirical Methods

The preceding methods for setting pass points rely entirely on the independent judgment of SMEs. That is, with the Angoff, Nedelsky, and Ebel methods, the SMEs typically make their respective ratings independently, and their results are simply averaged. Thus, each SME does not have access or knowledge of the other SMEs' ratings. Other methods, however, such as the Delphi technique, use informed judgments. That is, each SME makes his or her initial independent ratings, but then a moderator summarizes the initial ratings, and these data are then shared with all SMEs (usually only summary data with no individual SME names attached). Each SME is then allowed to make changes to his or her ratings based on the summary data provided by the moderator. No one *has* to change his or her ratings, however; they are simply afforded the opportunity to do so. In some instances, there may be several rounds of ratings and summary data before ratings are finalized.

You may be thinking, couldn't you accomplish the same thing by simply letting the SMEs talk about their ratings? Why go through such a potentially time-consuming and arduous process? Those of you who have taken a social psychology class probably already know the answer to this question, as it has to do with group dynamics. Not all group members, particularly new or younger group members, may feel comfortable disagreeing in public with other more senior SMEs. Thus, having a moderator and allowing for anonymous data feedback can be a good way to counteract certain group dynamics while still allowing SMEs to have feedback on the group's ratings.

Empirical/Judgmental Methods

While empirical/judgmental methods are more "data driven" than the preceding methods, purely empirical methods for setting cutoff scores are relatively rare. Some test users have applied rules of thumb, such as setting the pass point 1 standard deviation below the mean for the entire group, but these can be very difficult to justify in court. An example that combines empirical data with SME judgments is the contrasting groups method. In this method, SMEs identify two groups of individuals (e.g., proficient vs. nonproficient; successful vs. unsuccessful; masters vs. nonmasters). You then plot the distribution of scores for the two groups and set the cutoff score where the two distributions intersect (see Figure 14.1). The advantage of this method is that it equalizes the chance of making a false-positive and a false-negative decision. That is, once you set a pass point, you run the risk of mistakenly classifying someone as "passing" (false positive) or mistakenly classifying someone as "failing" (false negative). The contrasting groups method of setting pass points typically equalizes both errors.

However, there may be occasions when it is important to minimize one form of error over the other. For example, when selecting for positions that pose a substantial potential risk to the public, such as nuclear power plant operators or air traffic controllers, we tend to minimize false positives (hiring unqualified candidates) at the risk of increasing false negatives (not hiring potentially qualified candidates). Thus, the cutoff score in Figure 14.1 would be moved to the right in order to minimize the number of false positives, but, of course, resulting in an increasing number of false-negative decisions. As you might have guessed, your data will most likely not be as clear cut as those depicted in Figure 14.1. For example, the proficient and nonproficient groups might substantially (or completely) overlap. As a

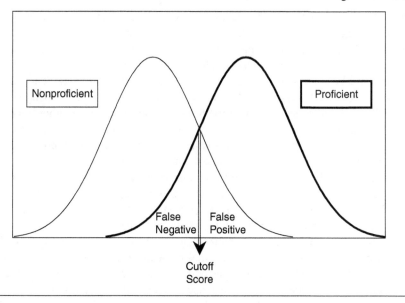

Figure 14.1   Setting Pass Points for Contrasting Groups

result, it may be difficult to set a cutoff score using the contrasting groups method. In such cases, other procedures may be needed to establish a passing score.

Subgroup Norming and Banding

Before the 1991 Civil Rights Act (CRA), it was fairly common to have different norms (or cutoff scores) for different groups. For example, a municipality may have established that an applicant had to score at the 85th percentile on a physical strength test to be hired as a firefighter. However, that was not the 85th percentile for the entire applicant pool; rather, it was within a given subgroup. Therefore, if you were a man, the 85th percentile may have translated to a raw score of 90 out of 100. The 85th percentile for a woman, however, may have equated to a raw score of 80 out of 100. Thus, while both male and female firefighter applicants had to score at the same percentile within their respective subgroup, those cutoff scores actually equated to different raw scores. This was done in order to reduce the **adverse impact** of the test on women. The 1991 CRA, however, bans the use of **subgroup norming**. Instead, everyone must be judged on the same absolute standard. Brown (1994), Gottfredson (1994), and Sackett and Wilk (1994) provided some interesting discussion on this controversial topic.

A second procedure sometimes used to deal with subgroup differences in the test is to set up "bands" of scores. For example, all scores are rank ordered from highest to lowest, and bandwidths are typically established using some psychometric (e.g., two standard errors of measurement) or logical (e.g., every five points) rationale. With fixed bands, the band must be exhausted before one moves on to the next band. For example, if the band goes from 96 to 100 (a bandwidth of 5) and there are seven people in that band, all seven individuals must be selected or disqualified before you can select an individual with a score less than 96. Assume we have the same scenario but now are using sliding bands. The person with a score of 100 is chosen and so the next highest score is 98. The band would slide down and now range from 94 to 98. The advantage of using either **banding** method is that it allows you to take "other things" into consideration for individuals within a given band. However, this issue, similar to within-group norming, has been controversial on psychometric, legal, and ethical grounds.

Campion et al. (2001) provided a comprehensive summary of some of the more salient issues involved in using banding as an alternative to setting a single pass point, particularly with regard to personnel selection. In particular, they addressed issues such as how wide the bandwidths should be, the psychometric and practical rationales for establishing bands, and legal issues with regard to the use of banding, as well as practical issues on whether and how to use banding. Their commentary, which includes the perspectives of advocates, opponents, and neutral observers, appears to reach a consensus that banding can serve legitimate organizational purposes of allowing other factors, such as diversity issues, to be incorporated into the decisions that result from the use of tests. However, there is still disagreement on the legitimacy of using psychometric rationales for establishing bands and on the potential legal implications of using bands. All the commentators appear to agree that additional research is needed that compares the actual outcomes of using banding with the outcomes that would be obtained from other procedures such as strict top-down selection or setting a single pass point (which, in a sense, is a banding procedure that has only two bands: pass and fail).

A Step-by-Step Example of Setting Cutoff Scores

In the step-by-step example provided in Module 13, we looked at the abridged results from a 74-item multiple-choice exam used in a tests and measurements class. Eight items were selected as examples for detailed psychometric examination. Assume a local private-sector employer that was interested in hiring an intern who had a specialization in test development and administration contacted us. The company has asked us to provide the names of at least five "technically qualified" candidates from whom they will make a selection decision. Thus, it will be up to us to determine who would be an MCP in this instance. Because the position requires technical knowledge regarding developing and administering both psychological and knowledge tests, we could use the 74-item tests and measurements exam, assuming it meets our standards for reliability and validity. Thus, we would need to administer the test and then identify those students who would be considered MCPs.

We could use one of the judgmental methods, such as the Angoff, Nedelsky, or Ebel method, for establishing the cutoff score. For these procedures, we would need to assemble a group of SMEs to provide ratings for all 74 items. How many SMEs do we need? As we discussed in Module 5 on reliability, other things being equal, the inter-rater reliability will increase the more raters we have. "More is better" is not much guidance, however. In this instance, three to five raters may be sufficient given the nature of the project. In practical terms, we may be lucky to get just one other person to provide ratings. Hopefully, at least some diversity (in terms of both demographics and technical competence) will be evident in however many raters we end up using. We should also incorporate some of the suggestions of Maurer and Alexander (1992) that we discussed previously, such as providing the SMEs with feedback and developing an agreed-upon single definition of the MCP. We may also want to provide raters with frame-of-reference training so that they have some practice providing such ratings. Such training also provides the SMEs with immediate feedback on how they are performing in the rating task. After the ratings are complete, we would also want to perform rater-total correlations to identify aberrant SMEs and potentially eliminate their responses. This all assumes, of course, that we have more than two SMEs.

Alternatively, we could use an empirical procedure such as the contrasting groups method discussed previously to set the pass point. Here we would have to identify "proficient" and "nonproficient" students in order to set the cutoff score. We could have SMEs identify each student as proficient or nonproficient; however, from a practical standpoint, that may be difficult. Alternatively, we could use some other standard to distinguish students on proficiency. In this case, we may choose to use the standard that those students who received a B or higher in the class were deemed proficient, while those who received a B– or lower were deemed nonproficient. Figure 14.2 displays the actual data from a class from which we had complete data on 33 students; one student dropped out before she received her final grade, so she could not be classified on proficiency. As we warned earlier, "real data" (such as the data in Figure 14.2) will not be as straightforward as the ideal data shown in Figure 14.1.

We said earlier to set the cutoff score where the two distributions (proficient and nonproficient) intersect. It appears, however, that the two distributions intersect several times in Figure 14.2. Which intersecting point should we use? Part of the problem is the small sample sizes for the two groups. Using the preceding criterion, we have 18 students in the proficient group and 15 students in the nonproficient group. Thus, within either group, most scores have only one student within each group, with only three scores (72, 89, and 107) having two students. No score had more than two students for either group. Thus, the shape of the curve may be somewhat deceptive, given the small sample sizes. Again, welcome to the reality of applied testing. Based on the data in Figure 14.2, we would recommend setting the cutoff score at either 82 or 85, because that is where the lines for the two groups cross. One practical constraint might be that with a higher cutoff score

Figure 14.2   Contrasting Groups Results for a Tests and Measurement Class

we may not have enough students to recommend. Alternatively, we may have too many to recommend with the lower cutoff score. Thus, other practical realities may also come into play when setting the cutoff score in this situation.

Concluding Comments

Both judgmental and empirical methods can be used to establish cutoff scores. Keep in mind, however, that setting cutoff scores is a very controversial issue with many practical and legal implications. For example, where we set the cutoff score will affect both the validity and the **utility** of our test. If we have an extreme cutoff score (i.e., almost no one passes), then we will have a highly restricted sample, and scores on the test will be unlikely to correlate with other variables due to the restriction of range. On the other hand, if almost everyone passes, then the utility of the test will be diminished, as we are not taking advantage of the fact that higher scores on the test are associated with higher criterion scores. In addition, the lack of variability will mean that our test scores will not correlate with other variables of interest.

Another practical issue is that we often use more than one test when making important decisions. How does the placement of a cutoff score on an early test hurdle influence how we make later cutoff score decisions? For example, if we are using several tests in a multiple-hurdle fashion and very few individuals are able to pass our first test, then we may have to set the cutoff score on later tests extremely low. As a result, we may end up hiring individuals who are "not proficient" on factors assessed by later measures, simply because we do not have enough individuals left in the pool due to overly restrictive early cutoff scores.

Finally, when we set the pass point, we make the decision of who "passes" (i.e., obtains a valued outcome) and who "fails" (i.e., does not obtain the valued outcome). As a result, some people may like our decision, and others may not. Therefore, we need to be able to defend and justify whatever procedure we ultimately end up using. Cascio, Alexander, and Barrett (1988) provided a comprehensive review of the legal, psychometric, and professional issues involved in establishing cutoff scores.

Best Practices

1. It is best to use some combination of informed, expert judgment as well as empirical data to make decisions regarding setting cutoff scores and pass points.
2. When using expert judgments, it is best to provide feedback to the SMEs regarding the other raters' rating (e.g., a Delphi technique).
3. Be sure to seriously consider not only psychometric criteria and expert judgment in setting cutoff scores and pass points, but also practical considerations such as the size of the applicant pool and the cost of testing in subsequent hurdles in the testing process.

Practical Questions

1. How do we best define the MCP when using judgmental methods such as the Angoff, Nedelsky, and Ebel methods?
2. When does a method for setting pass points go from being judgmental/empirical to empirical/judgmental? Does it really matter?
3. What legal issues do we need to be concerned with when setting cutoff scores?
4. Does where we set the cutoff score affect the validity of the test? The utility?
5. How do we know whether we should minimize false-positive or false-negative decisions? Will that decision impact the procedure we use to make the cutoff score decision?
6. Do we really even need to set cutoff scores? Why not just rank order all the test scores from highest to lowest and provide the valued outcome until it runs out?
7. What if we set a cutoff score and no one passes?

Case Studies

CASE STUDY 14.1: SETTING A CUTOFF SCORE ON A COMPREHENSIVE EXAMINATION

Alexius, a fifth-year doctoral student, had agreed to sit on the committee that was restructuring the doctoral comprehensive exams for his department. It seemed that every year students complained about the long essays they had to write, and professors complained about having to read and grade the essays with little guidance. Therefore, a committee of mostly full professors in the department was formed to explore the possibility of having a new two-part multiple-choice comprehensive exam. The first part would be a 250-question multiple-choice exam covering several general areas (e.g., history and systems, statistics, and research methods). The second part of the test would also have 250 multiple-choice questions, but in the student's area of concentration (e.g., social, cognitive, clinical, or I/O psychology). Thus, the test would consist of 500 multiple-choice questions in all. While a common standard of 80% correct or 90% correct could be used to set the pass point, the committee did not feel that was wise, as they knew the questions on the test would change each year. In addition, while all students in a given year took the same general portion of the test, students in different concentrations took different area-specific tests. Thus, it was felt that a new pass point should be established each year for each test segment. Several of the counseling professors on the committee sat on the state licensing board for counseling psychology, and they used a similar procedure to set the pass point for the professional licensing exam for counseling psychologists in their state for the written multiple-choice portion of the exam.

Because the number of students who took the comprehensive exams in a given year was relatively small (i.e., usually fewer than 20 students), an empirical strategy for setting the cutoff score did not seem feasible. However, the committee was uncomfortable with using a purely judgmental procedure for setting the cutoff score. In addition, multiple cutoff scores had to be set: one for the general portion of the test and a separate cutoff score for each specific test. The committee chair, who also happened to be the department chairperson, asked Alexius to provide the committee with a proposal of how best to set the cutoff scores for each portion of the test. Alexius felt a bit overwhelmed. Here were all these professors in the department, many who had been there for 30 years or more, and they were asking him for recommendations on how to set cutoff scores for the tests. Yes, he had just taken his comprehensive exams the year before, but that was under the old system when you had to write six or eight long essays, not this multiple-choice format. In some ways, he thought this was probably better than having to write all those questions. Therefore, Alexius went back to his notes from his applied psychological measurement class and started a literature search on the "best practices" for setting cutoff scores in such situations.

Questions to Ponder

1. If you were Alexius, where would you start your search for "best practices" for setting cutoff scores on a graduate comprehensive examination?
2. While a purely empirical method for setting the cutoff scores seems unrealistic given the small sample sizes, what things could Alexius do to make his judgmental procedures more empirical?
3. Who are the likely SMEs for setting the cutoff scores for the general test? The area-specific tests?
4. Is there a problem with the same individuals writing the questions and also helping to set the cutoff scores on the test they created?
5. Would information from past "pass rates" be of any use to the committee given that the format is being changed?

CASE STUDY 14.2: SETTING A CUTOFF SCORE ON A COLLEGE ENTRANCE EXAM

Lui-Ping (most people just called her Jasmin), a recent master's graduate, had decided to return home to Malaysia after graduation. After a short job search, she obtained a job with the Ministry of Education. One of Jasmin's first assignments was to help set the cutoff score for the national entrance exam for the three most sought-after public universities in Kuala Lumpur (the capital city of Malaysia). The three universities received tens of thousands of applications every year. It was no wonder; anyone who was admitted received free tuition. In addition, the top employers from across Malaysia (all of Southeast Asia, in fact) seemed to focus much of their recruitment effort for new employees at these three top public universities. Therefore, if a student was able to get into one of these three universities, he or she would be "set for life."

The Ministry of Education, however, had just recently reformatted the entrance exam to cover several new topics. As a result, a new cutoff score had to be "recommended" to the universities. Ultimately, the universities were free to choose their own cutoff scores, but they relied heavily on the expertise provided by the Ministry of Education, as that is where much of their funding came from. Therefore, Jasmin was asked to help determine the appropriate cutoff score for the three universities. This could be difficult, she thought, as the three universities seemed to be so different. The first was a technical university, focusing on STEM (science, technology, engineering, and math) disciplines. The second university was a more traditional liberal arts university, with a wide breadth of offerings and a much smaller student body. The third university had a strong focus on the professional degrees, with emphases in business, social work, medicine, law, and education. These all seemed so different. How could she set a single cutoff score for all three universities? It was time to sit down with her new boss and develop more clarification on what she should do next.

Questions to Ponder

1. Should Jasmin recommend the same cutoff score for each university, or should different cutoff scores be recommended?
2. Instead of having one overall cutoff score, might it be better to have separate cutoff scores for different portions of the exam?
3. Should Jasmin take into consideration the other criteria used by each of the universities to select its students? If so, how?
4. Given the large sample of data Jasmin will have to work with, how might she incorporate some empirical data into the cutoff score decision?
5. Who should be the SMEs for Jasmin in helping her to set the cutoff score(s)?

♲ ⟨•⟩ ♲

Exercises

EXERCISE 14.1: JUDGMENTAL PROCEDURES
FOR SETTING CUTOFF SCORES

OBJECTIVE: To practice setting cutoff scores using the Angoff and Nedelsky methods.

SCENARIO: The psychology department has decided to begin using graduate students to teach the lab portion of Psychology 210, Psychological Statistics. To ensure that students wishing to be graduate teaching assistants (GTAs) are "minimally competent," we will give the graduate statistics final exam from last year to those students wishing to be GTAs. The exam can be found in Table 14.1. Those "passing" the test will be allowed to interview for the GTA positions. Therefore, we must determine who is "minimally competent" in statistics by setting an appropriate cutoff score on the exam.

Table 14.1   Graduate Psychological Statistics Exam

1. A bivariate distribution is represented in most complete fashion by a
    A. Pearson r_{xy}.   *C. scatterplot.
    B. straight line.   D. line, whether curved or straight.

2. A causal relationship between X and Y can be inferred
    A. any time r_{xy} is other than zero.
    B. only for values of r_{xy} close to 1.00.
    C. whenever we use a test of group differences (e.g., t, F).
    *D. only on grounds that go beyond the statistics used to analyze the data.

3. Which, if any, statistic below is NOT subject to the influence of sampling variation (error).
    A. the mean   C. the standard deviation
    B. the correlation coefficient   *D. All of these are subject to sampling variation.

4. The correlation between job aptitude scores and job success ratings is computed to be +.29 for employees hired in the last 6 months. Which of the following is a legitimate guess as to the value for r_{xy} had all, rather than just the best-qualified, applicants been hired?
    A. < +.29   *C. > +.29
    B. +.29   D. insufficient information to even guess

5. Which of the following type of scores does NOT provide equal intervals when moving away from the center of the distribution by standard deviation units.
    A. z scores   C. raw scores
    B. T scores   *D. percentiles

6. The fundamental condition that permits proper statistical inference is
    *A. random sampling.   C. a normal distribution of scores.
    B. having large sample sizes.   D. knowledge of the population parameters.

7. "Degrees of freedom" refers to the number of
    A. samples in the sampling distribution.   C. tests we are free to use.
    *B. data points that are free to vary.   D. days to spring break.

8. In statistical work, a significant difference is one that is large enough
    A. that chance cannot affect it.   C. that it leads to retention of the null hypothesis.
    B. to be meaningful to the experimenter.   *D. that it would rarely be expected to occur by chance if Ho is true.

9. When samples are dependent, the standard error of the difference between two means will be
    *A. larger than when samples are independent.
    B. smaller than when samples are independent.

(Continued)

Table 14.1   (*Continued*)

C. smaller or larger depending on the situation.

D. unaffected by the degree of dependence of the samples.

10. Using paired observations (dependent observations) is most advantageous when

   A. sample sizes are equal.

   B. standard deviations must be estimated from samples.

   *C. the association between pairs of scores is high (e.g., large individual differences).

   D. Actually, it is never advantageous to have paired observations versus independent ones.

11. Interval estimates are generally preferred over point estimates because interval estimates

   A. have a firmer statistical basis.   *C. account for sampling error.

   B. result in greater statistical precision.   D. are based on more degrees of freedom.

12. We construct a 99% confidence interval for P, the population proportion of freshmen able to pass an English placement exam. The sample interval runs from .43 to .49. This tells us that

   A. there is a 99% probability that P falls between .43 and .49.

   *B. there is a 99% probability that an interval so constructed will include P.

   C. 99% of the time, P will fall between .43 and .49.

   D. 99% of intervals so constructed will fall between .43 and .49.

13. Suppose a 95% confidence interval for $\mu_x - \mu_y$ runs from -5 to $+2$. If Ho: $\mu_x - \mu_y = 0$ were tested against a two-tailed alternative hypothesis using $\alpha = .05$, our decision about Ho would be that we

   A. made a Type I error.   *C. should retain Ho.

   B. should reject Ho.   D. cannot determine from the information provided.

14. In general, reducing the risk of committing a Type I error

   A. reduces the risk of committing a Type II error.

   *B. reduces the power of the test statistic used.

   C. increases the power of the test statistic used.

   D. has no effect on any of these issues.

15. In a one-way ANOVA, the following results are obtained: SSb = 83.7, SStot = 102.6; thus the SSw = _____.

   A. 186.3   C. 51.3

   *B. 18.9   D. none of these

16. The assumption of homogeneity of variance in ANOVA designs means that

   *A. group population variance should be the same for all groups.

   B. within-group variance should be the same as the total variance.

   C. between-group variance should be the same as total group variance.

   D. within-group variance should be the same as between-group variance.

Table 14.1 (*Continued*)

17. In ANOVA for repeated measures, SSw is partitioned into

A. SSb and SSsubj.   C. SSsubj and SStot.

B. SSb and SSerror.   *D. SSsubj and SSerror.

18. A standard score regression equation reads: $Z = \beta Z_x$. If the correlation coefficient is +.5 and Johnny is two standard deviations above the mean on X, what standard score position will Johnny be predicted to have on Y?

*A. +1.0   C. +2.0

B. +1.5   D. none of these

19. In a one-way ANOVA involving three groups, the alternative hypothesis would be considered supported if, in the population,

1. All means were equal.

2. Two means were equal but the third was different.

3. All three means have different values.

A. 1   C. 3

B. 2   *D. either 2 or 3 is true

20. The purpose of the Fisher's r to z transformation is to correct for

*A. varying shape of the sampling distribution of r.

B. differing values of n (particularly when $n < 30$).

C. an unknown mean of the sampling distribution of r.

D. an unknown standard deviation of the sampling distribution of r.

21. A z score in a given distribution is 1.5. If the mean = 140 and s = 20, then the equivalent raw score is

A. 95.   C. 165.

B. 160.   *D. 170.

22. Suppose that a distribution of test scores is very negatively skewed. Mary obtains a raw score equal to the mean of the distribution. She proclaims, "I scored at the 50th percentile." You smile and calmly tell her that she

A. has indeed scored at the 50th percentile.   C. actually scored above the 50th percentile.

*B. actually scored below the 50th percentile.   D. actually scored at the 25th percentile.

23. If the distribution of raw scores above (in question 22) were transformed to Z scores, the new distribution will be

A. normally distributed.   *C. negatively skewed.

B. symmetrical but not normal   D. positively skewed.

24. ρ is to the sampling distribution of r as _____ is to the sampling distribution of the mean.

A. S_x C. σ_x

*B. μ_x D. η_x

(*Continued*)

Table 14.1   (*Continued*)

25. An interval estimate for the population parameter (e.g., ρ, σ, μ) is highly preferable to a point estimate when

    *A. N is small.   C. the sample statistic is small.

    B. N is large.   D. the sample statistic is large.

26. A 95% confidence interval for ρ is computed and is found to be −.75 to +.25. This suggests that

    A. ρ is probably negative.   C. a computational error was made.

    *B. a small sample size was used.   D. r is significantly different from zero.

27. The size of the standard error of the distribution of sample means will _____ the population standard deviation.

    A. always be the same as   *C. always be smaller than or equal to

    B. always be large than or equal to   D. sometimes be larger and sometimes be smaller than

28. Which of the following represents a Type II error?

    A. no effect when really there is an effect   C. an effect when really there is an effect

    B. no effect when really there is no effect   *D. an effect when really there is not an effect

29. Which combination below is most likely to lead to the most powerful study?

    A. small N, α = .01, two-tailed test   C. small N, α = .01, one-tailed test

    B. large N, α = .05, two-tailed test   *D. large N, α = .05, one-tailed test

30. The power of any statistical test can be represented as

    *A. $1 - \beta$.   C. $\alpha + \beta$.

    B. $1 - \alpha$.   D. $\alpha - \beta$.

31. Sample size affects the power of a statistical test because of its influence on the

    *A. standard error of the sampling distribution.   C. effect size "d."

    B. skewness the sampling distribution.   D. sample standard deviations.

32. Multiple regression and factorial ANOVA are similar conceptually in that

    A. all variable are continuous.   C. we have both multiple IVs and DVs.

    B. the IVs are independent of one another.   *D. you end up partitioning variance into explained and error.

33. I ran my analyses and got an ω^2 value that was negative. What likely happened?

    A. My F value must have been negative.

    B. Treatment effects were reversed.

    C. I had more error variance than treatment variance.

    *D. I must have made a calculational error because ω^2 can never be negative.

34. Which of the following is NOT an advantage of multiple regression (MR) over factorial ANOVA.

    A. I can use continuous and/or nominal IVs with MR.

    B. I can test for nonlinear relationships with MR but not with ANOVA.

Table 14.1   *(Continued)*

C. MR takes into account correlations among IVs.

*D. All are advantages of MR over factorial ANOVA.

35. Correlations are to covariance as _____ are to raw scores.

   *A. Z scores   C. percentiles

   B. standard deviations   D. means

36. The reason we should thoroughly describe our data before jumping into inferential statistics is because we

   A. have to see if our DV is normally distributed.

   B. need to find out if we have any outliers in our data.

   C. should get an ocular feel for our data to help us better explain our results.

   *D. All of the above are pretty legitimate reasons to do descriptive analyses before inferential ones.

37. The importance of sampling distributions of our statistics to statistical inference is that they

   *A. have known properties based on the central limit theorem.

   B. allow us to determine the probability of obtaining our statistic.

   C. guide us to which statistic will best answer our question of interest.

   D. tend to always reject the null hypothesis when we have very large sample sizes.

38. Which statement is true?

   *A. Any problem in hypothesis testing could be handled through estimation.

   B. Any problem in estimation could be handled through hypothesis testing.

   C. Hypothesis testing and estimation are mutually interchangeable.

   D. Hypothesis testing and estimation are never interchangeable.

   For the following four examples, indicate whether we should use an independent or dependent group design statistic to analyze data from the experiment described.

39. Thirty-three (33) Republicans were compared to 33 Democrats for signs of depression on November 4, 1992.

   *A. independent   B. dependent

40. A psychologist gave a pretest and matched each subject with another subject. Half the subjects were given a gin and tonic, and half were given plain tonic. All 40 subjects then learned statistics.

   A. independent   *B. dependent

41. The first 10 subjects to sign up for an experiment were asked to fill out a questionnaire. Then the next 10 subjects to sign up filled out a similar questionnaire, and the two groups were compared.

   *A. independent   B. dependent

42. The attitudes of 21 students toward statistics were compared to those of each one's "favorite professor."

   A. independent   *B. dependent

Table 14.1   *(Continued)*

43. The chairperson of the Psychology Department has asked you to determine whether the number of men who select psychology as their major differs significantly from that of women. The most appropriate way to answer the chair's question would be by doing

    A. an independent groups t test.

    B. a dependent groups t test.

    C. a preplanned contrast of men and women.

    *D. a z test for differences between proportions.

44. The chair of psychology recommended you to the VP for Student Affairs who wants to find out if there is a relationship between how far a student drives to school and his or her GPA. He has divided the students into five groups (< 15-minute commute, 15- to 30-minute commute, 31- to 45-minute commute, 46- to 60-minute commute, and > 60-minute commute). The most appropriate way to answer the VP's question would be to calculate

    *A. an F statistic for an independent groups one-way ANOVA.

    B. an F statistic for a dependent groups one-way ANOVA.

    C. a tetrachoric correlation coefficient.

    D. Tukey HSD statistics comparing the group means.

45. Harper and Wacker (1983) wished to examine the relationship between scores on the Denver Developmental Screening Test and scores on an individually administered intellectual measure for 555 children ages 3 to 4 years old (with both measures having interval scales). Which of the following would best assess the relationship between the two measures?

    A. a Kendall's Tau correlation

    B. an η^2 or ω^2 statistic to assess association

    C. a tetrachoric correlation coefficient

    *D. a Pearson's r statistic (assuming the relationship is linear)

46. Franklin, Janoff-Bulman, and Roberts (1990) looked at the long-term impact of divorce on college student's levels of optimism and trust. They compared students from divorced families and students from intact families. They found no differences on generalized trust, but children from divorced families showed less optimism about the future of their own marriages. In order to state the results as they did, they must have performed _____ to analyze their data.

    *A. an independent groups t test

    B. an η^2 or ω^2 statistic to assess association

    C. a tetrachoric correlation coefficient

    D. Pearson's r statistic (assuming the relationship is linear)

47. Olson and Shultz (1994) studied the influence of sex and source of social support (supervisor, friend, co-worker, or spouse) on the degree of overall social support reported being received by a sample of 314 employees from a large automotive manufacturer. Employees rated the amount of support they received from each of the above sources. This study is best represented by

    A. 2 × 4 factorial ANOVA.

    *B. 2 × (4) mixed-design ANOVA.

Table 14.1   (*Continued*)

C. (2) × 4 mixed-design ANOVA.

D. two repeated-measures ANOVA, one for men and one for women.

48. Cochran and Urbancyzk (1982) were concerned with the effect of height of a room on the desired personal space of subjects. They tested 48 subjects in both a high-ceiling (10 ft) and low-ceiling (7 ft) room. Subjects stood with their backs to a wall while a stranger approached. Subjects were told to say "stop" when the approaching stranger's nearness made them feel uncomfortable. The dependent variable was the distance at which the subject said "stop." Which of the following would be most appropriate to properly analyze the researchers' data?

A. independent groups *t* test   C. preplanned contrast of men and women

*B. dependent groups *t* test   D. *z* test for differences between proportions

49. The right side of a person's face is said to resemble the whole face more than does the left side. Kennedy, Beard, and Carr (1982) asked 91 subjects to view full-face pictures of 6 different faces. Testing for recall was conducted 1 week later, when subjects were presented with pictures of 12 faces and were asked to identify the ones they has seen earlier. At testing, subjects were divided into three groups of roughly equal size. One group was presented with full-faced photographs, one group saw only the right side of the face in the photograph, and one group saw only the left side. The dependent variable was the number of errors. Which of the following would be most appropriate to properly analyze the researchers' data?

*A. an *F* statistic for an independent groups one-way ANOVA

B. an *F* statistic for a repeated measures one-way ANOVA

C. an η^2 or ω^2 statistic to assess association in factorial designs

D. dependent groups t tests with follow-up ω^2's

50. I ran a one-way ANOVA and calculated $\eta^2 = .34$ (eta-square). If I dummy coded my IVs and ran a multiple regression, I would need to look at the _____ to get the equivalent measure in multiple regression.

*A. R^2 C. Wherry-corrected R^2

B. Adj R^2 D. Lord-Nicholson–corrected R^2

*Indicates the keyed answer.

EXERCISE: Half the class will use the Angoff method to set the cutoff score on the test. A rating sheet for the Angoff method can be found in Table 14.2. The other half of the class will use the Nedelsky method to set the cutoff score on the exam. A rating sheet for the Nedelsky method can be found in Table 14.3. If time permits, have the groups switch and use the other method they did not use the first time. Compare the cutoffs from the two separate groups of raters.

1. How do the two methods compare? Discuss possible reasons for the likely differences obtained.
2. Discuss issues surrounding the use of different methods and different groups of raters.

Table 14.2   SME Rating Sheet for the Angoff Method

Think of a group of "minimally competent students." Now, for each item, estimate the probability that a student from this minimally competent group could answer the given question correctly. Write this probability in the space provided for that question.

1. _____		19. _____		37. _____	
2. _____		20. _____		38. _____	
3. _____		21. _____		39. _____	
4. _____		22. _____		40. _____	
5. _____		23. _____		41. _____	
6. _____		24. _____		42. _____	
7. _____		25. _____		43. _____	
8. _____		26. _____		44. _____	
9. _____		27. _____		45. _____	
10. _____		28. _____		46. _____	
11. _____		29. _____		47. _____	
12. _____		30. _____		48. _____	
13. _____		31. _____		49. _____	
14. _____		32. _____		50. _____	
15. _____		33. _____			
16. _____		34. _____			
17. _____		35. _____			
18. _____		36. _____		$\Sigma p = $ ____	

EXERCISE 14.2: DELPHI METHOD FOR SETTING CUTOFF SCORES

OBJECTIVE: To practice using a judgmental/empirical method for setting cutoff scores.

This exercise requires that you first complete the steps in Exercise 14.1. Next, the professor or some other "moderator" will summarize the initial set of ratings for the class. You will then be provided with the results and be allowed to make changes to your initial ratings based on your review of the summary results. However, you need not make any changes if you believe your initial ratings are still an accurate assessment of your evaluation of each of the items. The moderator will then compute a second set of summary statistics based on the second set of ratings.

1. Did you find the summary ratings helpful to you as you reviewed your initial set of ratings?
2. If you changed some of your ratings, why did you make changes?
3. Did you notice any patterns in your ratings compared to the summary ratings? For example, did you tend to be more stringent or lenient in your ratings than the other raters?

Table 14.3   SME Rating Sheet for the Nedelsky Method

For each item, cross out the alternatives that you believe a minimally competent student should be able to eliminate. Then, in the space provided for each question, write the p value for that item (i.e., 4 alts. = .25, 3 alts. = .33, 2 alts. = .50, 1 alt. = 1.00).

1. _____		19. _____		37. _____	
2. _____		20. _____		38. _____	
3. _____		21. _____		39. _____	
4. _____		22. _____		40. _____	
5. _____		23. _____		41. _____	
6. _____		24. _____		42. _____	
7. _____		25. _____		43. _____	
8. _____		26. _____		44. _____	
9. _____		27. _____		45. _____	
10. _____		28. _____		46. _____	
11. _____		29. _____		47. _____	
12. _____		30. _____		48. _____	
13. _____		31. _____		49. _____	
14. _____		32. _____		50. _____	
15. _____		33. _____			
16. _____		34. _____			
17. _____		35. _____			
18. _____		36. _____		Σp = _____	

4. Do you feel that frame-of-reference training would have helped you provide more "accurate" ratings? Why or why not?
5. How do the two sets of summary ratings compare?

EXERCISE 14.3: CONTRASTING GROUPS METHOD FOR SETTING CUTOFF SCORES

Objective: To practice using empirical procedures to make passing score decisions.

The data set "Passing Score.sav" (see Appendix B) has fictitious data for 200 students' scores on the graduate statistics exam in Table 14.1. Using the data set, create a line graph that compares the proficient group and the nonproficient group (DESIG) in terms of their respective scores on the graduate statistics final exam (FINAL).

1. Based on your line graph, where would you set the passing score?
2. Can a case be made for more than one passing score (similar to the step-by-step example)?

Further Readings

Biddle, R.E. (1993). How to set cutoff scores for knowledge tests used in promotion, training, certification, and licensing. *Public Personnel Management, 22,* 63–79.

Campion, M.A., Outtz, J.L., Zedeck, S., Schmidt, F.L., Kehoe, J.F., Murphy, K.R., & Guion, R.M. (2001). The controversy over score banding in personnel selection: Answers to 10 key questions. *Personnel Psychology, 54,* 149–185.

Impara, J.C., & Plake, B.S. (1997). Standard setting: An alternative approach. *Journal of Educational Measurement, 34,* 353–366.

Module 15

Developing Measures of Typical Performance

This module is concerned with the development of measures of typical performance. Measures of typical performance assess an individual's typical preferences, or how he or she normally behaves or performs (Cronbach, 1970). Examples of these sorts of measures include personality inventories, attitude surveys, and self-reports of behavior. In creating such measures, authors should consider the recommendations discussed in Module 12, "Development of Tests of Maximal Performance."

A Necessary Forewarning

The development of a good measure of typical performance is a surprisingly difficult enterprise. Sure, it would seem easy enough to write personality or attitude items. The truth, however, is that development of a quality measure of typical performance requires consideration of a very wide range of issues. For example, did you know that even minor changes in question wording, item format, response options, or the ordering of questions can result in major changes in the responses obtained to measures of typical performance? Schwarz (1999) reviewed troubling examples of problems that can occur in survey research. For example, Schuman and Presser (1996) reported that when asked, "What is the most important thing for children to prepare them for life?" a little more than 61% of respondents to a constructed-response survey chose the response option, "To think for themselves." When this same question was asked using a free-response format, however, less than 5% of the sample provided this response. Perhaps even more disconcerting is the finding that respondents who hold no opinion on a topic will often construct one when queried by a researcher (Feldman & Lynch, 1988). Bishop, Oldendick, Tuchfarber, and Bennett (1980), for example, found that roughly a third of respondents expressed an opinion on whether the 1975 Public Affairs Act should be repealed, even though no such act existed. Schwarz (1999) argued that respondents make tacit assumptions about the pragmatic—not the literal—meaning of a question. Thus, respondents provide answers that use rules of "cooperative conversational conduct" to try to make sense of questions that are posed to them.

Such findings serve as crucial reminders of both the imperfection of psychological measures and the importance of assessing constructs that are truly meaningful to the sample of respondents. Still, there is no denying the importance of assessment of opinions, attitudes, and traits in today's society. The question, then, is how do we develop good measures of typical performance? Fortunately, you've come to the right place.

Test Specifications

At the risk of repeating ourselves, have you read Module 4 yet? As was the case for tests of maximal performance (see Module 12), the first step in the construction of a measure of typical performance is the careful development of test specifications. In developing these measures, the primary activity of the test specifications is to clearly define the construct of interest and to delineate it from related (but distinct) constructs. By painstakingly defining our construct, the process of writing items becomes far simpler (as do our later efforts in providing evidence of construct validity).

Free-Response Versus Constructed-Response Items

Choice of item format is an important decision during the test specification stage. In constructing a measure of typical performance, test developers may choose between free-response items and constructed-response items. Free-response items on measures of typical performance present a question or prompt and allow respondents to provide any answer they feel is appropriate. While the most common mode of response to these items is verbal, theoretically respondents could be asked to provide written responses. Written responses, however, are typically much shorter in length and may not reveal sufficient information about the respondent's beliefs or actions. Indeed, the more time or involvement required to provide a response, the less likely individuals will be to participate in the survey.

In providing answers to free-response items, respondents use their own frame of reference. Respondents are much less likely to be influenced by the researcher's preexisting expectations, which can be a concern with use of constructed-response items. Further, by providing respondents the option to respond in their own words, we are more likely to determine their most salient thoughts. Free-response items also allow respondents to qualify both their answers and their understanding of the item.

Unfortunately, when given the opportunity to provide a response in their own words, respondents may provide information that is largely irrelevant to the item.

A single respondent may also tend to repeat answers across a number of questions. Another concern with use of free-response items on a test of typical performance is that respondents are likely to differ in their ability to articulate answers. Differences in language and/or cognitive abilities may exert a large influence on the quality and depth of responses provided. Respondents may also use terms that have different meanings to them than to the researcher, leading the researcher to misinterpret an individual's response. A practical concern with the use of free-response items is that the variability of responses can be very difficult to code into a finite number of usable categories. Analyzing such qualitative data can be quite difficult.

This is not to say that the alternative, constructed-response items, is a panacea. While constructed-response items can often be administered and analyzed more easily, these items do not allow respondents to qualify their answers. Thus, pilot testing of constructed-response items is even more necessary than with free-response items in order to determine whether respondents interpret the items in the way the researcher intended. Even when the item is interpreted correctly, the presentation of response options often suggests answers to respondents that they otherwise would not have come up with on their own (Schwarz, 1999).

Additional Test Specification Issues

In a unique and intriguing book, Schuman and Presser (1996) explored a number of important issues regarding the development of a specific type of measure of typical performance: attitude surveys. Chapter by chapter, these authors present a single issue and then provide suggestions for scale development based on a combination of their own research and a review of the extant literature. Among the many issues addressed in their book are the following:

- *Does the ordering of items influence responses?* Sometimes. When order effects do occur, however, they can exert a large influence on the responses provided by test takers (Rasinski, Lee, & Krishnamurty, 2012). Order effects do not always result in greater consistency in responses to items. Rather, they can result in heightening differences in responses to items, as well. Unfortunately, it is difficult to predict when the ordering of items will influence responses. Order effects appear most likely to occur when multiple items assess the same (or very similar) issue and when respondents provide overall summary evaluations rather than more specific evaluations.
- *Should items include a "don't know" response option?* A corollary question might ask, "To what degree should respondents be pushed to provide a response?" Because researchers are typically after information from a respondent, some hesitation in the acceptance of a "don't know" response is understandable. After all, the researcher would want to communicate to the respondent that his or her opinions, attitudes, or beliefs are important. However, what if the individual really hasn't ever considered the issue assessed by the question? Encouraging respondents to provide a response would only increase error variance in the obtained data. Schuman and Presser (1996)

reported that when a "don't know" response is explicitly provided, an average of 22% more respondents will take this option. Some individuals will provide meaningful responses when the "don't know" response option is omitted, but will respond, "don't know" when the response option is presented as a possibility. The effect of provision of a "don't know" response option on the correlation between attitude variables is somewhat murky at this point. There is some evidence that correlations between attitude variables can be stronger when a "don't know" response option is presented to test takers. However, this effect is not always the case, in that sometimes correlations are stronger between items when the "don't know" response option is omitted.

- *Will respondents make up a response if they know nothing about the question posed?* Perhaps. In their research, Schuman and Presser (1996) found that about 30% of respondents will provide an opinion on a law they know nothing about if a "don't know" option is omitted. However, their research also found that a number of those respondents providing a "fictitious" response couched their responses in terms of great uncertainty, such as asserting, I "favor—though I really don't know what it is" (p. 159). It is likely that, in the absence of the "don't know" response option, respondents attempt to figure out what the obscure topic of the question is about and then provide a reasonable answer based on their interpretation of the item.

- *Does acquiescence influence responses in attitude measurement?* **Acquiescence** refers to the tendency of respondents to agree with an attitude statement. Given the ubiquitous use of Likert-type response scales with anchors ranging from "strongly disagree" to "strongly agree," the possibility of an acquiescence bias is a very real concern. However, does research indicate that acquiescence actually has a serious effect on survey responses? Quite simply, yes. In a study conducted by Schuman and Presser (1996), the percentage of acquiescent responses was somewhere in the range of 16%–26%. Further, evidence suggested that acquiescence could change the magnitude of the observed relationships between variables. Because acquiescence can occur whenever items are posed in a one-sided fashion, we might wonder whether acquiescence is also a concern for items that ask a one-sided question to which an individual might be required to respond "yes" or "no." For example, "Do you believe that liberals are more likely to fan the flames of partisanship than conservatives?" Again, the available research indicates that these sorts of one-sided questions are just as susceptible to acquiescence as are items that require respondents to indicate their level of agreement with a statement. Despite our awareness of concerns with acquiescence, the causes and effects of acquiescence are not yet fully understood. (See Module 16 for additional discussion of acquiescence as a response bias.)

These are but a sampling of the issues that Schuman and Presser (1996) explored. Anyone hoping to develop expertise in the area would be wise to read Schuman and Presser's entire book.

Item Writing

Once the issues related to test specification have been considered, it is time to draft the initial pool of items. Generally, the more items that can be initially generated the better, as a good portion of items will undoubtedly be discarded during subsequent steps in the test development process. Still, we should never sacrifice item quality for quantity. Below is a list of item-writing tips. These recommendations for item writing are admittedly incomplete. As Dillman (2007) points out, there are numerous rules, admonitions and principles for good item writing proffered by test development experts, but these recommendations frequently conflict with one another. With that caveat in mind, consider the following guidelines:

- *Keep items as simple as possible.* Respondents are likely to differ in educational level, as well as in vocabulary and language abilities.
- *Avoid or define ambiguous terms.* Respondents are often unfamiliar with terms that may be considered commonplace to the test developer. This concern speaks to the importance of pilot testing both items and instructions.
- *Assess choices respondents would make today, not what they plan to do in the future.* For example, inquire whom an individual would vote for if the election were held today, not whom they plan on voting for in an upcoming election. While individuals are notoriously poor at predicting their own future behavior, they can report what they would do now.
- *Carefully consider the advantages and disadvantages of using reverse-coded items.* In an effort to guard against acquiescence and random responding, test development experts once routinely recommended that one-third to one-half of items be reverse coded. Reverse-coded items are worded such that a favorable attitude requires respondents to disagree with the item. This practice is no longer universally recommended, however. Summarizing a large number of studies on the use of reverse-coded items, Hughes (2009) urges caution in the use of such items. Among the concerns for reverse-coded items are an increased susceptibility to misinterpretation by respondents, and findings that reverse-coded items can have unexpected impacts on factor structure, such as the formation of independent factors composed of reverse-coded items.
- *Ensure that response options (if provided) are logically ordered and mutually exclusive.*
- *Keep in mind that respondents often view the scale midpoint as a neutral point or typical amount.* This is especially important to keep in mind when assessing frequency of behavior (e.g., how much television watched per day). Balancing negative and positive response options can be helpful.
- *Include an "undecided" or "no opinion" response option along with the response scale.*

Just as important, be sure to *avoid* the following:

- *Awkward vocabulary or phrases.* Acronyms in particular should be avoided, as the understanding of the acronym may not be universal in the sample.

(The use of acronyms could be a major SNAFU for your data collection effort and may make your results FUBAR.) Likewise, pay close attention to idiomatic phrases (e.g., it's raining like cats and dogs) as the figurative meaning of the phrase may be lost on some respondents.

- *Double-barreled items.* These are items that assess more than one thing. For example, "My favorite classes in high school were math and science."
- *Double negatives.* Respondents required to respond on an agreement scale often experience difficulty interpreting items that include the word "not."
- *False premises.* These are items that make a statement and then ask respondents to indicate their level of agreement with a second statement. For example, "Although dogs make terrific pets, some dogs just don't belong in urban areas." If a respondent does not agree with the initial statement, how should he or she respond? Notice that this item has the further complication of including a double negative.
- *Leading or emotionally loaded items.* These items implicitly communicate what the "right" answer should be. For example, "Do you support or oppose restrictions on the sale of cancer-causing tobacco products to our state's precious youth?" The use of these items is sometimes appropriate, however, when respondents might otherwise be uncomfortable in reporting a certain attitude or behavior that might be considered socially deviant (e.g., self-reports of sexual practices).
- *Asking questions about which the respondent is likely to have very little interest.* Researchers all too often administer surveys to participants with little or no interest in the topic. One author of this textbook recently participated in a phone survey sponsored by a local municipality about the use of converting wastewater into drinking water. While the author had never previously considered this topic, he was able to respond fairly confidently to the first few questions. Twenty minutes later, however, when the phone interviewer continued to inquire about various attitudes on the topic, the quality of the provided responses might surely be considered questionable!

Rational or Empirical Test Development?

The use of the terms "rational" and "empirical" to identify the developmental process of a measure of typical performance is misleading, in that rational *and* empirical methods of test development involve both logic and empiricism (Gough & Bradley, 1992). However, the "rational" and "empirical" labels perhaps capture the emphasis of each of these developmental methods. Rational test development refers to a process that practically ensures the internal consistency of the test. With this approach, items are initially drafted to closely match the definition of the construct the test is intended to assess. Once the original pool of items is drafted, subject matter experts (SMEs) are used to confirm that these items are, indeed, relevant to the intended construct. For each item, each SME uses a rating scale to indicate how closely the item corresponds to the conceptualization of the construct. Items that are rated by SMEs as irrelevant to the construct are discarded.

The emphasis in empirically derived tests is on the relationship between test scores and an external criterion of interest, not on the internal consistency of items per se. In drafting items for an empirically derived test, less concern is placed on whether the items closely assess the underlying theoretical construct. Thus, it is often the case that the initial pool of items is much larger for an empirically devised measure than for a rationally developed measure. Using the empirical method, items that might be even tangentially related to the researcher's conception of the construct assessed are often included in the original pool of items. The pool of developed items is not subjected to the judgment of SMEs. Rather, the researcher identifies an external criterion of interest for which the items are intended to distinguish between various levels or categories. In a personnel selection test, for example, the criterion might be supervisor ratings of job performance. In a measure of psychopathology, the criterion might be the individual's psychiatric history (or lack thereof). After administering the items to a sample and collecting criterion information from the sample, item responses are correlated with the external criterion. Those items that distinguish between different levels of the criterion are retained for further pilot testing, while those items that do not differ across criterion levels are deleted.

Pilot Testing

The importance of **pilot testing** the measure cannot be overstated. At a minimum, measures of typical performance should be examined using a *think-aloud study* before administering the measure to a larger sample. Here, a small representative sample of the intended population is presented the measure and asked to verbalize their thoughts in deriving a response to each item. The goal of this procedure is to clarify *how* test takers interpret the items and their reasoning for their responses. Think-aloud studies help the test developer ensure the items are interpreted in the same way as intended. One of the authors of this text once attended a seminar in which a highly experienced test developer provided an excellent example of the utility of a think-aloud study. In this example, test administrators were baffled when an alarmingly high percentage of elementary school aged children reported "no" to a question asking if they lived with their parents. A think-aloud study quickly revealed that these children interpreted the question to mean "both parents," rather than either mother or father, as was intended by the researcher. A simple think-aloud study *prior* to administration of the measure would have avoided this problem.

The appropriate steps for additional pilot testing will depend on whether rational or empirical test development process was used. In either case, of course, larger sample sizes are preferable to smaller. In a rationally developed measure, data from the pilot test are factor analyzed to examine the underlying dimensionality of the measure. Reliability analysis is then conducted on emergent subdimensions of the scale (if any), as well as on the overall scale. An item may be discarded following either the factor analysis or the reliability analysis if it fails to demonstrate strong relationships with other items.

As discussed previously, the first step in pilot testing an empirically derived measure is the collection of data on both the newly developed measure and the criterion. Each item is then individually correlated with the criterion. Those items that are strongly related to the criterion are retained, while the remaining items are discarded. Due to concerns regarding the capitalization on chance, data are collected on the remaining items and the criterion using a second sample, and again the relationship between individual items and the criterion is examined. Items that again demonstrate a strong relationship with the criterion are retained for the final scale.

Survey Implementation

Don Dillman is perhaps the most influential author on the design and implementation of surveys. Dillman's (2007) tailored design method (TDM) is intended to increase response rates while decreasing error in responses. The TDM approach considers elements that might deter from the quality or quantity of responses, and looks at how to subsequently develop the survey to avoid such pitfalls. Dillman views survey response as a social exchange predicated on perceived rewards, costs, and trust. Survey design and implementation, then, must motivate participants by increasing perceived rewards (e.g., providing tangible rewards, communicating positive regard for the respondent) and trust (e.g., sponsorship by a legitimate authority, providing a token of appreciation for the respondent's time), while decreasing the respondent's costs (e.g., minimizing inconvenience, avoiding embarrassment). Dillman's TDM approach tailors the design and implementation of the survey to the specific needs of the population assessed, survey content, survey sponsor, and method of survey administration. According to Dillman (2007), the design of the survey, while important, has substantially less of an impact on response rate than does the way the survey is administered. Elements of the implementation of the survey include not only repeated contacts with potential respondents, but also thoughtful consideration of the cover letter, appearance of the envelopes used, explanation of the sponsorship of the survey, and incentives for participation.

Concluding Comments

Well, there you have it. Using the procedures outlined in this module, you are now ready to go out and create your own measure of typical performance. What? You don't think you're ready yet? Nonsense! Of course, you are. However, if you feel you're not quite ready for prime-time test construction, maybe it's best to first find an example or two. Gough and Bradley (1992) provided excellent examples of both empirical and rational methods of developing measures of typical performance, so you might want to start there. Dillman (2007) will prepare you for successful implementation of your newly constructed measure.

Best Practices

1. Development of a measure of typical performance begins once again with thorough test specifications.
2. Recognize that attitude and survey measurement is part of a social exchange. Respondents' decisions to participate in such measurement, and their interpretation of the items presented to them, are influenced by the social context.
3. Consult expert recommendations on the design and implementation of measures of typical performance. At the same time, use your own judgment of which rules, admonitions, and tips apply to your particular context, survey content, and purpose.
4. Always pilot test a measure prior to full implementation.

Practical Questions

1. This module begins by discussing serious concerns with self-report measures. Do such concerns indicate we should abandon this type of inquiry? Explain.
2. Why is defining the intended construct so essential to the development of a measure of typical performance?
3. In assessing someone's opinion, when might you prefer to use a free-response item format? When might you prefer to use a constructed-response item format?
4. Why is it sometimes appropriate to use emotionally loaded items when assessing self-report of a person's behavior?
5. What is acquiescence? What can a test developer do to reduce our concern with acquiescence?
6. Why shouldn't we ask respondents what they plan to do in the future? What should we do instead?
7. In reviewing the item-writing tips in this module, is there any particular tip that you feel is especially important? Why? Are there any item-writing tips that you would take issue with? Explain.
8. What is the major difference between rational and empirical methods of test development? Is rational test development unempirical? Is empirical test development irrational?

Case Studies

CASE STUDY 15.1: DEVELOPMENT OF THE MINNESOTA MULTIPHASIC PERSONALITY INVENTORY

The Minnesota Multiphasic Personality Inventory (MMPI) is one of the earliest and best-known empirically derived tests. Graham (1977, 1999) presented a detailed description of the development of the original version of the MMPI, based largely on the writings of the initial test developers, Starke Hathaway and J. Charnley McKinley.

Dissatisfied with the inefficiency and unreliability of individual interviews and mental exams, Hathaway and McKinley sought to develop a paper-and-pencil personality inventory that could be used for psychological diagnostic assessments. The test developers identified approximately 1000 personality-type statements from a wide variety of sources, including published attitude scales, psychiatric case histories, and textbooks. These 1000 items were then reduced to 504 relatively independent items.

As with any empirically derived test, the choice of a criterion was crucial. Hathaway and McKinley obtained two groups, whom Graham (1997, 1999) referred to as the Minnesota normals and the clinical participants. The Minnesota normals were composed of 1508 individuals, including visitors of hospital patients, recent high school graduates who attended precollege conferences at the University of Minnesota, hospital workers, and others. The clinical sample was composed of 221 psychiatric patients from the University of Minnesota Hospitals. These individuals were further divided into eight subgroups based on their clinical diagnosis.

The 504 potential items were administered to both the Minnesota normals and the specific clinical subgroups. Responses to each item were examined to determine whether an item differentiated between groups. Items that did differentiate between normal and clinical subgroup samples were retained and considered for inclusion in the MMPI scale for that particular diagnosis.

The test developers then cross-validated the clinical scales by administering retained items to new samples of normal and clinically diagnosed individuals. Items that were again able to differentiate between groups were subsequently included in the MMPI. The MMPI was then used to assist in the diagnosis of new patients.

Interestingly, the revision of the MMPI, which began in the early 1980s, adopted a somewhat more theoretical approach in that items were added to assess specific content areas (such as suicide potential and drug abuse) that SMEs deemed were underrepresented in the earlier version.

Questions to Ponder

1. Why did Hathaway and McKinley begin with such a large pool of potential items?
2. In what ways would item selection have differed if the original MMPI had been rationally developed?
3. Discuss the degree to which you feel the choice of criterion was appropriate for the MMPI.
4. Why did Hathaway and McKinley cross-validate the clinical scales?
5. Why would the process used to develop the MMPI be advantageous for diagnosing clinical patients?
6. Why would the revision of the MMPI include a somewhat more theoretical approach to test development?
7. The MMPI has sometimes been used in the selection of new employees. Is this an appropriate use of the test? Why or why not?

CASE STUDY 15.2: IDENTIFYING THE DIMENSIONALITY OF JOINERSHIP

"I knew this topic wasn't any good, but none of you listened to me, did you?" asked Doug, half in jest.

He and four other students in his graduate test construction seminar had recently begun working on a semester-long test construction project. Their assignment was to select a psychological trait, clearly define the domain, write items, and then conduct the usual steps for rational test development. Unfortunately, the semester was passing by quickly, and the students had just now begun to define the trait they had selected. Today, the group had decided to meet to hammer out a definition of the construct. Even so, there obviously remained some dissension as to whether the selected trait was really worth measuring at all.

"What sort of trait is *joinership* anyway?" continued Doug.

"You know, I really like the idea of this construct," retorted Kandice. "It seems to me that some people are more likely to join a lot of community groups and organizations, whereas others are never willing to join such organizations. As far as I know, there is no other scale intended to distinguish between these sorts of people."

Although she enjoyed this friendly bickering, Sangeeta was determined to get down to business. "Does anyone have any ideas as to how we should define the construct?"

Kristin had been waiting for this opportunity. "How about 'The number of groups a person joins'?"

"That's not bad," said Akira, "but does that mean we'll just measure how many groups a person is a member of? We could measure that with a single self-report item."

"No," protested Kristin, "I meant that we'd view the construct as a trait . . . more like someone's propensity for joining multiple groups."

"Would that mean that we are just interested in whether people *join* organizations? Or should we also measure their actual level of involvement in those organizations that they do join?" asked Akira.

Doug smiled. "Sorry, folks, but I see another problem. Without specifically saying so, I think we all have been thinking about the groups we're referring to as sort of social clubs and community organizations that generally have positive connotations. Are we also interested in a person's propensity for joining negative groups like gangs and cults?"

Sangeeta was ready to add her thoughts. "That's good, Doug, but maybe that's part of the dimensionality of the construct that we haven't talked about yet. Maybe there are different factors that would influence an individual to be attracted to different types of community groups. For example, maybe there exist different tendencies for people to join social groups versus religious groups versus violent groups."

Seeing an opening, Kandice jumped in, "You know, I did a little research last night in preparation for our meeting. I found a theory by Forsyth (1998) of why people join groups. According to Forsyth, people join groups to meet one of five functional needs, namely, belongingness, intimacy and support, generativity, influence, and exploration."

"Oh my," said Akira, obviously impressed. "Those needs sound like the dimensions of joinership we've been searching for. Wouldn't it make sense for us to write items that assess an individual's desire to join groups to satisfy those needs?"

"You bet," added Kristin. "And how's this for a formal definition? 'An individual's propensity to join multiple groups in order to satisfy each of Forsyth's (1998) needs.'"

"I think we're on to something big," said Sangeeta.

"Finally," added Doug.

Questions to Ponder

1. What special challenges might there be for defining a newly conceptualized construct such as joinership?

2. How would measurement of a personality trait differ from self-reported behavior? What implications would this have for the development of the scale?
3. A thorough test specification would likely discuss constructs that were similar, but distinct, from the construct assessed by the measure. What constructs might be used to compare and contrast joinership?
4. How important is it to define the context in which the scale is to be used? For what purposes could the joinership scale be used?
5. Explain how theory provided assistance in the development of the *joinership* scale. What role should theory play in the development of a psychological measure?
6. Now that the group has decided on the dimensionality of the construct, how should item writing proceed?

⊸⊸⊸

Exercises

EXERCISE 15.1: IMPROVING SURVEY ITEMS

OBJECTIVE: To identify and correct poorly written survey items.

Each of the items below share the following five-point Likert-type response scale:

Table 15.1   Five-point Likert-type Response Scale

1	2	3	4	5
Strongly Disagree	Disagree	Neither Agree nor Disagree	Agree	Strongly Agree

For each item, determine whether the item is clearly written or in need of improvement. If the item is in need of improvement, rewrite the item to eliminate the problem.

1. Many people fail to realize that the U.S. government is secretly run by a little-known, small group of individuals.
2. Advances in CAT and IRT have had a profound effect on the field of testing.
3. I will vote for Senator Wilson in the upcoming election.
4. The best times of my life were in high school and college.
5. I am in favor of our city council's revitalization plan.
6. Although the Christian Bible has revealed many essential truths, there are some passages of the Bible that we will never understand.
7. I tend to be shy.

8. Twenty-five pages of reading per week is an appropriate amount for a lower-division college course.
9. Doctors should never assist in a person's suicide.
10. I've volunteered in my community on many occasions.

PROLOGUE to Exercises 15.2–15.4: The following three exercises ask you to enact a number of steps required in scale construction. Items were developed to assess the fabricated construct of joinership. This construct can be defined as the propensity for an individual to join multiple groups. The scale is based loosely on the functional perspective, proposed by Forsyth (1998). The functional perspective assumes that the tendency for people to gather in groups reflects the usefulness of the groups to their members. The model proposes that individuals join groups to satisfy several functional needs. Although Forsyth originally proposed more than five needs, items were developed to assess an individual's drive to satisfy only the following functional needs:

1. *Belongingness:* The need for contact and inclusion with others
2. *Intimacy and Support:* The need for loving and supportive relationships
3. *Generativity:* The desire for goal achievement
4. *Influence:* The need for exertion of power
5. *Exploration:* The desire for personal growth

In accordance with the rational method of test development, specific items were written to assess each of these possible subdimensions of joinership. Care was taken to ensure that on the completed 42-item scale each subdimension of joinership was represented by a roughly equal number of items (approximately 8 or 9). Furthermore, a third of the items were negatively worded (i.e., required reverse coding), to help guard against acquiescence bias. The following 42 items resulted from this development process.

1. I would rather listen to others' instructions than get up and take command myself.
2. When problems arise, I look to others for support.
3. When working with people, I achieve more goals than I could on my own.
4. I think it is important to support community activities.
5. I don't feel a particular desire to try new things or learn new skills.
6. I feel that belonging to multiple organizations inhibits my personal growth.
7. Before making a decision, I ask for the advice of other people.
8. I am most happy when I am included in a group of my peers.
9. I am more likely to join groups when I can occupy a position of leadership.
10. In a group discussion, I am the person who talks the least.
11. I take advantage of opportunities to influence others.
12. Establishing caring relationships with others is a priority for me.
13. I like to work with others to reach the goals I have set for myself.

14. I like interacting with people who have similar interests.
15. I like to engage in a variety of new activities.
16. I take advantage of opportunities that increase my social status.
17. I prefer to solve problems by myself.
18. I can take care of myself, so I have little need for others.
19. Every person should have a cause or belief that they work toward.
20. I am open to new ideas and perspectives on life.
21. Sharing tasks decreases the amount of work I have to do.
22. I feel left out when I see others involved in a group.
23. The search for personal growth is done best when it is approached as a solitary endeavor.
24. I like to organize and lead the group.
25. Personal growth is a priority for me.
26. In general, I like being in charge of things.
27. I feel most satisfied when the goals I accomplish are achieved through my own efforts.
28. A goal-oriented person is less likely to join groups.
29. When I am having trouble, I count on others for support.
30. Exploring new ideas provides me with opportunities for personal growth.
31. Interaction with others motivates me to achieve my goals.
32. Forming supportive relationships with others is important to me.
33. I enjoy spending most of my free time doing activities that involve others.
34. I avoid organizations/groups because of pressures to conform.
35. Interacting with others helps me to develop my creativity.
36. I prefer being alone rather than being with others.
37. I feel uncomfortable sharing my problems with others.
38. In order to achieve my goals, I need the help of others.
39. Being with other people provides me with a sense of security.
40. I don't like being responsible for making important decisions.
41. I thrive on constant contact with other people.
42. I do not feel comfortable leading other individuals.

Thirty-five individuals served as SMEs to provide rational ratings of the items. Each rater was given detailed written and verbal instructions on how to complete the ratings. SMEs were provided with the definition of each of the five functional needs subdimensions and asked to rate the degree to which each item assessed its particular functional need. A five-point Likert-type scale was provided, with response options ranging from 0 for "No relevance" in assessing the defined functional need to 4 for "Highly relevant" to assessing the defined functional need. The resulting data file is titled "Joinership Rational Rating.sav" (see Appendix B).

A sample of 230 respondents was then administered the items. These individuals were asked to indicate how much they agreed with each item using the following five-point scale: 1 = strongly disagree, 2 = disagree, 3 = neither agree nor disagree, 4 = agree, 5 = strongly agree.

Data were entered into a file, and negatively worded items were reverse coded. The resulting data are included in the data file "Joinership Data Recoded.sav" (see Appendix B).

EXERCISE 15.2: EXAMINING SME RATINGS
OF THE JOINERSHIP ITEMS

OBJECTIVE: To refine the draft joinership scale using information provided by SME ratings.

Use the data file "Joinership Rational Rating.sav" to do the following:

1. Compute the mean and standard deviation of each item.
2. Determine a single cut score that you believe reflects SMEs' judgments that the item is too low in relevance to be included for further consideration. There are no rules of thumb here—you'll have to rely on your own judgment. However, don't set your cut score so high that you have too few items for the remaining steps.
3. Justify your choice of a cut score in item 2. Why should items that receive a rating at the cut score or above be retained for further analysis? Why should items below this cut score be discarded from further analysis?

EXERCISE 15.3: FACTOR ANALYZING THE JOINERSHIP ITEMS

OBJECTIVE: To examine the dimensionality of the remaining joinership scale items. (*Note:* If you have not yet covered Module 18, your instructor may ask you to skip Exercise 15.3 and proceed directly to Exercise 15.4.)

1. Using the data file "Joinership Data Recoded.sav," conduct an exploratory factor analysis of those items that were retained following examination of the SME ratings. Use the following options found within your data analysis software:

   • Choose principal axis factoring as the method of extraction.
   • Request a scree plot. Base the number of factors that emerge on your judgment of the results of the scree plot.
   • For the method of rotation, select Promax (see Module 18 for an explanation of why Promax is recommended).
   • Choose "sort by size" to display factor loadings.

2. Interpret the results of your factor analysis.

   a. How many interpretable factors emerged? This is the dimensionality of your scale. Label each interpretable factor by examining the items that it comprises.
   b. Which items load on each interpretable factor?
   c. Discard any items that fail to load on an interpretable factor.

EXERCISE 15.4: EXAMINING THE RELIABILITY
OF THE JOINERSHIP SUBSCALES

OBJECTIVE: To develop subscales of joinership with high internal-consistency reliability.

1. Using only those items retained following Exercises 15.2 and 15.3, conduct a reliability analysis of each dimension of the scale (as represented by the factors that emerged in Exercise 15.3) (*alternatively,* if your instructor omitted Exercise 15.3, develop scale dimensions based on your rational categorization of the items you expect to assess each of the five dimensions discussed in the prologue above). Choose the following options:

   • Compute alpha.
   • Select the options "scale if item-deleted" and "item-total correlations."

2. Examine the output for each reliability analysis. Compare the obtained alpha with the alpha estimated if each particular item was deleted. Would the alpha increase if an item were deleted from the scale? If the answer is no, retain all items. If the answer is yes, you may consider dropping the item with the lowest item-total correlation from the final version of the scale. First, however, ask yourself the following questions:

   • Would dropping the item increase the alpha substantially?
   • Is there a logical reason the item seems different from the other items loading on this factor?

If an item was dropped from a dimension, rerun the reliability analysis and repeat the process. Note that alpha is improved by dropping items with low item-total correlations.

3. Once the alphas of each dimension of the scale have been determined, compute the alpha of the overall scale.

Further Readings

Dillman, D.A. (2007). *Mail and Internet surveys: The tailored design method.* Hoboken, NJ: John Wiley & Sons.

Gough, H.G., & Bradley, P. (1992). Comparing two strategies for developing personality scales. In M. Zeidner & R. Most (Eds.), *Psychological testing: An inside view* (pp. 215–246). Palo Alto, CA: Consulting Psychologists Press.

Schuman, H., & Presser, S. (1996). *Questions and answers in attitude surveys: Experiments on question form, wording, and context.* Newbury Park, CA: Sage.

Module 16

Response Biases

W henever we administer a psychological test, we hope to obtain reliable individual differences on the measure. Without reliable individual differences, the measure is of little use to us in predicting our outcome of interest. Sometimes, however, we find few, if any, differences between test takers' responses. Other times, we may have substantially more variability in responses than we would expect based on previous administrations of the same or similar tests to comparable participants. In either possible scenario, we would want to determine *why* we obtained such different results than we had expected. There are a variety of reasons the results may be different than anticipated. In this module, we will discuss possible **response biases** that may influence the variability in test scores and, ultimately, the reliability, validity, and utility of those test scores. In this module, we define response biases to be strategies and methods that test takers use that are unrelated to the construct of interest.

Guessing on Knowledge and Aptitude Tests

One response bias that occurs with multiple-choice tests of knowledge and aptitude is guessing on items. That is, with these types of tests, there is only one correct (i.e., keyed) answer, and there are several distracter responses (also referred to as foils) for each item. Therefore, when a test taker answers an item correctly, it is either because he or she actually knew the answer or because he or she guessed correctly. Unfortunately, it is virtually impossible for us to know which the case is. In fact, even if you asked the respondent, he or she may not be able to tell you which was the case. Hence, one disadvantage of using multiple-choice (or constructed-response) tests is that respondents can answer an item correctly simply by guessing even though they have little or no knowledge of the subject matter being tested. Hence, in some instances, an individual's test score on a multiple-choice test may be telling you more about that person's level of test-wiseness or risk-taking behavior than his or her level of knowledge in a given content area. Therefore, one needs to be careful when developing tests to make sure that clues to the correct answer are not given within the item itself (e.g., grammatical errors that give away the answer) or that the answer is not given away by another item within the same test. Following the test construction principles outlined in Module 12 will go a long way toward reducing the potential influence of test-wiseness, and thus guessing, on test scores. Having a large number of items will help mitigate the influence of a "lucky guess," making it less likely that a few lucky guesses will make a large difference in any single test score.

Correcting for Guessing on Knowledge Tests

If we are unsure whether a given individual is answering an item correctly because he or she knows the correct answer or because he or she is guessing correctly, how can we "correct" test scores for the potential influence of guessing? There are several guessing models that can be applied to correct for the influence of guessing on test scores. In blind-guessing models, it is assumed that individuals have no idea what the correct answer is. Therefore, if there are four response options, any individual has a one-in-four (or 25%) chance of answering an item correctly simply by random guessing. In the past, it was thought that one way to reduce this probability was to simply insert more distracters. Hence, an individual would have five, six, or possibly more options to choose from. In theory, this is a good idea. In practice, however, it becomes clear that it is extremely difficult and time consuming to write distracter options that are attractive to respondents with little knowledge of the topic. As a result, it turns out that when a fifth, sixth, or additional response option is added, no one chooses it. Thus, in practice, it becomes a waste of time for test developers to rack their brains trying to come up with additional viable response options that no one is going to choose anyway.

Many test publishers have used the blind-guessing model (or assumption) when correcting scores for guessing. Thus, they use a correction formula such as

$$R_c = R - \frac{W}{k-1}$$

where R_c is the corrected-for-guessing score, R is the number of items answered correctly (right), W is the number of items answered incorrectly (wrong), and k is the number of alternatives for each question (e.g., A, B, C, D, and E would be five alternatives). Assume, for example, that an individual was administered a 35-item test with each item having five response options. She attempted 32 items and answered 20 correctly. Thus,

$$R_c = R - \frac{W}{k-1} = 20 - \frac{12}{5-1} = 17$$

Hence, we estimate that the individual knew 17 answers and made three lucky guesses of the 20 questions she answered correctly. Thus, you may remember being instructed when you took a standardized test (way back when) not to guess and to leave a question blank if you did not know the answer. This is because, you will notice, only items that are attempted are included in the correction formula. Thus, it will be to your disadvantage to guess on an item for which you have no clue as to the correct answer (i.e., you would have to guess randomly). This advice, of course, only applies in the rare instance when a correction-for-guessing formula is used and you are truly guessing randomly.

You are probably thinking that most guessing is not really blind guessing, and you would be correct. What typically happens on any given multiple-choice question is that you are able to fairly confidently eliminate one or two options. Therefore, it is no longer a one-in-five (20%) chance of answering a question correctly for a five-option multiple-choice test question, but rather a one-in-four (25%) or one-in-three (33%) chance of answering the item correctly. Another concern is that those who have the least knowledge have the most to gain from guessing. In addition, there may be certain personality characteristics associated with guessing. For example, if examinees are instructed not to guess, the more timid (or risk averse) test takers are more likely to follow the direction and not guess on items they do not know. They may do this even if they could eliminate one or two options, in which case guessing would be to their advantage.

So if you are the examinee, should you guess? Yes, if you can eliminate at least one of the incorrect options. In the long run, the correction formula undercorrects in such situations. If you are the test developer or test user, should you correct for guessing? If there are no omits (i.e., everyone answers every question), then there will be a perfect correlation between the original test score and the corrected test score. Hence, it will not make much of a difference in a practical sense. However, if there are omits and your purpose for instituting a **correction for guessing** is to obtain better true scores, to discourage random guessing, or to reduce measurement error (always a good thing), then why not?

Another, less direct way to "correct" for guessing is to use **computer adaptive testing (CAT)** methods. Using CAT methods, if an individual answers an item correctly (regardless of whether he knew it or whether he guessed), he then gets a harder question. However, it would be very unlikely that the individual then guesses correctly again (just by chance) on an even more difficult item. Thus, with the adaptive nature of CAT, the individual will eventually be directed back to questions of appropriate difficulty. Ultimately, then, his true underlying ability level will be accurately assessed without using a correction-for-guessing formula. This aspect of CAT is one of the reasons that the Educational Testing Service (ETS) no longer corrects for guessing on the general portion of the Graduate Record Examination. However, ETS still corrects for guessing on the subject test, which is given in paper-and-pencil format. More information on CAT is provided in Module 21.

Response Biases on Personality and Attitude Measures

A variety of different response biases can also occur on attitude measures. For example, **central tendency error** refers to the situation where the respondent tends to use only the middle of the scale and is reluctant (for whatever reason) to select extreme values. This happens when on a seven-point rating scale, for example, the respondent answers with predominantly 4s. Conversely, with **severity error** or **leniency error**, the respondent uses only the extreme ends of the continuum. Thus, again, the respondents are limiting themselves to a restricted portion of the rating scale and so engaging in response biases that will influence the reliability, validity, and utility of the resulting scores.

One of the most prominent forms of bias in attitude measurement is *acquiescence bias* (i.e., yea-saying), where respondents agree with everything that is presented in a survey. For example, you can query individuals on their attitudes regarding a variety of social issues from abortion to homosexuality to legalization of marijuana to gun ownership. Most individuals would agree with some, but probably not all, of the issues. However, the respondent who acquiesces will have a great tendency to agree with all the issues presented in your survey regardless of his or her true feelings regarding each topic. At the other end of the continuum is *nonacquiescence bias* (i.e., nay-saying), where the individual tends to disagree with everything that is presented. A common strategy to address both issues is to reverse approximately half the items on your survey so that individuals who have a tendency to acquiesce will not simply provide the highest or lowest rating for each item. That is, approximately half the items are worded positively, while the other half are worded negatively. However, you must remember to reverse score the negatively worded items so that they are positive before you compute the scale scores and realize that other, unintended, psychometric issues may occur such as the creation of subdimensions consisting of just the reverse-scored items (see Module 15).

An additional bias that can occur in personality measures in particular is *faking*. When respondents fake their answers to personality and attitude items, they are most likely trying to deliberately misrepresent themselves. For example, someone applying for a job as a salesperson may know that it is good to be extraverted to be a successful salesperson, so when the person fills out an extraversion questionnaire for employment as a car salesperson, he or she may well try to "fake good" on the extraversion dimension of a personality questionnaire to appear more extraverted than he or she really is. Alternatively, a defendant in a legal proceeding may be facing the death penalty in a capital murder trial. The only chance to avoid execution may be to "fake bad" on a personality measure (i.e., pretend he is criminally insane) in order to claim innocence by reason of insanity. In both instances, the person is not providing truthful or accurate assessments, but rather trying to fake answers in order to obtain a desirable outcome.

A concept somewhat similar to faking is that of *socially desirable responding*. Paulhus (1986, 1991) discussed two forms of socially desirable responding— namely, **self-deceptive enhancement (SDE)** and **impression management (IM)**.

With IM, the individual is deliberately trying to present a positive impression, similar to the faking-good situation discussed previously. The key is that the individual is consciously making a choice to respond so as to appear more socially acceptable than he or she truly is. On the other hand, an individual engaging in SDE may also be presenting himself or herself in an overly exaggerated positive light; however, the SDE individual is not conscious of doing so. For example, some three quarters of individuals typically report being above average in both intelligence and physical attractiveness. Here the individuals may not be consciously trying to deceive the questioner (although some may be trying to do so); rather, they actually believe, some obviously wrongly so, that they truly are "above average" in terms of intelligence and physical attractiveness. Social psychologists would attribute the reason individuals engage in SDE to related concepts such as self-image, self-esteem, and psychological defense mechanisms.

Another bias that occurs when individuals are rating others' behavior, or past performance (such as in performance appraisal ratings used in an organizational context), is *halo bias*. With halo bias, raters fail to discriminate among conceptually distinct aspects of the ratee's behavior. Unfortunately, it is almost impossible to determine whether the halo is true halo (i.e., the ratee really is excellent in all categories) or whether it is illusory (i.e., the ratee is very sociable, so is seen as good in all areas, even if he or she isn't). Disappointingly, there are no correction formulas for these biases as there are with knowledge tests.

We also need to make a distinction between response bias and response style. *Response biases* are measurement artifacts that emerge from the context of a particular situation. Thus, response biases can often be ameliorated with proper instructions or rater training. For example, individuals are likely to engage in IM and faking good on personality measures when a desirable outcome is attached (e.g., a job offer or academic placement). However, when the context does not involve a direct valued outcome (e.g., a career-counseling session), the individual will be much less likely to engage in response biases. **Response styles**, however, are not context specific. These measurement artifacts tend to be consistent across situations and so are more difficult to reduce. For example, there are clear cultural differences in how individuals respond to attitude questions. Thus, individuals from some cultures are more likely to agree with an item (i.e., acquiesce), regardless of the content of the item. In Module 11, we discuss in more detail these and related issues with regard to cross-cultural issues in testing.

What are some of the ways we can reduce response biases? First, we must make a distinction between detecting such biases and preventing such biases. Clearly, our primary concern should be to prevent such biases in the first place. Thus, for example, it is important to have clear instructions for both test proctors and test takers. It is also important to avoid implying that one response is preferred over another. Also, whenever possible, anonymity has been shown to lead to more honest responding. In addition, research convincingly indicates that subtle wording differences (particularly in attitude and public-opinion questionnaires) can make dramatic differences in how individuals respond to a question. Test developers have also used forced-choice item formats with comparable levels of social desirability for each option. In doing so, our hope is that respondents are unable to choose the most socially desirable answer and thus will answer in a more truthful and accurate manner. However, what is considered socially desirable may change depending on the context. For example, being extraverted may be desirable for a sales position, but it may be less socially desirable for an entry-level computer programmer. Respondents also tend to have a much easier time making comparative judgments rather than absolute judgments. Thus, it is better to ask, "Do you agree more with X or Y?" than to ask, "How much do agree with X? With Y?" Finally, use of unobtrusive observational measures may help to provide more accurate assessment of the constructs of interest.

No matter how much we try, however, we will not be able to totally prevent individuals from engaging in response biases. In addition, response styles are not context dependent; hence, it would be difficult to "prevent" such response biases. Therefore, we must be able to not only do our best to prevent such occurrences but also detect them once they occur. That is why popular measures such as the Minnesota Multiphasic Personality Inventory have several "lie" scales. In addition, there are numerous scales available to detect socially desirable responding. As Anastasi and Urbina (1997) pointed out, however, how we view such response biases has evolved over time. Initially, in the early to middle part of the 20th century, researchers assumed that any such response biases represented irrelevant error variance, and the goal was to eliminate them. By the late 20th century, however, many researchers began to see response biases such as faking, acquiescence, and socially desirable responding as their own unique traits that were worthy of measurement and study in their own right (Mersman & Shultz, 1998). Even today, however, it is still unclear how to deal with those who engage in such response biases and styles. Should they be removed from the data set? Should their scores somehow be "corrected" for such biases? In addition, we may not even be sure what causes some of the aberrant responding we may observe. Additional factors, such as fatigue, primacy, carelessness, or item-ordering effects, may be the "real" culprits. Thus, even though we have developed more sophisticated ways of identifying response biases, there is no consensus in the professional literature on what to do with such information once we have it.

A Step-by-Step Example of Identifying and Examining Response Biases

As a second-year graduate student, you have been asked to sit on a university-wide committee that is developing a questionnaire that will be given to faculty, staff, and students at your university to assess their attitudes regarding your university possibly converting from a quarter to a semester system. This issue has been raised numerous times in the past. In general, faculty members have been about equally split (50/50) on whether to convert to a semester system, with newer faculty members preferring to switch to semesters, while more senior faculty members generally oppose such a move. Students, though, overwhelmingly (75%+) do not want to switch from the quarter to the semester system. However, the views of the university staff have generally been much more variable, sometimes supporting and sometimes opposing such a conversion. The administration is strongly in favor of converting to semesters; however, it refuses to do so without the support of students, faculty, and staff.

Your role on the committee is to provide input regarding how to prevent certain biases from occurring in the survey before it is administered and how to identify any biases once the data are in and ready to be analyzed. You know that there are many advantages to assessing opinions via written attitude surveys—for instance, they are quick, inexpensive, efficient, and flexible. You also realize, however, that poor design and careless execution of the survey can lead to biased responding. You also know that error can be both random and systematic. Random error is typically thought of in terms of sampling error. Therefore, it is important that we choose our samples appropriately. However, other committee members will be addressing the issue of appropriate sampling methods. We are charged with evaluating possible systematic errors and, in particular, issues surrounding response errors (i.e., biases).

Systematic bias can arise from administrative errors (e.g., confusing directions on how to fill out the questionnaire) or respondent error. We will focus on respondent error because that is the focus of this module. A major source of respondent error is no response at all. That is, how do we interpret unreturned surveys or returned surveys that are only half completed? Were the respondents being careless, or were they trying to send a message with their lack of response? We also know that those with strong opinions are more likely to fill out and return attitude questionnaires; thus, those who are indifferent about the topic will likely be underrepresented in our final sample. Therefore, it is important that we do all that we can to maximize the response rate before, during, and after the administration of the survey. Doing so will dramatically reduce nonrespondent errors.

Then there are the response biases we discussed earlier, such as acquiescence, extremity (leniency and severity), central tendency, and socially desirable responding. For example, those strongly opposed to the potential conversion may be likely to engage in severity ratings that criticize every aspect of a potential conversion, even if they do not totally disagree with all such aspects, in order to ensure that their voice is heard. Others may be likely to acquiesce because they know that the administration is strongly in favor of such a conversion. In order to combat such potential response biases, we would want to guarantee anonymity, make the directions as clear and neutral as possible, and ensure that the items themselves are not worded in such a way as to elicit a response in favor of one position or another. We may even want to think about the possibility of adding some forced-choice items where each possible response is of equal social desirability; however, that may be difficult given the nature of this situation.

Assuming that we have taken the safeguards mentioned previously prior to the administration of the questionnaire, we then need to identify any possible response biases or styles that may be present in the respondents' answers once we collect the data. Depending on the number of respondents, it may be unwieldy to identify individual respondents who are demonstrating specific response biases or patterns. However, we may want to break down the data by major categories, such as faculty versus staff versus students. We may also want to look within subcategories, such as students within different colleges within the university or students in particular majors. However, we must be careful not to break down the data too finely, as we may be able to identify individuals (e.g., there may be only one Native American female who is a geology major at the university), thus violating our assurances of anonymity.

Clearly there are many details that need to be attended to when you attempt to undertake a major survey such as this one. Response biases are just a small part of the many decisions that need to be made. It is important, however, to keep potential response biases in mind as you make critical decisions along the way. For example, whether a face-to-face, mail, e-mail, telephone, or Internet survey is used can dramatically affect which response errors are likely to surface and in what fashion for each constituent group. Thus, being mindful of potential response biases will help you better prevent them before the survey is administered and identify and address them once you have collected the data.

Concluding Comments

With multiple-choice constructed-response knowledge questions, there is always the possibility that individuals might guess the correct answer. Most research shows that corrections for guessing tend to underestimate the extent of guessing, in that individuals can typically eliminate one or more incorrect responses. Hence, corrections for guessing should be used sparingly. In addition, if such corrections are used, it should be made clear to the test takers what the ramifications will be if they guess randomly. Response biases and response styles on attitude questionnaires also represent possible measurement artifacts that need to be dealt with. Several suggestions are offered to prevent (or at least reduce) and identify such biases, but in the end, it is difficult to assess whether such biases are true biases or illusory. Thus, how to address the issue of response biases in attitude questionnaires is still a controversial topic.

Best Practices

1. Any use of correction-for-guessing procedures should be well justified and carefully implemented.
2. It is always best to find ways to prevent response biases, rather than simply waiting until the data is collected to identify and deal with them post hoc.
3. It is important to distinguish between response biases (context dependent) and response styles (universal traits) and to recognize the need to deal with them in different ways.

Practical Questions

1. Is correcting for guessing appropriate in college-level courses where most individuals will not be guessing randomly, but rather will almost always be able to eliminate one or more distracter options?
2. In situations where individuals are unlikely to omit any of the questions on purpose, is it appropriate to correct for guessing?
3. What other personality characteristics, besides risk taking, do you think would be associated with guessing on multiple-choice tests?
4. What other factors, besides guessing, might contribute to extremely low or high levels of variability in knowledge test scores?
5. It was noted that if a test taker can eliminate at least one of the distracters, then corrections for guessing underestimate the extent of guessing. Is it possible to overestimate the extent of guessing with correction formulas? If so, how?
6. Given that you cannot guess on short-answer essay questions, would they, by default, be more reliable?
7. What is the difference between response biases and response styles?
8. What are the best ways to reduce response biases? Response styles?

Case Studies

CASE STUDY 16.1: COMPARABILITY OF DIFFERENT INTRODUCTORY PSYCHOLOGY TESTS

Ryan, a first-year PhD student, was teaching his own discussion sections of introductory psychology for the first time. At Ryan's university, the introductory psychology class consists of a 200-person lecture taught by a full-time professor in the department and ten 20-person discussion sections taught by first-year graduate students. There are five graduate students who teach two discussion sections each, every term. Every other week, the five discussion leaders for that term are to administer a 25-item quiz on the chapters covered in the lecture and discussion sections during that time frame. On the Monday before the scheduled quiz, the five discussion leaders meet with the professor and agree on the questions to be included in the quiz for that week.

Everything seemed to be going well until Ryan computed the results of the third quiz. He had noticed that students in the morning section had scored pretty much as usual, but that the grades in the afternoon section were rather odd. In particular, while he noticed that the afternoon class average was just slightly higher than the morning section's grades on the quiz for that week, what seemed really odd was that students in the afternoon section all received almost exactly the same score (i.e., all had a score of 21, 22, or 23). That is, there was basically no variability among the test scores. Figuring that the students in the afternoon section probably cheated and somehow got a copy of the quiz from the morning section, Ryan started examining the quizzes more closely. However, to his surprise, he noticed that while everyone had almost the exact same score, different students answered different questions correctly. That is, not everyone answered the same two, three, or four questions wrong. Hence, it didn't appear that individuals had copied from of one another. This left Ryan rather perplexed. Unsure of what was going on, Ryan decided that he had better check in with the other graduate student teaching assistants and see what they thought.

Questions to Ponder

1. What alternative explanation (besides cheating) do you think might explain the low variability in the afternoon section?
2. What might Ryan have done differently to reduce the possible "cheating factor"?
3. Would using a correction-for-guessing formula help Ryan in any way? If so, how?
4. Are there other statistical corrections Ryan could institute to correct for the low variability?
5. Is the low variability in test scores really a problem in a classroom situation such as this?

CASE STUDY 16.2: SUSPICIOUS SURVEY
DATA FROM A FRIEND

Dora was very excited about her committee's recent approval of her proposal for her master's thesis project. After several arduous sets of revisions, she was finally ready to collect her data. Unfortunately, the committee had added several new scales to her study, and suddenly, her six-page questionnaire had turned into 15 pages. As a result, the structural equation model she had proposed had also expanded. Thus, her original estimate of 150 subjects had doubled to more than 300. To add to her troubles, her target population was working parents. These were just the sort of people who didn't have time to fill out a lengthy questionnaire. Undaunted, Dora continued going to schools and day care centers to collect data, but the surveys seemed to be trickling in just a few at a time.

Just as Dora was about to throw up her hands in surrender, she had a stroke of good luck. Her friend in another city worked for a large school district as head of student counseling. Her friend said she could easily find 100–150 parents to complete her survey. So Dora quickly mailed off 200 surveys to her friend. About 6 weeks later, she called her friend to check in. Her friend said that she had been buried in work, but she reassured Dora that she would have the completed surveys back to her within 2 weeks. When Dora called her friend a month later, her friend was again rather vague on how many completed surveys she had, but the friend assured Dora once again that she would have the completed surveys mailed back to her by the end of the month. About ready to give up yet again, Dora received a box in the mail from her friend. Eagerly, she opened up the box and was shocked to see all 200 surveys inside. However, as she began entering the data that night, she noticed that all the responses were the highest value on the given scales (i.e., 5 on a five-point scale, 7 on a seven-point scale). She also noticed that while the ink color was different on some of the surveys, it seemed like the same handwriting was used on each of the 200 surveys. Did her friend simply go through and circle the highest value on all the surveys? Dora was desperate for more data, but was feeling rather uncomfortable with the current situation. Therefore, it seemed time to sit down with her thesis advisor and figure out what to do (if anything) with the "data" she recently received and where to go from here on her thesis.

Questions to Ponder

1. If you were Dora, would you use the surveys from her friend?
2. Would the data still be useful to Dora, assuming working parents, in fact, completed the data from her friend?
3. Again, assuming that the data are, in fact, legitimate, what response bias seems to be happening here?
4. Are there any statistical corrections that can be made to the data to make them useful?
5. If Dora were a fellow student colleague and friend, what suggestions would you provide to her with regard to collecting more data?

Exercises

EXERCISE 16.1: CORRECTION FOR GUESSING IN MULTIPLE-CHOICE KNOWLEDGE TESTS—COMPUTER EXERCISE

OBJECTIVE: To practice using the correction-for-guessing formula discussed in the module overview with computerized data.

The data set "GMA Data.sav" (see Appendix B) contains scores for 323 individuals on a 40-item general mental ability test that includes both verbal and quantitative questions. Each item has already been scored as incorrect (0) or correct (1). The data set also has a total raw score for each individual. Demographic data are also provided. Using the correction formula (discussed in the overview), compute a corrected-for-guessing score for each individual. Note that all questions have five possible responses (i.e., $k = 5$).

1. What is the relationship between the uncorrected and corrected scores?
2. Does guessing seem to help some respondents more than others? Discuss.
3. Respondents were not warned about the possibility of correcting for guessing. Is it fair, then, to correct for guessing in this situation? Discuss.
4. What alternatives to correcting for guessing could you use to increase the quality of the test scores?

EXERCISE 16.2: IDENTIFYING RESPONSE BIASES IN ATTITUDE ITEMS

OBJECTIVE: To practice identifying response biases in attitude items.

The "Geoscience Attitudes.sav" data set (see Appendix B) asks students about their attitudes toward the geosciences (archaeology, geography, and geology). The data set has 13 attitude items and 137 respondents (see Exercise 18.1 for a description of the content of each question). Examine the data set and try to identify individual cases (i.e., students) who appear to be engaging in some form of response bias. In particular, determine if any of the students are displaying signs of acquiescence, leniency, severity, central tendency, or socially desirable responding. For the latter, you will have to examine the wording of the items carefully and try to identify items that you believe to be highest in social desirability. Then, determine if any student's responses appear to differ for those items identified as socially desirable as compared to the less (or non-) socially desirable items.

1. Did you identify any individuals who appear to be providing biased responses?
2. Which cases appear to be demonstrating biased responses?
3. What forms of response biases did you identify?
4. What should we do with this information once we have it?

EXERCISE 16.3: DEVELOPING TEST MATERIALS AND PROCEDURES THAT WILL (HOPEFULLY) REDUCE RESPONSE BIAS IN PARTICIPANTS

OBJECTIVE: To gain practice in developing strategies to reduce biases in responding to attitude questionnaires.

Imagine you have been asked to develop a personality test that measures antisocial behaviors. The measure will be used for three different purposes. The first purpose will be to identify high school students who are having trouble in school and thus may be referred to an alternative high school for troubled youths. The second purpose is to determine whether parolees still pose a significant risk to society if they are paroled and thus allowed to rejoin society. In the third situation, the test will be used to screen candidates applying for the job of police officer with a small municipality (15,000 residents) that uses community policing as its major crime-fighting mechanism.

1. Would you expect to find different forms of response biases in the different populations under study? If so, which biases would you see as most prominent in each of the three scenarios?
2. What strategies would you suggest to prevent response biases in each of the three scenarios?
3. What strategies would you suggest to identify response biases in each of the three scenarios once the data have been collected?

Further Readings

Chan, D. (2009). So why ask me? Are self-report data really that bad? In C.E. Lance & R.J. Vandenberg (Eds.), *Statistical and methodological myths and urban legends: Doctrine, verity and fable in the organizational and social sciences* (pp. 309–336). New York: Routledge.

Moorman, R.H.P., & Philip, M. (1992). A meta-analytic review and empirical test of the potential confounding effects of social desirability response sets in organizational behaviour research. *Journal of Occupational & Organizational Psychology, 65,* 131–149.

Paulhus, D.L. (1986). Self-deception and impression management in test responses. In A. Angleitner & J.S. Wiggins (Eds.), *Personality assessment via questionnaires: Current issues in theory and measurement* (pp. 143–165). Berlin: Springer-Verlag.

Paulhus, D.L. (1991). Measurement and control of response bias. In J.P. Robinson, P.R. Shaver, & L.S. Wrightsman (Eds.), *Measures of personality and social psychological attitudes.* San Diego, CA: Academic Press.

Schaeffer, N.C., & Presser, S. (2003). The science of asking questions. *Annual Review of Sociology, 29,* 65–88.

Part 4
Advanced Topics

Module 17

Combining Predictors Using Multiple Regression

In Module 8, we said that evidence of criterion-related validity is demonstrated by correlating test scores with corresponding criterion scores. If the test is sufficiently related to the criterion of interest, regression can later be used to predict criterion scores in a sample of people for whom we have no actual criterion values, as long as the sample is drawn from the same population used in the original validation study. Obviously, the stronger the relationship between our test and the criterion, the more accurate will be our predicted criterion score. If a test is used in this way to *predict* a criterion score, the test is often referred to as a *predictor*. In most cases, we could increase the accuracy of predicting our criterion if we expanded the number of predictors beyond one.

Multiple regression allows us to use information from numerous predictors to predict a single criterion score. For example, if we wanted to predict tomorrow's high temperature in Poughkeepsie, New York, we would want to consider a number of factors, including today's temperature in Poughkeepsie, the amount of cloud cover, last year's high temperature in Poughkeepsie on tomorrow's date, and so on. The addition of multiple predictors would likely increase the accuracy of our prediction of tomorrow's high temperature beyond the accuracy we would obtain if we relied on any single measure alone. Similarly, if we wanted to predict an applicant's potential job performance, we would desire information from multiple valid selection tests rather than just a single one. This module will discuss issues associated with combining predictors when we use multiple regression procedures.

The Multiple Regression Equation

As in the single-predictor case, to use multiple regression for prediction purposes we would first conduct a study to determine the degree to which a set of predictors is related to scores on a criterion of interest. Thus, a sample is drawn, and scores on each predictor variable and criterion are collected. If the set of predictors is significantly related to the criterion, then we could use the information obtained from this original sample to produce the regression equation. As you will see below, a multiple regression equation is a linear equation that includes values for each of the predictor variables we choose to include. Each predictor variable receives a unique weight, or *regression coefficient*, based on (a) the means and standard deviations of the predictors, (b) the correlations between each of the predictors and the criterion, and (c) the correlations between the predictors themselves.

The regression equation can be presented in two forms: unstandardized or standardized. The unstandardized form of the multiple regression equation uses an individual's raw scores on each test to predict a raw score on the criterion. In addition to including regression weights and predictor raw score values, the unstandardized regression equation contains a value called the *intercept,* which is the value associated with the location where the regression line crosses the Y axis. The *unstandardized* multiple regression equation is as follows:

$$\hat{Y} = b_1 x_1 + b_2 x_2 + \cdots + b_k x_k + a$$

where $\hat{Y}$ is the predicted criterion raw score, b is an unstandardized regression coefficient, x is a predictor raw score, a is the intercept, and k is the number of predictors.

The standardized form of the equation requires the use of standardized predictor scores (such as z scores) to predict a standardized criterion score. The *standardized* multiple regression equation is

$$\acute{Z}_y = \beta_1 z_{x1} + \beta_2 z_{x2} + \cdots + \beta_k z_{xk}$$

Where $\acute{Z}$ is the predicted standardized criterion score, β is a standardized regression coefficient, and z_x is a standardized predictor score.

It should be noted that the two versions of the regression equation are equal in terms of accuracy in prediction. However, sometimes we prefer the use of the standardized regression equation because the magnitude of the resulting standardized regression coefficients, or beta weights (β), of each predictor can be directly compared to one another because all variables are measured on a common metric. Other times, it is preferable to use the unstandardized equation because the variables are in their original metrics.

As long as the new sample was drawn from the same population used in the development of the regression equation, the regression equation can be used to predict a criterion score for each member of a new sample of individuals. This is done by collecting predictor scores for each individual in the new sample, plugging these values into the regression equation, and computing predicted Y scores.

The Multiple Regression Equation: An Example

Let us consider a brief example of the use of the multiple regression equation, based on data in the "Volunteer Data.sav" data file (see Appendix B). (*Notes:* First, you will find a more detailed description of this data set in Exercise 17.2. Second, you are encouraged to follow the computations discussed in this example using your favorite data analysis program.) From this data set, we could examine whether the variables *perceived opportunity for reward* (reward), *role clarity* (clarity), and *leader consideration* (ledcons) as a set can be used to predict an individual's level of desire to remain in the organization due to an emotional bond. This is termed *affective commitment* (affectc). An examination of the zero-order correlations reveals that *affective commitment* is highly correlated with each of the predictors: $r = .64$ with *perceived opportunity for reward*, $r = .50$ with *leader consideration*, and $r = .64$ with *role clarity*. These relatively strong correlations suggest that a multiple regression equation using these three predictors will result in high prediction of the criteria (affectc).

Because we have three predictor variables, we would also have three regression coefficients in the equation. Assuming that the terms denoted with a subscript of 1 corresponded to *perceived opportunity for reward*, those denoted with a subscript of 2 corresponded to *leader consideration*, and those denoted with a 3 corresponded to *role clarity*, the resulting unstandardized multiple regression equation for the prediction of affective commitment would be written as

$$\hat{Y} = .48x_1 + .20x_2 + .38x_3 + (-.60)$$

Let us assume that we then randomly draw a sample from the same population and wish to predict these people's scores on affective commitment. For the sake of argument, suppose that an individual from this new sample scored a value of 5.17 on *reward*, 4.20 on *leader consideration*, and 3.83 on *role clarity*. (Note that this individual just so happened to score exactly the same values as the second case of our data file.) To estimate this individual's score on *affective commitment*, we would plug these values into the regression equation:

$$\hat{Y} = .48(5.17) + .20(4.20) + .38(3.83) + (-.60)$$
$$= 2.48 + .84 + 1.46 + (-.60) = 4.18$$

Thus, we would predict that a person with the given values on the predictor variables would have a value of 4.18 on *affective commitment*.

We would need to use the standardized version of the regression equation if we hoped to compare the magnitude of the regression coefficients across the predictor variables. In this case, the standardized regression equation is

$$\acute{Z}_y = .41z_{x1} + .11z_{x2} + .40z_{x3}$$

Note that scores on *perceived opportunity for reward* and *role clarity* receive nearly equal weighting, while scores on *leader consideration* receive a lesser weight. Virtually all statistical packages will provide a test of significance of each coefficient in a regression analysis. In SPSS, for example, a table labeled "coefficients" presents not only the standardized and unstandardized regression coefficients for each predictor, but also a test of the significance of each predictor's regression weight. In this example, the regression coefficients for both *perceived opportunity for reward* and *role clarity* are statistically significant, $p < .01$. The coefficient for *leader consideration*, however, is not statistically significant, $p > .05$. This suggests that we could eliminate the *leader consideration* variable from our regression equation without a significant loss in prediction accuracy.

Let us assume in this case that we did not want to eliminate any variables from our regression equation. If we wanted to estimate the individual's score on the criterion using the standardized regression equation, we would first need to standardize each of the predictor values. If z scores were chosen, the standardized regression equation for the same individual discussed previously (i.e., a person with the same values as the individual in case 2 of the data file) would yield the following:

$$\acute{Z}_y = .41z_{x1} + .11z_{x2} + .40z_{x3}$$
$$= .41(.61) + .11(.50) + .40(-.36)$$
$$= .25 + .06 + (-.14) = .17$$

It is important to remember that in this case the predicted score on *affective commitment* for this individual is also a z score.

Prediction Accuracy

Because we are predicting a criterion score for an individual, you might wonder just how accurate we are in predicting this particular individual's actual level of *affective commitment*. Unfortunately, we typically will never know, unless we obtain an actual criterion score. In the creation of this example, however, we cheated a bit, and the new individual for whom we just estimated a value for *affective commitment* just so happens to have the same exact value for all variables as the second case in our data set. Because we do actually have a criterion score for this person, we could see how accurate our prediction might be in this particular case. (Note that in the real world you would want to examine this question using data from a sample that was independent of the sample on which the coefficients were computed.) In the data set, the individual's actual raw score value for affective commitment is 4.29. Our prediction of 4.18 is therefore quite close. (Incidentally, the same individual's actual z score for *affective commitment* is .23, compared to our predicted z score of .17.)

Before we become too complacent in our ability to predict scores on *affective commitment*, we might want to compute another individual's predicted criterion score as well. Let us assume that our next individual randomly drawn from the population just so happens to have the same exact predictor values as the first individual in our data set. Thus, the individual received a value of 5.00 on *perceived opportunity for reward*, a 4.70 on *leader consideration*, and a 4.33 on *role clarity*. We could again compute the individual's predicted *affective commitment* score:

$$\hat{Y} = .48(5.00) + .20(4.70) + .38(4.33) + (-.60)$$
$$= 2.40 + .94 + 1.65 + (-.60) = 4.39$$

Well, if we had some way of knowing the *actual* criterion score for this individual, and we found that this also happened to be the same value as the individual in the first case in our data file, would we be happy with our predictive abilities? Certainly not. Taking a quick peek at the data file, we see that the actual *affective commitment* score for this individual is 2.43. That's quite far from our predicted value of 4.39, considering that the individual items comprising the criterion score were rated on a seven-point scale.

It should come as no surprise that unless our variables are perfectly reliable (which is quite unlikely) *and* as a set our predictors are perfectly related to our criterion (even less likely), we will have some error in prediction. Fortunately, in computing the regression equation, we can also derive some estimates of the overall degree of accuracy in our prediction.

In the single-predictor case, the squared correlation coefficient between the predictor and the criterion, r^2, provides an estimate of the accuracy of prediction. The larger the value of r^2, the greater the amount of reliable variance in criterion scores that can be explained by scores on the predictor. When we have multiple predictors, a similar estimate of accuracy in prediction is provided by the estimated squared **multiple correlation** coefficient, R^2. This value provides a basic estimate of how strongly the predictor set is related to the criterion. In the example prediction of *affective commitment* discussed previously, R^2 is equal to .57. This means that 57% of the variance in affective commitment is explained by the combination of the three predictors we examined.

The **standard error of estimate** provides a more direct measure of the accuracy of prediction in regression. Previously, we computed a few example cases in which we compared predicted criterion scores to actual criterion scores. Because the predicted criterion scores were not identical to the actual criterion scores, we knew that we had some amount of error in prediction. Conceptually, if we subtracted the estimated criterion score from the actual criterion score (e.g., $Y - \hat{Y}$) for every individual in our sample, squared these differences, computed the average squared difference, and, finally, took the square root, we would compute the standard error of the estimate. Thus, the standard error of the estimate is the square root of the average squared deviation from the regression line. More simply, it informs us how much, on average, a predicted criterion score differs from the actual criterion score. In the example prediction of *affective commitment*, the standard error of estimate is .92.

Predictor Interrelationships

In Module 8, we said that the coefficient of determination is computed by squaring a validity coefficient and multiplying the result by 100%. If a test had a criterion-related validity of .30, we would be able to explain 9% of the reliable variance in the criterion. Unfortunately, even when using this test, we would still leave 91% of the reliable variance in the criterion unexplained—our accuracy in prediction leaves much to be desired. Ah, but I can guess what you are thinking. Why not add more and more tests (predictors) until we have explained 100% of the reliable variance in the criterion? Unfortunately, there is a little problem called *collinearity* (or multicollinearity) that interferes with this potential solution.

Let us consider a hypothetical example in which three predictors are each valid predictors of the criterion. The validity of Predictor A is $r_{xy} = .30$, of Predictor B is $r_{xy} = .40$, and of Predictor C is $r_{xy} = .20$. Figure 17.1 presents a Venn diagram representing the idealized relationships between these predictors and the criterion. If Figure 17.1 correctly reflected the relationships among the variables, we would expect the combined percentage of reliable variance accounted for in the criterion to be $R^2 = 9\% + 16\% + 4\% = 29\%$. Note that because we are using more than one predictor, we now refer to the estimated squared multiple correlation coefficient (R^2) rather than r^2.

Unfortunately, in reality, the predictors themselves are likely intercorrelated, indicating that Figure 17.1 should be revised to depict some degree of overlap between predictors. Again consider the two examples presented at the very beginning of this module. In predicting tomorrow's high temperature in Poughkeepsie, New York, it is likely there will exist relationships among the following predictors: today's high temperature, the amount of cloud cover, and last year's high temperature on tomorrow's date. Similarly, an applicant's score on several selection tests such as an interview, a measure of cognitive ability, and a measure of personality are likely to be correlated to some degree as well. *Collinearity* refers to the extent to which predictors in a regression analysis are intercorrelated. The greater the collinearity between predictors, the less each additional predictor will contribute to the explanation of unique variance in the criterion; when predictors are highly correlated with each other, they provide redundant information with each other.

Thus, a more accurate representation of the relationship among Predictors A, B, and C would produce a diagram similar to Figure 17.2.

In this far less attractive, but more likely scenario, each of the predictors is associated not only with the criterion but also with each other. Because we cannot "double count" variance already explained by an earlier predictor, the unique contribution of

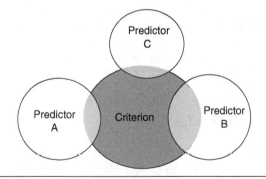

Figure 17.1   Three Orthogonal Predictors in Multiple Regression

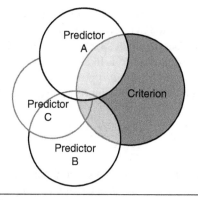

Figure 17.2   Three Oblique Predictors in Multiple Regression

each new predictor is lessened. Thus, the actual combined percentage of variance accounted for by the three predictors will be considerably less than 29%.

We have evidence that collinearity is a concern in our prediction of *affective commitment* as well. Recall that the zero-order correlations between *affective commitment* and each of the three predictor variables were all .50 and above. Yet when we examined the significance of the regression weights, we found that the inclusion of the variable *leader consideration* did not explain a significant portion of the variance in *affective commitment*. Inspection of the zero-order correlations both between the predictors and between the predictors and *affective commitment* helps to shed some light on this finding. Although all three predictor variables were highly related to the criterion of *affective commitment*, *leader consideration* was not as highly correlated with the criterion as were the other two predictors. Further, *leader consideration* is considerably correlated with both *perceived opportunity for reward* ($r = .44$) and *role clarity* ($r = .57$). Thus, when the other two predictors are included in the regression equation, *leader consideration* fails to explain a significant portion of unique variance in *affective commitment*. The information this variable provides is redundant with the other two predictors.

When contemplating the addition of a second, third, or fourth predictor, then, there are two factors to be considered. The first consideration is the predictor's correlation with the criterion. The second consideration is the predictor's correlation with the other predictor(s) already used. The ideal predictor will have a high correlation with the criterion and no relationship with the other predictors. In this way, the addition of this ideal predictor will explain a maximum amount of *unique variance* in the criterion—that is, variance not already explained by the predictors already in use. In multiple regression, greater beta weights are assigned to variables that explain higher amounts of unique variance in the criterion.

Stability of the Validity Coefficient

A second issue associated with the use of numerous predictors concerns the stability of the estimated squared multiple correlation coefficient, R^2. *Shrinkage* refers to the drop in validity that occurs if regression weights computed on one sample are used to predict the criterion in a second sample. Unless the sample size is very large relative to the number of predictors, some shrinkage is likely to occur. Put another way, our initial estimate of R^2 is likely to be overestimated. The **shrinkage formula** (also called *Wherry's formula*) provides an estimate of the "shrunken" squared validity coefficient for the population or what is known as the adjusted R^2:

$$\rho^2 = 1 - \left[\left(\frac{N-1}{N-k-1} \right) (1-R^2) \right]$$

where ρ^2 is the adjusted R^2, the estimated squared population multiple correlation coefficient; N is the sample size; and k is the number of predictors.

R^2 is the estimated squared multiple correlation coefficient between the predictors and the criterion.

Using Wherry's formula, we can compute an estimate of the squared population multiple correlation coefficient for our example prediction of *affective commitment*. The sample size in this example is 120. We have three predictor variables, and, as we stated previously, R^2 is .57. Thus,

$$\rho^2 = 1 - \left[\left(\frac{120-1}{120-3-1} \right) (1-.57) \right] = 1 - (1.03)(.43) = 1 - .44 = .56$$

In this example, the adjusted R^2 is nearly the same size as our original estimate of R^2, owing to our large sample size. For the sake of illustration, let us determine what the estimated squared population multiple correlation would be if our sample were composed of only 20 individuals rather than the 120:

$$\rho^2 = 1 - \left[\left(\frac{20-1}{20-3-1} \right) (1-.57) \right] = 1 - (1.19)(.43) = 1 - .51 = .49$$

Here we see a considerable increase in the amount of shrinkage when the estimate is based on a hypothetical sample with a smaller N. When reporting R^2 values, it is important to also report the adjusted R^2 as well so that readers can determine whether your R^2 value capitalized on chance (i.e., took advantage of unique sample idiosyncrasies). With large numbers of predictors and small samples, capitalization of chance can be a problem in multiple regression.

The estimated squared population multiple correlation coefficient provided by the Wherry formula can then be used to provide the *squared cross-validated correlation coefficient* (Cattin, 1980):

$$\rho_c^2 = \frac{(N-k-3)\rho^4 + \rho^2}{(N-2k-2)\rho^2 + k}$$

where ρ_c^2 is the squared cross-validated correlation coefficient, N is the sample size, k is the number of predictors, and ρ is the estimated population multiple correlation (square root of the value from the Wherry formula).

The Cattin (1980) formula provides an accurate estimate of the validity of a set of predictors when used on a new sample. If the criterion-related validity coefficient is based on a sufficiently large sample, the estimated population cross-validity estimate will be very close to the originally estimated validity coefficient. However, if the validity coefficient is based on a small sample relative to the number of predictors used, the observed validity coefficient can be much larger than the more accurate cross-validity.

Our example of the prediction of *affective commitment* can be concluded as follows:

$$\rho_c^2 = \frac{(120-3-3).32+.57}{(120-2(3)-2).57+3} = \frac{(114).32+.57}{(112).57+3} = \frac{37.05}{66.84} = .55$$

This value of .55 means that if we were to apply the regression coefficients calculated in our original sample with a different sample drawn from the same population, then we would expect the R^2 to be .55. Notice that the value of the ρ_c^2 is less than adjusted R^2, which is less than the uncorrected R^2. The difference between adjusted R^2 and uncorrected R^2 reflects the expected difference between estimating a population value from a sample value. The difference between ρ_c^2 and uncorrected R^2 reflects the expected difference between estimating one sample's value from another sample drawn from the same population. The latter inference takes into account that there may be unique same variation in both of the samples; hence, the difference between ρ_c^2 and uncorrected R^2 will be larger than the difference between adjusted R^2 and uncorrected R^2.

Adequate Sample Size

As you can see from our example, our original estimate of the squared correlation coefficient was quite stable. This finding is due to the relatively large sample size used in the computation of the regression equation. The estimate would have been far less stable had we used a small sample size. Concern with stability of a multiple correlation coefficient is lessened when we use a large sample size (N) relative to the number of predictors (k). The problem is determining just what is meant by a "large" sample size. A common recommendation is to ensure that, at a minimum, the N to k ratio (N/k) is no smaller than 15:1. Newton and Rudestam (1999) provided additional guidelines and simple formulas for determining adequate sample size, depending on whether the primary interest is in examining the multiple correlation coefficient (R) or in examining the individual predictor variables. To scrutinize the multiple correlation coefficient, the sample size should be at least $50 + 8k$ (where k is the number of predictors). To examine the individual predictor variables, the sample size should be at least $104 + k$. For most cases, Newton and Rudestam recommended computing both formulas and then using the larger sample size as a minimum.

Concluding Comments

The issues discussed in this module only begin to touch on the complexity of multiple regression. However, the issues discussed here will hopefully sensitize you to the utility of this widely used statistical procedure to test validation and prediction. For complete coverage of multiple regression, you would do well to consult Cohen, Cohen, West, and Aiken (2002) or Pedhazur (1997).

Best Practices

1. Choose variables that are relatively uncorrelated with each other to minimize collinearity.
2. Report adjusted R^2 and cross-validated R^2 when appropriate so that the reader can judge stability of prediction.

Practical Questions

1. What factors influence the relative weighting of each predictor in an unstandardized multiple regression equation?
2. How does a standardized regression equation differ from an unstandardized regression equation?
3. If we were currently using four predictors to explain 40% of the variance in our criterion, would the addition of four more predictors with equal combined validity allow us to explain 80% of the reliable variance in our criterion? Why or why not?
4. Why do we refer to the prediction of "reliable variance" in the criterion rather than just "variance"?
5. If in question 3 you added a fifth predictor to the original regression equation, what characteristics would you want from this predictor?
6. What information is provided by the standard error of estimate?
7. If we hoped to examine the predictive ability of four independent variables, what would you recommend as the minimum sample size?
8. Why is it necessary to compute the cross-validated correlation coefficient?

Case Studies

CASE STUDY 17.1: SELECTION OF GRADUATE STUDENTS

Reflecting concerns that standardized testing was unfair, the Psychology Department at South East State University (SESU) decided 6 years ago to eliminate the requirement that prospective students submit Graduate Record Examination (GRE) scores for admission to its popular master's program.

Although hired as an assistant professor only a year ago, Dr. Lisa Span already found herself questioning whether this policy was a wise decision.

Dr. Span's main concern was the quality of the graduate students in her classes. Although a number of students were highly talented academically, others appeared unable to grasp theoretical concepts and even seemed incapable of abstract thinking. Although Dr. Span had repeatedly questioned whether these problems were a consequence of her own teaching style, her concerns with the ability of the department's graduate students were mirrored by similar concerns expressed by other faculty in the department.

In an effort to understand how students were selected for the MA program, Dr. Span investigated the criteria used by the selection committee. She found that, in the absence of GRE scores, the selection committee relied heavily on three aspects of the student's application file: grade point average (GPA) as an undergraduate, the student's one-page statement of purpose, and three letters of recommendation.

Sensing an opportunity, Dr. Span decided to determine the validity of the selection system. The department agreed to give her access to the application files of all 110 students admitted and enrolled in the MA program since the GRE was discarded from the department's graduate student selection process. She was also able to obtain the GPAs these students had amassed while graduate students at SESU. Although undergraduate GPA and graduate GPA were easy variables to enter into a data file, the same could not be said for the statement of purpose and the three letters of recommendation. In the end, Dr. Span decided to code the statement of purpose on a four-point scale. This scale reflected a number of characteristics, including writing ability, ability to convincingly communicate the desire to attend graduate school, undergraduate involvement in research, and relevant work experience. The three letters of recommendation were coded as a single score of 0, 1, 2, or 3, reflecting the number of letters submitted that had only positive things to say about the applicant. Thus, if an applicant received two letters that said only positive things, and one that included at least one negative comment, the applicant received a score of "2" for this predictor. While inputting the data, Dr. Span realized that the vast majority of applicants received a score of "3" on this predictor.

With much anticipation, Dr. Span ran the multiple regression analysis examining the ability of the set of predictors to explain graduate GPA. The resulting multiple correlation coefficient was $R = .31$. Stunned, Dr. Span realized that, combined, these three predictors explained very little of the performance of graduate students. She was particularly surprised that two of the three selection tests—undergraduate GPA and letters of recommendation—received very low beta weights. Indeed, the zero-order correlation between undergraduate GPA and graduate GPA was an astonishingly low $r = .13$.

By chance, Dr. Span discovered that a student's application file contained a GRE reporting form. Opening several additional application files, she found that some other students had also reported their GRE scores to SESU. Although students were not required to do so, and although they were not considered in admission, some applicants had seemingly taken the GRE for other schools and had reported their scores to SESU as well. In all, Dr. Span was able to find GRE scores for 67 students. After quickly inputting these data into her file, she was pleased to see that the correlation between GRE scores and graduate GPA was $r = .36$. Convinced that the GRE should be reinstated as a requirement for graduate application to the department, Dr. Span prepared a report to her colleagues.

Questions to Ponder

1. What percentage of variance in graduate GPA is being explained by the current entrance criteria?
2. Is there any reason to expect that letters of recommendation would have a low criterion-related validity, even before conducting the statistical analysis? Explain.
3. Which of the current entrance criteria likely has the greatest criterion-related validity? How can you tell from the given information?
4. Would it be appropriate to conclude that undergraduate GPA is unrelated to graduate GPA in the psychology master's program at SESU? Why or why not? (*Hint:* You may want to review the issues we discussed in Module 8 in answering this question.)
5. Would it be appropriate to conclude that GRE scores will act as a better predictor of graduate GPA for future graduate students at SESU than the current entrance criteria? Explain.

CASE STUDY 17.2: THE PERFECT PERSONNEL
SELECTION BATTERY?

Although he had worked in human resources (HR) for a little more than a year, Connor Maxfield had been unexpectedly promoted to oversee the selection of new employees into MiniCorp after his boss resigned last month. Although he was now responsible for filling all vacancies in the organization, relatively low-level production workers would be hired most frequently. It seemed that every month there were at least two or three of these jobs that needed to be filled. The current personnel selection system for production workers had been in place for years. Applicants were given a paper-and-pencil job knowledge test and personality inventory. Those who passed the tests were then administered a

40-minute structured interview. In searching through records in the HR department, Connor was surprised to see that, combined, these tests accounted for a mere 25% of the reliable variance in job performance. Recognizing that more than 75% of the reliable variance in job performance remained unexplained by use of the current selection system, Connor vowed to improve things.

Connor spent every night for more than a week investigating a variety of selection tests that could be used to predict the future job performance of production worker applicants. Determining that the current three tests not only made logical sense but also demonstrated good validity, Connor decided he wouldn't attempt to replace these tests. Instead, he would add additional tests to the selection system until he was able to explain as close to 100% of the reliable variance in job performance as possible. He had a sneaking suspicion that measures of cognitive ability, biodata, and a work sample might go a long way to selecting the ideal candidate, but still other tests might be needed as well.

Although brief, Connor's work experience had convinced him of the importance of seeking validation evidence before implementing a new selection system. He planned to administer all of the possible new selection tests to his entire staff of production workers, which numbered 53 employees. He then expected to regress supervisor ratings onto these test scores to obtain a multiple correlation coefficient. Reflecting for a moment on his plan, Connor thought he had better get to it—he was certainly going to be busy.

Questions to Ponder

1. What type of criterion-related validity study does Connor plan on conducting?
2. What is the criterion-related validity of the current selection system for production workers at MiniCorp?
3. Is Connor's plan to attempt to explain nearly 100% of the reliable variance in job performance feasible? Explain.
4. What practical concerns might Connor encounter even if he did find that a selection battery of six or more tests was useful in predicting job performance for production workers?
5. How should Connor go about attempting to identify additional useful predictors of job performance for production workers?
6. What minimum sample size would be recommended for conducting a criterion-related validity study with three predictors? Six predictors?
7. Given the number of production workers at MiniCorp, what method of criterion-related validity should Connor consider using?

~⊖~⊙~⊖~

Exercises

EXERCISE 17.1: DETECTING VALID PREDICTORS (REVISITED)

OBJECTIVE: To reexamine the validity of predictors in a data set using multiple regression.

PROLOGUE: Exercise 8.2 examined a number of possible predictors of bus driver job performance. Using the entire set of predictors identified in Exercise 8.2, perform the following procedures to further examine the predictability of bus driver job performance, as indicated by the criterion of overall performance evaluation score (the variable *pescore*). As before, the relevant data set is titled "Bus Driver.sav" (see Appendix B).

Perform a multiple regression analysis using *pescore* as the dependent variable and each of the six predictors identified in Exercise 8.2 as the independent variables. Choose "enter" as the method.

1. What is the sample size analyzed?
2. What is the magnitude of the estimated multiple correlation coefficient (R) obtained in this analysis?
3. What is the magnitude of the estimated squared multiple correlation coefficient (R^2) obtained in this analysis?
4. What is the magnitude of the standard error of estimate obtained in this analysis?
5. Write out the unstandardized regression equation.
6. Write out the standardized regression equation.
7. What predictors have significant regression weights?

EXERCISE 17.2: PREDICTING THE WORK MOTIVATION OF VOLUNTEERS

OBJECTIVE: To examine the validity and cross-validity of a set of predictors.

PROLOGUE: Because volunteers are unpaid, the work motivation of these individuals can be complex. It is possible that individuals' work motivation depends on their perceptions of their own ability, along with elements of support provided by the organization. The SPSS data file "Volunteer Data.sav" (see Appendix B) contains data assessed from 120 volunteers in a number of small organizations. Each volunteer completed a survey, as shown in Table 17.1, assessing the following perceptions

Each of the scales was assessed using either a five-point or a seven-point Likert-type rating scale. An additional variable included in the data set, work motivation, will act as the criterion variable in Exercises 17.2 and 17.3.

Table 17.1   Example Predictor Variables From the "Volunteer data.sav" Data Set

Predictors	
Variable Name	Explanation of Perception
reward	The possible intrinsic rewards available by volunteering
ledinit	The amount of initiating-structure provided by the volunteer's immediate supervisor
ledcons	The amount of consideration provided by the volunteer's immediate supervisor
clarity	The degree to which one's role and task in the volunteer organization is unambiguous
conflict	The amount of intrarole and interrole conflict experienced as a result of volunteering
efficacy	The degree to which the individual perceives he or she is capable of handling the assigned work in the volunteer organization
goalid	The degree to which the individual believes the work of the volunteer organization is important
affectc	The affective commitment of the volunteer; the degree to which the volunteer wishes to remain a part of the volunteer organization due to an emotional tie
continc	The continuance commitment of the volunteer; the degree to which the volunteer wishes to remain a part of the volunteer organization due to perceptions of an obligation to remain in the organization

1. Examine the correlations between each of the possible predictors of work motivation. On the whole, how highly related to one another are these predictors? What is the range of magnitude of intercorrelation among this set of possible predictors?
2. Examine the correlations of work motivation with each of the possible predictors. Which predictors seem most highly related to work motivation?
3. Conduct a multiple regression analysis to determine the validity of the set of predictors for the criterion of work motivation. What is the magnitude of the multiple correlation coefficient (R)?
4. Which predictors have significant regression weights?
5. Compute the estimated population cross-validity of the entire set of predictors. How does this compare to the initial validity estimate?
6. Had you obtained the same regression results based on a sample of only 50 volunteers, what would be the estimated population cross-validity of this set of predictors? How does this new estimate of validity compare to the initial validity estimate, and to the cross-validated estimate based on 120 volunteers?

EXERCISE 17.3: PREDICTING SCORES USING
THE REGRESSION EQUATION

OBJECTIVE: To compare the accuracy of predicted criterion scores to actual criterion scores.

PROLOGUE: Use the data set discussed in Exercise 17.2 to answer the following items.

1. Conduct a multiple regression analysis using all nine predictors. Choose method equals "enter." Write out the unstandardized regression equation that would result if all nine predictors were retained.
2. Conduct a second multiple regression analysis, this time using *only* those predictors that had significant regression weights in the previous equation. Write out the unstandardized regression equation.
3. While the standard error of estimate provides an average level of prediction accuracy, we can examine the accuracy of prediction for a single individual who is included in the data set by comparing the individual's predicted work motivation score with his or her actual reported work motivation.

   a. Use the regression equation in item 1 to compute a predicted score on work motivation for the first volunteer in the data set (i.e., for case 1).
   b. Use the regression equation in item 2 to compute a predicted score on work motivation for the first volunteer in the data set (i.e., for case 1).
   c. Examining the actual work motivation score for the first volunteer in the data set (i.e., the "motivate" score for case 1), which regression equation provided the most accurate prediction of work motivation for this particular volunteer?
   d. Which regression equation had the smallest standard error of estimate?

4. Repeat the procedure in item 3 by randomly selecting two more volunteers in the data set and computing their predicted work motivation scores using both regression equations.

   a. Do you consistently find one of these equations is more accurate?
   b. If you continued this process for every individual in the data set, which equation would be more accurate? How do you know?

5. Are you surprised by either the accuracy or the inaccuracy of prediction when using the regression equations? Explain.

Further Readings

Aiken, L.S., West, S.G., & Reno, R.R. (1996). *Multiple regression: Testing and interpreting interactions.* Newbury Park, CA: Sage.

Cohen, P., Cohen, J., West, S.G., & Aiken, L.S. (2002). *Applied multiple regression: Correlation analysis for the behavioral sciences* (3rd ed.). Hillsdale, NJ: Erlbaum.

Licht, M.H. (1995). Multiple regression and correlation. In L.G. Grimm & P.R. Yarnold (Eds.), *Reading and understanding multivariate statistics* (pp. 19–64). Washington, DC: American Psychological Association.

Nunnally, J.C., & Bernstein, I.H. (1994). *Psychometric theory* (3rd ed., pp. 114–208). New York: McGraw-Hill.

Pedhazur, E.J. (1997). *Multiple regression in behavioral research* (3rd ed.). Pacific Grove, CA: Wadsworth.

Module 18

Exploratory Factor Analysis

F actor analysis is a complex set of statistical techniques that can be used to reveal or verify the underlying dimensionality of a newly developed measure or to refine an existing measure. Following administration of the measure to a large sample of respondents, we could examine the dimensionality of our scale through the use of factor analysis. If we were uncertain as to the possible dimensions underlying our scale, exploratory factor analysis (EFA) would be used. However, if we had strong theoretical expectations as to the new measure's dimensionality, then confirmatory factor analysis (CFA) could be applied. By examining how the items that compose a scale "cluster" together, we may gain an important understanding of our operationalization of the underlying construct we are assessing. In this module, we focus on EFA, whereas Module 19 concentrates on CFA.

Exploratory Factor Analysis

Do the items in our scale assess separate subdimensions, or is our scale unidimensional? If the scale is multidimensional, how many subdimensions are there? In the absence of strong theoretical expectations, EFA provides a way of examining these issues. EFA can be useful when developing measures of new constructs in which the test developers may have a vague understanding of the nature of the construct. For example, suppose you are asked to write a test to measure a construct that has never been measured before. It is likely that there are measures of similar constructs, and so you research those measures, figuring out what formats work and which do not work. In addition, you should document the nature of the construct as best as you can, knowing that after you conduct research, your understanding of the construct will likely change. Items may be written based on the initial understanding of the construct, but then researchers will want to use statistical analyses to determine the underlying structure of the data. EFA can be used to understand the structure of such a measure. These results can then be used to both refine the test, as well as to refine our understanding of the construct.

Factor analysis attempts to reduce the number of factors (from the original number of items) by accounting for the patterns of intercorrelations among items. To accomplish this, EFA procedures divide item variance into three different categories: common, specific, and unique variance. EFA attempts to extract factors based only on the common variance of the original items. The term communality refers to the variance that an item has in common with other items. The assumption is that there exist some underlying constructs that are responsible for the interrelationships among observed items. Consider a fictitious case in which we recently developed a brief personality inventory composed of eight items that we suspect (or perhaps, *intend to*) assess two of the Big Five personality dimensions: conscientiousness and extraversion. If there were multiple dimensions assessed by the eight items, we would expect to find that certain subsets of items would correlate highly with each other, whereas others would not correlate with these items but would instead correlate highly with each other. Thus, items assessing the personality dimension of conscientiousness would be expected to correlate highly with one another, but not with items assessing extraversion.

In test development terms, it is important to have items that have large amounts of communality, variance shared with other items. Invariably, items will also have unique variance that is unshared with other items. For example, if I have a reading comprehension test, hopefully each item will have significant amounts of common variance shared with other items that measure reading comprehension. If I ask students to respond to a writing passage, the specific contents of a particular reading passage might contribute to the unique variance of an item. For a reading passage that includes a question that contains information about St. Louis Cardinals' baseball, some students may be able to answer the item correctly because they are good at comprehending all of the information in a passage (that is what we want), or they may get the item right because they are a lifelong Cardinals fan (like one of the co-authors!). Such unique characteristics about items are often unavoidable, but in EFA we choose items that have small amounts of unique variance compared to the common sources of variance. Given the challenges that unique variance presents, it is not surprising that it is often called error variance.

A similar but distinct procedure is called principal components analysis (PCA). In PCA, the focus is not limited to common variance, but, rather, to total variance. The primary assumption of PCA is that the total variance of an item reflects both explained and error variance. Thus, the components that are formed using this procedure are linear combinations of the observed items. Although mathematicians often prefer the use of PCA due to its focus on modeling total variance, most applied social science and educational researchers favor factor analysis due to its usefulness for identifying latent variables that contribute only to the common variance in a set of measured variables. According to this logic, because tests are created to assess latent constructs, EFA should be preferred over PCA for test developers.

In conducting a factor analysis, it is crucial to obtain an adequate sample size. Without an adequate sample size, factor analytic results will be unlikely to generalize to other samples. How large a sample size is needed? As is the case with so many other statistical analyses, the answer is the more the better. At a bare minimum, however, we should use a sample size no smaller than 100 cases *and* a sample size relative to number of items (i.e., N/k ratio) of no less than 5 to 1. For complicated factor solutions, more cases will be needed. Velicer and Fava (1998) provide much more detailed procedures for determining appropriate sample sizes when conducting EFA.

How Many Components or Factors Are Present in My Data?

Because EFA does not a priori specify the number of underlying dimensions in our data, we must have some way of determining the number of factors to extract. Indeed, it is possible (though perhaps unlikely) that, in the development of our measure, no particular dimensionality is hypothesized. Use of EFA is intended to determine the number of latent constructs (e.g., personality dimensions) present in our measure.

There are numerous methods of extracting factors to choose from, and each method may indicate a slightly different number of factors. Methods that are available in commonly used statistical software packages include principal axis factor, maximum likelihood, generalized least squares, and alpha factoring, among others. Each of these extraction techniques vary mathematically. Perhaps the most commonly used method of determining the number of factors extracted is also the default in most statistical analysis software packages: the Kaiser eigenvalue criterion. The eigenvalue is a mathematical term that corresponds to the strength or magnitude of a particular factor; factors associated with large eigenvalues explain more variance, whereas those with small eigenvalues would explain less variance. The Kaiser method retains those factors whose eigenvalues are greater than or equal to 1.0. Although this method of determining the number of resulting factors is quite straightforward, Russell (2002) pointed out a number of problems with the use of the Kaiser criterion. One concern is that, when a large number of items are included in the factor analysis, it is likely that a relatively large number of factors with eigenvalues greater than or equal to 1.0 will be extracted, many of which will account for only a rather small percentage of the total variance.

Although not a perfect determinant of the number of factors in an EFA, the *scree test* (Cattell, 1966) is strongly preferred over the eigenvalue criterion. The scree test is provided as an option in most statistical software programs. Using the geological metaphor of stones that fall from a mountain (i.e., scree), the scree test provides a visual aid for determining the number of factors extracted. The magnitude of eigenvalues forms the Y axis, whereas the X axis presents the corresponding factor numbers. Within the plot itself, eigenvalues of each corresponding factor are plotted, and these are then connected with a line. This plot allows the user to visually determine the drop-off in the magnitude of eigenvalues from factor to factor. Typically, the user looks for an "elbow," or sudden flattening of the line. The resulting number of factors extracted is typically taken as one less than the factor associated with the elbow.

The Kaiser eigenvalue criterion and the scree plot are just two ways to determine the number of factors. An even more complicated method, called parallel analysis, requires that you generate random data (i.e., items that are uncorrelated with each other), which is fairly easy to do with a typical statistics package such as SPSS. You generate the same number of items and the same number of cases as in your focal data set. Next, you conduct a parallel factor analysis (using all of the settings as discussed later) on this random data set, just as you did with your real data set. Finally, you compare the scree plot of your random data set with the scree plot from your actual data analysis. By using the random data set as a comparison, it is possible to determine which factors are valid and which factors are just statistical noise. A good reference for conducting parallel analysis can be found at https://people.ok.ubc.ca/brioconn/nfactors/nfactors.html.

As you can see, EFA requires a lot of judgment, judgment that is informed by statistical output. One of the most important criteria in judging the number of factors is whether a particular factor solution makes sense. If a particular factor cannot be interpreted no matter how hard you try, then that combined with a low eigenvalue provides good evidence that the factor is not one that would replicate in additional samples. To figure out how to interpret factors, we need to consider the notion of a factor loading.

Which Items Are Loading on a Particular Factor?

After you have decided on the number of factors, it is important to interpret the meaning of those factors; realizing that, as mentioned previously, considering interpretability may help you revise your decision on the number of factors. To do so, you need to consider the *factor loadings*. Factor loadings are a regression between the item score and the underlying latent trait or factor. Items with large positive factor loadings will indicate that the item is a positive indicator of the factor, whereas items with large negative factor loadings indicate that the item is a negative indicator of the factor; those negative items will have to be reverse coded before scoring a test. Items with factor loadings close to zero indicate that the variance on the item does not relate to the factor.

Unlike other techniques such as multiple regression where you have one set of regression coefficients that best fit the data, there are a vast number of item factor solutions that are equally valid. The initial extraction provides one particular solution, though that solution is often difficult to interpret. To improve interpretability, researchers typically turn to a set of possible rotations, each of which attempt to reorient the factor loadings according to a set of mathematical principles (the mathematics of factor analysis can be quite complicated!).

There are again multiple choices in types of rotation, but the key is to determine whether to use orthogonal or oblique rotations. *Orthogonal rotations* force the resulting factors to be uncorrelated. Examples of orthogonal rotations include Varimax and Quartimax. Quartimax is the appropriate choice when you suspect that the items on your test represent a general factor (Gorsuch, 1983), as may be the case in the development of a classroom knowledge test.

Oblique rotations allow correlations between the factors. Examples here include Direct Oblimin and Promax. Oblique rotations are appropriate when the factors are expected to be interrelated, as might be the case in the development of a measure of extraversion in which multiple facets (e.g., warmth, assertiveness, excitement seeking) of the construct are being assessed. Fabrigar, Wegener, MacCallum, and Strahan (1999) recommended the use of oblique factor rotations. Russell (2002) pointed out that Promax allows correlations between factors only after initially performing an orthogonal Varimax rotation. Thus, uncorrelated factors would still be identified by use of a Promax rotation. Independent of which method of rotation is used, further ease of interpretation of output is aided by choosing the option to "sort by size," which arranges item loadings based on magnitude of relationship to the resulting factors rather than the order of listing in the data set.

The choice of rotation method is important because your choice will influence your final results. Some argue that oblique rotations should always be used because nearly every construct in nature is correlated at least at some modest level. In addition, in an oblique rotation, the correlations between factors are estimated and so if underlying constructs are truly uncorrelated, the oblique rotation will be able to let you discover that. Orthogonal rotations force constructs to be uncorrelated, allowing no possibility of correlated constructs. Like many statistical procedures, there is no right answer for which direction to go. Whatever method you choose, you must be prepared to defend the rationale behind your choice!

Interpreting EFA Output

Given the number of options for conducting the factor analysis, it should not be surprising that the interpretation of the output requires some expertise as well. The following discussion describes several elements of the output using the terms employed by SPSS (SPSS Inc., 2003). Labels may differ slightly for other statistical software packages.

The section of the output labeled "Total variance explained" provides information on the initial eigenvalues. All eigenvalues of 1.0 and above will be considered important factors when using the Kaiser criterion. The percentage of variance next to each of these values indicates the percentage of the variance in the original set of items that is captured by that particular factor. A cumulative percentage of variance accounted for by the factors is also listed. Remember that if you requested the scree plot option, the scree plot should also be consulted to determine the number of factors.

The section of the output labeled "factor matrix" provides factor-loading information computed prior to rotation of factors. "Extraction sums of square loadings" can be replicated by squaring each of the loadings on a particular factor and then summing across each of the original items. Similarly, squaring each of the loadings for an item across all of the factors and then summing will replicate extracted communalities.

The next part of the output differs depending on whether you requested an orthogonal or an oblique rotation method. With an orthogonal rotation, the output is presented in the "rotated factor matrix." With an oblique rotation, this output is presented in a "pattern matrix." Either way, this part of the output is likely to demand the greatest amount of your attention. If you chose the "sort by size" option when conducting the analysis, this matrix will display factor loadings arranged such that the item that loads highest on the first factor will be at the very top of the leftmost column, while the item with the second highest loading on the first factor will be listed next. This continues until the item with the highest loading on the second factor is presented, with subsequent item presentation following the same pattern as with the first factor. We will present a detailed example output and its interpretation later.

Typically, an item must have a loading in the range of at least .30 to be considered to load on a factor. Indeed, in conducting Monte Carlo studies, some researchers now use loadings of .4, .6, and .8 to represent low, medium, and high loadings, respectively (e.g., Enders & Bandalos, 2001). It is important to keep in mind that item loadings on a factor in one sample do not necessarily reproduce in another sample, particularly if the sample size is small relative to the number of items.

In examining the items that load on a particular factor, try to make some meaningful connection between the items. Do the items that load highly on a factor seem to have something in common? Does a single label seem appropriate for these items? If the answer to these questions is yes, then these items represent a subdimension on your scale.

Other items, however, may not load highly on a particular factor. If the test is empirically derived, it is unlikely that many of the items load onto neat, interpretable factors. That's not usually a problem for tests derived as such. On the other hand, the expectation with rationally derived tests is typically that certain general factors will emerge—namely, those consistent with the definition of the construct used to guide item generation. If this is the case, then most items should load on a limited number of interpretable factors. For rationally derived tests, items that do not load highly on any interpretable factor may be considered for elimination at this time.

On occasion, one or more items will load highly on more than a single factor. Such cross-loadings make the interpretation of factors more difficult. If only a small number of items cross-load, the items might be dropped from further consideration. Alternatively, a cross-loaded item can be inspected in terms of content and rationally categorized into the factor that is seemingly most relevant. Many significant cross-loadings, however, indicate that a smaller set of factors should likely be extracted in a subsequent factor analysis.

A Step-by-Step Example of EFA

At the outset of this module, we discussed the possibility of factor analyzing eight items that may or may not assess the conscientiousness and extraversion dimensions of personality. To illustrate an EFA, we will select eight items chosen from Saucier's Mini-Markers scale and analyze a subset of the data using a selected sample of the Mersman-Shultz (Mersman & Shultz, 1998) data set. You are strongly encouraged to follow along with this example by accessing the data set "Personality-2.sav" (see Appendix B). This data set contains responses from 314 individuals on eight items. We will conduct a factor analysis including all eight items. To conduct this factor analysis in SPSS, choose "principal axis factoring" as the method of extraction. Choose "Promax" as the method of rotation. Select the options to display a scree plot and choose to sort factor loadings by size.

Table 18.1 presents the entire SPSS output of this EFA. Results indicate two eigenvalues above 1.0. Indeed, in this instance, both factors have eigenvalues above 2.0. The first factor accounts for 30.56% of the variance explained, while the second factor accounts for 26.72% of the variance explained. The scree plot also suggests two factors. The pattern matrix reveals that four items (disorganized, organized, sloppy, and efficient) load on factor 1, with factor loadings on this factor ranging from .79 to .43. Four items (shy, quiet, bold, and extraverted) load on factor 2, with loadings ranging from .70 to .60. None of the items cross-loads highly on both factors. Clearly, factor 1 could be labeled conscientiousness, whereas factor 2 could be labeled extraversion. Finally, note that the factor correlation matrix indicates that the two factors are unrelated, with $r = .059$.

Table 18.1   Results of the Step-by-Step Example

FACTOR
  /VARIABLES bold disorgan efficien extraver organize quiet shy sloppy
  /MISSING LISTWISE /ANALYSIS bold disorgan efficien extraver organize quiet
  shy sloppy
  /PRINT INITIAL EXTRACTION ROTATION
  /FORMAT SORT
  /PLOT EIGEN
  /CRITERIA MINEIGEN(1) ITERATE(25)
  /EXTRACTION PAF
  /CRITERIA ITERATE(25)
  /ROTATION PROMAX(4)
  /METHOD=CORRELATION.

Communalities

	Initial	Extraction
BOLD	.302	.372
DISORGAN	.497	.619
EFFICIEN	.244	.237
EXTRAVER	.307	.365
ORGANIZE	.465	.591
QUIET	.382	.439
SHY	.406	.500
SLOPPY	.309	.388

Extraction method: principal axis factoring.

(Continued)

Table 18.1   (*Continued*)

Total Variance Explained

Factor	Total	% of Variance	Cumulative%	Total	% of Variance	Cum.%	Total
		Initial Eigenvalues			*Extraction Sums of Squared Loadings*		*Rotation Sums of Sq. Loadings*
1	2.445	30.560	30.560	1.894	23.679	23.679	1.803
2	2.137	26.717	57.277	1.618	20.221	43.900	1.725
3	.955	11.931	69.209				
4	.632	7.895	77.104				
5	.580	7.250	84.354				
6	.540	6.751	91.105				
7	.403	5.034	96.139				
8	.309	3.861	100.000				

Extraction method: principal axis factoring.

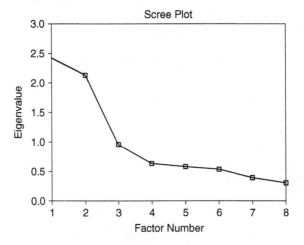

Scree Plot

Factor Matrix

	Factor	
	1	2
DISORGAN	.617	−.488
ORGANIZE	.566	−.521
SLOPPY	.535	−.381
EFFICIEN	.479	−.088
QUIET	.373	.548
BOLD	.341	.505
SHY	.499	.501
EXTRAVER	.416	.438

Table 18.1   (*Continued*)

Extraction method: principal axis factoring.
Two factors extracted. Seven iterations required.

Pattern Matrix

	Factor	
	1	2
DISORGAN	.788	−.044
ORGANIZE	.768	−.101
SLOPPY	.618	.048
EFFICIEN	.431	.204
SHY	.079	.698
QUIET	−.050	.664
BOLD	−.048	.611
EXTRAVER	.053	.598

Extraction method: principal axis factoring.
Rotation method: Promax with Kaiser normalization.
  Rotation converged in three iterations.

Structure Matrix

	Factor	
	1	2
DISORGAN	.786	.002
ORGANIZE	.762	−.056
SLOPPY	.621	.084
EFFICIEN	.443	.229
SHY	.120	.703
QUIET	−.011	.661
BOLD	−.012	.608
EXTRAVER	.088	.601

Extraction method: principal axis factoring.
Rotation method: Promax with Kaiser normalization.

Factor Correlation Matrix

Factor	1	2
1	1.00	.059
2	.059	1.00

Extraction method: principal axis factoring.
Rotation method: Promax with Kaiser normalization.

Concluding Comments

EFA has been an important statistical tool that has been used prolifically in the past to help test developers better understand the constructs that their tests measure, as well as to help refine tests by weeding out bad items. With the advent and popularization of CFA (the topic of Module 19), the popularity of EFA has decreased. Although we will get into CFA's details in the next module, in CFA you are able to dictate the number of factors, as well as which items load on a particular factor. And then you can test whether your proposed model fits the data. In many ways, this ability to test specific hypotheses in CFA has made EFA less important and has led to the proliferation of CFA techniques.

Some people argue that you should avoid exploratory techniques because you are likely to find solutions that are difficult to replicate and that lead to false conclusions. We believe that EFA techniques are important tools in the statistical toolbox and can provide some helpful insights into test development, especially at the early stages of test development. As communicated throughout this module, though, one of the challenges with EFA is that there are many decision points to make when conducting a factor analysis (e.g., rotation technique, level of factor loading to interpret, extraction method to use, number of factors to extract). Therefore, it is important that you document each of the choices that you make and that you do not rely strictly on the default options of the statistical package that you use (these defaults can vary widely across programs!). There is a lot of subjectivity involved in EFA. The decisions that you make should be informed by careful consideration of the vast amount of statistical output that guides each step of the way.

Best Practices

1. Use EFA early on in the development of your test. EFA can be helpful in understanding the factor structure of your test, as well as helping weed out bad items.
2. Unless you have a good reason to believe that your underlying constructs are uncorrelated, you should choose oblique rotations.
3. When using EFA to evaluate items, discard items that have high loadings on multiple factors (i.e., cross-loading items), as well as items that have low communality and high uniqueness.
4. Make sure to document all of the details of your EFA analysis when reporting the results. Document the rotation and estimation techniques, as well as your criteria used to determine the number of factors.

Practical Questions

1. Why would you want to understand the dimensionality of a set of items?
2. Under what conditions might you choose to use PCA? EFA?

3. Under what conditions might you choose to use an orthogonal rotation of factors in an EFA? An oblique rotation?
4. What would you do if the expected dimensionality of your scale were very different from the results suggested by your factor analysis?
5. In conducting an EFA, describe the procedure you would follow to determine whether items found to load on a factor actually form a meaningful, interpretable subdimension.
6. In conducting an EFA, what would you do if a factor in the rotated factor (or pattern) matrix were composed of items that seem to have nothing in common from a rational or theoretical standpoint?
7. List the different types of decisions that you need to make when conducting an EFA.
8. Upon their introduction to factor analysis, many students are likely to agree with Pedhazur and Schmelkin's (1991) assertion that factor analysis is like "a forest in which one can get lost in no time" (p. 590). Understanding, however, might be aided by identifying the elements that you find confusing. List two or three aspects of factor analysis that, if clarified, would help you to better understand this family of procedures.

Case Studies

CASE STUDY 18.1: A FIRST ATTEMPT AT EFA

Andra was on a roll, or at least she had been until she looked at the results of her EFA. At the request of the chair of the psychology department, she'd been working the past few weeks on the development of a scale to assess the citizenship behaviors of graduate students. Andra based her scale on the concept of organizational citizenship behavior, but she had quickly realized that the university context would require specific items that related more to graduate students. She expected her graduate student citizenship behavior (GSCB) scale to have four dimensions:

- *Helping behavior*—one's tendency to help other students in school-related tasks.
- *Conscientiousness*—following college, department, and program rules and regulations; maintaining visibility around the department; and so forth.
- *Professionalism*—avoiding complaining and gossiping about professors, students, and workload.
- *Civic virtue*—involvement in program-related activities, including serving on committees, presenting at departmental colloquia, and so on.

She'd followed a rigorous process of writing items intended to assess each of these dimensions and had then asked some of the psychology department faculty to look over the items. Based on this input, she had incorporated some revisions and thrown out some items altogether. In the end, her GSCB scale was composed of 43 draft items (with at least 10 items per hypothesized dimension). After obtaining approval from the university's human subjects review board, Andra had administered the draft items to 119 undergraduate students recruited through the psychology department's subject pool. Students received extra credit in their psychology class for voluntarily participating.

Once she had completed data collection, she had excitedly entered the data into an SPSS file. After checking the accuracy of her input, Andra moved on to the EFA. Not exactly familiar with all the possible options, Andra clicked away at a few of the options that sounded somewhat familiar. She ended up choosing to run PCA with Varimax rotation of factors. Unfortunately, the output was not very encouraging. According to the Kaiser criterion, she had seven factors. Seven. "I thought four dimensions of my scale would be complex enough, but seven," sighed Andra. She knew it was time to talk to her advisor about what to do next.

Questions to Ponder

1. The tryout sample is a crucial element in the test development process. Discuss the appropriateness of the following characteristics of Andra's sample for the development of this scale.

   a. Undergraduate students recruited through the psychology subject pool
   b. Sample size

2. Given the difficulty of obtaining a sizeable sample of graduate students, how could Andra obtain an appropriate sample?
3. Andra made a number of decisions in conducting the factor analysis. For each of the following decisions, discuss whether Andra's choice was the most appropriate option.

   a. Choosing exploratory procedures over CFA
   b. Choosing PCA over EFA
   c. Choosing Varimax rotation of factors
   d. Determining the number of factors based on the Kaiser criterion alone

4. If, following some modification of the analysis, Andra continued to find little support for her expected four factors, how would you suggest that she proceed?

CASE STUDY 18.2: CULTURAL DIFFERENCES
IN MARITAL SATISFACTION

"Will she ever be happy?" grumbled Chin, mostly to herself. Chin was, of course, referring to her thesis advisor. Everything, it seemed, revolved around her thesis right now. She and her fiancé had even arranged their wedding date so that it would come after her planned graduation date. Unfortunately, Chin had struggled mightily to develop a thesis topic before stumbling across a topic at the dinner table. Her parents, who had emigrated from China more than two decades ago, maintained close ties with their extended family—including those who remained in China and those who had similarly immigrated to the United States. At dinner 3 weeks ago, Chin's mother was talking about how unhappily married several of Chin's cousins were. Indeed, more than one of her older cousins had already been divorced. The cousins her mother was referring to were all, like Chin herself, born and raised in the United States. But then her mother said something that got Chin thinking, "I don't remember people being unhappy in their marriages in China. I wonder what it is with kids these days." That was it. Exactly what Chin was looking for. Her mind whirled. Wouldn't it be interesting to compare marital satisfaction between the United States and China?

Chin had always been interested in her heritage. Perhaps because of this, she'd also been an avid reader of the psychological literature on cultural value differences. Thus, by combining this interest with her other major life interest right now—marriage—Chin knew this would be a perfect starting point for her thesis. She couldn't imagine being more motivated by another topic.

Over the next few weeks, Chin pored over relevant literature, and she even developed a proposed model of the relationships between specific cultural values and their impact on marital satisfaction. She then began to think of methodological issues. She had already planned on visiting her grandmother in China that summer, so it seemed that she could collect data from a Chinese sample while she was there. She had even identified an often-used scale called the Marital Satisfaction Index that seemed perfect for her research. Much to her pleasant surprise, she learned that two research studies had already developed and used a Chinese-language version of the very same scale. Armed with her information, she scheduled a meeting with her thesis advisor.

Never had a meeting been so deflating. Her thesis advisor, Dr. Michelle Wordes, had initially seemed very interested in the project. Indeed, she approved of Chin's proposed research model and even seemed to agree with the hypotheses. However, when it came time to discuss methodology, Dr. Wordes became more and more negative about the idea. Dr. Wordes had focused most of her criticism on the Chinese version of the scale. "How do you know if the item wording is truly equivalent to the original?" she inquired. She didn't seem all that impressed that two other researchers had used the scale—and gotten their results published. Finally, Chin thought of a brilliant idea. She argued that since her parents were bilingual, she could have them help determine whether the items on the English and Chinese versions expressed the same ideas.

But was Dr. Wordes satisfied by this suggestion? Oh, no. Dr. Wordes then asserted that even if the wording were the same on the two versions, that maybe the items would be interpreted differently in the two cultures, or even that "marital satisfaction" as conceived in the United States might be a completely different concept in China.

Finally, Dr. Wordes asked the question that Chin could not get out of her mind: "So if you find differences in marital satisfaction between those in the United States and those in China, would the results be attributable to differences in cultural values or differences in versions of the test?" Even now, an hour after the meeting, Chin had yet to formulate a satisfactory response.

Questions to Ponder

1. Would Chin's parents serve as appropriate interpreters of the accuracy of the translation of the Marital Satisfaction Index? Why or why not?
2. How could EFA be used to determine whether equivalency exists across the translation and original version?

   a. What types of EFA-based statistics would you examine to determine whether there were differences?
   b. What samples would you like to collect for conducting your EFA?

3. Suppose that an EFA found that there were differences across the language translations. How would you act on these differences?
4. Besides EFA, what other statistical methods could you use to determine whether the translations were equivalent?

─◦─

Exercises

EXERCISE 18.1: CONDUCTING AN EFA

OBJECTIVE: To conduct and interpret an EFA using SPSS.

PROLOGUE: The SPSS data file "Geoscience Attitudes.sav" (see Appendix B) contains undergraduate responses to a survey assessing attitudes and interests related to the field of geoscience (geology, geography, and archaeology). Respondents rated their level of agreement to each of the following items using a five-point Likert-type rating scale ranging from 1 (strongly disagree) to 5 (strongly agree).

Item 1:   I have a good understanding of how scientists do research.
Item 2:   I consider myself well skilled in conducting scientific research.
Item 3:   I've wanted to be a scientist for as long as I can remember.
Item 4:   I have a good understanding of elementary geoscience.
Item 5:   I'm uncertain about what course of study is required to become a geoscientist.
Item 6:   I am considering majoring in geoscience.
Item 7:   I'd enjoy a career in geoscience.
Item 8:   I plan on taking math courses that would prepare me to major in a science.
Item 9:   I would enjoy going hiking or camping.
Item 10:   I would enjoy boating.
Item 11:   I'd prefer to work on a science project "in the field" than in a research laboratory.
Item 12:   I enjoy reading science fiction novels.
Item 13:   I enjoy reading nature and travel books and magazines.

Visually inspect the preceding geoscience attitude items. Which items would you expect to load on the same factors? What labels would you provide for these supposed factors?

Using the data set "Geoscience Attitudes.sav," conduct an EFA on the 13 items. Be sure to do the following:

- Choose principal axis factoring as your method of factor extraction.
- Choose Promax as the method of rotation.
- Ensure that the extraction of factors is determined by eigenvalues greater than 1.0.
- Select the option to produce a scree plot.
- Select the option to sort factor loadings by size.
- Ensure listwise deletion of missing cases.

   1. Interpret the findings of the factor analysis by completing the following:

      a. Is the sample size in the data set sufficiently large to conduct a factor analysis of the 13 items? Explain.
      b. How many factors with eigenvalues greater than 1.0 emerge from the EFA?
      c. What is the percentage of variance accounted for by each of these factors?
      d. What is the cumulative percentage of variance in items explained by factors with eigenvalues greater than 1.0?

    e. How many factors does the scree plot suggest? Does the scree plot provide a clear indication of the number of factors?

    f. In this particular case, do you feel the eigenvalue criterion or the scree plot is more useful for determining the number of factors present in the data?

    g. Identify which items load on each factor (use factors as determined by the eigenvalue criterion).

    h. Provide a possible label for each interpretable factor.

2. Although the EFA has suggested possible subscales within the geoscience attitude survey, these subscales may not have high internal consistency. Again using the data set "Geoscience Attitudes.sav," compute coefficient alpha for each of the emergent factors.

    a. What is the reliability of each of the factors?

    b. Would deleting one or more items from a factor considerably improve internal consistency reliability? If so, delete these item(s) and recompute the reliability of the factor.

    c. Which factors do you believe achieve a sufficiently high alpha to be considered viable subscales for use in research?

EXERCISE 18.2: REPRODUCING COMMUNALITIES AND EIGENVALUES

OBJECTIVE: To aid understanding of how exploratory factor analytic techniques compute extracted communalities and eigenvalues.

PROLOGUE: As discussed in the Module 18 overview, extracted communalities and eigenvalues can be computed from an unrotated factor matrix. An extracted eigenvalue is the sum of the squared loadings of the items on a factor. An extracted communality is the sum of the squared loadings for a variable across all factors. Table 18.2 is the unrotated factor matrix from the analysis requested in Exercise 18.1:

Extraction method: Principal axis factoring, four factors extracted, 20 iterations required.

Using information presented in this table, compute the following. Be sure to write out the relevant equation for each.

1. The extracted eigenvalue for factor 1.
2. The extracted eigenvalue for factor 2.
3. The extracted communality for item 1.
4. The extracted communality for item 2.

Note that you can verify your computations by comparing your computed values with those presented in the output of the EFA produced in Exercise 18.1.

Table 18.2   Factor Matrix

	Factor			
	1	*2*	*3*	*4*
V7	.664	−.311	−.363	7.290E–02
V3	.588	−.443	.156	−.262
V6	.557	−.531	−.247	.244
V8	.451	−.202	.101	−.263
V13	.407	.163	−.226	6.848E–02
V4	.328	2.132E–02	.264	.208
V12	.226	7.399E–03	−3.869E–02	−.212
V9	.571	.605	−9.928E–02	−.154
V10	.423	.578	−8.521E–02	−.164
V11	.278	.435	−.246	.312
V2	.461	2.486E–03	.612	.176
V1	.315	.215	.424	9.492E–02
V5	−3.964E–03	−5.199E–03	−9.033E–02	−6.165E–02

EXERCISE 18.3: EVALUATION OF EFA IN THE LITERATURE

OBJECTIVE: As mentioned throughout this module, there are lots of decisions that need to be made when conducting an EFA. In this exercise, we want you to review several journal articles that use EFA to see how other researchers have justified their choices.

Find two articles that have used EFA in the development of a psychological scale. Study these two articles, focusing on the documentation of the procedures that were used in conducting the EFA as well as understanding the decisions that were made.

When reading these articles, answer these questions:

1. What was the rationale given for conducting the CFA?
2. What extraction/rotation method was used? Was there a rationale given for the choice of this method?
3. How did the researchers determine the number of appropriate factors to extract?
4. What criteria were used to discard items?
5. How did the EFA help the researchers better understand the construct?
6. What unresolved questions do you have about the procedures conducted by the researchers?

Further Readings

Bryant, F.B., & Yarnold, P.R. (1995). Principal components analysis and exploratory and confirmatory factor analysis. In L.G. Grimm & P.R. Yarnold (Eds.), *Reading and understanding multivariate statistics* (pp. 99–136). Washington, DC: American Psychological Association.

Fabrigar, L.R., Wegener, D.T., MacCallum, R.C., & Strahan, E.J. (1999). Evaluating the use of exploratory factor analysis in psychological research. *Psychological Methods, 3,* 272–299.

Ford, J.K., MacCallum, R.C., & Tait, M. (1986). The application of exploratory factor analysis in applied psychology: A critical review and analysis. *Personnel Psychology, 39,* 291–314.

Pedhazur, E.J., & Schmelkin, L.P. (1991). *Measurement, design, and analysis: An integrated approach* (pp. 590–694). Hillsdale, NJ: Erlbaum.

Russell, D.W. (2002). In search of underlying dimensions: The use (and abuse) of factor analysis. *Personality and Social Psychology Bulletin, 28,* 1629–1646.

Tabachnick, B.G., & Fidell, L.S. (2011). *Using multivariate statistics* (6th ed). Boston: Allyn & Bacon.

Module 19

Confirmatory Factor Analysis

In the previous module, we considered exploratory factor analysis (EFA) and argued that it is an important statistical tool at the initial development stages when a researcher is uncertain about the underlying structure of his or her test. In fact, EFA methods are not even the first analyses that should be conducted when a scale is proposed. Basic item analysis techniques (Module 13) should be the initial analyses to see if items have acceptable means and variability as well as reasonable item-total correlations. EFA is often conducted after original item checks have been conducted. As one of the last line of analyses conducted in the scale evaluation process, methods in this module are used then to confirm whether the structure of a test conforms with a particular theory or structure hypothesized by the test developers. As a result, the techniques discussed in this module are powerful and are helpful in theoretically evaluating a test.

Suppose that you have strong expectations regarding the dimensionality of your measure. This is exactly the case for most rationally developed tests. Indeed, it is curious in the example described in the previous module as to why (or even how) we would create personality items without knowledge of the specific personality dimensions intended. More likely, the personality items were specifically developed to assess the conscientiousness and extraversion dimensions of personality. Confirmatory factor analysis (CFA) provides evidence of whether the responses of test takers are consistent with expectations regarding the scale's dimensionality. With this method, we can calculate statistical tests to determine whether data fit a particular model. CFA is based on the general technique of structural equation modeling (SEM), which has been used by psychologists, sociologists, and economists to model in a detailed manner the relationships between a complex set of variables.

Unlike EFA's rules for determining the number of factors that emerge (rules that require some subjective judgment), in CFA we specify a priori the number of factors that we expect to find and calculate a statistical test to determine whether the number of factors we specified is the correct number. Further, in CFA we must specify exactly which items we expect will load on each factor and what the relationships are between factors. Contemporary SEM programs, such as AMOS (Arbuckle, 2009), EQS (Bentler, 1995), LISREL (Jöreskog & Sörbom, 1996), and MPLUS (Muthén & Muthén, 2007), are typically used to conduct CFAs. Using these software packages, expected relationships between observed and latent variables are depicted through the use of a model. Figure 19.1 depicts a CFA model that we could employ to examine the eight variables previously discussed in the EFA example in Module 18. The circles at the top of the model represent factors (i.e., latent constructs), whereas rectangles are used to represent observed variables. Each observed variable is provided an error term (also represented in a circle). A factor loading is designated by drawing a single-headed arrow from the factor to the observed variable, indicating that the latent factor is causing the observed variable. Put in other words, scores on the latent factor are going to influence what the scores on the observed variables will be. The double-headed arrow between the two factors indicates that we would like to estimate the relationship between the proposed factors, but that we do not know which variable is influencing or causing the other variable. Just as important as the paths between variables are the absences of paths between other variables. When there are no paths between variables (latent or observed), that means that there are no direct relations between those variables.

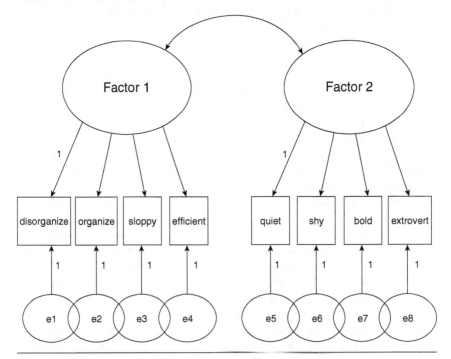

Figure 19.1   Two-Factor Structure Model for CFA Step-by-Step Example

Testing the Hypothesized Factor Model

In contrast to typical uses of EFA, CFA provides a number of indexes of how well our model actually fits the data. The problem in CFA is the decision as to which fit indexes to use to evaluate the model—there are literally dozens to choose from, though not all indexes are available from all SEM software packages. Each available index of fit addresses a slightly different issue and has different assumptions, and no index of fit is considered to be perfect. Therefore, several fit indexes are typically reported for any given model.

Chi-square. Perhaps the most commonly reported index of model fit is the Pearson chi-square, χ^2 (Widaman & Thompson, 2003). This index of fit indicates how likely it is that the model accurately represents the data. Good model fit is indicated by a nonsignificant chi-square. Unfortunately, the chi-square is likely to be significant if the sample size is larger than 200 regardless of model fit. Therefore, other fit indexes must also be considered. Despite its limitations, the chi-square statistic plays an additional important role in examining CFA model fit. In CFA, the fit of the hypothesized model is compared with the fit of at least two other models. One of these alternative models is typically a one-factor solution. Here, the CFA model is redrawn to indicate that all of the variables load on a common factor. On the opposite side of the spectrum, another alternative model is that each observed variable loads on its own, independent factor. This is termed the null, or independence, model and assumes that no observed variable in the scale is correlated with other variables. Most SEM programs generate fit statistics for the null model automatically when examining the hypothesized model, so it is unnecessary to draw this model (see Widaman & Thompson, 2003, for the conditions that must exist for a model to be an acceptable independence null model). In most cases, these two models are implausible, and so they are estimated for the purposes of creating baseline criteria. If your more complicated model cannot fit better than either of these extremely simple models, then that is a sign that your model is inaccurate.

To evaluate the hypothesized model, the chi-square value obtained from the hypothesized model is subtracted from the chi-square value of one of the alternative models. Similarly, the value for the degrees of freedom of the hypothesized model is subtracted from the degrees of freedom of the alternative model. If the resulting chi-square difference value is significant, given the resulting degrees of freedom value, then the hypothesized model is deemed to be a better fit than the alternative model. This process demonstrates whether the hypothesized model is a *better* fit to the data than the alternatives, but it does not provide convincing evidence that the hypothesized model is itself a *good* fit to the data. In general, comparisons with the null model and the one-factor solution often show that the proposed model fits better than those two models that have extreme assumptions (either that there is no correlation with any of the variables in the model or that there is only one factor that can explain the covariation). Given that it is likely that the chi-square statistic will show that your model is preferred, additional fit indexes are also considered.

Other Fit Indexes. Another popular fit index, referred to as the goodness-of-fit index (GFI), compares the relationships between the variables obtained from the sample with those hypothesized in the model. For each relationship hypothesized in the model, any difference between the model's specification and the actual data produces a residual. If the model fits the data very well, residuals will be near zero. If the model does not fit the data, then the residuals will be larger. Good model fit is indicated by GFI indexes greater than .90 (though some argue that .95 is necessary). Unfortunately, the number of parameters estimated affects this index of model fit. The GFI tends to be higher for more complex models (i.e., models with more parameters to estimate). The adjusted goodness-of-fit (AGFI) index takes this problem into account in determining model fit, but it, too, has been deemed problematic (Kline, 1998).

Another fit index is the comparative fit index (CFI). This index indicates the proportion of improvement in fit of the hypothesized model in comparison to the null model. Obtained CFI values above .90 indicate acceptable model fit. The CFI is less influenced by sample size than are other popular incremental fit indexes such as the normed fit index (NFI).

Finally, the root mean squared error of approximation (RMSEA) and root mean squared residual compare observed statistics (e.g., covariance estimates) with statistics that would be expected if the model were correct. These statistics are less affected by sample size, and confidence intervals can be computed around the RMSEA value so that researchers can determine the confidence levels involved for that particular fit index. For both of these indexes, smaller is better (standards of fit typically range from .05 to .08 for acceptable fit with the RMSEA).

It is important to keep in mind that the fit indexes discussed here are but a sample of the evolving number of model fit indexes. Scientific consensus as to which fit indexes are most appropriate is likely to change over time. In most CFA applications, a variety of fit statistics will be analyzed to determine if there is a consensus. When fit statistics indicate misfit, as discussed further in this module, there are methods for determining the source and type of misfit. This search for the sources of misfit can be helpful in further figuring out how your scale works.

A Step-by-Step Example of CFA

The model depicted in Figure 19.1 is a graphical representation of the expected loadings of our eight-item personality scale discussed in Module 18. The model was built in AMOS (Arbuckle & Wothke, 1999) (see Exercise 19.1 to obtain a free student version of popular SEM software, which will allow you to follow along with the analysis described here). As with other SEM packages, AMOS includes a graphical interface that helps us to build our hypothesized model. The model in Figure 19.1 was drawn to indicate that we have two expected factors, each with four expected factor loadings. Because observed variables likely include some error in measurement, error terms are drawn to each observed variable. These error terms include variance unrelated to the common factors.

In SEM, a model must be *identified* in order to be analyzed. A model is identified if, theoretically, it is possible to compute a unique estimate for each parameter in the model. If a model is not identified, then there exist an infinite number of possible solutions. This occurs when there are more parameters to be estimated than the number of variances and covariances in the model. To ensure identification, some parameters are fixed at 1.0. As can be seen in Figure 19.1, the path coefficients from each of the eight error variances and a path coefficient between each latent construct and one of the observed variables were constrained to a value of 1.0 to allow the model to be identified. Once the model is drawn and variable names are provided, it is necessary to indicate the data set we wish to analyze. The data set for this analysis is once again the "Personality-2.sav" data file (see Appendix B). For this analysis, all defaults were used, and standardized estimates were requested in the output. Finally, the estimates can be calculated.

Figure 19.2 depicts the CFA model with standardized path coefficients. As can be seen, the factors are uncorrelated. (Note this was also found in the EFA discussed in the previous module.) In contrast, the path coefficients between the observed variables and the expected factors are sizeable. Note, however, that Kline (1998) suggested that the squared multiple correlation (R^2) for each indicator should be at least .50. Otherwise, more than half of the indicator's variance is unrelated to the factor it is expected to measure. Unfortunately, the square of several

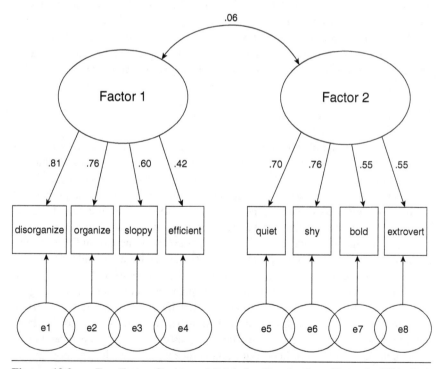

Figure 19.2   Two-Factor Structure Model for Step-by-Step Example With Path Coefficients

Table 19.1   Measures of Fit for Each Model

Model	$\chi^2(df)$	GFI	AGFI	CFI
Two-Factor	100.834 (19)	.921	.850	.870
One-Factor	353.606 (20)	.751	.552	.469
Null	656.524 (28)	.628	.522	.000

Chi-square difference tests: One-factor model versus two-factor model: $\chi^2(1) = 252.772$, $p < .01$. Null model versus two-factor model: $\chi^2(9) = 555.69$, $p < .01$.

of the factor loadings depicted in Figure 19.2 is considerably less than .50. Thus, the indicators "sloppy" and "efficient" fail to meet this strict criterion for factor 1, and "bold" and "extraverted" fail to meet this criterion for factor 2. Still, we are likely more interested in examining the overall fit of the model.

Table 19.1 presents some of the fit indexes for the two-factor model. Given the large sample size, we may not want to rely too much on the significant chi-square value, which would suggest poor model fit. Whereas the GFI value would suggest good model fit, the AGFI and CFI suggest the model may not adequately fit the data. Finally, we would want to compare the fit of our two-factor model with the fit of a one-factor model and the null model. Table 19.1 also presents the measures of fit for each alternative model. The chi-square difference between the two-factor model and the alternative models is significant in both models. Further, as we would expect, the additional fit indexes indicate that the hypothesized model provides a better fit than either of the alternative models. It is clear that the two-factor model is a much better fit than either of these two alternative models.

Revising Your Original Model

The process of model formulation and testing is a long process that involves many iterations. Even if your model fits satisfactorily in one sample, it is likely that the fit could be improved by making some changes to the model, especially early on in test and model development. In addition, sometimes the fit of a hypothesized model is unsatisfactory and so it becomes necessary to revise the model. Fortunately there are statistics that can be used to guide the process of model revision.

Model modification indexes indicate likely sources for increasing fit by freeing a coefficient that was previously set to be zero (i.e., there were no single- or double-headed arrows between two sources of variance). Coefficients that are likely to be identified as sources for increasing fit include paths between latent factors (e.g., if you estimated that two factors were uncorrelated, but they in fact are correlated, a modification index would show that) and paths between the error factors of individual items. It is quite common in CFA analyses that there will be several error terms that need to be correlated (i.e., double-headed arrows drawn between the error terms) in order to improve model fit.

Several points need to be made about this process of allowing correlated item error terms, as the process has been deemed controversial (see Landis, Edwards, &

Cortina, 2009). First, item error terms in CFA models indicate that there is variance in the item that is not explained by the latent factors in the model. The term error is a bit misleading because it can connote random uncertainty, but in the context of CFA models, the error term simply signifies all variance unexplained by the latent factor terms. Some researchers refer to this term as the residual, which may have an easier connotation to grasp. It makes sense that error terms for individual items may be correlated, suggesting that the correlation between individual items is higher than the correlation that would be expected given that they share common factors. There are lots of reasons that items may be correlated, besides shared latent factors, such as common response formats, shared idiosyncratic item content, and context factors. For example, it may be that on a scale of 10 items you have 2 items that are reverse coded. Those 2 items may share higher correlations than would be expected because of shared response bias.

There is no harm in investigating modification indexes to see where and how fit can be improved. The controversy consists of how you respond to the indexes. Simply freeing parameters and reestimating your model and reporting the increased and better fitting indexes is viewed as bad practice for several reasons. First, there are likely going to be some variations in your sample that will not be present in other samples. Therefore, simply freeing paths that have the highest modification indexes will likely result in an inflated fit index that when estimated in another sample would be much lower. In addition, freeing all parameters that would increase model fit, without any concern for the consequences of these changes, is viewed poorly as it fails to give proper deference to the original hypothesized model. Finally, the more that changes are made in an originally hypothesized model, the more that CFA starts to resemble an exploratory technique and not a confirmatory technique.

A healthy approach to dealing with model modification indexes is to use these statistics as a tool for thinking more deeply about the structure of your model and test. If there is a pattern among the modification indexes, such that all negatively worded items should have correlated error terms that would indicate that your test is measuring an additional construct beyond what was intended. You could either incorporate additional methodological constructs into your test to account for these sources of variance, or you could delete the reverse-coded items to eliminate that source of variance. Finally, changes to an originally hypothesized model based on data from a particular sample should be confirmed in a new independent sample to avoid the criticism of capitalization of chance. This need to replicate the changes in a new sample is more pronounced with more significant modifications in the original model. If one pair of item error terms (out of many) were allowed to correlate, then there might be little need to cross-validate your modified model.

Item Bundling

CFA analyses are very sensitive to idiosyncratic shared sources of variance across items, thereby often requiring correlated error terms. It may make some people uncomfortable to draw many correlated error terms in a model, even though that may be what it takes to increase model fit. Another solution would be to collapse items together to form item bundles (also referred to as item parcels). By combining several items into one bundle, you can cancel out the idiosyncrasies of individual items making it less likely that there will be correlated errors with other bundles. In most research that uses bundles, three or more bundles are formed within a particular scale. Therefore, if there are 12 items on a scale, there may be three bundles composed of 4 items. There are lots of methods that have been used to form item bundles (see Landis, Beal, & Tesluk, 2000). Some approaches use empirical analyses to choose items for a particular bundle that have strong correlations among each other. Other approaches use a content-based approach (e.g., combining all items that measure a particular subfacet of the larger trait). Another approach uses random selection methods to assign items to bundles. Once bundles have been formed, items are added together to form an uber-item. These bundles are then used in the CFA model instead of the individual items. Typically, the fit of a model is increased when item bundles are used instead of individual items. In addition to the benefit of increased fit, item bundles are useful in reducing the number of coefficients to estimate. This helps stabilize the estimates and can be useful especially when there are large numbers of terms to estimate relative to the number of cases. Rules of thumb for CFA analyses suggest anywhere from 5 to 10 cases per term (e.g., loading, pathway, error term) to estimate. By using item bundles in the model instead of individual items, this ratio can be made more favorable. One downside about bundling is that test takers respond to items, not bundles, and so there could be a loss of information that might be important for some purposes.

Concluding Comments

CFA is a powerful technique that helps researchers test specific hypotheses about their psychological measures. EFA methods (from Module 18) are useful earlier in the test development process when researchers have little idea about the underlying structure of their test. Conversely, CFA methods are more useful later in the test development process. This module presented some of the basic fundamentals regarding issues faced when using CFA. As we hope that you can fathom, there are many complexities to CFA, and decisions need to be made throughout the process.

Beginners wanting to delve deeper into factor analysis are strongly encouraged to read the very accessible works of Bryant and Yarnold (1995), Kline (2011), Lance and Vandenberg (2002), Tabachnick and Fidell (2012), and Thompson (2004).

Best Practices

1. Use CFA methods after you have developed a good theoretical and empirical understanding of your scale via scale development and exploratory practices.

2. Compare a variety of GIF indexes when judging whether your model fits the data.
3. Use modification indexes to gather insight into your scale, and make modifications with caution, focusing on whether the modifications make theoretical sense. Use the indexes to gain insight into your construct.
4. If major modifications were made, estimate your modified model on a new data set to avoid capitalization on chance.
5. Consider using item bundles to improve model fit and to reduce the number of parameters to estimate.

Practical Questions

1. List four differences between CFA and EFA. What are similarities?
2. In scale construction, when would CFA be preferable to EFA? When would EFA be preferable to CFA?
3. In CFA, how would you determine if the data were consistent with your hypothesized model?
4. If the fit indexes indicated poor fit of your expected CFA model, what would you do next?
5. How should modification indexes be used in revising a model? What are the dangers in using them?
6. How should item bundles be used when conducting a CFA? What are the advantages of bundles? What would be any disadvantages?
7. How can CFA be used to support validity evidence for a scale?

Case Studies

CASE STUDY 19.1: USING CFA TO ANALYZE A MULTITRAIT-MULTIMETHOD MATRIX

In an article published in the *Journal of Personality*, Marsh (1990) provided evidence that CFA can be very useful in analyzing a multitrait-multimethod (MTMM) matrix—as long as care is taken to specify the correct model.

Marsh (1990) examined the construct validity of three commonly used measures of preadolescent self-concept: the 80-item Piers-Harris (PH) instrument, the 76-item Self-Description Questionnaire I (SDQI), and the 28-item Perceived Competence Scale for Children (PCS). Although each of the scales examined has been found to be multidimensional, the number of previously identified dimensions differs across the scales. Marsh posited that each of the three measures assesses physical, social, and academic aspects of self-concept. Two of the three measures also include a general self-concept dimension, and two of the three measures assess other aspects of self-concept.

A sample of 290 Australian fifth graders was administered each of the scales. Marsh used the three different measures to represent different methods, while the previously identified dimensions of self-concept were taken as multiple traits. The resulting MTMM matrix was analyzed using both the Campbell-Fiske (1959) guidelines (see Module 9) and CFA.

Using the Campbell-Fiske approach, Marsh first found that similar dimensions across the measures were indeed substantially correlated with one another, providing evidence of construct validity. Second, Marsh examined whether convergent validities exceeded the correlations between different traits measured using different methods. Evidence indicated that the mean convergent validities were greater than heterotrait-heteromethod correlations for 60 out of 62 comparisons. This provided good evidence for this initial step in the examination of discriminant validity. Third, Marsh compared the convergent validities to the heterotrait-monomethod correlations. The expected pattern was found for two of the three measures of self-concept. However, mean heterotrait-monomethod correlations slightly exceeded the mean convergent validities for the PH measure. Thus, support for this criterion of discriminant validity was found for only the SDQI and PCS measures. Finally, the last Campbell-Fiske criterion was examined. This criterion argues that correlations among traits should be similar whether the methods are the same or different. Although this pattern was found for the SDQI and PCS, evidence was not supportive of the discriminant validity of the PH scales.

In reanalyzing the data using CFA, Marsh (1990) constructed four possible models to explain the data, based on Widaman's (1985) taxonomy of models that vary different characteristics of the trait and method factors. Model 1 is a trait-only model that proposes no effect of method. Model 2, the traits and uncorrelated methods factor, assumes that method effects associated with each of the measures are uncorrelated. Model 3 is a bit more complex, in that it does not assume that method effects are unidimensional across all variables assessed by a particular method. Rather, Model 3 represents method variance as correlated uniquenesses. These are correlations between pairs of variables measured by the same method once the trait effects are removed. Finally, Model 4 proposes that unidimensional method factors are correlated with each other. This model can be referred to as traits and correlated method factors.

For each of these four possible models, Marsh (1990) evaluated whether the solution was well defined for both a possible four-trait solution and a possible five-trait solution. Models 1 and 4 were found to be poorly defined for both possible solutions. Model 2 was found to be well defined for the four-trait solution, but only marginally defined for the five-factor solution. Model 3, however, was found to be very well defined for both the four- and five-factor solutions. Marsh pointed out that when method factors are considered, Model 3 typically provides solutions that are better defined than competing models. Inspection of the CFA results indicated that the correlated uniquenesses associated with the SDQI were considerably smaller than those associated with the other two measures, indicating the lesser influence of method effects for the SDQI. Although convergent validity was found for all three measures of preadolescent self-concept, evidence for discriminant validity was strongest for the SDQI.

Questions to Ponder

1. What concerns about the interpretation of an MTMM matrix are better addressed by CFA rather than the guidelines of Campbell and Fiske (1959)?
2. In what ways are the four CFA models proposed by Widaman (1985) similar? In what ways do these models differ from one another?
3. What are correlated uniquenesses?
4. What might cause a CFA model to be poorly defined?
5. What methods can be used to evaluate alternative CFA models? Are some methods more appropriate than others?
6. How can researchers who use advanced statistical analyses communicate with those who are less statistically savvy?

CASE STUDY 19.2: USING CFA TO TEST MEASUREMENT EQUIVALENCE

Module 11 discussed the idea of measurement equivalence in the context of cross-cultural research. CFA work has been very important in determining the measurement equivalence of instruments across cultures. Nye, Roberts, Saucier, and Zhou (2008) used CFA methods to test the equivalence of the Goldberg Adjective Checklist measure of the Big Five personality traits across Chinese, Greek, and American respondents. It is useful to consider their research to see how CFA methods can be used to determine whether a test structure holds up across various samples. As mentioned in Module 11, this equivalence is necessary to be able to use the instrument across cultures and to be able to compare results from one language to findings of another language.

In their research, Nye et al. used the software program LISREL to estimate a factor structure for the instrument in each of the three language samples, using a process called multigroup confirmatory factor analyses. As the first step in their analysis, they estimated a CFA model on one American sample (they had two separate American samples for cross-validation purposes) for each of the personality traits (i.e., five separate models). A single-factor model was rejected for each of the five personality traits suggesting that more complex models were needed. Next, they used EFA with an oblique rotation to get ideas for more complex models. Note that this is the reverse of the typical process where an exploratory model is used prior to a confirmatory approach; the interplay between exploratory and confirmatory methods is complex and, as this example shows, can go in a variety of directions. Their EFAs identified two factors for each dimension, with the factors largely being defined as a negative factor (i.e., words written to tap the negative end of the trait continuum) and a positive factor. Next, a CFA was fit to each scale that represented the two-factor solution identified in the EFAs. Each of these two-factor models (except Neuroticism, which fit satisfactorily at the first time) was tweaked based on modification indexes. For some scales, there needed to be cross-loadings for a few items (i.e., even though the item loaded primarily on one factor, there was still a significant loading on the other factor). For other cases, item error terms needed to be correlated for a few items. For example, the items *intellectual* and *unintellectual* loaded on separate factors (positive and negative respectively) on the Intellect scale, but the modification index suggested that the error terms for the two items should be correlated.

In the next stage, they tested three types of measurement equivalence across the two American samples. This test across two American samples allows the researchers to determine whether the factor structure identified in one sample fits well for the other sample, thus ruling out capitalizing on chance. They tested *configural equivalence* first, which tests whether both samples have the same number of factors and the same pattern of loadings across the two samples. Their analysis showed that there were no differences for any of the scales in terms of number of factors and the direction of loadings. Next they tested *metric equivalence* and *scalar equivalence*, which tests whether the factor loading estimates are equal across samples and then whether factor means are equivalent across samples. Their analyses demonstrated that there was equivalence in all of these steps, thus suggesting that the CFA models that they developed for each of the five scales was robust and fit the American samples well.

Next, they tested the equivalence of the American model with the Greek and Chinese samples, respectively. (*Note:* They did not test the equivalence of the Greek sample directly to the Chinese sample.) Across all comparisons, configural equivalence held suggesting that the factor structure was the same for these comparisons. The other analyses, scalar and metric, however, found that there were significant differences across samples. There were factor mean differences across samples, and there were differences in the magnitudes of factor loadings across language translations. If these differences in loadings were not accounted for, misleading conclusions could have been reached in terms of understanding mean differences across samples.

The Nye et al. (2008) article follows the traditional approach to testing the equivalence of scales across languages and cultures. They do a good job of detailing each step of their analysis, and so it is easy to follow and is worth reading in its entirety. At the end of their model-fitting analyses, they find differences between their baseline American sample and their Greek and Chinese samples. These statistical differences raise some interesting questions that we ask you to pursue in the following questions.

Questions to Ponder

1. What is the role of EFA with CFA?
2. Which of the following types of equivalence (configural, metric, and scalar) are more important?
3. How does the CFA approach to testing equivalence compare to other methods of testing cross-cultural equivalence mentioned in Module 11?
4. How do you untangle whether differences are due to poor translations versus true cross-cultural differences?
5. How can you make sure that your results estimated in one sample will generalize to other samples?
6. How can you test generalizability across cultures if you have small samples for at least one culture?

Exercises

EXERCISE 19.1: TUTORIAL IN STRUCTURAL EQUATIONS MODELING

OBJECTIVE: To provide a brief introduction to common SEM programs.

LISREL is one of the most popular SEM programs for conducting CFA. The subsequent links provide access to free demonstration versions of this software program for LISREL; download the free student version and the "Getting started with the Student Edition of LISREL" Word file at http://www.ssicentral.com/lisrel/downloads.html.

There is a "Getting started" document available at http://www.ssicentral.com/lisrel/techdocs/GSWLISREL.pdf. Open that up and refer to "Section 3: Fitting a Measurement model to SPSS data." This provides a step-by-step example of how to conduct a CFA in LISREL. Note that the depress.sav and depress0.spl files needed to conduct the step-by-step CFA example using LISREL should be in the directory "c:/Lisrel9 Student Examples/Tutorial" on your computer's hard drive as part of the installation of the student version.

EXERCISE 19.2: REVIEW OF CFA LITERATURE

OBJECTIVE: To see how CFAs are reported in the psychological literature.

Just as in any other statistical technique, there is a wide variety in terms of the practice and reporting of CFA. Find two studies that use CFA techniques to analyze the structure of a psychological measurement. Study how the CFAs are reported and note differences between the two different studies.

1. Describe the underlying models being tested in each article. Determine the rationale that the author(s) used to create the models. Did they rely on previous research to justify their model, or did they rely more heavily on theory?
2. What fit indexes and tests of model fit did the authors use?
3. Did the authors use modification indexes to revise their model? If so, how did they justify or explain their use?
4. Did the authors use item bundles? If so, how did they create those bundles?
5. How did the use of CFA help the authors to better understand their scale?

Further Readings

Bryant, F.B., & Yarnold, P.R. (1995). Principal components analysis and exploratory and confirmatory factor analysis. In L.G. Grimm & P.R. Yarnold (Eds.), *Reading and understanding multivariate statistics* (pp. 99–136). Washington, DC: American Psychological Association.

Klem, L. (2000). Structural equations modeling. In L.G. Grimm & P.R. Yarnold (Eds.), *Reading and understanding more multivariate statistics* (pp. 227–260). Washington, DC: American Psychological Association.

Kline, R.B. (2011). *Principles and practice of structural equation modeling* (3rd ed.). New York: Guilford Press.

Lance, C.E., & Vandenberg, R.J. (2002). Confirmatory factor analysis. In F. Drasgow & N. Schmitt (Eds.), *Measuring and analyzing behavior in organizations: Advances in measurement and data analysis* (pp. 221–254). San Francisco, CA: Jossey-Bass.

Tabachnick, B.G., & Fidell, L.S. (2012). *Using multivariate statistics* (6th ed.). Boston: Allyn & Bacon.

Thompson, B. (2004). *Exploratory and confirmatory factor analysis: Understanding concepts and applications*. Washington, DC: American Psychological Association.

Module 20

Item Response Theory

In Module 13, we discussed classical test theory item analysis (CTT-IA), where the focus was on how difficult and discriminating each item on a given test was within a particular sample. Under the CTT-IA framework, items on a given test are retained or discarded based on how difficult they are, as estimated by the percentage of respondents answering the item correctly—the p value—and how well they discriminate among our examinees, as estimated by an item-total correlation—the point-biserial correlation coefficient. In addition, our estimate of a person's underlying true score (or ability level) is simply the sum of the number of items correct, regardless of which items the individual answered correctly. CTT-IA has been a workhorse over the years for test developers and users who want to improve the quality of their tests. Given no other information, CTT-IA can be useful for local, small-scale test development and revision. However, there are newer, more psychometrically sophisticated models of item responding that provide much more useful and generalizable information to test developers and users who want to improve the quality of their tests, namely, **item response theory (IRT)**.

IRT Versus CTT

IRT (sometimes referred to as **modern test theory** to contrast it with CTT) models provide more detailed item, person, and test information than the CTT-IA procedures outlined in Module 13. Zickar and Broadfoot (2008) likened CTT-IA to an optical microscope, whereas IRT was more like an electron microscope. Although IRT is a more powerful method of item analysis, Embretson and Reise (2000) view them as related, with CTT-IA principles being special cases of the more general IRT model. Although there are some similarities between the approaches, the IRT approach to psychometric analysis provides more powerful and detailed analyses and allows for more sophisticated applications than CTT-IA. As such, many of the

CTT-IA principles that we all know and love (e.g., the principle that the longer a test is, the more reliable it will be as demonstrated by the Spearman-Brown prophecy formula) are simply not true under IRT. Thus, IRT is not simply a refinement of CTT-IA principles; rather, it is a new and different way of looking at the entire psychometric process, albeit one that is much more mathematically and conceptually complex and, as a result, requires a new and deeper level of thinking to appreciate.

Ellis and Mead (2002) noted that, to control error in test development, "CTT's approach resembles that of standardization (or matching) and randomization used in experimental design. IRT, on the other hand, relies on mathematical models to make statistical adjustments to test scores for 'nuisance' properties (e.g., difficulty, discrimination, and guessing) of items" (p. 333). IRT's use of a statistical model to represent the response process is different from CTT in which the model used ($X = T + E$) is so vague and elemental that it provides little insight into the response process used by test takers. Other distinctions between CTT and IRT noted by Ellis and Mead include IRT's focus on items rather than the overall test score, its use of nonlinear rather than linear models, as well as differences in how item parameters such as difficulty, discrimination, and guessing are estimated. In addition, Zickar and Broadfoot (2008) note that IRT models are falsifiable and CTT is not. Just as in confirmatory factor analysis (CFA) models, fit statistics can be used to evaluate whether a particular model fits a data set; the CTT approach does not provide any way to evaluate fit. Overall, Ellis and Mead provided a balanced comparison of the CTT-IA and IRT approaches to item analysis. In the end, Ellis and Mead "advocate that the CTT and IRT approaches be combined in conducting an item analysis" (p. 324), and they demonstrate how to do so in their chapter by applying both techniques to the analysis of a Spanish translation of a reasoning scale.

Given its complexity, we will not delve into the major underpinnings and nuts and bolts of IRT models here. For further information, we recommend excellent overview chapters and articles (e.g., Ellis & Mead, 2002; Zickar, 1998; Zickar & Broadfoot, 2008), as well as comprehensive book-length discussions (e.g., de Ayala, 2009; DeMars, 2010; Hambleton, Swaminathan, & Rogers, 1991). One of our favorites is Embretson and Reise (2000), who provided a very readable, nontechnical book-length introduction to IRT. Thus, we provide only a broad overview of the topic, and, as a consequence, we refer the reader to the preceding references (as well as others cited later and in Module 21) for more detailed discussions of the major current issues surrounding IRT, as well as detailed explications of its major underpinnings.

General Overview of IRT

IRT uses information from both the individuals (test takers) and the item to determine the likelihood of a person with a given level of ability (referred to as theta, θ, in IRT parlance) responding correctly to a given item. That is, IRT represents a set of probabilistic models that allow us to describe the relationship between a test taker's θ level and the probability of a correct response to any individual item.

Early IRT models (in the 1960s–1970s) were developed to examine dichotomous data (scored 0 = incorrect and 1 = correct) that focused primarily on mental abilities. However, researchers eventually realized that such models could easily be applied to other dichotomous data such as those used in many personality and attitude scales (e.g., agree/disagree or yes/no). By the 1980s, IRT models were being developed to examine polytomous data (more than two response options), such as Likert-type response scales of 1–5 (1 = strongly agree to 5 = strongly disagree). In this module, however, we will only discuss IRT models that use dichotomous responses (Zickar, 2002, provided a chapter-length overview on estimating polytomous item formats). In addition, we will assume unidimensionality of θ, as is traditional; however, newer multidimensional IRT models are becoming increasingly available, though often their data requirements (e.g., large sample size) are prohibitive for many psychologists.

A major advantage of IRT over CTT-IA is that IRT models provide test and item statistics that are population invariant. That is, the information provided by IRT models regarding item parameters (e.g., item difficulty and discrimination), unlike that provided by CTT-IA, is generally invariant to the population used to generate the item and test information. Thus, information obtained from one sample using IRT models, assuming it is sufficiently large but not necessarily representative of the target population, will be equivalent to that obtained from another sample, regardless of the average ability level of the examinees who took the two tests. The same cannot be said for CTT-IA.

For example, under the CTT-IA framework, an item measuring developmental psychology theories taken from an examination in an upper-division developmental psychology class may be viewed as very difficult for introductory psychology students, of moderate difficulty for students in the upper-division developmental psychology class, and extremely easy for students in a graduate-level developmental psychology class. However, IRT would provide a single (invariant across the three populations of students) estimate of difficulty and discriminability, regardless of which individuals were used to calibrate the item. In addition, under CTT-IA such items on the test would differentiate students in the upper-division developmental psychology class fairly well; however, they would not differentiate students in the introductory psychology or graduate-level class very well. The item might be too difficult for the former population and too easy for the latter population. The property of *parameter invariance* is an important one that allows applications such as computer adaptive testing (CAT) that are presented in Module 21 to be possible.

IRT is considered a strong test theory, whereas CTT-IA is considered a weak theory. This means that IRT provides more powerful applications and detailed level of analysis, but it also means that the theory requires more significant assumptions. Responses in IRT are assumed to be *locally independent*. What does that mean, you ask? Basically, it means that a test taker's response, for any given level of θ, is a function of only his or her level of θ. This can be problematic for items that measure more than one latent trait. Fortunately, IRT models can test whether the assumption of local independence is met in a particular sample. And if it is not strictly met, it is possible to determine the impact of the violations. Running IRT analyses, as with the CFA procedures discussed in Module 19, requires special software that is typically not part of most major statistical packages such as SPSS, SAS, and STATA. Embretson and Reise (2000) concluded their book with a chapter that compares and contrasts the major IRT programs available at that time. Historically, one of the challenges with conducting IRT analyses was that the software required specialized knowledge (often knowledge of DOS) and had poor user interfaces; fortunately, software packages have become more user-friendly, and the software used in our example, IRTPro 2.1, is much easier to navigate than earlier IRT programs. As a result, IRT analyses should be easier to produce—if not to understand.

Item Response Functions

Information in IRT models is often depicted in graphical form as item response functions (IRFs) or **item characteristic curves** (once again, different psychometricans use different phrases to signify the same thing; we will use IRF). Three such IRFs are plotted in Figure 20.1 based on data from Wiesen (1999), which will be discussed later in the step-by-step example. Note, however, that the item numbers presented here do not match the items on the Wiesen Test of Mechanical Aptitude (WTMA). These IRFs are nonlinear regressions (sometimes called S curves because of their shape) of the likelihood of responding affirmatively to an item given the individual's θ level (Zickar, 1998). Most items follow a cumulative normal distribution ogive. Although IRFs can take several forms, the three-parameter logistic (3-PL) model is the most general. Under this model, the three parameters of discrimination (a_i—the slope of the IRF, typically .5 to 1.5), difficulty (b_i—the point of inflection on the IRF, where the curve switches from accelerating to decelerating, typically −2.0 to +2.0), and pseudo-guessing (c_i—where the lower asymptote crosses the ordinate or Y axis, typically 0 to .20) are estimated. These parameters can be estimated in various ways. The most common practice is to use marginal maximum likelihood (MML) procedures to estimate the item parameters. In a two-parameter logistic (2-PL) model, the c_i parameter is assumed to be zero, while a_i and b_i are estimated; this model is useful for items in which no guessing would occur. In the one-parameter logistic (1-PL) model, also called the Rasch model, c_i is set to zero, while the a_i parameter is assumed to be constant across items; thus, only the b_i (difficulty) parameter is estimated. This highly restrictive model is often used when there are small sample sizes.

Examining Figure 20.1a, you can see that the first item (Item 12) is a relatively easy item. How can you tell? The b_i (difficulty) parameter is very low at −7.90. This means that a test taker only needs a very low (roughly 7.90 standard deviations below the mean) ability level (θ value) to have about an equal chance of answering this item correctly or incorrectly. In addition, the small a_i (discrimination) value (.18) indicates that it tends not to differentiate the test takers very well.

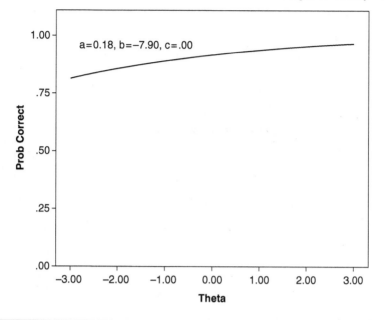

Figure 20.1a   Items 12 Item Response Function

This is seen by the very flat nature of the curve. Finally, the c_i (pseudo-guessing) parameter is somewhat deceptive in this graph. Typically, the line crosses the Y axis at about the value of the c_i parameter. However, given that this item is so easy, someone with even a θ value less than −3.00 has a better than 50/50 chance of getting this item correct.

Figure 20.1b shows that the second item (Item 9) is a relatively harder item. The b_i (difficulty) parameter is moderate at .35. In addition, the a_i (discrimination) value indicates that this is a better item than Item 12 at discriminating test takers, particularly in the middle of the score range (between say −1.0 and +1.0). That is, the slope of the line at the point of inflection is much steeper than it was for Item 12. Finally, the c_i (pseudo-guessing) parameter is more intuitive for this item, as the curve crosses the Y axis at about the value of the c_i parameter (.26). Overall, then, this would be a very good item for distinguishing individuals in the middle range of θ (i.e., it's a keeper).

In Figure 20.1c, the third item (Item 16) is the most difficult of the three items. Its b_i (difficulty) parameter is rather high at 1.92. As with Item 9, the a_i (discrimination) value for Item 16 indicates that it is better at discriminating test takers, however, this time at higher score ranges (between, say, 1.0 and 3.0). The c_i (pseudo-guessing) parameter in this case appears to be right on target, as the curve crosses the Y axis at the value of the c_i parameter (.11). Overall, then, this would be a useful item for distinguishing individuals in the upper range of θ.

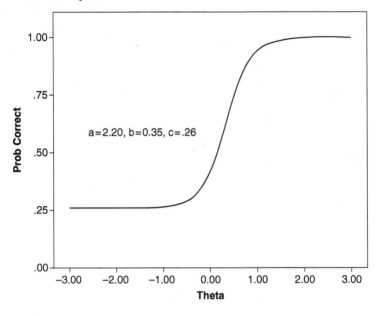

Figure 20.1b　　Items 9 Item Response Function

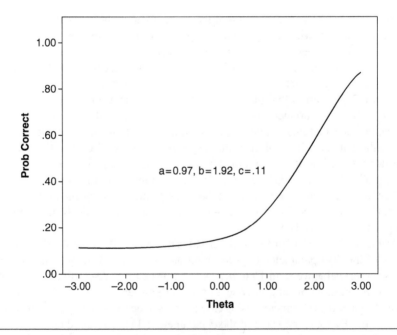

Figure 20.1c　　Items 16 Item Response Function

Item Information Functions

In CTT-IA, the concept of reliability applies to the entire test, whereas, with IRT, each item is assessed for the *information* it provides. As discussed in Module 6, the reliability estimate is used in CTT-IA to compute the standard error of measurement (*SEM*), which, in turn, is used to build confidence intervals around individual scores. In CTT-IA, however, the *SEM* is assumed to be the same at all ability levels. This is highly unlikely, in that extremely high or low scores will likely have more measurement error than moderate scores. In IRT, the *SEM* can be estimated for different ability levels, thus giving us much more accurate estimates of an individual's underlying ability, particularly at the extremes of the score distributions.

Figure 20.2 provides examples of *item information functions* (IIFs) for the previous three items. An IIF represents the amount of psychometric information that a given item contributes to a test's measurement precision. In general, the higher the value of a_i, the more information the item provides in estimating θ near the value of the difficulty parameter (b_i). Not surprisingly, then, the first item (Item 12) provides the most information for individuals at lower score ranges (θ between less than −3.0 and about .0), as it is a very easy item. Given that its discrimination is extremely low, though, the magnitude of the information is extremely low across all ranges. The second item (Item 9) provides the most information for individuals in the middle range of θ (between −1.0 and +1.0). Finally, the third item (Item 16)

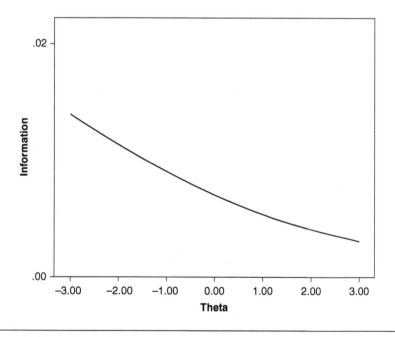

Figure 20.2a   Items 12 Item Information Function

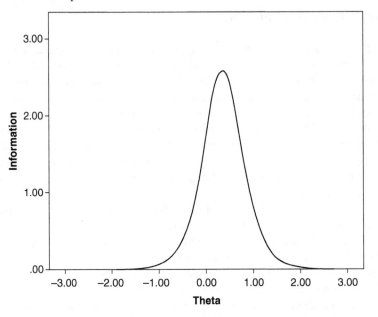

Figure 20.2b   Items 9 Item Information Function

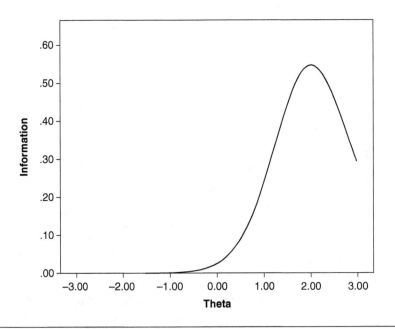

Figure 20.2c   Items 16 Item Information Function

provides the most information for individuals at the upper ranges of θ (from 1.0 to +3.0). When interpreting the shapes of individual information functions, please notice that the y-axis differs across items. For example, note that the maximum information for Item 12 is .02, whereas the maximum information for Item 9 is nearly 3.0. Although we prefer to have a common metric on our graphs, in this case it is common practice for the maximum of the y-axis to vary. So always pay attention! When we are building a test, we want items with a variety of difficulty levels. We also want items with high discrimination values. Thus, we would most likely keep Items 9 and 16; however, we would only keep item 12 if we could not find other easy items with better discrimination values. Because most traits we study tend to follow roughly a normal distribution, we would want to have more items of moderate difficulty (such as Item 9) than items of high or low difficulty, although, again, we need a wide range of difficulty levels. In addition, if we were working with special populations, such as gifted or mentally disabled students, we would clearly need more items at the appropriate ends of the distributions.

A Step-by-Step Example of Conducting an IRT Analysis

Wiesen (1999) discussed the administration, scoring, development, and validation (among other things) of the WTMA—PAR Edition. This test is similar to tests such as the Bennett Mechanical Comprehension Test, the Differential Aptitude Test—Mechanical Reasoning, Science Research Associates Mechanical Concepts Test, the Career Ability Placement Survey—Mechanical Reasoning, and Applied Technology Series—Mechanical Comprehension (see Wiesen, 1999, Appendix F, p. 45). These tests measure (to varying degrees) an individual's ability to learn mechanical and physical principles. Given many of these tests are well established with known reliability, validity, and utility, why is there a need for yet another mechanical aptitude/comprehension test? Wiesen (1999) noted that the WTMA "was developed to achieve four goals: (a) to measure mechanical aptitude using questions based on common everyday objects and events rather than those encountered primarily in academic physics or chemistry courses, (b) to present modern test content, (c) to minimize gender and racial/ethnic bias in test content, and (d) to provide a tool for further academic research on mechanical aptitude" (p. 1).

The WTMA consists of 60 questions that measure three broad classes of object types (kitchen, nonkitchen household, and other everyday objects) of 20 questions each. Each question has three options (A, B, and C). The sample question on the WTMA is typical of most items on the test. It shows two pitchers of water (one labeled A, the other B) with different amounts of ice in them. The question asks, "Which pitcher of water will stay cold longer? (A) A, (B) B, or (C) There is no difference." In addition to the three broad classes of object types, there are eight mechanical/physical principles of seven to eight items each (basic machines, movement of objects, gravity, basic electricity/electronics, transfer of heat, basic physical properties, miscellaneous, and academic). The program IRTPro was used to analyze the items from the 20-item everyday-objects scale. Exercise 20.2 gives the URL for the software publisher, where you can download a student version of the software. For a review of IRTPro 2.1 published in the journal *Applied Psychological Measurement*, please consult Paek and Han (2012). Table 20.1 displays the output of a Rasch analysis using IRTPro; we have simplified the output to focus on the primary interest. The first part of the output displays the discrimination and difficulty parameter estimates for all 20 items on the scale; you can observe that each item has an *a* parameter but they are all the same value (.62). Also reported on this page are the standard errors for each item difficulty. These standard errors give an index of the amount of uncertainty for each parameter. Values that are relatively high indicate large uncertainty. Examining the difficulty column, we can see that Item 8 is the easiest item in that a person with a θ value of –4.26 (more than four standard deviations below the mean) still has a 50/50 chance of answering this item correctly. In CTT-IA terms, Item 8 has a *p* value of .96 (i.e., 96% of respondents answered the item correctly). On the other hand, Item 16 is the most difficult item. For this item, a θ value of 1.85 would be needed to have a 50/50 chance of correctly answering this question. Item 16 has a *p* value of only .30. In general, the higher the *p* value the lower the b_i value.

Table 20.1   IRTPro 1PL IRT Computer Program Outputs (Excerpts)

1PL Model Item Parameter Estimates for Group 1 (Back to TOC)

Item	Label	a	s.e.	b	s.e.
1	i04	0.62	0.03	–2.63	0.17
2	i05	0.62	0.03	–3.84	0.24
3	i06	0.62	0.03	0.32	0.11
4	i10	0.62	0.03	0.09	0.11
5	i11	0.62	0.03	–0.62	0.11
6	i13	0.62	0.03	–1.23	0.12
7	i14	0.62	0.03	–2.63	0.17
8	i15	0.62	0.03	–4.26	0.26
9	i17	0.62	0.03	–0.35	0.11
10	i24	0.62	0.03	–1.94	0.15
11	i29	0.62	0.03	1.41	0.13
12	i30	0.62	0.03	–2.42	0.16
13	i31	0.62	0.03	–1.36	0.13
14	i37	0.62	0.03	–0.25	0.11
15	i38	0.62	0.03	–3.66	0.23
16	i45	0.62	0.03	1.85	0.14
17	i48	0.62	0.03	–0.93	0.12
18	i54	0.62	0.03	0.82	0.12
19	i58	0.62	0.03	–3.78	0.23
20	i60	0.62	0.03	0.11	0.11

(Continued)

Table 20.1   *(Continued)*

Summed-Score-Based Item Diagnostic Tables and X^2s for Group 1 (Back to TOC)
S-X^2 Item Level Diagnostic Statistics

Item	Label	X2	d.f.	Probability
1	i04	32.07	13	0.0023
2	i05	29.81	11	0.0017
3	i06	16.53	13	0.2213
4	i10	37.89	13	0.0003
5	i11	20.74	13	0.0781
6	i13	13.31	12	0.3487
7	i14	20.91	13	0.0746
8	i15	10.15	12	0.6037
9	i17	38.06	13	0.0003
10	i24	12.60	12	0.4004
11	i29	116.53	13	0.0001
12	i30	46.83	13	0.0001
13	i31	23.18	13	0.0395
14	i37	34.41	13	0.0010
15	i38	39.84	12	0.0001
16	i45	18.66	12	0.0967
17	i48	33.26	13	0.0016
18	i54	13.01	13	0.4484
19	i58	19.78	11	0.0483
20	i60	32.00	13	0.0024

After the presentation of item parameter estimates and their associated standard errors, Table 20.1 also provides chi-square values for each item as an indicator of how well the Rasch model fits the data of each individual item. In this output, 12 of the 20 items exceed the critical value of chi-square ($p < .05$), indicating that the Rasch model may not fit the data. Given that the Rasch model is restrictive, this is not especially surprising. In addition, the chi-square value is highly dependent on sample size, which, in this case, is rather large ($N = 1000$). Hence, chi-square may not be an appropriate indicator of fit in this instance. We will test items against the 2-PL and 3-PL IRT models later on to see if items display a better fit.

Table 20.2 displays the abridged output for a two-parameter MML IRT analysis using IRTPro. Unlike the previous output, you can see in this output that both a and b parameter estimates vary across items, consistent with the 2PL model. Item 1 is the most discriminating ($a = 1.34$), whereas Item 11 is the least discriminating

($a = .02$). In fact, two items have extremely low discrimination parameters along with extreme difficulty parameters (Items 11 and 15). This may indicate the model is not appropriate for those items or that those items belong on a different scale. Finally, we can compare the fit statistics for the 2PL and compare the fit to the Rasch model. Given that the 2PL model is more flexible (e.g., discrimination parameters can vary), everything else being equal, we would expect it to fit the data better. And indeed it does fit better; now only four items have significant chi-square statistics.

Table 20.2   IRTPro 2PL IRT 3Computer Program Outputs (Excerpts)

1PL Model Item Parameter Estimates for Group 1   (Back to TOC)

Item	Label	a	s.e.	b	s.e.
1	i04	1.34	0.17	−1.48	0.14
2	i05	1.14	0.18	−2.36	0.27
3	i06	0.80	0.10	0.26	0.09
4	i10	0.84	0.11	0.07	0.09
5	i11	0.83	0.11	−0.49	0.10
6	i13	0.95	0.12	−0.88	0.11
7	i14	1.22	0.16	−1.57	0.15
8	i15	0.75	0.16	−3.63	0.69
9	i17	1.28	0.14	−0.21	0.06
10	i24	0.80	0.12	−1.57	0.20
11	i29	0.02	0.09	38.75	160.29
12	i30	0.17	0.10	−8.07	4.62
13	i31	0.87	0.11	−1.04	0.13
14	i37	0.12	0.08	−1.19	0.95
15	i38	0.06	0.13	−35.85	77.75
16	i45	0.63	0.10	1.82	0.28
17	i48	0.37	0.09	−1.48	0.37
18	i54	0.50	0.09	0.98	0.21
19	i58	1.18	0.18	−2.28	0.26
20	i60	0.22	0.08	0.29	0.30

Summed-Score Based Item Diagnostic Tables and X^2s for Group 1   (Back to TOC)

S-X^2 Item Level Diagnostic Statistics

Item	Label	X2	d.f.	Probability
1	i04	10.04	12	0.6132
2	i05	17.61	10	0.0617

(Continued)

Table 20.2   (*Continued*)

Item	Label	X2	d.f.	Probability
3	i06	15.58	13	0.2720
4	i10	40.18	13	0.0001
5	i11	17.64	12	0.1266
6	i13	8.44	12	0.7509
7	i14	15.89	12	0.1958
8	i15	8.60	12	0.7370
9	i17	17.05	11	0.1061
10	i24	13.19	12	0.3571
11	i29	39.47	14	0.0003
12	i30	18.28	14	0.1937
13	i31	22.96	12	0.0280
14	i37	8.22	13	0.8294
15	i38	17.06	12	0.1468
16	i45	21.11	12	0.0486
17	i48	23.39	14	0.0541
18	i54	11.13	13	0.6014
19	i58	4.97	11	0.9327
20	i60	16.62	13	0.2167

Table 20.3 displays the abridged output for a three-parameter MML IRT analysis using IRTPro.

Table 20.3   IRTPro 3PL IRT Computer Program Outputs (Excerpts)

3PL Model Item Parameter Estimates for Group 1 (Back to TOC)

Item	Label	a	s.e.	b	s.e.	g	s.e.
1	i04	1.43	0.29	−1.36	0.53	0.05	0.35
2	i05	1.17	0.40	−2.33	0.58	0.00	0.00
3	i06	2.06	0.82	0.95	0.15	0.29	0.05
4	i10	45.43	9.69	0.81	0.16	0.37	0.03
5	i11	1.36	0.47	0.34	0.35	0.29	0.13
6	i13	1.00	0.23	−0.85	0.16	0.00	0.00
7	i14	1.74	0.69	−0.78	0.43	0.37	0.18
8	i15	0.84	0.33	−3.29	0.90	0.00	0.00
9	i17	2.20	0.62	0.35	0.24	0.26	0.10
10	i24	1.00	1.75	−0.68	4.70	0.32	1.39
11	i29	54.83	9.34	1.75	0.29	0.28	0.02

Table 20.3   (*Continued*)

Item	Label	a	s.e.	b	s.e.	g	s.e.
12	i30	0.18	0.19	−7.90	8.33	0.00	0.00
13	i31	1.18	1.68	−0.25	2.98	0.29	1.02
14	i37	0.28	5.13	−0.59	16.27	0.00	1.38
15	i38	0.37	2.76	−5.84	48.98	0.01	4.52
16	i45	0.97	0.83	1.92	0.38	0.11	0.13
17	i48	4.91	1.90	1.29	0.28	0.58	0.03
18	i54	0.53	0.11	0.94	0.20	0.00	0.00
19	i58	1.41	2.07	−1.34	4.16	0.49	1.41
20	i60	2.22	4.14	2.04	0.78	0.45	0.05

Summed-Score Based Item Diagnostic Tables and X^2s for Group 1   (Back to TOC)

S-X^2 Item Level Diagnostic Statistics

Item	Label	X2	d.f.	Probability
1	i04	9.64	10	0.4743
2	i05	23.87	9	0.0045
3	i06	5.43	11	0.9089
4	i10	18.60	11	0.0685
5	i11	14.06	11	0.2293
6	i13	5.71	11	0.8925
7	i14	12.39	10	0.2591
8	i15	8.67	10	0.5648
9	i17	14.79	11	0.1919
10	i24	13.62	11	0.2538
11	i29	26.29	13	0.0155
12	i30	18.38	13	0.1432
13	i31	20.83	12	0.0528
14	i37	9.72	12	0.6414
15	i38	26.99	12	0.0077
16	i45	10.10	12	0.6079
17	i48	14.51	12	0.2685
18	i54	9.60	12	0.6519
19	i58	6.08	10	0.8090
20	i60	14.12	12	0.2923

By letting the *c* parameter vary (remember IRTPro refers to this as the *g* parameter), you can see that some items have estimated lower asymptotes that are 0, indicating that little or no guessing is present for those items. Other items have lower asymptotes that are much greater than zero, indicating that significant guessing is possible for those items. For example, Item 19 has a g parameter of .49, indicating that even people with extremely low ability can guess the correct answer right almost 50% of the time; perhaps for that item, the wrong answers are not particularly attractive. Another observation is that there are several parameter estimates that are quite extreme (e.g., Item 4's a parameter is 45.43) and that have large standard errors. These extreme values should be taken with caution. They can occur with complex models (remember the 3PL is more complex than the previously estimated models). These items with extreme values should be further studied to figure out why they are outliers. Finally, it should be noted that the 3PL model has only four items that have significant chi-square values, the same number of items as the 2PL model. There are other ways to test competing models, but the methodology is beyond the scope of this book. Please refer to the book-length treatments for more in-depth treatment of investigating model-fit.

Concluding Comments

CTT-IA can be useful, especially in small-sample (e.g., classroom) situations. Such procedures can greatly facilitate the construction of new tests and the evaluation and revision of existing tests in these limited situations. However, a major problem with CTT-IA is that the parameter estimates of difficulty and discrimination are sample dependent. In local situations, this may not be as big an issue because the test takers may not differ much in ability level from one administration to another. However, for tests and instruments that are developed with the intention of being used across a wide span of ability levels, use of CTT-IA may be at best incomplete and at worse misleading. In addition, the precision of IRT models allows researchers to ask specific questions that are hard to answer using CTT-IA. Thus, IRT models, whose parameter estimates are sample invariant, are more appropriate and informative when constructing, evaluating, administering, and scoring tests. In addition, IRT models allow for use of CAT techniques of test administration, thus allowing each "test" to be tailored to the individual's ability level, as well as estimation of item bias. Both of these issues will be discussed in the next module.

Best Practices

1. Consider estimating IRT item statistics when you have a roughly unidimensional test with a sample size of 250 or more.
2. Conduct an exploratory factor analysis to show that your test is roughly unidimensional before proceeding with the IRT estimation.
3. Estimate several IRT models to determine which one better fits your data. If your model misfits for many items, consider a less restrictive model.
4. Eliminate items that contribute low information in ranges of θ that you wish to discriminate.
5. Choose items that span the range of θ so that you have a test that discriminates across a wide spectrum.

6. If you have a small sample size, consider a more restrictive model. If you have a large sample size, choose a less restrictive model.

Practical Questions

1. What are the major advantages of IRT over CTT-IA?
2. How do you determine the difficulty, discrimination, and pseudo-guessing parameters in IRT? How are they different from CTT-IA?
3. When might it be preferable to use CTT-IA instead of IRT?
4. What are the advantages and disadvantages of the 1-PL, 2-PL, and 3-PL IRT models?
5. What advantages do IRFs (i.e., graphs) have over simply examining the item parameters in table form?
6. What does it mean to say that item and person parameters are invariant (i.e., locally independent) in IRT models, but not in CTT-IA?
7. What unique information do IRFs and IIFs provide for test development and revision?

Case Studies

CASE STUDY 20.1: ANALYSIS OF A HIGH SCHOOL ENGLISH PROFICIENCY EXAM USING IRT

Elena, a first-year educational measurement graduate student, vaguely remembered a discussion of IRT in her undergraduate tests and measurements class, but never thought that she might actually conduct such a study one day. The whole concept of IRT seemed so complex and appeared to require a level of mathematical sophistication that was well beyond her. In addition, the IRF graphs she remembered seemed like the apparent random lines that she recalled seeing on her father's oscilloscope when she was a child. How could she possibly understand all of it, let alone help a professor conduct such a study using IRT?

However, she had recently agreed to serve as a paid graduate research assistant for Professor Koshino in the college of education. Professor Koshino was contracted to help a large local school district evaluate the English competency exit exam it had recently developed and administered to seniors in the district's four high schools. The district graduated more than 2500 students each year from its four high schools combined. Not surprisingly, students varied widely in their English ability, both within and across schools. Given the large sample sizes and wide ability ranges, Professor Koshino decided that IRT would be a good way to examine items on the test to determine which items should be kept and which should be revised or discarded. However, Professor Koshino was no expert in IRT. He was hoping he could just turn over the analysis part of the project to Elena and some other graduate students in the educational measurement PhD program. However, Elena and the other graduate students were feeling rather uncomfortable trying to apply what little they had learned about IRT so far to this very real-life situation. It seemed time to sit down and have a frank discussion with Professor Koshino.

Questions to Ponder

1. What would be the advantages and disadvantages of using CTT-IA in this situation instead of IRT?
2. What would be the advantages and disadvantages of using the 1-PL IRT model? The 2-PL IRT model? The 3-PL IRT model?
3. Where should Elena start to "get up to speed" with the IRT procedures?
4. Should the four high schools be analyzed separately or together?
5. What should Elena and Professor Koshino be focusing on in their IRT computer printouts?
6. What advantages are there to examining the IRFs in this situation?

CASE STUDY 20.2: CREATION OF A CERTIFICATION EXAM FOR CORRECTIONS AGENTS

Dr. Agars was recently hired by the state of California as a senior research analyst in the Department of Corrections (DoC). His degree was in industrial and organizational psychology, with a minor in forensic psychology, while his undergraduate degree was in criminal justice. Thus, his boss knew that Dr. Agars had some expertise in psychological testing as well as the job duties of a parole agent. The DoC was recently mandated by the state legislature to develop a certification exam for parole agents. Corrections in the state of California is a $5.2 billion industry, by far the largest in the United States. A large part of the reason for the exorbitant cost is that 66% of the 125,000 annual parolees from the state's 33 prisons are reincarcerated before their 3-year parole is up. That's more than twice the national average. It's not all that surprising, however, because 75% of parolees have drug or alcohol problems, 50% are illiterate, and 80% have no job when they get out. Thus, the goal of the state legislature in passing the certification requirement was to hire additional parole agents (who typically have a load of between 80 and 100 ex-convicts at any one time) to work more closely with current felons to prepare them for their eventual release from prison. This, the legislature hopes, will dramatically reduce the number of reincarcerated felons, thus more than making up for the cost of new parole agents. However, there is no way of knowing if the current parole agents are qualified to perform these additional functions, hence, the new certification requirement.

The DoC has close to 1000 applicants for the parole agent job each year. Thus, the DoC typically offered the civil service exam for parole agents four times a year. However, with the certification prerequisite, there will be an additional requirement that individuals pass not only the civil service exam to be a parole agent, but also a new certification exam. In addition, current parole agents will need to take and pass the yet-to-be-implemented certification exam.

The State Personnel Board has hundreds of multiple-choice test items that it has given to tens of thousands of job applicants over the last 20 years (when it started its electronic scoring procedures) for the job of parole agent. The DoC would like to create a computerized version of the certification test that could be offered on an as-needed basis. Professor Agars knows a little about computer-based testing but is by no means an expert. However, given that the DoC was interested in continuous testing and there were lots of questions and data to get things started, it seemed to Dr. Agars that using IRT to create a computer adaptive test would be a logical choice. Use of IRT would allow the test to be tailored (or adapted) to each test taker. In addition, because each individual would, in a sense, have his or her own exam with a different mixture of questions, unlike the state civil service exam, problems with cheating and remembering items would be minimized. Thus, applicants who had already passed the state civil service exam for parole agent could come into a testing center at a designated time and take the certification exam. Finally, using IRT to create a CAT version of the certification exam would also allow individuals currently in the position to take the certification exam multiple times over a short time period until they passed. Thus, it seemed that using IRT to create a CAT version of the certification exam was a logical choice. When Dr. Agars presented the idea, his boss was not only excited about it but also wanted to know if he could do the same thing (i.e., use IRT to create a CAT version) for the civil service exam for parole agents. Suddenly, Dr. Agars was beginning to wonder what he had gotten himself into.

Questions to Ponder

1. Does it appear that IRT is a viable option for creating a written exam (CAT or paper-and-pencil) in this situation?
2. Given the changing nature of the job of parole agent, should Dr. Agars be using questions from prior civil service exams for the selection of new parole agents?
3. Are there any unique issues concerning the use of IRT for certification and/or licensing exams? If so, what are they?

4. Would the development and use of a test using IRT procedures be any different for the civil service exam (which typically rank orders job applicants) and the certification exam (which typically sets a pass point; those above are "certified," whereas those falling below the pass point are not "certified")?
5. Based on the information presented in the case study, does it appear that a new certification exam is the answer to the state's reincarceration problem? What unique information do you think it will provide?
6. What would be the advantage of using IRT methods over CTT-IA procedures to develop the certification test in this instance?
7. Should the applicants and current incumbents be treated any differently in this situation?

━◦━

Exercises

EXERCISE 20.1: 1-PL (RASCH), 2-PL, AND 3-PL COMPUTER RUNS

OBJECTIVE: To provide a brief introduction to common IRT programs by downloading a demo version and running 1-PL (Rasch), 2-PL, and 3-PL models for example data.

1. The website http://www.sscicentral.com provides information on several IRT programs, including BILOG-MG, MULTILOG, PARSCALE, and IRT-Pro. The website has a student version of IRTPro available for download.
2. Once IRTPro is downloaded and installed on your computer, start the program. You should get a screen that looks like Figure 20.3a. From the menu, select "Open," and from type of file choose "IRTPro Data file" as the type of file. Choose "Chapter 20 data.ssig." It is possible to open regular ASCII data files in the student version, but at this point, it is easier for you to open a file already prepared for you. After opening this file, you should see the data set open on your screen (see Figure 20.3b). This data set is composed of 10 items from the GMA test used in Module 16. Next click on the "Analysis" tab on the Command Menu at the top of the screen and then choose "Unidimensional Analysis." Next, choose the "Items" tab in the middle of the screen. At this point you should see the following (see Figure 20.3c).

Add all of the items from the list of variables in the column on the left to the "Items" column on the right (use the shift key to easily move them over at one time). Click on the "Models" tab, and you can see that the 2PL model will be run for all 10 items.

Click "Run," and the program will initiate the parameter estimation. If your computer is fast, it should take less than 1 second before the output is completed (see Figure 20.3d).

3. Examine the output file. There are lots of interesting bits of information there. You can see the a and b parameters for each item. Be aware that the column that has the c parameter should be ignored at this point. This program uses c to signify a different value than what we typically think of as the guessing parameter. That value, when you estimate the 3-PL model, will be signified with the letter g for IRTPro. Notice which items are most discriminating (large values of a) and which items are relatively easy and relatively difficult. From this output file, if you click on the "Analysis" tab this time, you will see a "Graphics" command. Click on that, and you will see the IRFs for each item. (See Figure 20.3e).

4. Now that you have estimated the 2-PL model for these 10 items, you can rerun the program using the 3-PL model and the 1-PL Rasch model. To rerun the 3-PL model, go back to the models section and where you see 2-PL for each item, right-click and you will be given the option to change to the 3-PL model. Rerun the analysis and see how the parameter estimates change (noting that the g parameter in the output is what we normally refer to as the c parameter in the text). If you want to run the Rasch model, make sure that the model chosen is the 2-PL model and click the button "Constraints." From there, highlight all of the values in the a parameter column (i.e., selecting the a parameters for all 10 items).

Figure 20.3a   Initial IRTPro Computer Program Window

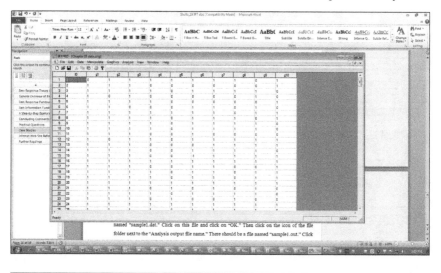

Figure 20.3b   IRTPro Data File for Chapter 20 data.ssig File

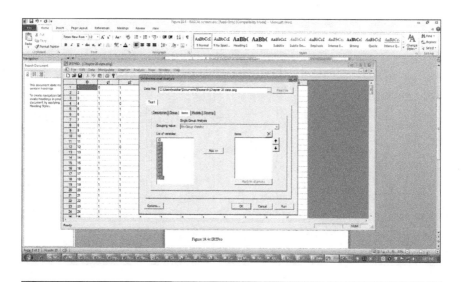

Figure 20.3c   IRTPro Computer Program Window for Running the Analyses

Right-click over these highlighted *a* parameters, and you will be given an option to "Set Parameters Equal." Click on that option, and then you will be running the Rasch model. You can verify that you have run the Rasch model because in the output all of the *a* parameter estimates should be equal across items.

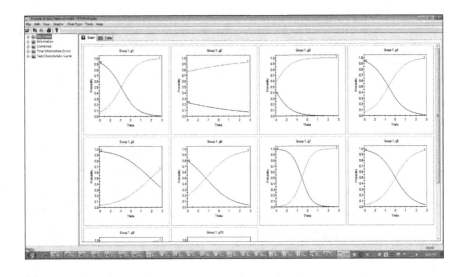

Figure 20.3d   IRTPro Output for 2PL Model

Figure 20.3e   IRTPro Graphic Output for 2PL Model

Questions

1. What are the basic descriptive statistics for the data? (*N*, average number correct, number of items, etc.)
2. Which items were most and least discriminating, and how did that change across models?

3. If you had to choose just three items for a test that provided the most information at low ability, which would you choose? What about for high ability?

4. Which of the three models seems to best fit the data? What did you base your answer on?

EXERCISE 20.2: IRT LITERATURE SEARCH

OBJECTIVE: To become familiar with applications of IRT in the literature.

Either individually or in small groups, perform a literature search to find a recent empirical article that provides an example of the application of IRT to an applied testing situation. IRT literature can be very complex, so make sure to choose an article where the primary focus is a substantive issue. Then write a brief summary and/or make a short presentation to the class summarizing the application of IRT with a focus on critiquing the use of IRT for that particular application. Focus on why the authors chose to use IRT and how IRT helped answer substantive research questions.

Further Readings

de Ayala, R.J. (2009). *The theory and practice of item response theory*. New York: Guilford Press.

DeMars, C. (2010). *Item response theory*. New York: Oxford University Press.

Ellis, B.B., & Mead, A.D. (2002). Item analysis: Theory and practice using classical and modern test theory. In S.G. Rogelberg (Ed.), *Handbook of research methods in industrial and organizational psychology* (pp. 324–343). Malden, MA: Blackwell.

Embretson, S.E., & Reise, S.P. (2000). *Item response theory for psychologists*. Hillsdale, NJ: Erlbaum.

Hambleton, R.K., Swaminathan, H., & Rogers, H.J. (1991). *Fundamentals of item response theory*. Newbury Park, CA: Sage.

Paek, I., & Han, K. T. (2012). IRTPro 2.1 for Windows. *Applied Psychological Measurement, 20*, 1–11.

Zickar, M.J. (2002). Modeling data with polytomous item response theory. In F. Drasgow & N. Schmitt (Eds.), *Measuring and analyzing behavior in organizations: Advances in measurement and data analysis* (pp. 123–156). San Francisco, CA: Jossey-Bass.

Zickar, M.J., & Broadfoot, A.A. (2008). The partial revival of a dead horse? Comparing classical test theory and item response theory. In C.E. Lance & R.J. Vandenberg (Eds.), *Statistical and methodological myths and urban legends* (pp. 37–59). New York: Routledge.

Module 21

Applications of Item Response Theory

Computer Adaptive Testing and Differential Item Functioning

Two major applications of item response theory (IRT) noted in Module 20 were the development of computer adaptive testing (CAT) and the examination of differential item functioning (DIF). There are numerous other less well-known applications of IRT beyond these, such as appropriateness measurement and test equating, which unfortunately we do not have the space to expand on here. However, given the technical—and, to many, mysterious—nature of IRT, we believe that it is important to discuss at least a few of the more prominent applications of this technique. In doing so, we hope to demonstrate IRT's practical relevance and entice you to learn more about IRT and its application to a variety of measurement issues. As with IRT itself, however, both of these topics are rather involved. Therefore, we provide only a brief overview of these topics and refer you to Camilli and Shepard (1994), de Ayala (2009), Embretson and Reise (2000), Raju and Ellis (2002), and Wainer, Dorans, Flaugher, Green, and Mislevy (2000) for more detailed discussions on the nuts and bolts of implementing such procedures in practice.

Computer Adaptive Testing

Throughout the history of testing, the vast majority of tests, whether measuring cognitive ability or achievement or aptitude or attitude, were administered in the traditional paper-and-pencil format. Increasingly, however, we are seeing tests being administered via computer, many via the Internet. When a paper-and-pencil test is simply transferred from paper to a computer, it is commonly referred to as **computer-based testing (CBT)**. Such tests may provide many practical advantages, including immediate scoring with no need for a separate answer sheet, use of multimedia questions, easy test delivery via the Internet, and easier creation of test score databases. However, there is no real psychometric advantage to simply transferring a paper-and-pencil test to a CBT. In fact, research has demonstrated that in most cases, there is nearly perfect concordance between tests administered on paper-and-pencil compared to the identical test administered via computer. Conversely, when IRT, as discussed in Module 20, is used to develop, administer, and score computerized tests, then there are distinct psychometric, as well as practical, advantages.

In particular, CAT, as compared to traditional paper-and-pencil tests, can be both more effective and more efficient. By effective, we mean that CAT is generally more accurate in estimating individuals' ability levels. Another way of thinking about it is that CAT tends to have less measurement error than traditional paper-and-pencil tests because the tests are specifically tailored to an individual's estimated ability level. In addition, traditional tests based on classical test theory (CTT) assume that measurement error is uniform across the ability score distribution. As discussed in Module 20, IRT makes no such assumption. Instead, measurement error is estimated for all levels of ability. This property allows test takers lots of flexibility in administering tests adaptively. For example, test developers can program an adaptive test to continue administering items to an individual until the standard error of measurement reaches an acceptable level. Whereas, for fixed-administration tests, you may be stuck with unacceptable levels of standard errors for many test takers.

CAT is also more efficient because it can be tailored to the individual's ability level; thus, test takers do not have to answer as many questions as in a traditional paper-and-pencil test to obtain comparable, or better, estimates of ability. That is, the questions become easier or harder as test takers correctly, or incorrectly, answer each question. As a result, most computer adaptive tests tend to be about half as long (i.e., 50% shorter) than their paper-and-pencil counterparts and yet have equal or better measurement properties. In addition, because individuals with low ability are not wasting their time answering extremely difficult questions, and, conversely, individuals with high ability levels are not wasting their time answering questions that are extremely easy for them, CAT is more efficient. This efficiency is gained by the fact that each item in CAT provides more useful information than a typical paper-and-pencil test, thus allowing the test user to more efficiently distinguish test takers at various levels of ability (Wainer et al., 2000). If you are reading this textbook, asking you to answer the item "24 x 4 = ?" would be pointless. It will provide no psychometric information for people whose mathematical ability is above the grade-school level. That item, however, might be extremely informative in differentiating between high- and low-ability sixth graders.

In addition to the practical advantages noted previously for CBTs (e.g., use of multimedia, no need for separate answer sheets, easier creation and maintenance of test score databases), CAT also has the practical advantage of increased test security. With a large item pool (along with standard practices that go beyond this book), it can be extremely unlikely that two test takers will receive more than a trivial number of identical items. This decrease in item exposure gives tests a much longer shelf life. For example, back in the authors' day, the Graduate Record Examination (GRE) was administered only a few times a year in paper-and-pencil format. As a result, in order for the first author to meet certain graduate admissions application deadlines, he ended up having to go to Canada to take his GREs. Now that the GRE is administered continuously via CAT, it is simply a matter of making an appointment and, of course, paying your fee. Another advantage is that test takers typically receive their scores (although, in many cases, they are treated as unofficial until they are later certified) in minutes. Again, in the authors' day, it was an anxious few months before GRE results were received. Assuming the test taker is comfortable using a computer, CAT is likely to be a less stressful testing environment than the traditional experience of mass testing in a crowded school gymnasium. Thus, overall, there are many practical and psychometric advantages to CAT over traditional paper-and-pencil tests.

As you might guess, however, CAT poses some potential challenges, as well. For example, in most cases, CAT requires many questions to be available at all ability ranges; having a large number of good items is necessary to make sure that there is a pool of discriminating items for a wide range of test takers as well as making it possible to keep item exposure for any individual item low. As noted in Module 12, it can be very difficult and time consuming to create a single good item, let alone a cadre of good items for each level of ability. In addition, CAT is based on IRT, which is a model-based theory. If your data do not meet the assumptions of the model or simply do not fit your proposed model very well, then the results obtained from CAT will likely not possess all of the advantages noted previously. As a result of these practical and technical constraints, CAT has until recently been limited to large-scale testing operations, such as the Educational Testing Service (ETS) and the U.S. military. Although there are now commercially available software programs that can allow organizations to administer CAT, there still remains a need for **psychometricians** to monitor the performance of CAT over time. In addition, many testing organizations add new items to existing computer adaptive tests and retire items as their exposure rates get too high. This continual development makes CAT a powerful technique but also makes it necessary that it be run by someone with strong psychometric skills. Consequently, in our experience, researchers with strong IRT skills have had excellent job security!

So how does CAT actually work? With CAT, the test is adapted to an individual's level of ability as she progresses through the test. For example, a test taker is typically first given an item of moderate difficulty (i.e., $\theta = .0$ or between, say, $-.50$ and $+.50$). If the person is known to be substantially above or below average on the trait being measured, however, an appropriately harder or easier item can be used to begin the testing session. Assuming, though, that we start with a moderately difficult item and the individual answers the first item correctly, her θ level is assessed (presumably as being above the mean) and she is given a more difficult item (i.e., $\theta > .0$); whereas if she answers the first item wrong, she is given an easier item (i.e., $\theta < .0$). This adaptive form of question administration is continued until a certain predetermined level of confidence (i.e., standard error of measurement) in the estimate of the individual's level of ability (θ) is obtained.

As you might surmise, early estimates of a test taker's θ based on a small number of responses will have much higher measurement error than estimates of a test taker's θ after he or she has taken a large number of items. In addition, individuals who respond in an unsystematic fashion will also have a lot of measurement error associated with their θ value. As a result, some individuals may need only a few items to accurately estimate their ability level, whereas others, who may be responding less systematically, may require many more items. In some instances, the computer is preprogrammed to administer a minimum and/or maximum number of items. As a result, there may be some instances where an individual's ability level (θ) is unable to be estimated with enough precision within the maximal number of allowable questions or time limit.

Several prominent examples of the use of CAT include the GRE general exam, which you may well have taken yourself in CAT form; the Armed Services Vocational Aptitude Battery, used to select and place armed services recruits; and the National Council Licensure Examination for Registered Nurses (NCLEX-RN). In all three examples, IRT is used to develop and administer CAT versions of the respective tests. That is, the test developers have written and calibrated a wide range of items with varying levels of difficulty (b_i). In addition, item discrimination (a_i) for most items will be high at designated levels of ability. There is an important difference in these three tests, however. For the former two, the goal is to estimate as precisely as possible a test taker's level of ability (θ). For the NCLEX-RN (or any professional licensing exam, for that matter), the goal is not a precise estimate of θ, but rather to estimate if θ is above or below a given critical passing score. Thus, licensing exams administered via CAT may require fewer items because of the goals of the measurement process (i.e., pass/fail); however, when the test taker's θ level is very close to the cutoff point, a CAT may actually require more questions to confidently establish a pass/fail grade than would be required if we were simply estimating θ. Thus, with traditional tests, we typically desire a wide range of items with varying difficulty levels, whereas with licensing examinations we need many more items that are near the cutoff score.

Nearly all large-scale testing companies now use CAT techniques, though the use of CAT for lower volume tests still remains somewhat low. The benefits of CAT are enormous, but the expenses of maintaining computer adaptive tests make them less popular for tests that do not have thousands of test takers per year.

Differential Item Functioning

As noted throughout this book, starting in Module 1, psychological and educational testing is not just a psychometric process but can also be influenced by politics and personal values. As a result, individuals who do not receive valued outcomes as a result of testing may well claim that it was due to the test itself being biased. In Module 11, we discussed the issue of test bias and how best to estimate it. What happens, however, once a test is found to display some evidence of test bias? Do we discard the entire test? Hopefully not. As you have seen throughout this book, the test development and validation process is a long and arduous one. Therefore, we do not want to simply discard an entire test that may have been years in the making, especially one with well-established and promising psychometric properties. Conversely, even though we may have a large investment into the development of a particular test, we certainly do not want to be administering tests that display clear evidence of test bias. So what is the alternative?

It may well be that only a few items on the test are the major contributors to the observed test bias. Therefore, we would want to establish whether individual items are biased and modify or discard those particular items and replace them with items that display less (hopefully no) bias. So how does one go about identifying biased items? Detection of item bias is a holistic process that involves both qualitative and quantitative evidence. In this module, we are going to focus on a particular form of quantitative or empirical evidence for item bias known as **differential item functioning (DIF)**. (In Exercise 21.3, you will perform a qualitative item bias review.) An item displays DIF when individuals from different groups with the same ability level (θ) have different probabilities of correctly answering an item. Although we can look at more than two groups, we will focus here on comparing only two groups at one time, typically referred to as the focal and referent groups. For example, if you wanted to see if certain cognitive ability items were biased against women, women would be identified as the focal group and men would be identified as the referent group. Thus, groups can be based on a variety of characteristics; however, demographic groups based on gender, race, and ethnicity are typically used because individuals in these groups are protected under major civil rights laws.

Before we discuss the IRT approach to item bias, it should be noted that other non-IRT methods are common and have a long history. For example, the Mantel-Haenszel (M-H, chi-square) technique has been used extensively to assess item bias. The key information for this analysis is a 2 (focal vs. referent group) by i (where i is the number of items on the test) table set up for each item. Item endorsement rates are compared across the two groups for individuals who receive the same score on the remaining test items. For example, on a 20-item test, we will compare item endorsement rates for men who received 10 items correct on the rest of the exam with women who also received 10 items correct. If men who received 10 items correct on the rest of the exam had a 58% probability of answering the particular item correct, whereas women with 10 items correct received only a 42% probability of answering that item correct, then that would be convincing evidence that the item is biased against women. These endorsement rates are computed across all possible test scores, and the resulting table is tested for statistical significance using the M-H statistic, which is based on the chi-square statistic. A significant M-H statistic would be an indication that a particular item evidences bias. One challenge with the M-H technique is that we will have too few (and sometimes no one) from a particular group at a given score level. Therefore, in practice, score groups (e.g., deciles or quartiles) may be established instead of individual raw scores in order to obtain adequate sample sizes. Note that the M-H approach is a non-IRT technique; it is based on test and item scores and does not rely on any latent traits.

Another prominent non-IRT technique for estimating item bias is the use of logistic regression (LR). With LR, one predicts the item outcome (i.e., pass/fail) using three predictors: (1) the total test score, (2) the variable that designates group membership, and (3) the interaction term between total test score and group membership. If the regression weight for group membership is significant, but the interaction is not, this is referred to as uniform DIF (Raju & Ellis, 2002). Uniform DIF occurs when the item differs in difficulty level across the focal and referent groups but is not different in terms of discrimination. Alternatively, if the regression weight for the interaction between group membership and total test score is significant (regardless of whether the group membership weight is significant by itself), then this is an indication of nonuniform DIF. As you might guess, nonuniform DIF means that the item displays both differences in difficulty and discrimination for individuals in different groups with the same ability levels. This procedure is analogous to, though not the same as, the use of moderated multiple regression to establish test bias in the form of slope and intercept bias (i.e., uniform DIF being similar to intercept bias and nonuniform DIF being similar to slope bias). With item-level data, however, we are evaluating **measurement bias** (i.e., if the item represents the underlying construct equally well for different groups). Conversely, with test bias, we are establishing **predictive bias** (i.e., if the test differentially predicts some criterion of interest). Thus, although item and test bias are similar, they represent the evaluation of fundamentally different forms of bias.

Several IRT-based methods for detecting DIF are discussed by Raju and Ellis (2002). These include a visual inspection of differences in item response functions (IRFs; such as those displayed in Figure 20.1) for the focal and referent groups on a given item. Similar to the LR procedure discussed previously, both uniform and nonuniform DIF can be found. Uniform DIF would be present when the b_i (difficulty) parameters differ for the two groups, whereas differences in the a_i (discrimination) parameters would indicate nonuniform DIF. This can be seen when the two IRF curves cross one another. A statistical test of the significance of the difference in these parameters is available using Lord's chi-square statistic. Thus, inspection of the IRFs provides visual evidence of the DIF, and Lord's chi-square provides statistical evidence; however, neither procedure provides an actual index of the amount of DIF present. With large sample sizes, even trivial differences between IRFs can be found to be significant. Conversely, with small samples, large differences in IRFs might fail to reach significance. Raju and Ellis (2002) discussed several statistics that actually map the differences in area between the two IRFs and thus serve as an index of the level of DIFs. Recent advances have come up with additional statistics to help researchers not only determine the statistical significance of DIF but also quantify the effect sizes of DIF, helping test takers make more informed decisions about retaining or removing individual items.

The process of computing DIF statistics under an IRT framework can be quite complicated, though. Before item parameters from different groups can be compared, however, the two groups must first be linked. That is, the scores from different groups must be equated so that the item parameters represent meaningful differences and not just artifacts associated with the two distributions. The two groups may differ in terms of ability, and so those differences need to be accounted for when comparing parameters across the two groups. An in-depth discussion of linking item parameters is beyond the scope of this overview. Briefly, however, a subset of items from your scale is used as the linking items to equate the tests. The problem with this is deciding which items to use. Ideally, you will want to use items that do not display DIF. To determine DIF, however, you must first do the linking procedure. As a result, most IRT users run an iterative process where DIF items are identified, then removed, and the linking study is run again until no DIF items are identified. The remaining items are then used for linking purposes. Alternatively, newer IRT programs (e.g., BILOG-MG and MULTILOG) use a likelihood ratio procedure that allows for multigroup IRT modeling, thus ameliorating the need for the linking step (Embretson & Reise, 2000). In summary, regardless of which DIF procedure is used, our key goal is to identify, and remove if necessary, items that have different levels of difficulty and/or discrimination across groups that have the same ability level.

IRT-based DIF approaches, although complicated, can help improve the quality of testing in many ways by helping pinpoint the sources of item bias. Although CTT-based methods can give a rough indication of which items work poorly for a particular group, IRT-based methods can provide a much better understanding of the nature of the differences. One challenge with using IRT-based methods to detect DIF, though, is the increased sample size requirements compared to CTT methods. This can be a challenge for many types of item bias analyses where the focal group is a minority group, which in particular samples may have small sample sizes. In those cases, initial analyses may be conducted via CTT-based methods, and later IRT analyses can be conducted after more data have been collected.

Concluding Comments

In the previous module, we presented some of the fundamental IRT concepts and demonstrated how they could be used to evaluate the quality of items. In this module, we focused on two IRT-based applications, which can help better explain the importance and power of this testing framework. IRT procedures still remain a mystery to many classically trained psychologists. However, the use of IRT is becoming more prominent as specialty software becomes more user-friendly and less technical references are available to explain its basic principles. In addition, as new graduates who have wider exposure to IRT enter the field, its use should continue to increase. As a result, application of IRT models is clearly becoming more widespread, yet by no means mainstream. Therefore, our goal in writing this module was not so much to provide technical details on the applications of IRT, but rather to pique your interest in the possible applications of IRT and to provide a few examples of how IRT can be applied.

Best Practices

1. CAT procedures work best when large numbers of unidimensional items can be written and it is possible to collect large amounts of data to calibrate the item response parameter estimates. Consequently, CATs are feasible if a psychometrican can monitor the test closely on an on-going basis.
2. CATs are effective in that they provide superior measurement while being more efficient. In addition, they increase test security by providing different tests for each respondent. IRT-based DIF methods are effective because they can pinpoint the source and types of item bias. For smaller sample sizes, however, it may be necessary to use non-IRT based methods such as the M-H technique.

Practical Questions

1. What are the major advantages of CAT administration over traditional paper-and-pencil test administration?
2. Could CAT be used in small-scale applications? If so, explain how.
3. What is the difference between a test that is simply administered on a computer (sometimes called CBT) and a computer adaptive test?
4. How do DIF procedures extend CTT-IA analyses?
5. What are the advantages and disadvantages of using non-IRT DIF versus IRT-based DIF?
6. Why do we need to equate item parameters before running a DIF analysis?
7. How do item bias and test bias procedures differ? How are they similar?

Case Studies

CASE STUDY 21.1: EXPLAINING CAT TO A LAY AUDIENCE

Scott, a second-year graduate student in educational measurement, had just gotten off the phone with his sister Gail, who had recently finished her nursing degree. Gail and her friend, Tammy, had taken the CAT version of the NCLEX-RN a few weeks earlier. Gail and Tammy had just received their results. Gail had passed, and Tammy had failed. Passing this licensing exam is required of all nursing students who hope to practice as registered nurses in a given state within the United States. While Gail was glad that she had passed, she was disappointed for her friend Tammy. Gail didn't really understand how the CAT worked, and, reflecting back on their conversation, Scott felt he had had a difficult time trying to explain it to her.

"It doesn't seem fair that Tammy and I actually took different tests. Don't the tests have to contain the same items to be able to compare them?" asked Gail.

"Well, it doesn't have to," Scott began as he tried to explain. "The test is called 'adaptive' because it adapts to your ability level."

"How does a computer know what my ability level is if I haven't taken the test yet?" asked Gail, somewhat perplexed.

"Well, the computer starts with a moderately difficult item and then, depending on whether you answer that one correctly or not, it gives you an easier item if you get it wrong, or a harder item if you get it correct," Scott explained. "Then the computer uses that information to compute an estimate of your ability in nursing," Scott added.

"But how could it do that with just a few questions?" Gail wondered out loud.

"Well, the estimate of your ability isn't very good at first. That's why the computer has to give you more than just a couple of questions," Scott tried to explain. "In fact, I just looked up information on the NCLEX-RN on the Internet, and it says that they have to administer a minimum of 75 questions."

"I kind of understand, but I still don't know why Tammy had to answer so many more questions than I did and she still failed. In fact, she was there for 5 hours, and it only took me about half that time to complete the test," said Gail, somewhat frustrated.

"Well, you must have been more consistent in your responding than Tammy. In addition, for a licensing exam, the key is to score above the cutoff score, so as soon as the computer is relatively confident that you are above the cutoff score, it will stop administering questions. So, my guess is that the computer was able to say with confidence that you were above the cutoff, but it took much longer for Tammy. In fact, the information I found on the NCLEX-RN says the maximum time limit is 5 hours, so Tammy simply ran out of time and never reached the maximum number of 265 questions," Scott explained.

"Ah, I think I'm starting to understand," said Gail with a wry smile on her face. "But, I still don't understand why Tammy and I couldn't just answer the same questions."

Somewhat discouraged, Scott said, "Okay, let me try to explain it to you another way. . . ."

Questions to Ponder

1. If you were Scott, how would you go about explaining what CAT was to Gail?

2. What are some of the major differences between CAT and a paper-and-pencil test that might highlight the advantages of CAT over paper-and-pencil testing for Gail?
3. Are there other reasons that Tammy might have had to answer more questions than Gail? Is there a better way to explain this than what Scott said?
4. What other stopping procedures might CAT use to decide when to end the testing session besides a maximum number of items or a time limit? Will it be different for licensing exams versus other more traditional testing situations?
5. Are there other examples of the use of CAT that you can think of that might help Gail better understand what CAT is?

CASE STUDY 21.2: DIF

The ETS identified DIF on an analogy question from the SAT exam. The question was an analogy that asked: "Strawberry: red as (a) peach:ripe, (b) leather:brown, (c) grass:green, (d) orange:round, or (e) lemon:yellow." The test question demonstrated DIF against Hispanic test takers in that they were more familiar with lemons that are green, not yellow. As a result, they were more likely to select option (c) instead of the correct answer, option (e). The procedure that ETS used to determine DIF was a statistic developed by psychometricians at ETS called the Delta statistic, which compares how difficult different groups found the item. In addition to the DIF analysis, ETS also gathered a panel of experts who were the ones who identified that Hispanic examinees would be more likely to associate lemons with being green and not yellow. Thus, this item was ultimately discarded because the question was intended to assess one's knowledge of analogies, but for at least one group, Hispanics, it was more an assessment of one's knowledge of different fruit colors.

Questions to Ponder

1. What additional information might the use of IRT procedures for DIF analysis provide that is not available with use of the Delta statistic?
2. Psychometricians at ETS no doubt know a lot about IRT procedures. In fact, ETS psychometricians were among the earlier pioneers in IRT research and development. Why, then, do you think they opted not to use IRT procedures to assess DIF in this instance?
3. As noted in the module overview, in order to perform IRT DIF procedures, item parameters need to be linked or equated across groups. Do you think such equating would also be required if other statistics, such as ETS's Delta procedure, are used to establish DIF?

4. If you plotted the IRFs for the different ethnic groups noted in this example, what do you think you are likely to see?
5. Could this item be revised instead of simply being discarded? If so,
   how?

⤳ ⟷ ⤴

Exercises

EXERCISE 21.1: CAT ONLINE REVIEW

OBJECTIVE: To become familiar with IRT and CAT through an investigative of
current adaptive tests.

BACKGROUND: In the module overview, we discussed the key elements of IRT
and how it can be applied to CAT and DIF. We mentioned that many large-scale
tests are now administered in an adaptive format. Many of these tests have detailed
descriptions geared to test takers about the nature of the adaptive test process.

1. Find two different adaptive tests and compare and contrast how these two
   tests explain the adaptive testing procedure to test takers.
2. If you were publishing your own adaptive test, how would you communicate the test-taking experience to test takers?

EXERCISE 21.2: ITEM BIAS/FAIRNESS REVIEW

OBJECTIVE: To provide an opportunity to use item bias/fairness review to critically evaluate test items for possible bias.

The web page http://pareonline.net/getvn.asp?v=4&n=6 by Ronald Hambleton
and H. Jane Rogers is titled "Item Bias Review." The page provides a number of
questions that test creators can ask themselves in order to reduce bias in test items.
After reviewing the brief write-up at the website, use the "Sample questions addressing fairness" and the "Sample bias questions" to review the 13 organizational
behavior items found in Table 13.4 for possible item bias with regard to both
gender (men vs. women) and race/ethnic group (Caucasian vs. African American
and Caucasian vs. Hispanic).

1. Did you find any questions that appear to demonstrate bias based on sex? If
   so, which items and on what basis do they appear to show bias?
2. Did you find any questions that appear to demonstrate bias based on race
   (Caucasian vs. African American)? If so, which items and on what basis do
   they appear to show bias?

3. Did you find any questions that appear to demonstrate bias based on ethnic group status (Caucasian vs. Hispanic)? If so, which items and on what basis do they appear to show bias?

EXERCISE 21.3: A CAT/DIF LITERATURE SEARCH

OBJECTIVE: To become familiar with the CAT and DIF literature.

Either individually or in small groups, perform a literature search to find a recent empirical article that provides an example of the application of IRT to an applied testing situation that specifically addresses CAT or DIF. Then write a brief summary and/or make a short presentation to the class summarizing the application of IRT with a focus on critiquing the use of IRT for that particular application of CAT or DIF.

Further Readings

Camilli, G., & Shepard, L.A. (1994). *Methods for identifying biased test items.* Thousand Oaks, CA: Sage.

de Ayala, R.J. (2009). *The theory and practice of item response theory.* New York: Guilford Press.

Embretson, S.E., & Reise, S.P. (2000). *Item response theory for psychologists.* Hillsdale, NJ: Erlbaum.

Raju, N.S., & Ellis, B.B. (2002). Differential item and test functioning. In F. Drasgow & N. Schmitt (Eds.), *Measuring and analyzing behavior in organizations: Advances in measurement and data analysis* (pp. 156–188). San Francisco, CA: Jossey-Bass.

Wainer, H., Dorans, N.J., Flaugher, R., Green, B.F., & Mislevy, R.J. (2000). *Computerized adaptive testing: A primer.* New York: Routledge.

Module 22

Generalizability Theory

S uppose that you realize that your test has many different potential sources of error: rater error, item sampling error, and temporal instability. How do you figure out which sources of error are significant concerns and which might be trivially small? We have visited several different test theories throughout this book, some of which can help answer this question, though not directly. The most prevalent one has been classical test theory (CTT), which has provided a foundation for many of the scale development techniques that we have considered. With CTT, you could conduct separate studies to investigate test-retest, internal consistency, and inter-rater reliabilities, though it would be difficult to incorporate all of these different reliabilities into one meaningful statistic. In the last few modules, we have considered item response theory (IRT), which has led to more detailed insights about test behavior, though again that framework seems perhaps even less equipped to untangle different sources of error. In this final module, we consider one final test theory paradigm, **generalizability theory** (GT), and demonstrate some of the powerful insights that can come from using this paradigm. And yes, GT will be able to untangle all of our different sources of error.

In many ways, GT is an expansion of CTT. With CTT, one of the limitations is that the error term in the special formula $X = T + E$ can include variance that you might otherwise care about, and/or the true score term may include irrelevant variance, depending on how you have operationalized reliability in your particular study. For example, if you have operationalized error through coefficient alpha, then, unfortunately, any kind of error due to temporal instability will be included in the true score. So if you take an important test and you have a splitting migraine throughout the test, the diminished score that you had due to the migraine would be treated as true score, given that there was no opportunity to consider another testing time. The source of error considered under coefficient alpha is consistency across a set of items; given that you had the splitting migraine across the set of items, it would be impossible to incorporate this headache into your error term.

GT expands CTT by utilizing the logic of experimental design to be able to better pinpoint and understand the sources of error in particular test scores. In many ways, GT uses the logic of analysis of variance (ANOVA) to improve on the simplified notion of error that has been used in CTT. Unfortunately, GT has been more influential in the theoretical development of test theory compared to the actual practice of test evaluation and development. This is because GT requires more thought and effort on data collection; hence, the data needs are often greater than for CTT studies. In CTT evaluations of reliability, one source of error is studied at a time. Therefore, test-retest reliability focuses on time-related error, ignoring other sources of error such as domain sampling error and rater error. Internal consistency focuses on domain sampling error (i.e., error due to imperfectly sampling the construct domain) but ignores any time-related error or error due to rater inconsistency. The isolation of a single source of error is convenient and simplifies data collection, but this simplified design prevents a deeper understanding of the magnitude of various aspects of error.

In addition, GT studies simultaneously model different aspects of error by using the logic of experimental design. GT studies will often incorporate a series of different manipulations, thereby collecting data for the same construct across items, across raters (if appropriate), across different lengths of time, and perhaps across different modes of administration. The name came about because the goal of a GT study is to see how *generalizable* a particular measure is across a variety of different settings. To the extent that a GT study can incorporate a large variety of sources of error, it becomes possible to make judgments such as 40% of the error in a particular measure is related to time-related error, 20% is related to inconsistency across items, 20% is related to rater error, and 20% is related to the interaction between rater and item content. This type of breakdown of the error term is impossible to do with a traditional CTT analysis. In addition, the advanced methodology of IRT is useful for understanding how items work but still is unable to decompose different sources of error in a particular measure.

As a result, GT has unique contributions to make to test development and evaluation. The results of a good GT study can, for example, be used to pinpoint what aspects of a test need to be refined and what potential sources of error can be treated as relatively unimportant. Unfortunately, GT is complex and requires sophisticated data collections; hence, it has been relatively neglected compared to IRT and CTT methods. In this final module, we will point out some key concepts about GT that we hope will inspire you to learn more about this technique.

The GT Framework

The key to GT studies is that multiple sources of error as well as possible multiple sources of construct variance are manipulated within a particular study. In CTT, the focus is on the *reliability* of a particular test score, the ratio of true score variance over total variance. In GT, the focus is on understanding the *generalizability* of a particular test score, or as Shavelson, Webb, and Rowley (1989) state, "how accurately observed scores permit us to generalize about persons' behavior in a defined universe of situations" (p. 922). In GT, there are a variety of coefficients and statistics that can be computed that help researchers make better decisions about how their tests and measures can be applied when making decisions. In addition, GT can provide excellent insights into how to improve your particular measurements.

Before getting into the mathematics of GT, it makes sense to begin with a concrete research example to illustrate some of its general aims and goals. Highhouse, Broadfoot, Yugo, and Devendorf (2009) used GT to understand how financial and human resource management (HRM) experts made judgments about the corporate reputations of large American companies. These corporate reputations are often collected in rankings such as the Harris Interactive poll that compute a *reputation quotient* that is based on a variety of public perceptions. Given that little is known about the nature of the construct of corporate reputations, Highhouse et al. conducted a GT study to determine the stability of reputations over time, companies, expert groups, and type of question. They conducted a study where they examined the variance of rankings across items (i.e., how much consistency there was across the set of three items that they used to measure reputation), time (i.e., how much stability there was across two data points collected 2 weeks apart), targets (i.e., how much variance there was across nine different companies that were being evaluated), types of expert groups (i.e., whether there were differences across marketing professors, finance professors, and HRM professors), and, finally, individuals within a profession (i.e., how much variance there was among professors within a particular specialization). This data collection was complex because there were multiple types of respondents reporting corporate reputation across three items for nine different companies across two time periods! Actually there were three time periods, but the number of respondents decreased significantly for the third time period, and so many of the analyses were computed across the two time periods.

The analysis and reporting of GT results can be complex, especially when many factors are measured. One of the key statistics in any GT analysis is the *variance component estimate* associated with each factor, along with the many associated interaction terms (e.g., time by company rating). These variance component estimates divide the observed variance for the ratings across each of the components, and so by comparing the magnitude of each component, it is possible to determine which factors are important sources of variance and which factors account for trivial amounts. This type of analysis is called a *generalizability study* (or **G study**) within the GT framework. The G study output for Highhouse et al. is re-created in Table 22.1. As you can see in the table, there are variance component effects for single factors as well as effects estimated for interactions of factors.

Highhouse et al. found that there was a large amount of variance due to the company being evaluated, which was a good thing ($\sigma^2 = .233$). If there were little

Table 22.1 Variance Component Estimates for Highhouse et al.

Effect	Variance Component Estimate
Companies	.233
Items	.000
Time	.000
Expert Group	.001
Persons[1]	.039
Companies × Items	.023
Companies × Time	.000
Companies × Expert Group	.003
Companies × Persons[1]	.281
Items × Time	.000
Items × Expert Group	.001
Items × Persons[1]	.010
Time × Persons[1]	.002

Source: This table was adapted from Highhouse et al. (2009).

[1]Persons were nested within Expert Group.

variance due to the company, then that would have meant that either the raters were unable to distinguish between companies or that the researchers chose companies that were nearly identical. There was little variance accounted for by items or by time ($\sigma^2 < .001$), suggesting that the three items that were chosen were internally consistent (consistent with the coefficient alpha for the scale of .88) and that there was high stability across the 2-week interval ($\sigma^2 < .001$). If there were low stability across time, the variance component estimate across time would have been higher in magnitude. There was also very little variance due to the type of expert group ($\sigma^2 = .001$), suggesting that marketing, finance, and HRM professors had few differences. Finally, there was a small amount of individual variation ($\sigma^2 = .039$), which means that some individuals are tougher in general on corporations, whereas others tend to be more lenient.

These were the main effect differences, but interaction terms were also evaluated. The items by time term showed that there was no variance associated with the interaction ($\sigma^2 < .001$), suggesting that how people responded to particular items did not vary as a function of time. Other interaction terms were larger. The companies by individual raters interaction was the largest variance term of all ($\sigma^2 = .281$), suggesting that individual raters had unique reactions to individual companies, unpredicted by their type of expertise category. This is not surprising given that people often have unique experiences (both good and bad) with various companies so that there will rarely be consistency in the pattern of responses across individuals. The item by individuals interaction term also accounted for some variance ($\sigma^2 = .010$) as did the corporation by item interaction term ($\sigma^2 = .023$). The other interaction terms (e.g., item by time, item by expert group) had trivial variance component estimates.

This initial analysis allowed Highhouse et al. to derive some meaningful conclusions about their measure of corporate reputation as well as the nature of the construct itself. They concluded that the items functioned coherently across time and across several categories of raters, and that the items showed meaningful differences across several different companies. Each of these bits of information could have been figured out through previously mentioned CTT-based techniques, though separate studies would need to have been conducted. For example, an initial data collection could have concluded that internal consistency was high, and then a separate test-retest study could have concluded that this reliability statistic was reasonably high. Finally, an interrater agreement study could have been conducted to show that different types of raters tend to come up with the same judgments about companies. Instead of conducting these different studies, however, the GT approach allows one to conduct all of these investigations in one unitary analysis. In addition, as can be seen in Table 22.1, the magnitude of the different sources of variation can be compared with each other.

Distinctions Within the GT Framework

There are several types of analyses and designs that can be used within GT analyses. One distinction is a *crossed* or *nested* design. **Crossed designs** mean that the measurements have scores on all possible factors or **facets**. **Nested designs** signify that there are some measurements that do not fully span all possible factors or facets. The Highhouse et al. study is a nested design because individuals are nested within a particular specialization. If it was a fully crossed design, individuals would have responded as if they were marketing professors, and then as if they were finance professors, and finally as if they were HRM professors. Given that having people respond as if they were in another field than the one they are employed in probably would lead to meaningless responses, Highhouse et al. had to rely on a nested design where individuals were nested within profession; all other factors were fully crossed within their design. Fully crossed designs are preferred, as they provide simpler analytic frameworks, but as the Highhouse et al. example shows, sometimes they simply are not possible.

Just like in ANOVA, manipulated factors can be considered *fixed* or *random*. Factors are considered **random factors** if the values chosen to represent them were sampled randomly (or quasi-randomly) from a larger possibility of choices; factors are considered fixed if the values chosen to represent them were chosen specifically and there is little desire to generalize beyond those chosen values. In the Highhouse et al. study, clearly the type of expertise would be considered a fixed variable as the three categories of experts (e.g., marketing, finance, and human resources) were not chosen at random. And clearly the authors of that study would not generalize their findings on those three experts to other types of experts not in their study. They did not specify the nature of the factors in their paper, but the time period was likely treated as a **fixed factor** as well.

However, if factors were chosen randomly, it is possible to generalize beyond the range of conditions chosen by the researcher. If the factors were treated as fixed, then the researchers would not be able to generalize beyond the conditions chosen in their research. Given that time and type of expertise were treated as fixed by Highhouse et al., it would not make sense for them to apply their findings to industrial-organizational psychology professors or to time periods that were 2 years in length!

The GT framework can also be used to tailor a test to help it make better decisions. As opposed to G studies, which are used to estimate variance component estimates, *decision studies* (or D studies) are used to make decisions about the number of items, raters, or time points needed to achieve a certain level of precision needed for a particular purpose. The logic of a **D study** is similar to the logic behind the Spearman-Brown prophecy formula presented in Module 13, which allows one to take an existing measure of reliability and to extrapolate what the reliability would be if the test was expanded (or decreased) by a set number of items. Just as was shown in previous modules, this formula can be extremely useful in terms of guiding future development of tests. D studies take this similar logic and combine it with the power of GT to allow researchers to examine the effects of simultaneously modifying several components of a test to determine how decisions could be improved.

Within the GT framework, two different types of test uses are distinguished, and depending on which way your test is used, you will need to take a slightly different approach to the D study. Decisions that require you to consider the relative ranking of individuals, such as using a test to identify the top five scorers to hire, are called *relative decisions*. In many ways, this usage of a test requires more measurement precision because errors in multiple individuals can impact the final decision of any single individual. For example, suppose you have the highest true score of all individuals who have taken a firefighter entrance exam. Even though you might have the highest true score, you might not have the highest observed score, either because you had some negative error or somebody who had a lower true score than you managed to have a high error term that allowed her to surpass your observed score. Relative decisions are contrasted with *absolute decisions*. With absolute decisions, an individual score is being compared to a particular standard. So with the firefighter example, suppose that it is not important how you rank compared to other applicants, only that you answer correctly 90% of the items on the entrance exam. In that case, your decision is impacted only by error related to your score; error in others' scores cannot impact whether you get hired or not.

The formulae for computing D studies, along with the formulae used to compute the variance component estimates, are beyond the scope of this book but can be found in the references in the Further Readings section. In the Highhouse et al. study, the researchers conducted a D study to determine the number of raters that would be needed to achieve different levels of reliability. They manipulated the number of raters because they felt as though the G study demonstrated that increasing the number of time points and number of expert groups would have resulted in few increases in reliability. The index of reliability that they used was called the **generalizability coefficient** *for relative decisions*. This index can be considered roughly similar to other types of reliability coefficients, though it is calculated within the GT framework. With one rater, the index was .40, and it increased as the raters were increased. With eight raters, the index reached .81, and it took until 18 raters to achieve .90. The authors concluded that five raters would result in a sufficient coefficient (.75) for most research purposes. Note that if they were more concerned with using the test for absolute decisions, the number of raters needed to achieve similar results would have been smaller. Thus, D studies are extremely useful in helping to tailor a particular instrument.

Conducting a GT Analysis

Like IRT analyses, GT analyses can be difficult to compute because there are no easy options to click a few buttons in SPSS or SAS or R to obtain the GT results. However, there is specialized software that can be used to conduct GT analyses. Highhouse et al. used one of the GENOVA-suite programs (Brennan, 2001), which can be found at http://www.education.uiowa.edu/centers/casma/. There are three sets of programs available at that website, including a program for balanced designs, another for **nested designs**, and another one for multivariate designs (see Exercise 22.2 for more details). These programs are all downloadable for free and include extensive user manuals. Mushquash and O'Connor (2006) provided syntax programs that can be used to run GT analyses within SPSS, SAS, and MATLAB, thus making these analyses more accessible for individuals who use these common statistical programs.

Before running these analyses (and before collecting data), it is very important that you plan out your likely analyses, deciding what the number of factors are that you have as well as which factors can be fully crossed and which, by necessity, must be nested. GT analyses, although used much less frequently than CTT analyses, are especially useful when you have many different domains that can be tested or measured. As a result, GT can be used to clarify all of these complex measurements. Consequently, GT has begun to be used somewhat frequently in areas of physical measurements, where it is possible to sample physical measurements such as heart rate over a series of times, contexts, and measuring devices. Although this module has presented only some of the foundational material for GT, focusing on concepts instead of formulae, we believe that continued study of GT will provide many psychometric rewards!

Concluding Comments

GT provides a comprehensive approach to evaluating measures and lets researchers judge the magnitude of various sources of error simultaneously. These analyses require much forethought in terms of designing the data collection but when done can be quite powerful and can greatly expand on lessons learned from traditional CTT analyses. GT analyses really excel when a large number of sources of variation can be manipulated in a single GT study analysis, and so it is important that GT studies be as comprehensive as possible. The results of the GT analyses, especially the D studies, can be used to derive best practices for using a particular measurement instrument, especially with regard to the number of raters and items needed to achieve a particular level of decision accuracy. Even when it is not possible to conduct GT analyses, understanding this technique can help researchers better think about the underlying dynamics and factors that impact the variation of test scores.

Best Practices

1. Brainstorm as many potential sources of error as possible that could influence your measure and then consider how you could collect data manipulating these sources of error.
2. Collect a comprehensive set of data, manipulating as many sources of variance as you can.
3. Estimate variance components to determine which sources of variance matter most and which matter little.
4. Decide on whether an absolute or relative D study is appropriate and compute the appropriate statistics. If you are unsure, compute the statistics for both types of decisions.
5. Based on the D study, update test recommendations to provide adequate levels of accuracy for test usage.
6. Realize that the test construction process is a continuous one. As a test sees expanded uses, consider that additional sources of error may be encountered. Develop future GT-based studies to consider the magnitude of these new types of errors.

Practical Questions

1. What are the main differences between GT and CTT?
2. What are typical sources of error that are investigated in GT studies?
3. What does the variance component estimate tell us?
4. What is the difference between a fixed and a random facet?
5. What is the difference between a fully crossed design and a nested design?
6. What is the purpose of a D study?
7. What are the differences between absolute and relative decisions?
8. Why has GT been slow to be adopted in many research areas?

Case Studies

CASE STUDY 22.1: DEVELOPING A PROJECTIVE TEST

Your advisor wants to develop a new measure of negative affectivity to complement existing measures that are traditional response formats. Your advisor believes that existing measures are limited because they only tap conscious aspects of negative affectivity, whereas she believes that there is a significant aspect of personality that lies beyond conscious understanding. To address her concerns, you have been tasked with developing a projective test that measures the unconscious aspects of negative affectivity.

For your initial version of the test, you have found 10 pieces of abstract art and present these images on the computer, asking respondents to type up to five sentences about their instant and initial reactions to the abstract art. You have randomly sampled 100 undergraduate students from your research subject pool. After you have collected these data, your advisor asks "Okay, how do we score these tests?" (Yes, you should have thought of this before you collected the data!) You propose that you score each of the items based on your interpretation of the number of negative statements made in response to each piece of abstract art. Your advisor says, "Well, we shouldn't just rely on your judgment, so I will rate each of the responses to each piece of abstract art so we can test each other's reliability."

Finally, your advisor suggests that people's responses to art may be influenced by their mood when they took the test, and so she proposes that you follow up with each of your 100 respondents and ask them to complete the test 2 weeks later.

You have collected all of the data, and now your advisor says, "How do we analyze all of this?" Given that you have just read this module, you suggest GT analyses, to which she says "I have never done one of those; tell me how we do it." She asks the following questions for you to ponder.

Questions to Ponder

1. What are the factors of variation that you would compute for your G study? For each of these factors, would you consider that factor random or fixed? Is your design fully crossed, or are some factors nested within others?
2. What statistics would you report back to your advisor to help her better understand whether the projective test is working well?

3. When conducting a D study, would you be most interested in absolute or relative decisions for this new measure?
4. Explain to your advisor how the information gathered from your GT analysis compares to information that could have been found from traditional CTT-based investigations of reliability as well as IRT-based investigations.
5. Suppose that the GT study shows that there is reasonable consistency over time and raters. Develop a new GT-based study to investigate other sources of variation and error. Think of these other sources of variation and decide how you would measure them.

CASE STUDY 22.2: DEVELOPMENT OF A STRUCTURED INTERVIEW SYSTEM

Structured interviews are some of the most popular measurement devices used for hiring purposes because they tap into managers' affinity for employment interviews, but they also do so in a way that provides structured data that has higher reliability than typical employment interviews.

Suppose you are hired as a consultant to Alfaxto Inc., a start-up organization that wants to hire a large sales force to push their hot new products. The vice president for human resources (VP-HR) who hired you wants you to develop the best possible structured interview system. He says, "I want this to be the scientific state of the art, and so I don't want you to skip anything in demonstrating its reliability and validity." The VP-HR is giving you free rein to develop your own structured interview as well as free rein for collecting data to support its use.

Based on job analyses, you have identified four dimensions that you want to assess in the interview: enthusiasm, verbal ability, problem-solving capability, and goal driven. You have written a series of 10 items per dimension.

The VP-HR prides himself on knowing a lot about measurement given that he took a psychological testing course back in college. He wants to know exactly how you are going to evaluate your new structured interview. You try to explain the basic concept of GT and how you will conduct a GT study along with a D study to figure out the best scenario on how to use this test.

He tells you, "Remember, I give you carte blanche to design the best study. On the other hand, I don't want you wasting my applicants' time unnecessarily either. Make it just right!" He also says, "I want you to get it right this time around . . . don't come back 6 months later and tell me that we need to include additional factors that weren't considered this time!"

Questions to Ponder

1. What are the factors that you will analyze in your GT study? For each factor, decide whether it is fixed or random. Are any of the factors nested within each other?
2. What type of D study will you conduct to satisfy the VP-HR?
3. From a pragmatic perspective, which factors will be necessary to focus on in the D study?
4. The VP-HR remembers something about inter-rater reliability from his single testing class. He asks, "Why do we need to do this fancy design? Can't we just correlate how my ratings compare to yours and be done with it?" How would you answer him?
5. Do you think the additional effort needed to conduct the GT study is worth it, compared to alternatives?

⦿⧫⦿

Exercises

EXERCISE 22.1: REVIEW TWO G STUDIES

OBJECTIVE: To observe how GT studies are reported in practice and to observe the different rationales that researchers use for motivating GT analyses.

Find two empirical studies that use GT to evaluate a test or measure (make sure to choose different sets of authors). Study those two articles, paying particular attention to the aspects of GT. Answer the following questions, comparing and contrasting both empirical articles.

1. What was the rationale given for using GT? What rationale did the authors give for using GT analyses compared to other techniques discussed in this book?
2. What sources of error did the authors manipulate in their articles? Did they treat these factors as random or fixed?
3. If the authors conducted a D study, did they use relative or absolute criteria to guide the analyses?
4. What factors were found to be significant sources of error, and which were found to be trivial?
5. How did the authors use their GT findings to refine their instrument?

EXERCISE 22.2: EVALUATE COMPUTER PROGRAMS TO RUN GT ANALYSES

OBJECTIVE: To gain some familiarity with popular GT analysis programs and to better understand some of the design features used to develop GT studies.

One of the leading centers of research on GT has been Center for Advanced Studies in Measurement and Assessment at the University of Iowa, where Dr. Robert Brennan has worked for many years. Check out their website at http://www. education.uiowa.edu/centers/casma/ for excellent resources on measurement in general but also for GT in particular. There are notices for conferences and workshops, usually on advanced measurement topics, research reports, and monographs, again usually on topics that are extensions and more advanced than the material in this book (but if you are inspired, by all means dig into them!). Click on the Computer Programs section of this page and download the three different GT analysis programs, under the rubric GENOVA Suite Programs: GENOVA, urGENOVA, mGENOVA.

Each of these programs is designed for different types of GT analyses and designs. When you download the programs, a PDF manual accompanies each program. Open up each of these manuals and read them, focusing on the types of data that can be analyzed with each different version as well as the types of different statistics each can compute.

Pretend that you are reviewing these software packages for your company because your boss is interested in running GT analyses in the future. Your boss would be interested in the following questions:

1. Why types of designs can each piece of software best handle? How are the three different pieces of software distinguished from each other?
2. Exercise 22.1 presents a scenario where you have a series of items being responded to by two judges over a period of time. Which program would be best to analyze those data?
3. The Highhouse et al. project used one of these programs to analyze their data. Based on your understanding of their project, which of the three software programs would be most appropriate? (Hint: You can find the right answer by perusing the original article.)

Further Readings

Brennan, R.L. (2001). *Generalizability theory*. New York: Springer-Verlag.
DeShon, R.P. (2002). Generalizability theory. In F. Drasgow & N. Schmitt (Eds.), *Measuring and analyzing behavior in organizations: Advances in measurement and data analysis* (pp. 189–220). San Francisco, CA: Jossey-Bass.
Shavelson, R.J., Webb, N.M., & Rowley, G.L. (1989). Generalizability theory. *American Psychologist, 44,* 922–932.

Appendix A

Course-Long Exercise
on Psychological Scale Development

This continuing exercise will require you and your classmates to apply information from many of the modules that constitute this book. The intent of this continuing exercise will be to develop a rationally derived measure of typical performance of your choosing. Development will progress through test specifications, item writing, administration of the scale, consideration of issues related to reliability and validity, item refinement through use of exploratory factor analysis, and specification of test scoring. In the end, you will be encouraged to create a test manual that outlines the development of your measure.

This continuing exercise has elements of both group and individual work. In a group with other classmates, you will choose a psychological construct to measure, decide on test specifications, develop items, obtain both subject matter expert (SME) ratings and responses to items, and construct data files. Individually, you will then be responsible for making decisions based on the SME ratings, examining the reliability and dimensionality of the scale, discarding items, proposing methods for examining the scale's validity, and creating the test manual.

Important note: In creating this book, the authors have followed what we consider to be a logical organization of the material needed to understand the process of test construction. The order in which the modules are presented, however, is not likely to be the order in which a test developer creates a test. For the purpose of this continuing exercise, we suggest conducting the continuing exercise in the following order:

Part 1: Introduction (Module 1)

Objective: To gain experience in all steps of development of a rationally derived psychological measure of typical performance.

Table A.1   Steps in the Psychological Scale Development Process

Group Work	Relevant Module
Part 1: Introduction	Module 1
Part 2: Test preparation and specification	Module 4
Part 3: Item writing and administration	Module 15
Individual Work	Relevant Module
Part 4: Examining SME ratings	Module 7
Part 5: Exploratory factor analysis	Module 18
Part 6: Reliability analysis	Modules 5 and 6
Part 7: Criterion-related validity	Module 8
Part 8: Construct validity	Module 9
Part 9: Development of a test manual	Uses information from all modules

In part 1 of this continuing exercise, we ask you to begin looking forward to and mentally preparing for some of the activities that will go into the development of a measure of typical performance. It's likely going to be more work than you think. Now is a good time to begin to identify a psychological construct that you might like to operationalize.

Part 2: Test Preparation and Specification (Module 4)

Objective: To begin development of a psychological measure by developing test specifications.

By this time, your instructor has specified how many people will make up a group for the initial parts of this continuing exercise, and you have hopefully determined who your group members will be. We're about to get started on this project in earnest.

1. Together with your group members, identify a psychological construct that could benefit from additional measurement. Perhaps consider a construct that

   - is currently not well measured,
   - is currently available only from a test publisher,
   - could be useful for an upcoming research project or thesis, and
   - captures your interest.

2. Clearly define the domain to which this test will apply. Carefully consider each of the sub-questions (Steps 2a–2d) presented in the overview of Module 4. (*Note:* This is the most important step of this continuing exercise.)
3. Choose the item format that will be used. This is an important element of test specifications. For this continuing exercise, choose a Likert-type rating scale for your items. Determine the scale anchors that will be used.

Part 3: Item Writing and Administration (Module 15)

Objective: To develop quality items to assess a psychological construct.

1. Determine how many items will be written.

   Great! You finally get to write some items. Before you do, we must consider an important dilemma concerning how many items should be written. On the one hand, the more items your group develops, the better. That way, after conducting some analyses, you will be able to discard poor items without worrying too much about ending up with too few items in the final scale. On the other hand, with a class exercise such as this, we often have a limited sample to which we can administer our scale. Because some important statistical procedures such as exploratory factor analysis require a large sample size relative to the number of items, we'd like to ensure that we don't have too many items.

   So what's the plan? We recommend the following. Determine the largest possible tryout sample size your group will commit to obtaining (your instructor will likely give you a minimum sample size). Then divide that number by 5. The resulting number is the number of items your group will want to create for initial administration. Let's say, for example, the sample size of your tryout sample will be 180. Because at a minimum we'll want to ensure five respondents per item (see Module 18), then we divide 180 by 5 and determine that we need to include no more than 36 items in the initial draft.

   If your group has six members, then each person is responsible for drafting six items (36 total items divided by 6 members × 6 items each). In planning how many items to create, your group may want to specify that each member should initially draft more than the minimum number of items so that, as a group, you can select the best items to be initially administered to the tryout sample. Continuing with the example, each of the six group members might want to draft nine items initially, for a group total of 54 items. Together, the group can then decide which 36 of the 54 possible items should be administered to the tryout sample.

2. Write items to assess the construct specified in part 2.

   To ensure quality items, remember to do the following:

   Review your definition of the construct.
   Write items to assess each of the dimensions of your construct (if multidimensional).
   Consider whether you want to include reverse-coded items in the measure. Review Module 15 to consider the advantages and disadvantages of such items.
   Review the item-writing tips presented in Module 15.

3. As a group, determine the set of items that will be administered to the tryout sample.
4. Obtain SME ratings of the items.

   SMEs should be asked to rate each of your draft items. Several scales could be used, including the rating scale used to assess the content validity ratio as discussed in the overview of Module 7. Here, each SME rates whether the item is "essential," "useful," or "not necessary" to the operationalization of the theoretical construct. Alternatively, you could use a scale of relevance to the intended construct that includes anchors such as "not at all relevant," "somewhat relevant," "relevant," and "highly relevant." Your instructor may have additional suggestions and will specify the minimum number of SME ratings your group should obtain.

   When obtaining SME ratings, ensure the following:

   SMEs are presented a clear definition of your construct.
   SMEs are informed that items that assess the opposite pole of your construct (i.e., reverse-scored items) are just as relevant to your construct as other items.
   SMEs understand they are making judgments about the items themselves. They are not being administered the items.

5. Administer the items to your tryout sample.
6. Construct two data sets. One should contain all of the SME responses obtained by group members; the other should contain all of the responses of the tryout sample obtained by group members.

   This is the last step of the group work phase of the project. From here on, you will be making all important decisions on your own (or perhaps with some advice from your instructor).

Part 4: Examining SME Ratings (Module 7)

Objective: To refine the draft scale by using information provided by SME ratings.

1. Using the SME ratings data file created by your group, compute the mean and standard deviation of all items.
2. Determine a cut score that you believe reflects SME judgments that the item is too low in relevance to be included for further consideration. There are no rules of thumb here—you'll have to rely on your own judgment. Keep the following in mind when determining what cut score to use:

   Be sure you are able to justify your choice of a cut score. Why do you think all items at or above this mean should be included for further analysis, while all other items should be discarded?

Use the same cut score for all items on the scale. Even if you expect your scale to be multidimensional, use a single cut score across all items.

Do not set your cut score so high that you eliminate too many items. Remember, additional items may be dropped following reliability and/ or factor analysis.

3. Eliminate from further consideration those items that do not meet your cut score. Use only those items that are at or above your cut score for all remaining parts of this continuing exercise.

Part 5: Exploratory Factor Analysis (Module 18)

Objective: To examine the dimensionality of the remaining scale items.

1. Using the tryout sample data file, conduct an exploratory factor analysis of those items that were retained following examination of the SME ratings. Use the following options found within your data analysis software:

Choose the principal axis factoring method.
Choose Promax as the method of rotation.
Request a scree plot. Determine the number of factors by examining your scree plot.
Choose "sort by size" to display the factor loadings.

2. Examine the output from your factor analysis. Does the output support the expected dimensionality of your scale? Which items are loading on the major factors? Can you provide a logical label for the group of items loading on a particular factor?

It is often the case that exploratory factor analysis does not support the expected dimensionality of a newly created scale. Perhaps you expected a multidimensional scale and found that almost all of the items load on a single factor. Perhaps you expected a single dimension, and the items form distinct, interpretable factors. If the initial exploratory factor analysis suggests a very different factor structure from what you expected, you may want to conduct an additional factor analysis requesting a specified number of factors to be extracted. Does the new factor analysis provide a more logical grouping of items? Select the output from the factor analysis that seems to make the most logical sense for the remaining steps of this part of the continuing exercise.

3. Interpret the results of your factor analysis.

a. How many interpretable dimensions emerged? This is the dimensionality of your scale. Label each interpretable factor by examining the items that compose it.

b. Which items load on each interpretable factor?
c. Delete items that fail to load on any interpretable factor. Only those items that are retained should be used in the remaining parts of the continuing exercise.

Part 6: Reliability Analysis (Modules 5 and 6)

Objective: To develop scales with high internal consistency reliability.

Using only those items still retained in the tryout sample, conduct a reliability analysis of each dimension of the scale. Choose the following options:

Compute alpha.

Select the options *scale if item-deleted* and *item-total correlations*.

1. Examine the output for each reliability analysis. Compare the obtained alpha with the alpha estimated if each particular item were deleted. Would the alpha increase if the item were deleted from the scale? If the answer is no, you will obviously retain the item. If the answer is yes, you may consider dropping the item from the final version of the scale. First, however, ask yourself the following:

   Would dropping the item increase alpha substantially?
   Is there a logical reason that the item seems different from the other items loading on this factor?

If an item was dropped from a dimension, rerun the reliability analysis and repeat the process. Note that alpha is improved by dropping items with low item-total correlations.

2. Once the alphas of each dimension of the scale have been determined, compute the alpha of the overall scale.

Part 7: Criterion-Related Validation (Module 8)

Objective: To propose appropriate criteria to assess the criterion-related validity of the scale.

Identify criteria that *could* be used to assess the criterion-related validity of your newly developed scale. Consider the following:

Ensure that the criteria you propose are practical, relevant, and reliable.
Justify why your recommended criteria would be useful for validating your scale.
Determine whether the proposed criterion-related validation design will be concurrent, predictive, or postdictive.

Part 8: Construct Validation (Module 9)

Objective: To propose appropriate measures to provide evidence of the construct validity of the scale.

Identify psychological measures that *could* be used to provide evidence of the construct validity of your newly developed scale. Consider the following:

> In part 2, you specified constructs that were related to your measure. Accepted measures of these constructs could be used to provide evidence of the convergent validity of your scale.
>
> Psychological measures that you expect to be unrelated to your scale, but that are measured on a similar Likert-type scale, would be useful in examining the discriminant validity of your newly developed scale.
>
> It is important to explain why the measures you are recommending could be useful for providing evidence of the convergent and discriminant validity of your scale.

Part 9: Development of a Test Manual

Objective: To conclude the experience of the development of a psychological measure by production of a written report.

This final part of this continuing exercise asks you to document the entire process you conducted in developing your psychological measure. Be sure to include the following:

> Clearly define the psychological construct.
>
> Identify the number of SMEs used and the size and characteristics of the tryout sample.
>
> Document and discuss the procedures you followed in each step of the scale's development, including revisions.
>
> Discuss the decision points you encountered in the development of the scale and justify the decisions you made.
>
> Discuss the proposed validation of your scale.
>
> Use appendices to present the items in the initial scale, as well as the final version of the scale.
>
> Include any additional elements suggested by your instructor in your test manual and/or appendices.

Appendix B

Data Set Descriptions

This appendix contains a description of all the computerized data files needed for the exercises used in this book. All data files can be found in electronic (SPSS) format at http://www.routledge.com/9780415644792 at the Routledge Academic Press website. The exercises that use each data set are listed in parentheses after the data set name. Data sets are listed in alphabetical order.

Bus Driver.Sav (Exercises 3.2, 8.2, and 17.1)

This data set consists of 1441 incumbent bus drivers who completed a job analysis questionnaire, as well as personality and ability tests, as part of a large-scale employment test validation project. Job performance criteria were also collected and are included in this version of the data set. This version of the data set represents only a fraction of the 1375 variables that made up the entire data set for the large-scale study.

Variable	Description
rand id#	Random ID number
r_hpi	Hogan Personality Inventory reliability (e.g., integrity) subscale
st_hpi	Hogan Personality Inventory stress tolerance subscale
so_hpi	Hogan Personality Inventory service orientation subscale
jobtitle	Current job title
	1 = Light bus driver
	2 = Heavy bus driver
	3 = Replacement bus driver
	4 = Driver trainee

        5 = Training supervisor

tenure	Years on current job
	1 = Less than 1 year
	2 = 1–5 years
	3 = 6–10 years
	4 = 11–15 years
	5 = More than 15 years
degree	Level of education
	1 = Less than high school
	2 = High school degree
	3 = Some college
	4 = College degree
	5 = Graduate-level work
race	Racial category
	1 = Asian
	2 = Black
	3 = Filipino
	4 = Hispanic
	5 = Native American
	6 = Pacific Islander
	7 = White
	8 = Other
sex	Sex of bus driver
	0 = Male
	1 = Female
time	Full- or part-time driver
	1 = Full time
	2 = Part time
sickdays	Number of sick and personal days in last year
srti	Number of self-reported traffic incidents in last year
drivetst	Score on driving performance test
pescore	Overall performance evaluation score
age	Age in years
TF001	Task 1—Frequency (following response scale used for all TF items)
	1 = Almost never
	2 = Hardly ever
	3 = Regularly
	4 = Often
	5 = Very often
TT001	Task 1—Relative time spent (following response scale used for all TT items)
	1 = Almost none
	2 = Little
	3 = Moderate
	4 = Much
	5 = Almost always
TI001	Task 1—Importance (following response scale used for all TI items)
	1 = Unimportant
	2 = Borderline
	3 = Important

4 = Very important
5 = Critical

TF002	Task 2—Frequency
TT002	Task 2—Relative time spent
TI002	Task 2—Importance
TF003	Task 3—Frequency
TT003	Task 3—Relative time spent
TI003	Task 3—Importance
TF004	Task 4—Frequency
TT004	Task 4—Relative time spent
TI004	Task 4—Importance
TF005	Task 5—Frequency
TT005	Task 5—Relative time spent
TI005	Task 5—Importance
TF006	Task 6—Frequency
TT006	Task 6—Relative time spent
TI006	Task 6—Importance
TF007	Task 7—Frequency
TT007	Task 7—Relative time spent
TI007	Task 7—Importance
TF008	Task 8—Frequency
TT008	Task 8—Relative time spent
TI008	Task 8—Importance
TF009	Task 9—Frequency
TT009	Task 9—Relative time spent
TI009	Task 9—Importance
TF010	Task 10—Frequency
TT010	Task 10—Relative time spent
TI010	Task 10—Importance

Geoscience Attitudes.Sav (Exercises 16.2 and 18.1)

This data set has 15 variables (items) measured on 137 cases. Respondents rated their level of agreement to each of the following items using a five-point Likert-type rating scale ranging from 1 = strongly disagree to 5 = strongly agree.

Variable	Description
item 1	I have a good understanding of how scientists do research.
item 2	I consider myself well skilled in conducting scientific research.
item 3	I've wanted to be a scientist for as long as I can remember.
item 4	I have a good understanding of elementary geoscience.
item 5	I'm uncertain about what course of study is required to become a geoscientist.
item 6	I am considering majoring in geoscience.
item 7	I'd enjoy a career in geoscience.
item 8	I plan on taking math courses that would prepare me to major in a science.
item 9	I would enjoy going hiking or camping.
item 10	I would enjoy boating.

item 11   I'd prefer to work on a science project "in the field" than in a research laboratory.
item 12   I enjoy reading science fiction novels.
item 13   I enjoy reading nature and travel books and magazines.
sex   Participant sex
           1 = Female
           2 = Male
classyr   Class year
           1 = HS frosh or sophomore
           2 = HS junior or senior
           3 = College frosh or sophomore
           4 = College junior or senior

GMA Data.Sav (Exercise 16.1)

These data come from a study by Mersman and Shultz (1998) on the fakeability of personality measures, which consisted of 323 students who worked at least part time.

Variable	Description
g1–g40	The 40 general mental ability (GMA) items
	0 = Incorrect
	1 = Correct
gsum	Total score on the GMA scale
gender	Sex of respondent
	1 = Female
	2 = Male
age	Age of respondent in years
ethnicity	Respondent's race/ethnicity
	1 = Caucasian
	2 = Hispanic
	3 = African American
	4 = Asian
	5 = Native American
	6 = Other
	7 = Filipino
	8 = Asian Pacific Islander
class	Academic rank of respondent
	1 = Freshman
	2 = Sophomore
	3 = Junior
	4 = Senior
	5 = Graduate student

Joinership Data Recoded.Sav (Exercises 15.3 and 15.4)

Each of the items below shares the following five-point Likert-type response scale: 1 (strongly disagree), 2 (disagree), 3 (neither agree nor disagree), 4 (agree), and 5 (strongly agree). An "R" indicates that the item has already been recoded. There are 230 subjects in the data set. (See the description of Exercises 15.2–15.4 in Module 15 for the actual items and a more detailed description of the data set.)

Variable	Description
item1– item42R	Scores for each of the 42 items
age	Age in years
gender	Gender
	1 = Male
	2 = Female

Joinership Rational Rating.Sav (Exercise 15.2)

Subject matter expert rational ratings ($N = 35$) for the 42 items in the joinership study described in Module 15, Exercises 15.2–15.4.

Variable	Description
r1–r42	Rational rating for the 42 items
age	Age in years
gender	Gender
	1 = Male
	2 = Female

Mechanical Comprehension.Sav (Exercises 2.1, 2.2, and 11.2)

This data set was from an applied research project where 474 current employees of a large automobile manufacturer completed two tests of mechanical aptitude. Job performance data (supervisory ratings) were also collected on all 474 employees. A variety of demographic information was also collected.

Variable	Description
id	Employee code
sex	Sex of employee
	0 = Male
	1 = Female
	9 = Missing value
age	Age of employee
edlevel	Education
	0 = Missing value
	1 = Less than HS
	2 = HS diploma or GED
	3 = Some college
	4 = Associates degree
	5 = Bachelors degree
	6 = Graduate or professional degree

work   Work experience in years
jobcat   Job category
          0 = Missing value
          1 = Clerical
          2 = Office trainee
          3 = Security officer
          4 = College trainee
          5 = Exempt trainee
          6 = MBA trainee
          7 = Technical
minority Minority classification
          0 = White
          1 = Non-White
          9 = Missing value
          sexrace Sex and race classification
          1 = White males
          2 = Minority males
          3 = White females
          4 = Minority females
mech1   Current mechanical aptitude test score
mech2   Proposed mechanical aptitude test score
perf   Job performance rating
          1 = Unacceptable
          2 = Well below standard
          3 = Below standard
          4 = Meets standard
          5 = Above standard
          6 = Well above standard
          7 = Outstanding

Nomonet.Sav (Exercise 9.2)

These data are from an applied project where 255 individuals completed several psychological tests.

Variable	Description
overt	Overt integrity measure
cogab	Cognitive ability measure
masked	Personality-based integrity measure

Passing Score.Sav (Exercise 14.3)

This data set contains data on 200 student scores for a graduate statistics exam.

Variable	Description
final	Final exam grade in graduate statistics—ideal
final2	Final exam grade in graduate statistics—realistic

desig   Designation as successful or unsuccessful
         1 = Successful
         2 = Unsuccessful

Personality.Sav (Exercise 11.1)

These data come from a study by Mersman and Shultz (1998) on the fakeability of personality measures, which consisted of 323 students who worked at least part time.

Variable	Description
im	Impression management scale score
sd	Social desirability scale score
conmean1	Mean on con scale for honest
conmean2	Mean on con scale for fake
intmean1	Mean on intellect scale for honest condition
gender	Sex of respondent
	1 = Female
	2 = Male
age	Age of respondent in years
ethnicity	Respondent's race/ethnicity
	1 = Caucasian
	2 = Hispanic
	3 = African American
	4 = Asian
	5 = Native American
	6 = Other
	7 = Filipino
	8 = Asian Pacific Islander
class	Academic rank of respondent
	1 = Freshman
	2 = Sophomore
	3 = Junior
	4 = Senior
	5 = Graduate student

Personality-2.Sav (Module 18 and 19 overviews)

This data set is a subset of the study by Mersman and Shultz (1998) that examined the fakeability of personality measures. This subset of the larger data set consists of responses from 314 students who worked at least part time. Eight personality variables from Saucier's (1994) Mini-Markers scale (see http://pages.uoregon. edu/gsaucier/gsau41.htm) in this subset of the data use the following nine-point rating scale: 1 = extremely inaccurate, 2 = very inaccurate, 3 = moderately inaccurate, 4 = slightly inaccurate, 5 = ?, 6 = slightly accurate, 7 = moderately accurate, 8 = very accurate, and 9 = extremely accurate.

Variable	Description
bold	Bold
disorgan	Disorganized
efficien	Efficient
extraver	Extraverted
organize	Organized
quiet	Quiet
shy	Shy
sloppy	Sloppy

Reliability.Sav (Exercise 6.1)

This data set consists of a small subset of data from Wave 1 (1992) of the Health and Retirement Study (http://hrsonline.isr.umich.edu). This subset includes 1560 persons who had retired "early" as of 1992.

Variable	Description
V1	DS (depression scale)—Depression
	1 = All the time
	2 = Most
	3 = Some
	4 = None
V2	DS—Tiring
V3	DS—Restlessness
V4	DS—Happiness (R)
V5	DS—Loneliness
V6	DS—People unfriendly
V7	DS—Enjoyed life (R)
V8	DS—Sadness
V9	DS—People dislike me
V10	DS—Can't get going
V11	DS—Poor appetite
V12	DS—Lots of energy (R)
V13	DS—Tired
V14	DS—Rested when woke up (R)
V15	LS (life satisfaction)—House
	1 = Very satisfied
	2 = Somewhat satisfied
	3 = Even
	4 = Somewhat dissatisfied
	5 = Very dissatisfied
V16	LS—Neighborhood
V17	LS—Health
V18	LS—Financial
V19	LS—Friendships
V20	LS—Marriage
V21	LS—Job
V22	LS—Family life

V23	LS—Way handle problems
V24	LS—Life as a whole
V25	Reason retired (RR)?—Bad health

1 = Very important
2 = Moderately important
3 = Somewhat important
4 = Not important at all

V26	RR—Health of family member
V27	RR—Wanted to do other things
V28	RR—Didn't like to work
V29	RR—Didn't get along with the boss
V30	RR—Didn't need to work/had sufficient income
V31	RR—Couldn't find any work
V32	RR—My work not appreciated
V33	RR—My spouse was about to retire
V34	RR—Employer policy toward older workers
V35	Good about retirement (GAR)—Lack of pressure

1 = Very important
2 = Moderately important
3 = Somewhat important
4 = Not important at all

V36	GAR—Being own boss
V37	GAR—Taking it easy
V38	GAR—Having time with spouse
V39	GAR—Spending more time with kids
V40	GAR—Spending more time on hobbies
V41	GAR—Time for volunteer work
V42	GAR—Having chance to travel
V43	Bad about retirement (BAR)—Boring/too much time

1 = Bothered a lot
2 = Bothered somewhat
3 = Bothered a little
4 = Bothered not at all

V44	BAR—Not productive/useful
V45	BAR—Missing co-workers (0 = didn't work)
V46	BAR—Illness/disability
V47	BAR—Not enough income
V48	BAR—Inflation
sex	Sex of respondent

1 = Male
2 = Female

age	Age of respondent

Sales.Sav (Exercise 8.3)

A sales manager hoping to improve the personnel selection process for the position of product salesperson compiled the data file with variables listed below consisting of scores on three tests as well as a job performance score and demographic data for 229 sales employees.

Variable	Description
sex	Sex of employee
	0 = Female
	1 = Male
ethnic	Ethnicity of employee
	0 = Caucasian
	1 = African American
w1–w50	Each indicates the employee's score on a separate item on the test of cognitive ability
	0 = Incorrect
	1 = Correct
cogab	Employee's total cognitive ability score
sde	Employee's score on a test assessing one's level of self-deception
impress	Employee's score on a test of impression management
selling	Number of products employee sold in the past month

Volunteer Data.Sav (Module 17 overview, Exercises 17.2 and 17.3)

This data set contains data assessed from 120 volunteers in a number of small organizations. Each of the volunteers completed a survey assessing the following perceptions.

Variable	Description
reward	Perceived reward
ledinit	Leader-initiating structure
ledcons	Leader consideration
clarity	Role clarity
conflict	Role conflict
efficacy	Job-related self-efficacy
goalid	Goal identification
affectc	Affective commitment
continc	Continuance commitment
motivate	Work motivation

Glossary of Key Terms

B elow, we provide definitions for key terms used within this text, as well as other key terms used more broadly in the field of psychological measurement and psychometrics. Please be aware that multiple definitions of these key terms can be found in the extant literature on psychological testing. Therefore, we have tried to strike a balance between technical and common usage, but given the nature of the book, we have emphasized the former. Note that italicized words within the definitions of key terms below are also defined elsewhere in this glossary.

Ability   The capacity for performing different tasks, acquiring knowledge, or developing skills within cognitive, psychomotor, or physical domains. In *classical test theory,* ability is represented by the true score. In *modern test theory* (*item response theory,* or *IRT*), ability is represented by a theoretical value (theta, q).

Ability Testing   The use of *tests* to determine an individual's current level of ability in cognitive, psychomotor, or physical domains.

Accommodation   In testing and assessment, the adaptation of an assessment device or testing procedure, or the substitution of one device for another, to make the test more appropriate for individuals with special needs (e.g., a physical disability such as blindness).

Achievement Test   A test that emphasizes what an individual currently knows or can do with regard to a particular subject matter.

Acquiescence   A *response style* characterized by agreement with whatever is presented in a given assessment device.

Adaptive Testing   A form of testing that individually tailors the presentation of test items to the *test taker.* See also *Computer Adaptive Testing (CAT).*

Adverse Impact   A situation where individuals in one group (typically a "protected group" under federal statute) pass a test at a substantially different rate than other comparable groups. The "80% rule" is typically applied to establish adverse impact.

Alternate Forms Reliability   An estimate of the degree to which the items used on two versions of the same assessment device are associated with one another. Also called *Parallel Forms Reliability.*

Anchor Test or Items   A common set of items from two forms of a test that allows a test user to equate the two forms of the test. Creating an anchor test is necessary when *item response theory* procedures are used to investigate the possibility of item bias.

Aptitude Test   A test that emphasizes innate potential and informal learning and is used to predict future performance and/or behavior.

Armed Services Vocational Aptitude Battery (ASVAB)   A series of tests used for military selection and placement. The ASVAB consists of 10 subtests that assess individuals' strengths and weaknesses in aptitudes including general science, arithmetic reasoning, word knowledge, paragraph comprehension, numerical operations, coding speed, auto and shop information, mathematics knowledge, mechanical comprehension, and electronics information.

Assessment   A broad method of obtaining information that may include the use of test scores, as well as other information that describes individuals, objects, or some other target of the assessment.

Attitude   One's disposition, thoughts, and/or feelings regarding a particular stimulus that is relatively stable in nature.

Back Translation   The translation of a test, which has already been translated from its original language, back into its original language. The original test and the back-translated version are then compared to determine the quality of the translation.

Banding   A procedure for setting a *cutoff score* where scores within a particular range are treated as equivalent. The range of scores is typically determined based on statistics such as the *standard error of measurement.*

Battery   A combination of several tests given in sequence in order to obtain a combined assessment score. See also *Armed Services Vocational Aptitude Battery (ASVAB).*

Bias   Variance in test scores due to deficiencies or *contamination* that differentially affects scores within different groups of individuals, such as men versus women or minority versus majority *test takers.*

Bivariate Distribution   A joint distribution for two variables. This can include two tests or a test and a criterion variable. Bivariate distributions are typically visualized using a *scatterplot* graph.

Calibration   In *item response theory,* the process of estimating the parameters (i.e., difficulty, discrimination, and guessing) for an item. In equating test scores, the process of setting test statistics (i.e., *central tendency, variability,* and shape) in order to equate scores across distributions.

Central Tendency   A statistical estimate of the "average" or "typical" score in a given distribution. Examples include the arithmetical *mean, median,* and *mode.*

Central Tendency Error   When an evaluator rates *test takers* using only the central portion of a rating scale regardless of the test takers' actual level of performance.

Classical Test Theory (CTT)   A theory of testing that says that any observed score is a function of an individual's true score plus error. The basis for common estimates of *reliability*, *validity*, and estimations of error, such as the *standard error of measurement*.

Coefficient Alpha   An estimate of test *reliability* based on the inter-correlations among items.

Coefficient of Determination   The squared value of a bivariate correlation coefficient. It represents the percentage of variance in one variable that is attributable to variance in the other variable.

Common Method Variance (CMV)   Refers to a problem in which correlations between constructs are artificially inflated because the data were obtained using the same method of data collection for each variable.

Compensatory Scoring   The combining of several test scores where high scores on one test can offset low scores on another.

Composite Score   The combining of individual test scores into a single score based on some specified formula, such as unit weighting or empirically derived regression weights.

Computer Adaptive Testing (CAT)   A form of assessment where the test is administered via computer and the items administered are tailored to each individual based on his or her responses to previous items. See also *Item Response Theory* (*IRT*).

Computer-Based Testing (CBT)   A method of test administration where a test is administered (and possibly scored) on a computer, thus allowing for branching of items and use of multimedia materials.

Concurrent Validity   Providing evidence for the *validity* of a measure by determining the degree of association between it and a *criterion* that is presently available.

Confidence Interval   The estimation of a population parameter (e.g., a population mean) by creating an interval that is determined based on a designated probability value (e.g., critical Z value) and a standard error statistic (e.g., standard error of the mean).

Constant Ratio Model   A model of test *fairness* where the proportion of individuals successful on the *criterion* must be equal to the number that pass the test *cutoff score* across designated subgroups in order for the test to be considered fair.

Constituents, Testing   Individuals or stakeholders who have a vested interest in the testing process. These include the *test taker*, *test developer*, *test user*, and society as a whole.

Construct   A characteristic or *trait* that individuals possess to differing degrees that a test is designed to measure.

Construct Equivalence   The degree to which a given *construct* measured by a given test is comparable across different cultural or linguistic groups, or the degree to which a given *construct* is the same across different tests.

Construct Validity   The evidence gathered to support the inferences made regarding the scores obtained on an assessment instrument and the degree to which they represent some intangible characteristic of the *test taker*. The extent to which a measurement instrument assesses the hypothesized *construct* of interest.

Contamination   The extent to which irrelevant sources of systematic variance account for a portion of the total variance in test scores.

Content Domain   The set of knowledge, skills, abilities, related characteristics, and behaviors that is proposed to be measured by a given assessment device.

Content Validity   The degree to which the content of a given measure is representative of the hypothesized *content domain*, as judged by *subject matter experts (SMEs)*.

Content Validity Index (CVI)   A quantitative index of the average CVR value across items for a given test. See Module 6 for the formula for, and the interpretation of, the CVI.

Content Validity Ratio (CVR)   A quantitative index of the degree to which *subject matter experts (SMEs)* agree in their ratings of item content. See Module 6 for the formula for, and the interpretation of, the CVR.

Convergent Validity   A way of supporting the *construct validity* of a measure by demonstrating the association between theoretically similar measures of the same *construct* or *trait*. See also *Multitrait-Multimethod (MTMM) Matrix* and *Divergent Validity*.

Correction for Attenuation   A formula that yields an estimate of relationship between two variables if they are both measured without error (i.e., the population relationship).

Correction for Guessing   A procedure/formula used with multiple-choice items to better estimate a person's true score by removing from their observed score that portion that is a function of guessing (see Module 16 for the correction-for-guessing formula).

Correlation Coefficient   A statistical index of the degree of association between two variables.

Criterion   The yardstick by which a test or test scores are assessed. Alternatively, an outcome of interest (e.g., job performance) with which the test is predicted to be associated.

Criterion Contamination   The extent to which irrelevant variance contributes to the measure of a *criterion* of interest.

Criterion Deficiency   The extent to which important and relevant variance is missing from a *criterion* of interest.

Criterion-Referenced Testing   Deriving the meaning of a test score by comparing it to a given standard. Contrast with *Norm-Referenced Testing*.

Criterion-Related Validity   The degree of association between a *test* and *criterion* variable.

Critical Score   The specific point on a distribution of scores that distinguishes successful from unsuccessful *test takers*. Unlike the *cutoff score,* which may have many factors influencing it (e.g., size of the test applicant pool, number of openings), the critical score is *criterion referenced* and thus should be the same regardless of other contextual factors.

Crossed Design   A type of *generalizability theory* research design where the measurements have scores on all possible *facets*.

Cross-Validation The application of a set of scoring weights derived from one sample of *test takers* to another sample of test takers in order to assess the stability of the weights across samples.

Cutoff Score The designated point in a distribution of scores where individuals at or above the point are considered successful on the test, whereas those below are considered unsuccessful. It is distinguished from the *critical score* in that it may be based on a variety of contextual factors in addition to *criterion-referenced testing* performance.

Descriptive Statistics A collection of statistical procedures used to summarize a sample of data. Includes measures of *central tendency*, dispersion or *variability*, and shape.

Differential Item Functioning (DIF) When individuals in different groups, who possess the same level of estimated ability or total test score, respond differently to a given test item.

Discriminant Validity See *Divergent Validity.*

Divergent Validity A way of supporting the *construct validity* of a measure by demonstrating the association between theoretically dissimilar measures of the same *construct* or *trait*. Also referred to as discriminant validity. See also *Multitrait-Multimethod (MTMM) Matrix* and *Convergent Validity.*

Domain Sampling When items are selected for a *test* so that they represent a specified universe or area of interest.

D Study A decision study is typically the second phase of a *generalizability theory* analysis where the researcher uses results of the first-phase *G study* to make decisions regarding future measurement strategies by estimating the generalizability of various combinations of *facets.*

Equivalent Forms Reliability See *Alternate Forms Reliability.*

Expectancy Charts A graphical technique that expresses the *validity coefficient* as the ability of a *test* to make correction predictions.

Facets The various factors or dimensions assessed as part of a *generalizability theory* study analysis.

Face Validity The extent to which a *test* or *assessment* device appears to be valid.

Factor Analysis A set of statistical procedures by which a set of items is reduced to a fewer number of factors, based on the interrelationship among the items. If item-factor relationships are specified a priori, it is known as confirmatory factor analysis; if not, it is designated as exploratory factor analysis.

Fairness A sociopolitical concept where the outcome of the testing process is examined separately for various subgroups of *test takers*. Several definitions of fairness have been proposed over the years (e.g., constant ratio, equal probability, conditional probability, constant ratio), but no consensus definition currently exists.

False Negative A term used to define those individuals who are not selected or do not pass a test but would have been successful had they been selected or passed.

False Positive   A term used to define those individuals who were selected or passed a test but ended up not being successful once selected.

Fixed Factor   In *generalizability theory*, fixed factors represent measurement variables where each level of the variable (or *facet*) is specifically chosen and generalizability to other levels of the *facet* is not desired.

Frequency Distribution   A tabular representation of individual test scores in terms of how frequently a given score occurs in a given distribution of scores.

Generalizability Coefficient   Values obtained in a *generalizability theory* analysis *D study* that help determine the number and levels of a given *facet* needed to achieve a certain level of precision. These coefficients differ somewhat for relative versus absolute generalizability decisions.

Generalizability Theory   Estimates of *reliability* that extend classical forms of reliability by using analysis of variance (ANOVA)–like procedures to assess the generalizability of test scores beyond a given sample of persons, items, or other related study dimensions.

General Mental Ability (GMA)   One's capacity to learn and reason across a wide variety of situations and content domains.

Grouped Frequency Distribution   A tabular representation of groups of test scores in terms of how frequently each group of scores occurs in a given distribution of scores.

G Study   A generalizability study is the first phase in *generalizability theory* (GT) analysis where the researcher seeks to determine the magnitude of variance associated with various *facets* and combination of facets in the proposed GT model.

Heteroscedasticity   Unequal variability along the entire range of the regression line.

Hit Rate   The proportion of *test takers* who are accurately identified as possessing a given *trait* or characteristic purported to be measured by a test. Contrast with *False Negatives* and *False Positives*.

Homoscedasticity   Equal variability along the entire range of the regression line.

Impression Management (IM)   The degree to which a *test taker* responds in a socially desirable fashion in order to purposefully inflate his or her test score.

Incremental Validity   The extent to which additional *predictors* added to a *multiple regression* prediction equation improve the overall *predictive validity* of the multiple predictors.

Individual Differences   The dissimilarity observed on a single *construct* or *trait* of interest across individuals (*inter-individual differences*) or within the same individual over time or across constructs (*intra-individual differences*).

Intercept Bias   A form of *predictive bias* where the prediction lines for each group are parallel, but cross the *Y* axis (the intercept) at different points. Contrast with *Slope Bias*.

Internal Consistency   A reliability estimate based on the intercorrelation (i.e., homogeneity) among items on a *test*, with alpha being a prime example.

Inter-Individual Differences   An analysis of a single construct across *test takers* common with *norm-referenced testing*.

Interquartile Range A statistical measure of variability or dispersion equal to the difference between the 75th percentile and the 25th percentile of a distribution of scores. This measure of variability is typically computed for ordinal-level data or highly skewed interval-level data.

Inter-Rater Reliability The extent to which two or more raters agree in their assessment of target objects, such as individuals.

Interval Scale The level of measurement where the distance between score points is uniform, but the zero point on the scale is arbitrary.

Intra-Individual Differences An analysis of a single construct within a given *test taker* over time or an analysis of multiple constructs within the same individual.

Item Analysis Statistical procedures used to assess the properties of *tests* and specific test items. Statistics calculated typically include *item difficulty*, *item discrimination*, item-total correlations, and related indexes.

Item Characteristic Curve (ICC) A mathematically derived function used in *item response theory* models to depict the probability of correctly answering a given item for various levels of ability (designated as theta). Also called item response curves (IRCs) or item response functions (IRFs).

Item Difficulty An item analysis statistic that quantifies how easy or difficult an item is by computing the percentage of respondents who answered the item correctly or the difference in percentages between high- and low-scoring groups. The former is typically referred to as the p value, while the latter is called the d statistic for contrasting groups.

Item Discrimination An item analysis statistic that quantifies the degree to which *test takers* answering an item correctly is associated with their total test score. Typically computed using biserial, point-biserial, tetrachoric, or phi coefficients, depending on the nature of the data.

Item Response Theory (IRT) A mathematical model of the relationship between performance on a test item and the test taker's level of the construct being assessed, typically designated as q. The probability of a given response for a given level of q is typically determined using a logistic function that resembles a cumulative normal distribution (i.e., ogive).

Kappa Statistic An index of the degree of inter-rater agreement for nominal scales.

Kurtosis A statistical index of the degree to which scores in a distribution are clumped together. A distribution of test scores that has a positive kurtosis (i.e., the distribution of scores piling up in the center) is said to be leptokurtic. A distribution of test scores that has a kurtosis of zero (i.e., the distribution of scores closely follows a normal distribution) is said to be mesokurtic. A distribution of test scores that has a negative kurtosis (i.e., the distribution of scores is very flat, as in a uniform distribution) is said to be platykurtic.

Leniency Error A form of systematic rater error in which the rater is being insufficiently critical of the individual being assessed. Contrast with *Severity Error*.

Likert Scale A procedure for scaling individuals where items typically have five response options (e.g., 1 = Strongly Disagree to 5 = Strongly Agree). Individual item responses are then summed to get a total score.

Local Independence   A term used in *item response theory* to indicate that item characteristics or parameters are independent of the sample used to derive those characteristics.

Mean   The arithmetic average of a distribution of scores.

Measurement   The systematic quantification of a characteristic of *test takers* according to clearly explicated rules.

Measurement Bias   When test items do not represent the underlying *construct* they are intended to measure equally well for different subgroups of *test takers*.

Measurement Theory   See *Psychometrics*.

Median   The middle score (50th percentile) of a distribution of scores.

Mental Measurements Yearbook (MMY)   A reference volume that publishes reviews and critiques of a wide variety of tests and assessment instruments.

Meta-Analysis   A statistical method for quantitatively reviewing and summarizing findings from empirical studies within a given area.

Mode   The most frequently occurring score of a distribution of scores.

Moderator Variable   A variable that explains additional variance in a *criterion* of interest beyond that of the selected *predictor* variable due to its nonlinear (i.e., interactive) association with the predictor variable.

Modern Test Theory   A theory used to explain the relationship between individuals' responses to test items and their underlying *traits* or *abilities*.

Multidimensional Scaling (MDS)   A statistical procedure where the number of dimensions underlying a *construct* is identified and then quantified (i.e., scaled).

Multiple Correlation   The degree of association among three or more variables.

Multiple Regression   The use of two or more *predictor* variables in predicting a *criterion* variable.

Multitrait-Multimethod (MTMM) Matrix   A matrix used to depict the relationship among variables representing two or more *traits*, as well as two or more methods. The MTMM is used to provide evidence of the *construct validity* of a test.

Nested Design   A type of *generalizability theory* research design where the measurements do not have scores on all possible *facets*.

Nominal Scale   A scale of measurement where values represent qualitative (rather than quantitative) differences.

Normal Distribution   A theoretical, symmetrical distribution of scores.

Norm-Referenced Testing   Deriving the meaning of a test score by comparing it with the test scores of other *test takers*. Contrast with *Criterion-Referenced Testing*.

Ordinal Scale   The scale of measurement where data are ordered or ranked.

Parallel Forms Reliability   See *Alternate Forms Reliability*.

Percentile Rank   The percentage of *test takers* who score lower than a given score within a given sample of scores.

Phi Coefficient   An index of association between two dichotomously scored variables.

Pilot Testing   Administration of a test or test items to a sample of *test takers* in order to evaluate the test or items in terms of the clarity or appropriateness of instructions, items, options, or other test characteristics, thus allowing for necessary changes to be made before full-fledged testing occurs.

Point-Biserial Correlation Coefficient   A Pearson product moment correlation coefficient of the degree of association between a dichotomous variable (e.g., pass/fail) and a continuous variable (e.g., job performance measured in dollar sales).

Postdictive Validity   The degree of association between test scores measured in the present and criterion scores that were already measured (e.g., current test scores and prior absenteeism rates).

Power Test   A test that has a very comfortable time limit, thus allowing the typical individual to complete the test within the allotted time. Contrast with *Speed Test.*

Predictive Bias   When a test score systematically under- or overpredicts a criterion of interest for designated groups.

Predictive Validity   The degree of association between test scores measured in the present and criterion scores measured in the future (e.g., current test scores and future promotions).

Predictor   A measure, often a test, used to predict a criterion of interest, such as job or school performance.

Psychometrician   The name given to an individual who has extensive advanced formal training in the area of psychological measurement and assessment.

Psychometrics   The science of the assessment of individual differences. Usually refers to the quantitative aspects of psychological measurement. Also called *Measurement Theory.*

Qualitative   The degree to which variables differ in terms of type.

Quantitative   The degree to which variables differ in terms of amount.

Range   A *descriptive statistic* that estimates the variability or dispersion of a set of scores. Defined as the difference between the highest and lowest scores in a distribution.

Random Factor   In *generalizability theory*, random factors represent measurement variables where the levels of the variable (or *facet*) are chosen at random and generalizability to other levels of the *facet* is desired.

Ratio Scale   The scale of measurement where the intervals are equal and the zero point represents the complete absence of the construct of interest.

Regression Coefficient   In linear regression analysis, an index of the linear relationship between a *predictor* and *criterion* variable. In unstandardized form, its size is influenced by the variance of the two variables.

Reliability   The degree to which test scores are free of measurement error for a given group of *test takers*. Also the extent to which test scores are consistent over time or across forms of the test.

Reliability Coefficient   The quantification of the degree of association between two parallel tests.

Response Biases   The extent to which *test takers* respond to test items in such a way as to create construct-irrelevant error in the test scores. These *biases* are typically associated with the context of the testing situation. Examples include test takers engaging in guessing on multiple-choice knowledge tests, faking on personality measures, or impression management tactics in interviews.

Response Styles   The extent to which *test takers* respond to test items in such a way as to create construct-irrelevant error in the test scores. These biases are typically associated with personality or cultural characteristics of the test taker. Examples include *acquiescence, leniency,* and *severity* response errors in attitude measures.

Restriction of Range   A situation where test scores do not represent the entire possible range for a given variable, thus resulting in a deflated *correlation coefficient.*

Scaling   Quantification of *constructs* according to a designated set of rules.

Scatterplot   A graphical depiction of the relationship between two variables in which individuals' scores are shown simultaneously on the same graph.

Selection Ratio   An index reflecting the proportion of individuals who are selected, compared to all those assessed, as a result of the use of some assessment device.

Self-Deceptive Enhancement (SDE)   The degree to which a *test taker* responds in a socially desirable fashion, which is not purposeful but inflates his or her test score regardless.

Severity Error   A form of systematic rater error in which the rater is being overly critical of the individual being assessed. Contrast with *Leniency Error.*

Shrinkage Formula   A correction statistic used in *multiple regression* that adjusts the index of fit (e.g., R^2) due to the fact that the regression weights for a given sample are maximized for that sample and as a result are likely to be lower than in any other sample. The correction becomes more pronounced as the number of *predictor* variables in the multiple regression equation increases.

Skewness   An index of the degree to which a distribution of scores is symmetrical about a central value. A distribution of scores with a skew of zero generally follows a normal distribution. A negatively skewed distribution has scores piled in the upper end of the distribution, while a positively skewed distribution has scores piled in the lower end of the distribution.

Slope Bias   A form of *predictive bias* where the prediction lines for at least two groups are not parallel and as a result have different predictive power for the two groups. Contrast with *Intercept Bias.*

Spearman-Brown Prophecy Formula   An equation that estimates the *reliability* of a set of items if the number of the items is increased or decreased by a given factor.

Speed Test   A test that has a short time limit where most candidates will not be able to complete the instrument. Contrast with *Power Test.*

Split-Half Reliability Coefficient   An estimate of reliability created by correlating two halves of a given test. This figure is then corrected by using the *Spearman-Brown prophecy formula.*

Standard Deviation An index of the degree of dispersion of a set of scores about their *mean*.

Standard Error of Estimate An index of the degree of error associated with using one variable to predict another variable. Sometimes referred to as the standard error of prediction.

Standard Error of Measurement An index of the degree to which scores will vary over repeated assessments across parallel tests.

Stanine A standard score distribution with nine values, which has a *mean* of 5 and a *standard deviation* of approximately 2.

Statistical Artifacts Negative characteristics of an empirical study (e.g., small sample size, use of unreliable measures, restriction of range) that distort the results of the study. In *meta-analysis*, researchers often correct for such artifacts within each study.

Subgroup Analysis An analysis of the relationship between a *predictor* variable and a *criterion* variable separately for different subgroups (e.g., men vs. women) in order to determine if *moderator variables* differentially influence the predictor-criterion relationship across subgroups.

Subgroup Norming The separate ranking of individuals within subgroups based on their test scores as compared to only members within their group.

Subject Matter Expert (SME) An individual with expertise in a given area who provides expert ratings or assessments as part of a measurement process.

Technical Manual A document produced by *test developers* (e.g., test publishers) that explains the development of the test, its administration, and the *psychometric* evidence available to support inferences made from use of the test.

Test An assessment device based on a sample of *test-taker* behavior.

Test Battery A collection of *tests* and/or *assessment* devices that is used to assess a wide range of psychological constructs. For an example, see *Armed Services Vocational Aptitude Battery (ASVAB)*.

Test Developer The individual or group of individuals (i.e., *constituents*) responsible for the creation of the test and for documentation that supports the inferences to be drawn from use of the test (e.g., *technical manual*).

Test Information Function (TIF) A mathematical function in *item response theory* of the relationship between *ability* level and the reciprocal of the conditional measurement error variance. The TIF is equivalent to reliability scores in classical true score theory.

Test-Retest Reliability The assessment of *reliability* by correlating the scores of two administrations of the same test on the same groups of individuals after a given period of time between test administrations.

Test Taker The individual (i.e., *constituent*) who is assessed by the measurement device.

Test User The individual or agency (i.e., *constituent*) responsible for administration and, possibly, scoring, interpretation, and implementation decisions based on the test.

Trait A persistent or enduring characteristic of an individual that is often represented by his or her score on a test purported to measure that trait.

True Score Theory   The *classical test theory* that an individual's true score (T, i.e., underlying attribute) is a function of his or her observed score (X) and measurement error (E), depicted as $T = X + E$.

***T* Score**   A standardized score that has a *mean* of 50 and a *standard deviation* of 10.

Utility   In *measurement theory*, the degree to which a test proves useful in terms of its *psychometric* properties (e.g., *validity*) and cost-effectiveness (e.g., cost, ease of use).

Validation   The process of gathering, analyzing, and reporting theoretical and empirical evidence that supports the intended uses of a *test* or *assessment* device.

Validity   The body of theoretical and empirical evidence gathered to support the intended uses of a *test* or *assessment* device.

Validity Coefficient   An index of the degree to which inferences drawn from the use of a *test* are appropriate. Typically depicted as a *correlation coefficient* between test scores and a criterion variable.

Validity Generalization   The degree to which the *validity coefficients* established in one setting for a given population generalize to other settings and populations.

Variability   The extent to which test scores are distributed. Typically depicted as the extent to which test scores differ from some central value, such as the *mean* or *median*.

Variance   A statistical measure of variability or dispersion equal to the arithmetic average of the squared difference between each score in the distribution and the mean of the distribution. This measure of variability requires interval-level data.

Z Score   A standardized score with a *mean* of zero and a *standard deviation* of one.

References

AERA/APA/NCME. (1999). *Standards for educational and psychological testing.* Washington, DC: American Educational Research Association.

Aguinis, H., Culpepper, S.A., & Pierce, C.A. (2010). Revival of test bias research in pre-employment testing. *Journal of Applied Psychology, 95,* 648–680.

Albermarle Paper Company v. Moody., 422 U.S. 405 (1975).

Allen, M.J., & Yen, W.M. (2001). *Introduction to measurement theory.* Long Grove, IL: Waveland Press.

Anastasi, A., & Urbina, S. (1997). *Psychological testing* (7th ed.). Upper Saddle River, NJ: Prentice Hall.

Anderson, L.W., & Krathwohl, D.R. (Eds.). (2001). *A taxonomy for learning, teaching, and assessing: A revision of Bloom's taxonomy of educational objectives.* Boston: Allyn & Bacon.

Arbuckle, J. (2009). *Amos 18 user's guide.* Armonk, NY: IBM/SPSS Incorporated.

Arnold, B.R., & Matus, Y.E. (2000). Test translation and cultural equivalence methodologies for use with diverse populations. In I. Cuellar & F.A. Paniagua (Eds.), *Handbook of multicultural mental health: Assessment and treatment of diverse populations* (pp. 121–136). San Diego, CA: Academic Press.

Arvey, R.D., & Faley, R.H. (1988). *Fairness in selecting employees* (2nd ed.). New York: Addison-Wesley.

Barrett, G.V., Phillips, J.S., & Alexander, R.A. (1981). Concurrent and predictive validity designs: A critical reanalysis. *Journal of Applied Psychology, 66,* 1–6.

Barrett, R.S. (1992). Content validation form. *Public Personnel Management, 21,* 41–52.

Barrett, R.S. (1996). Content validation form. In R.S. Barrett (Ed.), *Fair employment strategies in human resource management* (pp. 47–56). Westport, CT: Quorum Books/Greenwood.

Beehr, T.A. (1986). The process of retirement: A review and recommendations for future investigation. *Personnel Psychology, 39,* 31–55.

Bentler, P.M. (1995). *EQS structural equations program manual.* Encino, CA: Multivariate Software.

Berk, R.A. (Ed.). (1982). *Handbook of methods for detecting test bias.* Baltimore: Johns Hopkins University Press.

Berk, R.A. (1986). A consumer's guide to setting performance standards on criterion-referenced tests. *Review of Educational Research, 56,* 137–172.

Biddle, R.E. (1993). How to set cutoff scores for knowledge tests used in promotion, training, certification, and licensing. *Public Personnel Management, 22,* 63–79.

Bishop, G.F., Oldendick, R.W., Tuchfarber, A.J., & Bennett, S.E. (1980). Pseudo-opinions on public affairs. *Public Opinion Quarterly, 44,* 198–209.

Bloom, B. S. (Ed.). (1956). *Taxonomy of educational objectives: The classification of educational goals; Handbook I, cognitive domain.* New York: Longmans, Green.

Borden, L. W., & Sharf, J. C. (2007). Developing legally defensible content valid selection procedures. In D. Whetzel & G. R. Wheaton (Eds.), *Applied measurement: Industrial psychology in human resources management* (pp. 385–401). New York: Taylor & Francis Group/Erlbaum Associates.

Bornstein, R. F. (1996). Face validity in psychological assessment: Implications for a unified model of validity. *American Psychologist, 51,* 983–984.

Brennan, R. L. (2001). *Generalizability theory.* New York: Springer-Verlag.

Brown, D. C. (1994). Subgroup norming: Legitimate testing practice or reverse discrimination. *American Psychologist, 49,* 927–928.

Bryant, F. B., & Yarnold, P. R. (1995). Principal components analysis and exploratory and confirmatory factor analysis. In L. G. Grimm & P. R. Yarnold (Eds.), *Reading and understanding multivariate statistics* (pp. 99–136). Washington, DC: American Psychological Association.

Burns, R. S. (1996). Content validity, face validity, and quantitative face validity. In R. S. Barrett (Ed.), *Fair employment strategies in human resource management* (pp. 38–46). Westport, CT: Quorum Books/Greenwood.

Buster, M. A., Roth, P. L., & Bobko, P. (2005). A process for content validation of education and experienced-based minimum qualifications: An approach resulting in federal court approval. *Personnel Psychology, 58,* 771–799.

Camilli, G., & Shepard, L. A. (1994). *Methods for identifying biased test items.* Thousand Oaks, CA: Sage.

Campbell, D. T., & Fiske, D. W. (1959). Convergent and discriminant validation by the multitrait-multimethod matrix. *Psychological Bulletin, 56,* 81–105.

Campion, M. A., Outtz, J. L., Zedeck, S., Schmidt, F. L., Kehoe, J. F., Murphy, K. R., & Guion, R. M. (2001). The controversy over score banding in personnel selection: Answers to 10 key questions. *Personnel Psychology, 54,* 149–185.

Cascio, W. F., Alexander, R. A., & Barrett, G. V. (1988). Setting cutoff scores: Legal, psychometric, and professional issues and guidelines. *Personnel Psychology, 41,* 1–24.

Cattell, R. (1966). The meaning and strategic use of factor analysis. In R. B. Cattell (Ed.), *Handbook of multivariate experimental psychology* (pp. 174–243). Chicago: Rand McNally.

Cattin, P. (1980). Estimation of the predictive power of a regression model. *Journal of Applied Psychology, 65,* 407–414.

Chan, D. (2009). So why ask me? Are self-report data really that bad? In C. E. Lance & R. J. Vandenberg (Eds.), *Statistical and methodological myths and urban legends: Doctrine, verity and fable in the organizational and social sciences* (pp. 309–336). New York: Routledge.

Chan, D., Schmitt, N., DeShon, R. P., & Clause, C. S. (1997). Reactions to cognitive ability tests: The relationships between race, test performance, face validity perceptions, and test-taking motivation. *Journal of Applied Psychology, 82,* 300–310.

Cohen, J. (1988). *Statistical power analysis for the behavioral sciences* (2nd ed.). Hillsdale, NJ: Erlbaum.

Cohen, P., Cohen, J., West, S. G., & Aiken, L. S. (2002). *Applied multiple regression: Correlation analysis for the behavioral sciences* (3rd ed.). Hillsdale, NJ: Erlbaum.

Cohen, R. J., & Swerdlik, M. E. (2002). *Psychological testing and assessment: An introduction to test and measurement* (5th ed.). Boston: McGraw-Hill.

Cole, D.A. (1987). Utility of confirmatory factor analysis in test validation research. *Journal of Consulting and Clinical Psychology, 55,* 584–594.

Cole, M., Gay, J., Glick, J., & Sharp, D.W. (1971). *The cultural context of learning and thinking.* New York: Basic Books.

Cortina, J.M. (1993). What is coefficient alpha? An examination of theory and applications. *Journal of Applied Psychology, 78,* 98–104.

Crocker, L.M., & Algina, J. (1986). *Introduction to classical and modern test theory.* Belmont, CA: Wadsworth.

Cronbach, L.J. (1970). *Essentials of psychological testing* (3rd ed.). New York: Harper & Row.

Cronbach, L.J., & Meehl, P.E. (1955). Construct validity in psychological tests. *Psychological Bulletin, 52,* 281–302.

de Ayala, R. J. (2009). *The theory and practice of item response theory.* New York: Guilford Press.

DeMars, C. (2010). *Item response theory.* New York: Oxford University Press.

DeShon, R.P. (2002). Generalizability theory. In F. Drasgow & N. Schmitt (Eds.), *Measuring and analyzing behavior in organizations: Advances in measurement and data analysis* (pp. 189–220). San Francisco, CA: Jossey-Bass.

Dillman, D. A. (2007). *Mail and Internet surveys: The tailored design method.* Hoboken, NJ: John Wiley & Sons.

Doering, M., Rhodes, S.R., & Schuster, M. (1983). *The aging worker: Research and recommendations.* Thousand Oaks, CA: Sage.

Downing, S. M. (2006). Twelve steps for effective test development. In S.M. Downing & T.M. Haladyna (Eds.), *Handbook of test development* (pp. 3–25). Mahwah, NJ: Lawrence Erlbaum.

DuBois, D.A., & DuBois, C.L.Z. (2000). An alternate method for content-oriented test construction: An empirical evaluation. *Journal of Business and Psychology, 15,* 197–213.

Ebel, R.L. (1982). Proposed solutions to two problems of test construction. *Journal of Educational Measurement, 19,* 267–278.

Ebel, R.L., & Frisbie, D.A. (1986). *Essentials of educational measurement.* Englewood Cliffs, NJ: Prentice Hall.

Eid, M. (2000). A multitrait-multimethod model with minimal assumptions. *Psychometrika, 65,* 241–261.

Ellis, B.B., & Mead, A.D. (2002). Item analysis: Theory and practice using classical and modern test theory. In S.G. Rogelberg (Ed.), *Handbook of research methods in industrial and organizational psychology* (pp. 324–343). Malden, MA: Blackwell.

Embretson, S.E., & Reise, S.P. (2000). *Item response theory for psychologists.* Hillsdale, NJ: Erlbaum.

Enders, C.K., & Bandalos, D.L. (2001). The relative performance of full information maximum likelihood estimation for missing data in structural equation models. *Structural Equation Modeling, 8,* 430–457.

Fabrigar, L.R., Wegener, D.T., MacCallum, R.C., & Strahan, E.J. (1999). Evaluating the use of exploratory factor analysis in psychological research. *Psychological Methods, 3,* 272–299.

Ford, J. K., MacCallum, R. C., & Tait, M. (1986). The application of exploratory factor analysis in applied psychology: A critical review and analysis. *Personnel Psychology, 39,* 291–314.

Feldman, J. M., & Lynch, J. G. (1988). Self-generated validity and other effects of measurement on belief, attitude, intentions, and behavior. *Journal of Applied Psychology, 73,* 421–435.

Fitzpatrick, A. R. (1983). The meaning of content validity. *Applied Psychological Measurement, 7,* 3–13.

Forsyth, D. R. (1998). *Group dynamics* (3rd ed.). Belmont, CA: Wadsworth.

Fouad, N. A., & Chan, P. M. (1999). Gender and ethnicity: Influence on test interpretation and reception. In J. W. Lichtenberg & R. K. Goodyear (Eds.), *Scientist-practitioner perspectives on test interpretation* (pp. 31–58). Needham Heights, MA: Allyn & Bacon.

Frisby, C. L. (1998). Culture and cultural differences. In J. Sandoval, C. L. Frisby, K. F. Geisinger, J. D. Scheuneman, & J. R. Grenier (Eds.), *Test interpretation and diversity: Achieving equity in assessment* (pp. 51–73). Washington, DC: American Psychological Association.

Ghiselli, E. E., Campbell, J. P., & Zedeck, S. (1981). *Measurement theory for the behavioral sciences.* New York: W. H. Freeman.

Glass, G. V. (1976). Primary, secondary and meta-analysis of research. *Educational Researcher, 5,* 388.

Glass, G. V., McGaw, B., & Smith, M. L. (1981). *Meta-analysis in social research.* Beverly Hills, CA: Sage.

Gorsuch, R. L. (1983). *Factor analysis* (2nd ed.). Hillsdale, NJ: Erlbaum.

Gottfredson, L. S. (1994). The science and politics of race-norming. *American Psychologist, 49,* 955–963.

Gough, H. G., & Bradley, P. (1992). Comparing two strategies for developing personality scales. In M. Zeidner & R. Most (Eds.), *Psychological testing: An inside view* (pp. 215–246). Palo Alto, CA: Consulting Psychologists Press.

Graham, J. R. (1977). *The MMPI: A practical guide.* New York: Oxford University Press.

Graham, J. R. (1999). *MMPI-2: Assessing personality and psychopathology* (3rd ed.). New York: Oxford University Press.

Guildford, J. P. (1954). *Psychometric methods.* New York: McGraw-Hill.

Guion, R. M. (1965). Synthetic validity in a small company: A demonstration. *Personnel Psychology, 18,* 49–63.

Haladyna, T. M. (1999). *Developing and validating multiple-choice test items* (2nd ed.). Mahwah, NJ: Erlbaum.

Hambleton, R. K., Swaminathan, H., & Rogers, H. J. (1991). *Fundamentals of item response theory.* Newbury Park, CA: Sage.

Haney, W. M., Madaus, G. F., & Lyons, R. (1993). *The fractured marketplace for standardized testing.* Boston: Kluwer.

Hanh, E., Gottschling, J., & Spinath, F. M. (2012). Short measurements of personality—Validity and reliability of the GSOEP Big Five Inventory (BFI-S). *Journal of Research in Personality, 46,* 355–359.

Highhouse, S., Broadfoot, A., Yugo, J. E., & Devendorf, S. A. (2009). Examining corporate reputation judgments with generalizability theory. *Journal of Applied Psychology, 94,* 782–789.

Hogan, T. P. (2013). *Psychological testing: A practical introduction* (3rd ed.). Hoboken, NJ: Wiley.

Hughes, G. D. (2009). The impact of incorrect responses to reverse-coded survey items. *Research in the Schools, 16,* 76–88.

Hunter, J. E., & Schmidt, F. L. (1990). *Methods of meta-analysis: Correcting error and bias in research findings.* Newbury Park, CA: Sage.

Hunter, J.E., Schmidt, F.L., & Jackson, G.B. (1982). *Meta-analysis: Cumulating research findings across studies.* Beverly Hills, CA: Sage.

Impara, J.C., & Plake, B.S. (1997). Standard setting: An alternative approach. *Journal of Educational Measurement, 34,* 353–366.

Johnson, J.W., Steel, P., Scherbaum, C.A., Hoffman, C.A., Jeaneret, P.R., & Foster, J. (2010). Validation is like motor oil: Synthetic is better. *Industrial and Organizational Psychology: Perspectives on Science and Practice, 3,* 305–328.

Johnson, R. L., Penny, J. A., & Gordon, B. (2009). *Assessing performance: Designing, scoring, and validating performance tests.* New York: The Guildford Press.

Jöreskog, K.G., & Sörbom, D. (1996). *LISREL 8: User's reference guide.* Chicago: Scientific Software International.

Kehoe, J.F., & Murphy, K.R. (2010). Current concepts of validity, validation, and generalizability. In. J.L. Farr & N.T. Tippins (Eds.), *Handbook of employee selection* (pp. 99–123). New York: Routledge/Taylor & Francis Group.

Kim, J.E., & Moen, P. (2001). Moving into retirement: Preparation and transitions in late midlife. In M.E. Lachman (Ed.), *Handbook of midlife development* (pp. 487–527). New York: Wiley.

Klem, L. (2000). Structural equations modeling. In L.G. Grimm & P.R. Yarnold (Eds.), *Reading and understanding more multivariate statistics* (pp. 227–260). Washington, DC: American Psychological Association.

Kline, R. B. (1998). *Principles and practice of structural equation modeling.* New York: Guilford.

Kline, R.B. (2011). *Principles and practice of structural equation modeling* (3rd ed.). New York: Guilford Press.

Krathwohl, D. R. (2002). A revision of Bloom's taxonomy: An overview. *Theory into Practice, 41,* 212–218.

Lammlein, S.E. (1987). *Proposal and evaluation of a model of job knowledge testing* (Unpublished doctoral dissertation). University of Minnesota, Minneapolis.

Lance, C.E., & Vandenberg, R.J. (2002). Confirmatory factor analysis. In F. Drasgow & N. Schmitt (Eds.), *Measuring and analyzing behavior in organizations: Advances in measurement and data analysis* (pp. 221–254). San Francisco, CA: Jossey-Bass.

Landis, J.R., & Koch, G.G. (1977). The measurement of observer agreement for categorical data. *Biometrics, 33,* 159–174.

Landis, R. S., Beal, D. J., & Tesluk, P. E. (2000). A comparison of approaches to forming composite measures in structural equation models. *Organizational Research Methods, 3,* 186–207.

Landis, R. S., Edwards, B. D., & Cortina, J. M. (2009). On the practice of allowing correlated residuals among indicators in structural equation models. In C. E. Lance & R. J. Vandenberg (Eds.), *Statistical and methodological myths and urban legends* (pp. 193–215). New York: Routledge.

Landy, F.J. (1986). Stamp collecting versus science: Validation as hypothesis testing. *American Psychologist, 41,* 1183–1192.

Lawshe, C.H. (1952). What can industrial psychology do for small business? *Personnel Psychology, 5,* 31–34.

Lawshe, C.H. (1975). A quantitative approach to content validity. *Personnel Psychology, 28,* 563–575.

Licht, M.H. (1995). Multiple regression and correlation. In L.G. Grimm & P.R. Yarnold (Eds.), *Reading and understanding multivariate statistics* (pp. 19–64). Washington, DC: American Psychological Association.

Lievens, F., De Corte, W., & Schollaert, E. (2008). A closer look at the frame-of-reference effect in personality scale scores and validity. *Journal of Applied Psychology, 93,* 268–279.

Lipsey, M. W., & Wilson, D. B. (2001). *Practical meta-analysis.* Thousand Oaks, CA: Sage.

Lonner, W. J. (1990). An overview of cross-cultural testing and assessment. In R. W. Brislin (Ed.), *Applied cross-cultural psychology* (pp. 56–76). Newbury Park, CA: Sage.

Maclure, M., & Willett, W. C. (1987). Misinterpretation and misuse of the kappa statistic. *American Journal of Epidemiology, 126,* 161–169.

Magnusson, D. (1967). *Test theory.* Palo Alto, CA: Addison-Wesley.

Marsella, A. J., & Kameoka, V. A. (1989). Ethnocultural issues in the assessment of psychopathology. In S. Wetzler (Ed.), *Measuring mental illness in psychometric assessment for clinicians* (pp. 231–256). Washington, DC: American Psychiatric Press.

Marsh, H. W. (1990). Confirmatory factor analysis of multitrait-multimethod data: The construct validation of multidimensional self-concept responses. *Journal of Personality, 58,* 661–692.

Maurer, T. J., & Alexander, R. A. (1992). Methods of improving employment test critical scores derived by judging test content: A review and critique. *Personnel Psychology, 45,* 727–762.

McKeachie, W. J. (1994). *Teaching tips* (9th ed.). Lexington, MA: D. C. Heath.

Mersman, J. L., & Shultz, K. S. (1998). Individual differences in the ability to fake on personality measures. *Personality and Individual Differences, 24,* 217–227.

Messick, S. (1989). Validity. In R. Linn (Ed.), *Educational measurement* (3rd ed., pp. 13–103). New York: Macmillan.

Messick, S. (1995a). Standards of validity and the validity of standards in performance assessment. *Educational Measurement: Issues and Practice, 14,* 5–8.

Messick, S. (1995b). Validity of psychological assessment: Validation of inferences from persons' responses and performances as scientific inquiry into score meaning. *American Psychologist, 50,* 741–749.

Millman, J., & Greene, J. (1989). The specification and development of tests of achievement and ability. In R. L. Linn (Ed.), *Educational measurement* (3rd ed., pp. 335–366). New York: American Council on Education/Macmillan.

Moorman, R. H. P., & Philip, M. (1992). A meta-analytic review and empirical test of the potential confounding effects of social desirability response sets in organizational behaviour research. *Journal of Occupational & Organizational Psychology, 65,* 131–149.

Murphy, K. R. (2009). Content validity is useful for many things, but validity isn't one of them. *Industrial and Organizational Psychology: Perspectives on Science and Practice, 2,* 453–464.

Murphy, K. R., & Davidshofer, C. O. (2005). *Psychological testing: Principles and applications* (6th ed.). Upper Saddle River, NJ: Pearson Education.

Murphy, K. R., & Newman, D. A. (2003). The past, present, and future of validity generalization. In K. R. Murphy (Ed.), *Validity generalization: A critical review* (pp. 403–424). New York: Routledge Academic Press.

Mushquash, C., & O'Connor, B. P. (2006). SPSS and SAS programs for generalizability theory analyses. *Behavior Research Methods, 38,* 542–547.

Muthén, L. K., & Muthén, B. O. (2007). *MPlus users' guide* (7th ed.). Los Angeles, CA: Muthén & Muthén.

Newton, R. R., & Rudestam, K. E. (1999). *Your statistical consultant: Answers to your data analysis questions.* Thousand Oaks, CA: Sage.

Nunnally, J. C., & Bernstein, I. H. (1994). *Psychometric theory* (3rd ed.). New York: McGraw-Hill.

Nye, C. D., Roberts, B. W., Saucier, G., & Zhou, X. (2008). Testing the measurement equivalence of personality adjective items across cultures. *Journal of Research in Personality, 42,* 1524–1536.

Ory, J. C., & Ryan, K. E. (1993). *Tips for improving testing and grading.* Newbury Park, CA: Sage.

Osterlind, S. J. (1998). *Constructing test items: Multiple-choice, constructed-response, performance, and other formats.* Boston: Kluwer.

Padilla, A. M. (2001). Issues in culturally appropriate assessment. In L. A. Suzuki, J. G. Ponterotto, & P. J. Meller (Eds.), *Handbook of multicultural assessment: Clinical, psychological, and educational applications* (2nd ed.) (pp. 5–27). San Francisco, CA: Jossey-Bass.

Paek, I., & Han, K. T. (2012). IRTPro 2.1 for Windows. *Applied Psychological Measurement, 20,* 1–11.

Paulhus, D. L. (1986). Self-deception and impression management in test responses. In A. Angleitner & J. S. Wiggins (Eds.), *Personality assessment via questionnaires: Current issues in theory and measurement* (pp. 143–165). Berlin: Springer-Verlag.

Paulhus, D. L. (1991). Measurement and control of response bias. In J. P. Robinson, P. R. Shaver, & L. S. Wrightsman (Eds.), *Measures of personality and social psychological attitudes* (pp. 17–59). San Diego, CA: Academic Press.

Pearson, K. (1903). Mathematical contributions to the theory of evolution XI: On the influence of natural selection on the variability and correlation of organs. *Philosophical Transactions of the Royal Society, Series A, 200,* 1–66.

Pedhazur, E. J. (1997). *Multiple regression in behavioral research* (3rd ed.). Pacific Grove, CA: Wadsworth.

Pedhazur, E. J., & Schmelkin, L. P. (1991). *Measurement, design, and analysis: An integrated approach.* Hillsdale, NJ: Erlbaum.

Peter, J. P. (1979). Reliability: A review of psychometric basics and recent marketing practices. *Journal of Marketing Research, 16,* 6–17.

Raju, N. S., & Ellis, B. B. (2002). Differential item and test functioning. In F. Drasgow & N. Schmitt (Eds.), *Measuring and analyzing behavior in organizations: Advances in measurement and data analysis* (pp. 156–188). San Francisco, CA: Jossey-Bass.

Rasinski, K. A., Lee, L., & Krishnamurty, P. (2012). Question order effects. In H. Cooper (Ed. in Chief), *APA handbook of research methods in psychology: Vol. 1. Foundations, planning, measures, and psychometrics* (pp. 229–248). Washington, DC: American Psychological Association.

Reid, R. (1995). Assessment of ADHD with culturally different groups: The use of behavioral rating scales. *School Psychology Review, 24,* 537–560.

Resnick, L. B., & Resnick, D. (1992). Assessing the thinking curriculum: New tools for educational reform. In B. R. Gifford & M. C. O'Connor (Eds.), *Changing assessments: Alternative views of aptitude, achievement and instruction* (pp. 37–75). Boston: Kluwer.

Rodriguez, M. C. (2002). Choosing an item format. In G. Tindal & T. M. Haladyna (Eds.), *Large-scale assessment programs for all students: Validity, technical adequacy, and implementation* (pp. 213–231). Mahwah, NJ: Erlbaum.

Rothstein, H. R., McDaniel, M. A., & Borenstein, M. (2002). Meta-analysis: A review of quantitative cumulation methods. In F. Drasgow & N. Schmitt (Eds.), *Measuring and analyzing behavior in organizations: Advances in measurement and data analysis* (pp. 534–571). San Francisco, CA: Jossey-Bass.

Russell, D. W. (2002). In search of underlying dimensions: The use (and abuse) of factor analysis. *Personality and Social Psychology Bulletin, 28,* 1629–1646.

Saad, S., & Sackett, P.R. (2002). Investigating differential prediction by gender in employment-oriented personality measures. *Journal of Applied Psychology, 87,* 667–674.

Sackett, P.R., Laczo, R.M., & Lippe, Z.P. (2003). Differential prediction and the use of multiple predictors: The omitted variables problem. *Journal of Applied Psychology, 86,* 1046–1056.

Sackett, P.R., & Wilk, S.L. (1994). Within-group norming and other forms of score adjustment in preemployment testing. *American Psychologist, 49,* 929–954.

Samuda, R.J. (1998). Cross-cultural assessment: Issues and alternatives. In R.J. Samuda, R. Feuerstein, A.S. Kaufman, J.E. Lewis, R.J. Sternberg, & Associates, *Advances in cross-cultural assessment* (pp. 1–19). Thousand Oaks, CA: Sage.

Saucier, G. (1994). Mini-marker: A brief version of Goldberg's unipolar big-five markers. *Journal of Personality Assessment, 63,* 506–516.

Schaeffer, N.C., & Presser, S. (2003). The science of asking questions. *Annual Review of Sociology, 29,* 65–88.

Schmidt, F.L., & Hunter, J.E. (1977). Development of a general solution to the problem of validity generalization. *Journal of Applied Psychology, 62,* 529–540.

Schmidt, F.L., & Hunter, J.E. (1980). The future of criterion-related validity. *Personnel Psychology, 33,* 41–60.

Schmidt, F.L., & Hunter, J.E. (1996). Measurement error in psychological research: Lessons from 26 research scenarios. *Psychological Methods, 1,* 199–223.

Schmidt, F.L., & Hunter, J.E. (2001). Meta-analysis. In N. Anderson, D.S. Ones, H.K. Sinangil, & C. Viswesvaran (Eds.), *Handbook of industrial, work and organizational psychology* (Vol. 1, pp. 51–70). Thousand Oaks, CA: Sage.

Schmidt, F.L., Hunter, J.E., & Urry, V.W. (1976). Statistical power in criterion-related validity studies. *Journal of Applied Psychology, 61,* 473–485.

Schmitt, N. (1996). Uses and abuses of coefficient alpha. *Psychological Assessment, 8,* 350–353.

Schmitt, N., Gooding, R., Noe, R.A., & Kirsch, M. (1984). Meta-analyses of validity studies published between 1964 and 1982, and the investigation of study characteristics. *Personnel Psychology, 37,* 407–422.

Schmitt, N., & Klimoski, R. (1991). *Research methods in human resource management.* Cincinnati, OH: Southwest.

Schmitt, N., & Ostroff, C. (1986). Operationalizing the "behavioral consistency" approach: Selection test development based on a content-oriented strategy. *Personnel Psychology, 39,* 91–108.

Schmitt, N., & Stults, D.M. (1986). Methodology review: Analysis of multitrait-multimethod matrices. *Applied Psychological Measurement, 10,* 1–22.

Schuman, H., & Presser, S. (1996). *Questions and answers in attitude surveys: Experiments on question form, wording and context.* Newbury Park, CA: Sage.

Schwarz, N. (1999). Self-reports: How the questions shape the answers. *American Psychologist, 54,* 93–105.

Section 60-3, Uniform Guidelines on Employee Selection Procedures, 43 Fed. Reg. 38295 (August 25, 1978).

Shavelson, R.J., Webb, N.M., & Rowley, G.L. (1989). Generalizability theory. *American Psychologist, 44,* 922–932.

Shultz, K.S. (1995). Increasing alpha reliabilities of multiple-choice tests with linear polychotomous scoring. *Psychological Reports, 77,* 760–762.

Shultz, K.S., Morton, K.R., & Weckerle, J.R. (1998). The influence of push and pull factors in distinguishing voluntary and involuntary early retirees' retirement decision and adjustment. *Journal of Vocational Behavior, 53,* 45–57.

Shultz, K.S., & Taylor, M.A. (2001, August). The predictors of retirement: A meta-analysis. In K.S. Shultz & M.A. Taylor (Co-Chairs), *Evolving concepts of retirement for the 21st century.* Symposium conducted at the 109th Annual Conference of the American Psychological Association, San Francisco, CA.

Spearman, C. (1904). General intelligence: Objectively determined and measured. *American Journal of Psychology, 15,* 201–293.

SPSS Inc. (2003). *SPSS 11.5 base user's guide.* Chicago: Author.

Steenkamp, J.-B.E.M., & Baumgartner, H. (1998). Assessing measurement invariance in cross-national consumer research. *Journal of Consumer Research, 25,* 78–90.

Sternberg, R.J., & Grigorenko, E.L. (2001). Ability testing across cultures. In L.A. Suzuki, J.G. Ponterotto, & P.J. Meller (Eds.), *Handbook of multicultural assessment: Clinical, psychological, and educational applications* (2nd ed., pp. 335–358). San Francisco, CA: Jossey-Bass.

Storholm, E.D., Fisher, D.G., Napper, L.E., Reynolds, G.L., & Halkitis, P.N. (2011). A psychometric analysis of the Compulsive Sexual Behavior Inventory. *Sexual Addiction & Compulsivity, 18,* 86–103.

Styers, B., & Shultz, K.S. (2009). Perceived reasonableness of employment testing accommodations for persons with disabilities. *Public Personnel Management, 39 (3),* 119–140.

Sussmann, M. (1986). The validity of validity: An analysis of validation study designs. *Journal of Applied Psychology, 71,* 461–468.

Tabachnick, B.G., & Fidell, L.S. (2012). *Using multivariate statistics* (6th ed.). Boston: Allyn & Bacon.

Tenopyr, M.L. (1977). Content-construct confusion. *Personnel Psychology, 30,* 47–54.

Thompson, B. (2004). *Exploratory and confirmatory factor analysis: Understanding concepts and applications.* Washington, DC: American Psychological Association.

Torgerson, W.S. (1958). *Theory and methods of scaling.* New York: Wiley.

Traub, R.E. (1994). *Reliability for the social sciences: Theory and application.* Thousand Oaks, CA: Sage.

Tuckman, B.W. (1988). *Testing for teachers* (2nd ed.). New York: Harcourt, Brace, Jovanovich.

van der Ven, A.H.G.S. (1980). *Introduction to scaling.* New York: Wiley.

Velicer, W.F., & Fava, J.L. (1998). Effects of variable and subject sampling on factor pattern recovery. *Psychological Methods, 2,* 231–251.

Wainer, H., Dorans, N.J., Flaugher, R., Green, B.F., & Mislevy, R.J. (2000). *Computerized adaptive testing: A primer.* New York: Routledge.

Wanous, J.P., Sullivan, S.E., & Malinak, J. (1989). The role of judgment calls in meta-analysis. *Journal of Applied Psychology, 74,* 259–264.

Widaman, K.F. (1985). Hierarchically nested covariance structure models for multitrait-multimethod data. *Applied Psychological Measurement, 9,* 1–26.

Widaman, K.F., & Thompson, J.S. (2003). On specifying the null model for incremental fit indices in structural equation modeling. *Psychological Methods, 8,* 16–37.

Wiersma, W., & Jurs, S.G. (1990). *Educational measurement and testing* (2nd ed.). Boston: Allyn & Bacon.

Wiesen, J.P. (1999). *WTMA™ Wiesen Test of Mechanical Aptitude™ (PAR edition) professional manual.* Odessa, FL: Psychological Assessment Resources.

Wiggens, G. (1989, May). A true test: Towards a more authentic and equitable assessment. *Phi Delta Kappan, 71,* 803–813.

Williams, R.L. (1972). *The black intelligence test of cultural homogeneity.* St. Louis, MO: Black Studies Program, Washington University.

Wilson, F.R., Pan, W., & Schumsky, D.A. (2012). Recalculation of the critical values for Lawshe's content validity ratio. *Measurement and Evaluation in Counseling and Development, 45,* 197–210.

Wonderlic Inc. (2002). *Wonderlic Personnel Test and Scholastic Level Exam user's manual.* Libertyville, IL: Wonderlic.

Zappe, S.E. (2010). Response process validation of equivalent test forms: How qualitative data can support the construct validity of multiple test forms. *Dissertation Abstracts International: Section A; Humanities and Social Sciences, 70*(11-A), 4184.

Zickar, M.J. (1998). Modeling item-level data with item response theory. *Current Directions in Psychological Science, 7,* 104–109.

Zickar, M.J. (2002). Modeling data with polytomous item response theory. In F. Drasgow & N. Schmitt (Eds.), *Measuring and analyzing behavior in organizations: Advances in measurement and data analysis* (pp. 123–155). San Francisco, CA: Jossey-Bass.

Zickar, M. J., & Broadfoot, A. A. (2008). The partial revival of a dead horse? Comparing classical test theory and item response theory. In C. E. Lance & R. J. Vandenberg (Eds.), *Statistical and methodological myths and urban legends* (pp. 37–59). New York: Routledge.

Author Index

Subject Index